Looking Forward

Looking Forward

A GUIDE TO FUTURES RESEARCH

OLAF HELMER

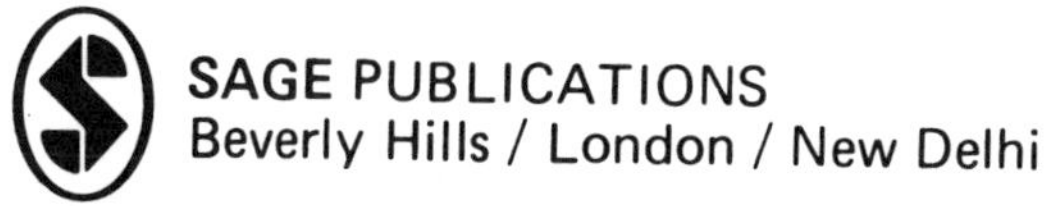
SAGE PUBLICATIONS
Beverly Hills / London / New Delhi

For information address:

SAGE Publications, Inc.
275 South Beverly Drive
Beverly Hills, California 90212

SAGE Publications India Pvt. Ltd.
C-236 Defence Colony
New Delhi 110 024, India

SAGE Publications Ltd
28 Banner Street
London EC1Y 8QE, England

Printed in the United States of America

Library of Congress Cataloging in Publication Data

Main entry under title:

Helmer, Olaf, 1910-
Looking forward.

Bibliography: p.
1. Forecasting—Methodology. 2. Forecasting—Research. I. Title.
CB158.H415 1983 003'.2 83-4520
ISBN 0-8039-2017-2

FIRST PRINTING

Contents

Preface

This book is concerned with generic methods of exploring the future and the application of such methods to long-range planning. The material presented here should be useful to anyone professionally engaged in planning the future of a given area or organization or activity, be it international trade, human values, criminal justice, computer applications, warfare, space exploration, a particular country, a particular city, a particular corporation, or whatever.

The book should also be of value to aspiring planners, that is, to students taking courses in subjects related to the future, including public-sector and corporate planning. In such courses it can be used as a primary or supplementary text. In addition to professionals and would-be professionals in planning, there are by now many thousands of others with an increasing interest in the rapidly growing field of futures research to whom the book will give an informative overview of what this field is all about.

Furthermore, I hope that those actively engaged in basic research in this field will find numerous suggestions throughout this book of directions in which it may be worthwhile to seek further advances in the state of the art. Futures research is still very much under development, and graduate students in search of thesis topics may well find this a challenging area to investigate.

About half of the material in this volume I have previously published in the open literature. Another 30 percent or so has been drawn from in-house printings of the Rand Corporation, the Institute of Government and Public Affairs at the University of California at Los Angeles, the Institute for the Future, the Center for Futures Research at the University of Southern California, and the International Institute for Applied Systems Analysis. The remainder consists of largely new material, interspersed to provide continuity and to cover aspects not taken up explicitly in the articles I wrote earlier. The result, it is hoped, amounts to a coherent treatment of the field of futures research, especially its conceptual and methodological aspects, along with excursions into substantive applications.

Several of the previously published pieces included here were co-authored with others; these are:

"The Epistemology of the Inexact Sciences", *Management Science,* 1959; co-author: Nicholas Rescher;

"An Experimental Application of the Delphi Method to the Use of Experts", *Management Science,* 1963; co-author: Norman Dalkey;

"Future Opportunities for Foundation Support", Institute of the Future, R-11, 1970; co-author: Helen Helmer;

"Report on a Long-Range Forecasting Study", Rand publication P-2982, 1964 (later published as an appendix in my book *Social Technology,* Basic Books, 1966); co-author: Theodore Gordon;

"Some Potential Societal Developments—1970–2000", Institute for the Future, R-7, 1970; co-author: Raul de Brigard;

"An Approach to the Study of a Developing Economy by Operational Gaming", Rand publication P-2718, 1963; co-author: Edward Quade;

"The Use of Futures Analysis in Transportation Research Planning", *Transportation Journal,* vol. 16, 1976; co-author: Paul Gray.

I am greatly indebted to my collaborators on these contributions to this volume and appreciate their willingness to have this material reproduced on this occasion.

I would not have undertaken to put this volume together had it not been for the persuasiveness of my friend David Loye and for the unpersuasiveness of my wife, Helen, who did not think much of the idea at first. Therefore her saintly patience, moral support and, above all, her invaluable editorial contribution are especially appreciated by me.

Carmel, California

Chapter I

The Future of X

1 INTRODUCTION

Fascination with the future is an age-old and forgivable indulgence. The future, as has been remarked aptly though perhaps not very profoundly, is, after all, where we will spend the rest of our lives; and our persistent curiosity in this regard is understandable. The focus of all our hopes and fears is in the future, and everything we do today, is inevitably affected by our expectations for tomorrow.

However, the way people think about the future has changed profoundly in recent years, and a new intellectual climate in this regard is in the making in many parts of the world. It is evidenced by a wholly new attitude toward the future that has become apparent in public and private planning agencies as well as in the research community. The effect has been to extend customary planning horizons into a more distant future and to replace haphazard intuitive gambles, as a basis for planning, by sober and craftsmanlike analysis of the opportunities the future has to offer.

The general public has not been unaffected by this change in the orientation toward the future among professionals, with the result that the last twenty years have seen the emergence of what has become known as a futures movement, with hundreds of futures societies all over the world, numerous journals devoted to the future, and congresses attended by thousands.

The change in attitude toward the future is manifesting itself in several ways: philosophically, in that there is a new understanding of what it means to talk about the future; pragmatically, in that there is a growing recognition that it is important to do something about the future; and methodologically, in that there are new and more effective ways of in fact doing something about the future.

By the change in philosophical attitude I mean that defeatism regarding the possibility of exploring the future is being replaced with a growing awareness that a great deal can be said about future trends in terms of probability and, moreover, that through proper planning we can exert considerable influence over these probabilities. Thus fatalism has become a fatality. The future is no longer viewed as unique, unforeseeable, and inevitable; instead, it is realized that there are a multitude of possible futures, with associated probabilities that can be estimated and, to some extent, manipulated.

As for the new pragmatic attitude, it derives from the general perception that not only are technology and our environment undergoing change, but the pace of change in our time is accelerating. No longer does it take generations for a new pattern of living conditions to evolve, but several major adjustments in our lifestyles and the ways of making our livelihood are imposed on many of us these days, and continual adaptation may well become our children's way of life. For such adaptation to occur without major psychological or economic disruption, it has become mandatory for us to strive to anticipate changes in our environment rather than to attempt to deal with them belatedly and inadequately only after it is obvious that they are upon us. The recognition of this need for anticipation has had visible effects, perhaps most notably in the form of legislation creating an Office of Technology Assessment under congressional auspices. By "technology assessment" is meant the assessment, in advance, of the likely impact on society of technological innovations, for the purpose of averting undesirable (and often unanticipated) side effects of such new technologies or, at least, of alleviating their deleterious consequences. The institutionalization of such precaution may well be viewed as the first concrete evidence that the message of the futures movement has been accepted at the highest governmental levels.

The third point I mentioned, our growing ability to do something about the future, is, in fact, the lesson I am hoping to transmit through the entire span of this volume. The discipline of futures research, which seeks to explore these potentialities of interactive intervention in future developments, is gradually emerging as a highly multidisciplinary branch of operations research. It is still very much under development, still inadequate in many respects, yet highly promising in what it may one day be able to offer when it comes to full fruition. It does not seem unreasonable to assume that much progress in this regard will come about even within another decade. But even now, while still immature, futures research is making a useful and far from negligible contribution to the improvement of the planning process.

Like its parent discipline, operations research, futures research is pragmatic in its orientation, its principal task being considered the delivery of operationally meaningful assistance to decision makers. In contrast to the so-called pure scientist, who sees his role as the discoverer and establisher of laws of nature, on the basis of which forecasts can then be made, the futures analyst adopts a more pragmatic attitude: He aims at helping the decision maker arrive at a rational decision, even if that help, in the absence of an established theory permitting scientific derivation, consists merely in systematically collecting and presenting intuitive judgment on the problem in question.[1] In futures research emphasis is placed on

1. Here, and throughout, I have avoided the awkward "his or her" in the hope that the reader will interpret the word "his" and other masculine pronouns in their now obsolete generic meaning.

- the construction of mathematical models that permit sophisticated extrapolation from the past;
- a thoroughly cross-disciplinary treatment of its subject matter;
- the systematic use of intuitive expert judgment; and
- a systems-analytical approach to its problems, which does not neglect paying close attention to resource constraints and cost-effectiveness considerations.

2 *ORIENTATIONS TOWARD THE FUTURE*

It is not uncommon for Americans to be future-oriented in their thinking. Even at a time of relative economic stagnation, we do not indulge excessively in nostalgia about the good old days or lose ourselves in regretful musings about past mistakes. Instead we are more likely to accept the situation as it is and to seek effective ways and means of bringing about a better personal or national future. This emphasis on a pragmatic, constructive outlook may well be a heritage of the pioneering days.

But the future as an object of systematic exploration and planning is not entirely an American invention. The roots of the so-called futures movement go back to the Europe of the 1950s, where the first two men who may rightly be called futurists were Bertrand de Jouvenel and Dennis Gabor. De Jouvenel, a well-known writer in the fields of economics and political science, has produced many future-oriented publications, among which his 1967 book *The Art of Conjecture* is an undisputed classic in the field. In the 1960s, de Jouvenel headed an informal group of scholars, mostly French, known as "Futuribles", which met occasionally and published numerous articles on future political, social, and economic developments. Gabor, who received the Nobel prize for his invention of holography, first examined the subject of the future in his 1963 book *Inventing the Future,* which he followed later, in 1972, with a very thoughtful work called *The Mature Society.*

Gabor's writings on the future, particularly his earlier ones, are typical of many futurist efforts at self-defeating prophecies, intended as warnings of possible catastrophes that might occur unless timely interventive steps are taken. (Perhaps the most notable such undertaking, in the early 1970s, was the Meadows study, *Limits to Growth,* carried out under the auspices of the Club of Rome.) Self-defeating predictions, such as Gabor's, of dire future developments are often optimistic in nature; that is, they are made in the hope that, by bringing the likely consequences of inaction to people's attention, countermeasures will be taken in time to prevent these predictions from becoming reality.

Such self-defeating prophecies are in contrast to self-fulfilling prophecies, which perhaps are somewhat more prevalent. For instance, a pessimistic economic forecast by the nation's president or by the chair of the Federal Reserve Board surely would tend to depress the economy; conversely, an authoritative statement that, say, cheap solar energy will become available might well give potential investors the courage to make appropriate commitments and thus bring the prediction closer to fulfillment.

As for prophecies with self-defeating intent, many have been in the realm of utopian or, rather, dystopian writing. Not all of these have been successful in reversing the trends toward realization of the predicted developments. Both Huxley's *Brave New World* and Orwell's *1984* are cases in point. We are getting perilously close to a state of the world resembling their descriptions: electronic surveillance à la Orwell is already on our technological menu; and the possibility of mass production of identical humans through cloning, à la Huxley, is around the corner.

People, as said before, have always had a natural curiosity about their future. But it is only in the last few decades that supposedly divine oracles or the use of tea leaves and crystal balls have given way to serious intellectual attempts at exploring the future. The early efforts in this direction, by such pioneers as Gabor and de Jouvenel, provided some of the philosophical bases for such an approach, mainly by emphasizing that we are faced not with one unknowable future whose character can only be guessed or divined, but with a multitude of possible futures, and that planning can help determine which of these will become the real one.

The key to progress in this field has been the recognition that in dealing with the future, especially in "soft" areas such as social, political, and economic developments, we have no firm laws providing the kind of predictive power associated with the laws of physics but must rely largely on intuitive understanding and perceptiveness of experts in the relevant areas. Some experience in the systematic use of expertise was gained in the development of operations research, which originally primarily served military purposes, and many of the futures research methods invented in the 1960s were inspired by, or transferred from, operations research and applied to the broad social arena. Systematic methods of this kind are of quite recent origin and have been, or are being, developed largely in the United States; they are known by such names as "trend extrapolation", "the Delphi technique", "cross-impact analysis", "simulation gaming", and "scenario-writing".

Once invented and seen to promise applicability to long-range social, technological, and corporate planning, these methods quickly spread to Europe and other parts of the world. Delphi, first developed at Rand in 1953 and then, in 1963, applied to large-scale technological forecasting, was first successfully employed for internal corporate planning by Thompson-Ramo-Wooldridge in the mid-1960s, and then its use proliferated rapidly. It has now been applied in innumerable cases throughout the world, with special interest exhibited in such widely divergent countries as France, Sweden, Japan, the Soviet Union, and China. Cross-impact analysis, too, is receiving increasing attention abroad and, interestingly, has been applied regularly and on a large scale to governmental planning in Czechoslovakia. Interactive gaming, thus far, is still awaiting widespread acceptance, except for rather narrowly defined business gaming, which seems to have become a routine instructional device at the business schools of many universities, both in the United States and abroad. Other methods, such as a variety of trend-extrapolation routines and scenario-writing, have been widely employed, often in conjunction with some of the other techniques already mentioned.

Regardless of which particular methods of studying the future are favored, there is no doubt that the idea of a constructive, no-nonsense attitude toward the future has been firmly accepted throughout the developed world. There is a widespread recognition that our social and technological environment is changing much more rapidly than in former days and that this circumstance has important consequences for any kind of long-range planning. Whether plans are made in the public or in the private sector, whether they are made in Norway or Romania or the United States, there is a growing awareness that sound planning must be based on as clear an accounting as possible of expected changes in the operating environment for which the plans are being formulated. Hence the elaborate efforts everywhere to obtain probabilistic forecasts of the future technological, economic, social, and political setting and to seek an understanding of the probable consequences of alternative strategies vis-à-vis this changed environment.

3 THE PLAN FOR THIS BOOK

The letter X has customarily been used either to designate a mysterious, unknown quantity or else to function as a variable, that is, as a stand-in for any one of many possible entities. The second of these alternatives applies to the X in "The Future of X", the title of this first chapter, and it was used to emphasize the generic character of the kind of "looking forward" that this book is all about.

The title of this chapter goes back to a pleasant memory of my experience as a teacher at the University of Southern California, where, for a course called Methods of Futures Analysis, I had developed a special computer program named The Future of X for use by the students. As I explained to them on the first day, the format of this program was a multipurpose one, into which, by filling in the X part of it, they could fit whatever their preferred subject of study might be—the future of the Japanese steel industry, the future of telecommunications, the future of Social Security, or whatever. I hope that, similarly, no matter on what subject matter a reader's interest may focus, this book will be of some help in studying and planning the future of X.

Preparing this book has given me an opportunity to collect together in one place those of my previous writings that bear directly on the subject of exploring the future. That is not the main purpose of this volume, however. I am hopeful that the result is a coherent treatment of the field of futures research, with emphasis on aspects of special professional interest to me, namely, those relating to concepts and methods, but not neglecting their applications to some of the urgent problems of the real world that face us in this troubled century.

Chapter II includes two treatises that were precursors of futures research proper. In retrospect, it can be seen that they contributed to laying the conceptual and attitudinal groundwork for that newly emerging field. They are *On the Epistemology of the Inexact Sciences,* written with Nicholas Rescher in 1959, in which, in particular, an attempt was made to clarify the conceptual difference between explanation and prediction; and *Social Technology,* which came out in 1966 and advocated the application of operations-research techniques to the solution of pressing social problems. Both stress the need for multidisciplinary approaches.

Chapter III follows through with a discussion of the role and scientific status of operations research and its relationship to systems analysis and futures research. The history and development of futures research is then taken up in Chapter IV. This is followed, in Chapter V, by a number of papers on the Delphi technique, including the original paper on this topic, *An Experimental Application of the Delphi Method to the Use of Experts,* written with Norman Dalkey in 1963.

Chapter VI is devoted to cross-impact analysis, illustrated by use of an example dealing with global resources (the subject matter of *Limits to Growth* by Meadows et al.).

Chapter VII, then, undertakes a systematic examination of the planning process, adding to the passive exploration of probable futures the deliberate enhancement of the probabilities of desirable futures. The chapter includes a discussion of technology assessment and of the role of game theory in long-range planning. An example of "normative forecasting" is provided at the end of the chapter.

In Chapter VIII we begin to turn to some specific applications in the form of technological, scientific, and societal forecasts. One section of this chapter consists of a reprint of the original *Report on a Long-Range Forecasting Study,* written with Theodore Gordon in 1964.

Chapter IX consists primarily of excerpts from a paper entitled *On the Future State of the Union,* which is concerned with various aspects, both conceptual and methodological, of long-range planning in the public sector. This essay takes up, in particular, the possibility of using judgmental social indicators, called "satisfaction indices", as a means of measuring the condition of our society. The chapter also contains a brief report on a study related to the future of transportation.

The future of international relations and methods for dealing with domestic and global economic problems are treated in Chapters X and XI, respectively. A final chapter, XII, after a brief recapitulation, presents some personal forecasts, both factual and normative, on the future of our society, as well as some notes on the future of futures research.

Chapter II

The Need for Interdisciplinarity

4 THE NATURE OF LONG-RANGE PLANNING

Long-range planning, no matter what the specific subject matter, cannot fail to require contributions from a variety of disciplines. At the time a plan now formulated becomes reality, if it is indeed a long-range plan, many aspects of the environment are likely to have changed: new technologies may have emerged, and economic and sociopolitical conditions may no longer be the same. Thus, aside from the immediate area in which plans are being made (which, for example, might be health care, space travel, aid to a developing country, or the marketing of a new product), the planner has to give some thought to probable developments in various fields that determine the parameters of the future environment in which the plan needs to prove itself. To be truly effective, such planning must of necessity be multidisciplinary.

Most of the disciplines relevant here are not the so-called hard sciences, and it may be well for that reason to start out, as we do in this chapter, with some reflections on the epistemological nature of these relatively "softer" sciences.

5 EXPERIMENTATION IN THE NONEXPERIMENTAL SCIENCES[1]

Among the empirical sciences, some have traditionally been recognized as experimental, while others have not been considered susceptible to experimentation. Some sciences, notably biology and later psychology, have gradually shifted from the nonexperimental into the experimental domain.

Peculiarly, among the nonexperimental sciences, there are two totally different types, which might almost be said to represent opposite poles among the sciences as far as amenability to precise analytic treatment is concerned: they are astronomy, on the one hand, and several of the social sciences, such as economics and political science (which may serve as illustrations forthwith), on the other. The reasons for the absence of experimentation in these fields are quite different. In astronomy it is the hugeness of the objects that form its subject matter that precludes experimentation; in economics and

1. The passages in this section are taken from a 1953 internal Rand Corporation memorandum of the same title.

political science it is our unwillingness and, often, inability to interfere with social institutions as well as the seeming impossibility of achieving the prerequisites of all experimentation, the reproducibility of like circumstances.

Now, while it is not being claimed here that experimentation in the usual sense can after all be introduced into these sciences, nevertheless, something close to experimentation does seem feasible. In order to get a clue as to what this next best thing might be, let us look at another one of the physical sciences, which, like astronomy, at least faces certain barriers to direct experimentation, namely, atomic physics. Its subject matter concerns objects too small (rather than too large) to be explored by experimentation in the usual sense, where the effects of manipulation are directly observable. To be sure, the situation is quite different from that found in astronomy; experimentation does in fact take place, and it is merely the manipulation and observation of the particles concerned that is less immediate than in the other physical sciences. Nevertheless, no matter what the obstacles may have been, the fact is that atomic physics has at times been compelled to resort to procedures close to, but not identical with, experimentation in the strict sense. It is these techniques which, it seems, begin to show some promise of paying off similarly in the nonexperimental sciences, especially at the social-science end of the scale.

What is being referred to here is the device, well known by now, of constructing a mathematical model of certain atomic or nuclear processes, and of then using so-called Monte Carlo sampling techniques to conduct not real, but paper, experiments, in which the paths of fictitious particles of the model are "observed" as they go through a series of random collisions, deflections, or what not. In short, the real world is first replaced by an analogue (usually mathematical, sometimes physical), the experiment with real objects is replaced by one with fictitious objects, and in this "experiment" the features supposedly not under the control of the "experimenter" are assumed to be subject to given probability distributions, so that the chance fluctuations that would naturally occur can be simulated in the model by the operation of an artificial chance device.

Astronomy, because it possesses adequate analytical tools to give us a very thorough understanding of the interaction of celestial bodies, has little need for pseudo-experimentation of this kind, although in principle there is no obstacle to its use in this field, and it is even quite conceivable that, in the application of astronomy to the problems of space navigation, substantial aid might be derived from Monte Carlo experimentation.

In the case of the social sciences, on the other hand, progress toward integrated theory has been impeded so greatly by the absence of a structural framework and of experimental devices that the introduction of pseudo-experimentation within models of the real world offers some definite hope of stimulating a new trend of research in this field. Much of the vast accumulation of knowledge, especially in economics and political science, might be systematized by the introduction of mathematical analogues and thus be opened up to further analysis and to verification both by direct observation and by Monte Carlo experimentation within these models. The social sciences would thus have a chance of gaining parity with the physical sciences in the sense that they might share with them the achievement that is the ultimate goal of all scientific inquiry, namely, the prediction and control of our environment.

What evidence is there that this approach may be fruitful? Even the economist, who is apt to be quite familiar with mathematical techniques, has every right to be skeptical. As for the political scientist, to whose background mathematical constructs and systematic experimentation are likely to be foreign, initial sympathy with this approach is even less likely. Thus the evidence has to be strong if the potential beneficiaries are to be convinced.

There is no denying that, in this respect, it would be premature to hope for the support of the social-science community. But this support is not immediately indispensable. Some of our "think tanks", such as Rand, by now have a tradition of investing in pioneer research in areas of potentially great payoff, even if the probability of payoff would appear insufficient to satisfy a banker's conscience. In the case under discussion, some payoff by way of a better understanding of certain social-science issues by now seems certain. The probability of an even more substantial payoff in the form of prediction and, consequently, some measure of control in the arenas of economics and international relations does not seem negligibly small. ■

Epistemology, according to Webster, is the theory of the methods and grounds of knowledge. My suggestion of introducting at least pseudo-experimentation into the nonexperimental sciences opens up the epistemological question of the extent to which we can properly expect these "softer" (or inexact) sciences to emulate the "hard" (or exact) sciences. This question is addressed in the following section. While in the exact sciences explanation and prediction have the same logical structure, this is not so in the inexact sciences. This permits various methodological innovations in the inexact sciences, such as the use of expert judgment and the conduct of pseudo-experiments within simulation models of the real world.

6 *ON THE EPISTEMOLOGY OF THE INEXACT SCIENCES*[2]

6.1 *The Myth of Exactness*

It is a fiction of long standing that there are two classes of sciences, the exact and the inexact, and that the social sciences by and large are members of the second class—unless and until, like experimental psychology or some

2. This essay, first published under the same title in 1959, was written jointly with my former Rand colleague (now Professor of Philosophy at the University of Pittsburgh), Nicholas Rescher. It is reprinted here by permission of the Institute of Management Sciences from *Management Science*, vol. 6, no. 1 (October 1959), copyright 1959.

parts of economics, they mature to the point where admission to the first class may be granted.

This widely prevalent attitude seems to us fundamentally mistaken, for it finds a difference in principle where there is only one of degree, and it imputes to the so-called exact sciences a procedural rigor that is rarely present in fact. For the sake of a fuller discussion of these points, let us clarify at the very outset the terms "science", "exact science", and "inexact science", as they are intended here.

For an enterprise to be characterized as *scientific* it must have as its purpose the explanation and prediction of phenomena within its subject-matter domain and it must provide such explanation and prediction in a reasoned, and therefore intersubjective, fashion. We speak of an exact science if this reasoning process is formalized in the sense that the terms used are exactly defined and reasoning takes place by formal logico-mathematical derivation of the hypothesis (the statement of the fact to be explained or predicted) from the evidence (the body of knowledge accepted by virtue of being highly confirmed by observation). That an exact science frequently uses mathematical notation and concerns itself about attributes that lend themselves to exact measurement, we regard as incidental rather than defining characteristics. The same point applies to the precision, or exactness, of the predictions of which the science may be capable. While precise predictions are indeed to be preferred to vague ones, a discipline that provides predictions of a less precise character, but makes them correctly and in a systematic and reasoned way, must be classified as a science.

In an inexact science, conversely, reasoning is informal; in particular, some of the terminology may, without actually impeding communication, exhibit some inherent vagueness, and reasoning may at least in part rely on reference to intuitively perceived facts or implications. Again, an inexact science rarely uses mathematical notation or employs attributes capable of exact measurement, and as a rule does not make its predictions with great precision and exactitude.

Using the terms as elucidated here—and we believe that this corresponds closely to accepted usage—purely descriptive surveys or summaries, such as the part of history that is mere chronology or, say, purely descriptive botany or geography, are not called *sciences.* History proper, on the other hand, which seeks to explain historical transactions and to establish historical judgments having some degree of generality, is a science; it is in fact largely coincident with political science, except that its practitioners focus their interest on the past while the political scientists' main concern is the present and the future.

As for *exactness,* this qualification, far from being attributable to all of the so-called natural sciences, applies only to a small section of them, in particular to certain subfields of physics, in some of which exactness has even been put to the ultimate test of formal axiomatization. In other branches of physics, such as parts of aerodynamics and of the physics of extreme temperatures, exact procedures are still intermingled with unformalized expertise. Indeed the latter becomes more dominant as we move away from the precise and usually highly abstract core of an exact discipline and toward its applications to the complexities of the real world. Both architecture and medicine are cases in point. Aside from the respective activities of building structures and healing people, both have a theoretical content—that is, they are predictive and explanatory ("this bridge will not collapse, or has not collapsed, because . . ."; "this patient will exhibit, or has exhibited, such and such symptoms because . . ."). They must therefore properly be called sciences, but they are largely inexact since they rely heavily on informal reasoning processes.

If in addition to these examples we remember the essentially in-between status of such fields as economics and psychology, both of which show abundant evidence of exact derivations as well as reliance on intuitive judgment (exhibiting intermittent use of mathematical symbolism and of measurable attributes and an occasional ability to predict with precision), it should be obvious that there is at present no clear-cut dichotomy between exact and inexact sciences, and, in particular, that inexactness is not a prerogative of the social sciences.

However, leaving aside their present comparative status, it still might be possible to hold the view that there exists an epistemological difference in principle between the social sciences on the one hand and the natural or physical sciences on the other, in the sense that the latter, though not necessarily quite exact as yet, will gradually achieve ultimate exactness, while the former, due to the intangible nature of their subject matter and the imperfection in principle of their observational data, must of necessity remain inexact. Such a view would be based upon false premises, viz., a wholly misguided application of the exactness versus inexactness distinction. Indeed, the artificial discrimination between the physical sciences with their (at least in principle) precise terms, exact derivations, and reliable predictions as opposed to the vague terms, intuitive insights, and virtual unpredictability in the social sciences has retarded the development of the latter immeasurably.

The reason for this defeatist point of view regarding the social sciences may be traceable to a basic misunderstanding of the nature of scientific endeavor. What matters is not whether or to what extent inexactitudes in procedures and predictive capability can eventually be removed; rather it is *objectivity,* i.e., the intersubjectivity of findings independent of any one person's intuitive judgment, that distinguishes science from intuitive guesswork however brilliant. This has nothing to do with the intuitive spark that may be the origin of a new discovery; pure mathematics, whose formal exactness is beyond question, needs that as much as any science. But once a new fact or a new idea has been conjectured, no matter on how intuitive a foundation, it must be capable of objective test and confirmation by anyone. And it is this crucial standard of scientific objectivity rather than any purported criterion of exactitude to which the social sciences must conform.

In rejecting precision of form or method as well as degree of predictability as basic discriminants between the social and the physical sciences it thus remains to be seen whether there might not in fact be a fundamental epistemological difference between them with regard to their ability to live up to the same rigorous standard of objectivity. Our belief is that there is essentially no such difference—in other words, that the social sciences cannot be separated from the physical on methodological grounds. We hope to convince the reader of the validity of our position by offering, in what follows, at least some indications as to how the foundations for a uniform epistemology of all of the inexact sciences might be laid—be they social sciences or "as yet" inexact physical sciences.

Our goal is more modest than that of presenting a comprehensive epistemology of the inexact sciences. We merely wish to outline an epistemological attitude toward them that we would like to see adopted more widely. Since epistemology is concerned with the role of evidence in the attainment of scientific laws and with the scientific procedures implied by that role, we need to reexamine the status of such things as laws, evidence, confirmation, prediction, and explanation, with special reference to the case of inexact sciences.

6.2 Historical Laws

Let us first take a brief look at historical science in order to obtain some illustrative examples of the form of laws in the social sciences and of the function they perform. An *historical law* may be regarded as a well-confirmed statement concerning the actions of an organized group of men under certain restrictive conditions (such group actions being intended to include those of systems composed conjointly of people and nonhuman instrumentalities under their physical control). Examples of such laws are: "A census takes place in the U.S. in every decade year", "Heretics were persecuted in seventeenth-century Spain", "In the sea fights of sailing vessels in the period 1653-1803, large formations were too cumbersome for effectual control as single units". Such statements share two features of particular epistemological importance and interest: they are *law-like* and *loose*. These points require elaboration.

To consider law-likeness, let us take for example the statement about the cumbersomeness of large sailing fleets in sea fights. On first view, this statement might seem to be a mere descriptive list of characteristics of certain particular engagements: a shorthand version of a long conjunction of statements about large-scale engagements during the century and a half from Texel (1653) to Trafalgar (1803). This view is incorrect, however, because the statement in question is more than an assertion regarding characteristics of certain actual engagements. Unlike mere descriptions, it can serve to explain developments in cases to which it makes no reference. Furthermore, the statement has counterfactual force. It asserts that in literally any large-scale fleet action fought under the conditions in question (sailing vessels of certain types, with particular modes of armament, and with contemporaneous communications methods), effectual control of a great battle line is hopeless. It is claimed, for example, that had Villeneuve issued from Cadiz some days earlier or later he would all the same have encountered difficulty in the management of the great allied battle fleet of over thirty sail of the line, and Nelson's strategem of dividing his force into two virtually independent units under prearranged plans would have facilitated effective management equally well as at Trafalgar.

The statement in question is thus no mere descriptive summary of particular events; it functions on the more general plane of law-like statements, specifically, in that it can serve as a basis for explanation, and that it can exert counterfactual force. To be sure, the individual descriptive statements which are known and relevant do provide a part of the appropriate evidence for the historical generalization. But the content of the statement itself lies beyond the sphere of mere description, and in taking this wider role historical laws become marked as genuine law-like statements.

The second important characteristic of historical laws lies in their being "loose". It has been said already that historical laws are (explicitly or obliquely) conditional in their logical form. However, the nature of these conditions is such that they can often not be spelled out fully and completely. For instance, the statement about sailing fleet tactics has (among others) an implicit or tacit condition relating to the state of naval ordnance in the eighteenth century. In elaborating such conditions, the historian delineates what is typical of the place and period. The full implications of such reference may be vast and inexhaustible; for instance, in our example, ordnance ramifies via metalworking technology into metallurgy, mining, and so on. Thus the conditions which are operative in the formulation of an historical law may only be indicated in a general way and are not necessarily (indeed in most cases cannot be expected to be) exhaustively articulated. This characteristic of such laws is here designated as *looseness.*

It is this looseness of its laws which typifies history as an inexact science in the sense in which we have used the term: in a domain whose laws are not fully and precisely articulated there exists a limit to exactitude in terminology and reasoning. In such a sphere, mathematical precision must not be expected. To say this implies no pejorative intent whatever, for the looseness of historical laws is clearly recognized as being due, not to slipshod formulation of otherwise precise facts, but to the fundamental complexities inherent in the conceptual apparatus of the domain.

A consequence of the looseness of historical laws is that they are not universal but merely quasi-general in that they admit exceptions. Since the conditions delimiting the area of application of the law are often not exhaustively articulated, a supposed violation of the law may be explicable by showing that a legitimate (but as yet unformulated) precondition of the law's applicability is not fulfilled in the case under consideration. The laws may be taken to contain a tacit caveat of the "usually" or "other things being equal" type. An historical law is thus not strictly universal in that it must be taken as applicable to all cases falling within the scope of its explicitly formulated conditions; rather it may be thought to formulate relationships which obtain generally, or better, *as a rule.* (This point has been made by various writers on historical method. Charles Frankel [1957, p. 142], for example, puts it as follows in his lucid article, "Explanation and Interpretation in History": "It is frequently misleading to take statements such as 'Power corrupts, and absolute power corrupts absolutely', when historians use them, as attempts to give an exact statement of a universal law. . . . But such remarks may be taken as statements of strategy, rules to which it is best to conform in the absence of very strong countervailing considerations.")

Such a "law" we will term a *quasi-law.* In order for the law to be valid, it is not necessary that no apparent exceptions occur; it is necessary only that, if an apparent exception should occur, an adequate explanation be forthcoming, an explanation demonstrating the exceptional characteristic of the case in hand by establishing the violation of an appropriate (if hitherto unformulated) condition of the law's applicability.

For example, the historical law that in the prerevolutionary French navy only persons of noble birth were commissioned is not without apparent exceptions, since in particular the regulation was waived in the case of the great Jean Bart, son of a humble fisherman, who attained great distinction in the naval service. We may legitimately speak here of an *apparent* exception; for instead of abandoning this universal law in view of the cited counterexample, it is more expedient to maintain the law but to interpret it as endowed with certain tacit amendments, which, fully spelled out, would read somewhat as follows: "In the prerevolutionary French navy, as a rule, only persons of noble birth were commissioned, that is, unless the regulation was explicitly waived or an oversight or fraud occurred or some other similarly exceptional condition obtained." While it may be objected that such a formulation is vague—and indeed it is—it cannot be said that the law is now so loose as to be vacuous; for the intuitive intent is clear, and its looseness is far from permitting the law's retention in the face of just any counterexample. Specifically, if a reliable source brings to light one counterinstance for which there is no tenable explanation whatsoever to give it exempt status, an historian may still wish to retain the law in the definite expectation that some such explanation eventually be forthcoming; but should the historian be confronted with a succession or series of unexplained exceptions to the law, he or she would no doubt soon feel compelled to abandon the law itself.

We thus have the indisputable fact that in a generally loose context, that of history being typical of the inexact sciences, it would be hopeless to try to erect a theoretical structure that is logically, perhaps even esthetically, on a plane with our idealistic image of an exact theory. Yet, if we consider the situation not from the standpoint of the wishful dreamer of neat and tidy theory construction, but from that of the pragmatist in pursuit of a better understanding of the world through reasoned methods of explanation and prediction, then we have good reason to take heart at the sight even of quasi-laws, and we should realize that the seemingly thin line between vagueness and vacuity is solid enough to distinguish fact from fiction reasonably well in practical applications.

6.3 Quasi-Laws in the Physical Sciences

We have chosen to illustrate the nature of limited generalizations (quasi-laws) by means of the graphic example of historical laws. Use of this example from a social-science context must not, however, be construed as implying that quasi-laws do not occur in the natural, indeed even the physical, sciences. In many parts of modern physics, formalized theories based wholly on universal principles are (at least currently) unavailable, and use of limited generalizations is commonplace, particularly so in applied physics and engineering.

Writers on the methodology of the physical sciences often bear in mind a somewhat antiquated and much idealized image of physics as a very complete and thoroughly exact discipline in which it is never necessary to rely on limited generalizations or expert opinion. But physical science today is very far from meeting this ideal. Indeed some branches of the social sciences are in better shape as regards the generality of their laws than various departments of physics, such as the theory of turbulence phenomena, high-velocity aerodynamics, or the physics of extreme temperatures. Throughout applied physics in particular, when we move (say in engineering applications) from the realm of idealized abstraction ("perfect" gases, "homogeneous" media, and so on) to the complexities of the real world, reliance on generalizations that are, in effect, quasi-laws becomes pronounced. (Engineering practice in general is based on "rules of thumb" to an extent undreamed of in current theories of scientific method.)

Thus no warrant whatever exists for using the presence of quasi-laws in the social sciences as validating a methodological separation between them on the one hand and the physical sciences on the other. A realistic assessment of physical science methods shows that quasi-laws are here operative too, and importantly so.

With this in mind, let us now turn to a closer examination of the role played by laws—or quasi-laws—in prediction and explanation.

6.4 Explanation and Prediction

A somewhat simplified characterization of scientific explanation—but one that nonetheless has a wide range of applicability, particularly in the physical sciences—is that explanation consists in the *logical derivation* of the statement to be explained from a complex of factual statements and well-established general laws. One would, for example, explain the freezing of a lake by adducing (1) the fact that the temperature fell below 32°F and (2) the law that water freezes at 32°F. These statements, taken together, yield the statement to be explained deductively. (For a full discussion of this matter, see C. G. Hempel and P. Oppenheim, 1948, pp. 135-175.)

This deductive model of explanation, while adequate for many important types of explanations encountered in the sciences, cannot without at least some emendation be accepted as applying to all explanations. For one thing there are probabilistic explanations, which can be based on statistical (rather than strictly universal) laws ("I did not win the Irish Sweepstakes because the chances were overwhelmingly against my doing so"). Then there are what we have been referring to as quasi-laws, occurring in the inexact sciences, which because of their escape clauses cannot serve as the basis of strict *derivation,* yet can carry explanatory force.

The uncertainty of conclusions based on quasi-laws is not due to the same reason as that of conclusions based on statistical laws. A statistical law asserts the presence of some characteristic in a certain (presumably high) percentage of cases, whereas a quasi-law asserts it in all cases for which an exceptional status (in some ill-defined but clearly understood sense) cannot be claimed.

We note for the moment, however, that the schema of explanation when either type of nonuniversal law is involved is the same and in fact identical with what it would be were the law universal; and an explanation is regarded as satisfactory if, while short of logically entailing the hypothesis, it succeeds in making the statement to be explained highly credible in the sense of providing convincing evidence for it. (We shall return to a discussion of the concept of evidence below.)

With regard to prediction as opposed to explanation, analyses of scientific reasoning often emphasize the similarities between the two, holding that they are identical from a logical standpoint, inasmuch as each is an instance of the use of evidence to establish an hypothesis, and the major point of difference between them is held to be that the hypothesis of a prediction or of an explanation concerns respectively the future or the past. This view, however, does not do justice to several differences between prediction and explanation that are of particular importance for our present purposes. (On the contrast between prediction and explanation, see Scheffler, 1957, pp. 293-309, and Rescher, 1958, pp. 281-290.)

First of all, there are such things as unreasoned predictions—predictions made without any articulation of justifying argument. The validation of such predictions lies not in their being supported by plausible arguments, but may, for example, reside in proving sound *ex post facto* through a record of successes on the part of the predictor or predicting mechanism.

It is clear that such predictions have no analogue in explanations; only reasoned predictions, based on the application of established theoretical principles, are akin to explanations. However, even here there is an important point of difference. By the very meaning of the term, an explanation must *establish* its conclusion, showing that there is a strong warrant why the fact to be explained—rather than some possible alternative—obtains. On the other hand, the conclusion of a (reasoned) prediction need not be well established in this sense; it suffices that it be rendered *more tenable than comparable alternatives.* Here then is an important distinction in logical strength between explanations and predictions: an explanation, though it need not logically rule out alternatives altogether, must beyond reasonable doubt establish its hypothesis as *more credible than its negation.* Of a prediction, on the other hand, we need to require only that it establish its hypothesis simply as *more credible than any comparable alternative.* Of course predictions may, as in astronomy, be as firmly based in fact and as tightly articulated in reasoning as any explanation. But this is not a general requirement to which predictions *must* conform. A doctor's prognosis, for example, does not have astronomical certitude, yet practical considerations render it immensely useful as a guide in our conduct because it is far superior to reliance on guesswork or on pure chance alone as a decision-making device.

Generally speaking, in any field in which our ability to forecast with precision is very limited, our actions of necessity are guided by only slight differences in the probability that we attach to possible future alternative states of the world, and consequently we must permit predictions to be based on far weaker evidence than explanations. This is especially true of a science such as history, or rather its predictive counterpart—political science. Here, in the absence of powerful theoretic delimitations that narrow down the immense variety of future possibilities to some manageable handful, the *a priori* likelihood of any particular state of affairs is minute, and we can thus tolerate considerable weakness in our predictive tools without rendering them useless. Consider, for example, the quasi-law that in a U.S. off-year election the opposition party is apt to gain. This is certainly not a general law, nor is it intended to be a summary of statistics. It has implicit qualifications of the *ceteris paribus* type, but it does claim to characterize the course of events "as a rule" and it generates an expectation of the explainability of deviations. On this basis, an historical (or political) law of this sort can provide a valid, though limited, foundation for sound predictions.

The epistemological asymmetry between explanation and prediction has not, it seems to us, been adequately recognized and taken into account in discussion of scientific method. For one thing, such recognition would lead to a better understanding of the promise of possibly unorthodox items of methodological equipment, such as quasi-laws, for the purposes of prediction in the inexact sciences. But more generally it would open the way to explicit consideration of a *specific methodology of prediction*—a matter that seems to have been neglected to date by the philosophers of science. As long as one believes that explanation and prediction are strict methodological counterparts, it is reasonable to press further with solely the explanatory problems of a discipline, in the expectation that only the tools thus forged will then be usable for predictive purposes. But once this belief is rejected, the problem of a specifically predictive method arises, and it becomes pertinent to investigate the possibilities of predictive procedures autonomous of those used for explanation.

6.5 Some Examples of the Use of Evidence in Prediction

The simplest use of evidence occurs when there is a direct reference to prior instances. Will my car start on this cold morning? Its record of successful starting on previous cold mornings is around 50 percent. I would be unduly hopeful or pessimistic in assigning as personal probability of its starting today a number significantly different from one-half. This use of a record of past instances as a basis for probability assignments with regard to future events is a common, and generally justified, inductive procedure. However, under some circumstances it is a very poor way indeed of marshalling evidence.

Consider the case of Smith, who has been riding the bus to work for a year, the fare having been 10 cents. One morning he is required to pay 15 cents. Smith may wonder if his return fare that evening will be 10 cents. It is highly unlikely—despite the great preponderance of 10-cent rides in Smith's sample. Smith well knows that public transportation fares do change, and not by whim but by adoption of a new fare structure. In the light of this item of background information, it is unreasonable for Smith to base his personal probability directly on the cumulative record of past instances.

This illustrates the need for the use of background knowledge as indirect evidence, in the sense of furnishing other than direct instance confirmation. This need is encountered constantly in the use of evidence. Consider another example: Will my new neighbor move away again within five years? He is a carpenter (the average carpenter moves once every ten years) and a bachelor (the average bachelor moves once every three years). I can assess the likelihood of my neighbor's moving within the next five years relative to either the reference class of carpenters or that of bachelors. Which one I should choose, or what weight I should give to each, must depend strongly on my background information concerning the relative relevance of occupation versus marital status as a determining factor in changes of domicile.

Such reference-class problems arise even with statistical information of the simplest kind. Consider a sample of 100 objects drawn at random from a population, with the following outcome as regards possession of the properties P and Q:

	has Q	has not Q
has P	1	9
has not P	89	1

Given this information, what is the probability that another object drawn from the population, which is known to have the property P, will also have the property Q? Should we use a value around 0.1 (since only 1 of 10 observed Ps is a Q) or a value around 0.9 (since altogether 90 percent of the observed sample has the property *Q*)? Here again, an expedient use of the statistical evidence before us must rely on background information, if any, regarding the relevance of *P*-ness to *Q*-ness. If we know that most Texans are rich and most barbers poor, and are given as the only specific item of information about a man by the name of Jones that he is a Texan barber, we would do well to assign a low probability to the statement that Jones is rich, precisely because occupation is known to us to be more relevant to financial status than is location.

6.6 The Role of Expertise in Prediction

The implication of the examples we have been discussing is that a knowledge about past instances or about statistical samples—while indeed providing valuable information—is not the sole and sometimes not even the main form of evidence in support of rational assignments of probability values. In fact the evidential use of such *prima facie* evidence must be tempered by reference to background information, which frequently may be intuitive in character and have the form of a vague recognition of underlying regularities, such as analogies, correlations, or other conformities whose formal rendering would require the use of predicates of a logical level higher than the first.

The consideration of such underlying regularities is of special importance for the inexact sciences, particularly the social sciences (but not exclusively; see below), because in this sphere we are constantly faced with situations in which statistical information matters less than knowledge of regularities in the behavior of people or in the character of institutions, such as traditions and customary practices, fashions and mores, national attitudes and climates of opinion, institutional rules and regulations, group aspirations, and so on. For instance, in assessing the chances of a Republican presidential victory in 1960 [remember that this essay was written in 1959], a knowledge of the record of past election successes matters less than an insight into current trends and tendencies; or in answering a question as to the likelihood, say, of U.S. recognition of Communist China by 1960, it is hard to point to any relevant statistical evidence, yet there exists a host of relatively undigested but highly relevant background information. (Use of background information, to temper the application of statistical information, is just as operative in the physical sciences—e.g., in engineering—so that no difference in principle is involved here.)

This nonexplicitness of background knowledge, which nonetheless may be significant or even predominantly important, is typical of the inexact sciences, as is the uncertainty as to the evidential weight to be accorded various pieces of *prima facie* information in view of indirect evidence provided by underlying regularities. Hence the great importance that must be attached to experts and to expertise in these fields. For the expert has at his ready disposal a large store of (mostly inarticulated) background knowledge and a refined sensitivity to its relevance, through the intuitive application of which he is often able to produce trustworthy personal probabilities regarding hypotheses in his area of expertise.

The important place of expert judgment for predictions in the inexact sciences is further indicated by the prominence of quasi-laws among the explanatory instrumentalities of this domain. Since the conditions of applicability of such generalizations are neither fully nor even explicitly formulable, their use in specific circumstances presupposes the exercise of sound judgment as to their applicability to the case in hand. The informed expert, with his resources of background knowledge and his cultivated sense of the relevance and bearing of generalities in particular cases, is best able to carry out the application of quasi-laws necessary for reasoned prediction in this field.

6.7 The Problem of the Predictive Use of Evidence in an Inexact Context

In summary, the foregoing illustrations of the predictive use of evidence may be said to indicate that we are frequently confronted with what must be considered as a problematical, and far from ideal, epistemological situation. The examples we have been considering show that in assessing the probability of an hypothesis—typically a description of some future event—we are in many instances required to rely not merely on some specific and explicit evidence but also on a vast body of potentially relevant background knowledge, which is in general not only vague in its extent but also deficient in explicit articulation or even articulability. One is unable to set down in sentential form everything that would have to be included in a full characterization of one's knowledge about a familiar room; the same applies equally, if not more so, to a political expert's attempt to state all he or she knows that might be relevant to a question such as that of U.S.-China relations.

Faced with this situation, we must either renounce all claims to systematic prediction in the inexact sciences or turn to unorthodox methods that rely on expert judgment. That is, an expert's subjective estimate of the probability of a particular hypothesis, given certain evidence, may be taken as an estimate, on our part (as users of that expert), of the probability in question.

It might seem that in resorting to this device we conjure up a host of new problems, because—to all appearances—we are throwing objectivity to the winds. Of course, since we insist on remaining within our own definition of scientific activity, we do not propose to forego objectivity. However, before attempting to analyze the possibility of salvaging objectivity in this situation, it may be well to look at a few examples illustrating the application of expertise in the sense just described.

6.8 The Intrinsic Use of Experts for Prediction

A source of characteristic examples of the predictive use of expert judgment is provided by the field of diagnostics, especially medical diagnostics. (An extensive and useful discussion of medical prediction is contained in Mehl, 1954.) A patient, let us assume, exhibits a pattern of symptoms such that it is virtually certain that he has either ailment A or ailment B, with respective probabilities of .4 and .6, where these probabilities derive from the statistical record of past cases. Thus the entire body of explicit symptomatic evidence is (by hypothesis) such as to indicate a margin in favor of the prediction that the patient suffers from disease B rather than A, and thus may respond positively to a corresponding course of treatment. But it is quite possible that an examining physician, taking into consideration not only the explicit indicators that constitute the "symptoms" (such as temperature and blood pressure) but also a host of otherwise inarticulated background knowledge with regard to this particular patient, the circumstances of the case, and so on may arrive at a diagnosis of disease A rather than B. Thus the use of background information in a way that is not systematized but depends entirely on the exercise of informal expert judgment may appropriately lead to predictive conclusions in the face of *prima facie* evidence that points in the opposite direction.

Quite similar in their conceptual structures to the foregoing medical example are various other cases of predictive expertise in the economic sphere. The advice of an expert investment counselor, for example, may exhibit essentially the same subtle employment of nonarticulate background knowledge that characterized the prediction of the diagnostician.

Other examples, drawn from the applied sciences, engineering, industry, politics, and so forth, will easily suggest themselves. What they have in common is the reliance, in part or wholly, on an expert, who here functions in an intrinsic rather than an extrinsic role. By *extrinsic expertise* we mean the kind of inventiveness, based on factual knowledge and the perception of previously unnoticed relationships, that goes into the hypothesizing of new laws and the construction of new theories; it is, in other words, the successful activity of the scientist *qua* scientist. *Intrinsic expertise,* by contrast, is not invoked until after an hypothesis has been formulated and its probability, in the sense of degree of confirmation, is to be estimated. The expert, when performing intrinsically, thus functions within a theory rather than on the theory-constructing level.

6.9 The Role of Prediction as an Aid to Decision-Making

The decisions that professional decision makers—governmental administrators, company presidents, military commanders, and the like—are called upon to make inevitably turn on the question of future developments, since their directives as to present actions are invariably conceived with a view to future results. Thus a reliance on predictive ability is nowhere more overt and more pronounced than in the area of policy formation, and decision-making in general.

For this reason, decision makers surround themselves by staffs of expert advisers, whose special knowledge and expertise must generally cover a wide field. Some advising experts may have a great store of factual knowledge and can thus serve as walking reference books. Others may excel through their diagnostic or otherwise predictive abilities. Others may have a special analytical capacity to recognize the structure of the problems in hand, thus aiding in the proper utilization of the contributions of the other two types of experts (e.g., operations analysts and management consultants). The availability of such special expertise constitutes for the decision maker a promise of increased predictive ability essential to the more effective discharge of his own responsibilities. Thus the ultimate function of expert advice is almost always to make a predictive contribution.

While the dependence of the decision makers on expert advisers is particularly pronounced in social-science contexts, for instance, in the formulation of economic and political policies, such dependence on expertise ought by no means to be taken to contradistinguish the social from the physical sciences. In certain engineering applications, particularly of relatively underdeveloped branches of physics (such as the applied physics of extremes of temperature or velocity) the reliance on "know-how" and expert judgment is just as pronounced as it is in the applications of political science to foreign-policy formation. The use of experts for prediction does *not* constitute a line of demarcation between the social and the physical sciences, but rather between the exact and the inexact sciences.

Although we have held that the primary functions of expert advisers to decision makers is to serve as "predictors", we by no means intend to suggest that they act as fortune-tellers, trying to foresee specific occurrences for which the limited intellectual vision of the nonexpert is insufficient. For the decision-supporting uses of predictive expertise, there is in general no necessity for an anticipation of particular future occurrences. It suffices that the expert be able to sketch out adequately the general directions of future developments, to anticipate—as we have already suggested—some of the major critical junctures ("branch points") on which the course of these developments will hinge, and to make contingency predictions with regard to the alternatives associated with them.

While the value of scientific prediction for sound decision-making is beyond question, it can hardly be claimed that the inexact sciences have the situation regarding the use of predictive expertise well in hand. Quite to the contrary, it is our strong feeling that significant improvements are possible in the predictive instruments available to the decision maker. These improvements are contingent on the development of methods for the more effective predictive use of expert judgment. In the final section we shall give consideration to some of the problems involved in this highly important, but hitherto largely unexplored, area.

6.10 Justification of the Intrinsic Use of Expertise

We come back to the problem of preserving objectivity in the face of reliance on expertise. Can we accept the utilization of intrinsic expert judgment within the framework of an inductive procedure without laying ourselves open to the charge of abandoning objective scientific methods and substituting rank subjectivity?

To see that explicit use of expert judgment is not incompatible with scientific objectivity, let us look once more at the medical-diagnosis example of the preceding section. Consider the situation in which a diagnostician has advised that a patient be treated for ailment A (involving, say, a major surgical operation) rather than B (which might merely call for a special diet). Our willingness, in this case, to put our trust in the expert's judgment surely would not be condemned as an overly subjective attitude. The reasons our reliance on the expert is objectively justified are not difficult to see. For one thing, the selection of appropriate experts is not a matter of mere personal preference but is a procedure governed by objective criteria (about which more will be said in the ensuing section). But most important, the past diagnostic performance record makes the diagnostician an objectively reliable indicator (of diseases), in the same sense as one of any two highly correlated physical characteristics is an indicator of the other. ("If most hot pieces of iron are red, and vice versa, and if this piece of iron is red, then it is probably hot.")

Even if the expert's explicit record of past performance is unknown, reliance on his predictions may be objectively justified on the basis of general background knowledge as to his reputation as an expert. The objective reliability of experts' pronouncements may also be strongly suggested by the fact that they often exhibit a high degree of agreement with one another, which—at least if we have reason to assume the pronouncements to be independent—precludes subjective whim.

Epistemologically speaking, the use of an expert as an objective indicator—

as illustrated by the example of the diagnostician—amounts to considering the expert's predictive pronouncement as an integral, intrinsic part of the subject matter and treating his reliability as a part of the theory about the subject matter. Our information about the expert is conjoined with our other knowledge about the field, and we proceed with the application of precisely the same inductive methods that we would apply in cases where no use of expertise is made. Our "data" are supplemented by the expert's personal probability valuations and by his judgments of relevance (which, by the way, could be derived from suitable personal probability statements), and our "theory" is supplemented by information regarding the performance of experts.

In this manner the incorporation of expert judgment into the structure of our investigation is made subject to the same safeguards that are used to assure objectivity in other scientific investigations. The use of expertise is therefore no retreat from objectivity or reversion to a reliance on subjective taste.

6.11 Criteria for the Selection of Predictive Experts

The first and most obvious criterion of expertise is of course knowledge. We resort to an "expert" precisely because we expect his information and the body of experience at his disposal to constitute an assurance that he will be able to select the needed items of background information, determine the character and extent of their relevance, and apply these insights to the formulation of the required personal probability judgments.

However, the expert's knowledge is not enough; he must be able to bring it to bear effectively on the predictive problem in hand, and this not every expert is able to do. It becomes necessary also to place some check on his predictive efficacy and to take a critical look at his past record of predictive performance.

The simplest way in which to score an expert's performance is in terms of "reliability": his *degree of reliability* is the relative frequency of cases in which, when confronted with several alternative hypotheses, he ascribed to the eventually correct alternative among them a greater personal probability than to the others.

This measure, while useful, must yet be taken with a grain of salt, for there are circumstances where even a layman's degree of reliability, as defined above, can be very close to 1. For instance, in a region of very constant weather, a layman can prognosticate the weather quite successfully by always predicting the same weather for the next day as for the current one. Similarly, a quack who hands out bread pills and reassures his patients of recovery "in due time" may prove right more often than not and yet have no legitimate claim to being classified as a medical expert. Thus what matters is not so much an expert's absolute degree of reliability but his relative degree of reliability, that is, his reliability as compared to that of the average person. But even this may not be enough. In the case of the medical diagnostician discussed earlier, the layman may have no information that might give him a clue as to which of diseases A and B is the more probable, while anyone with a certain amount of rudimentary medical knowledge may know that disease A generally occurs much more frequently than disease B; yet his prediction of A rather than B on this basis alone would not qualify him as a reliable diagnostician. Thus a more subtle assessment of the qualifications of an expert may require his comparison with the average person having some degree of general background knowledge in his field of specialization. One method of scoring experts somewhat more subtly than just by their reliability is in terms of their "accuracy": the *degree of accuracy* of an expert's predictions is the correlation between his personal probabilities p and his correctness in the class of those hypotheses to which he ascribed the probability p. Thus of a highly accurate predictor we expect that of those hypotheses to which he ascribes, say, a probability of 70 percent, approximately 70 percent will eventually turn out to be confirmed. Accuracy in this sense, by the way, does not guarantee reliability, but accuracy in addition to reliability may be sufficient to distinguish the real expert from the specious one.

The following example may further clarify the difference between reliability and accuracy. Suppose experts A and B each gave 100 responses, assigning probabilities .2, .4, .6, and .8 to what in fact were the correct alternatives among 100 choices of H and ~H, as follows:

p	*A*	*B*
.2	10	0
.4	20	0
.6	30	60
.8	40	40

Then A is perfectly accurate (e.g., exactly 60 percent, or 30, of the 20 + 30, or 50, cases to which he assigned .6 were correct), but he is only 70 percent reliable; B, on the other hand, is 100 percent reliable, but his accuracy is quite faulty—since 100 percent, rather than 60 percent, of the 60 cases to which he assigned .6 were correct.

6.12 The Dependence of Predictive Performance on Subject Matter

Not only are some experts better predictors than others, but subject-matter fields differ from one another in the extent to which they admit of expertise. This circumstance is of course in some instances due to the fact that the scientific theory of the field in question is relatively undeveloped. The geology of the moon or the meteorology of Mars is less amenable to prediction than mundane counterparts, although no greater characteristic complexity is inherent in these fields. In other cases, however, predictive expertise is limited despite a high degree of cultivation of a field, because the significant phenomena hinge on factors that are not particularly amenable to prediction.

In domains in which the flux of events is subject to gradual transitions and constant regularities (say astronomy), a high degree of predictive expertise is possible. In those fields, however, in which the processes of transition admit of sharp jolts and discontinuities, which can in turn be the effects of so complex and intricate causal processes as to be "chance" occurrences for all practical purposes, predictive expertise is inherently less feasible. The assassination of a political leader can altogether change the policies of a nation, particularly when such a nation does not have a highly developed complex of institutions that ensure gradualness of its policy changes. Clearly no expert on a particular country can be expected to have the data requisite for a prediction of assassinations; that is, his relevant information is virtually certain not to include the precisely detailed knowledge of the state of mind of various key figures that might give him any basis whatsoever for assigning a numerical value as his personal probability to the event in question. This situation is quite analogous to that of predicting the outcome of a particular toss of a coin; only the precise dynamic details of the toss's initial conditions might provide a basis for computing a probability other than one-half for the outcome, and these details again are almost certainly unavailable. We may here legitimately speak of "chance occurrences", in the sense that not even an expert, unless he has the most unusual information at his disposal, is in a better position than the layman to make a reliable prediction.

In the inexact sciences, particularly in the social sciences, the critical causal importance of such chance events makes predictive expertise in an absolute sense difficult and sometimes impossible, and it is this, rather than the quality of his theoretical machinery, that puts the social scientist in a poor competitive position relative, say, to the astronomer.

However, when the expert is unable to make precise predictions, due to the influence of chance factors, we can expect him to indicate the major contingencies on which future developments will hinge. Even though the expert cannot predict the specific course of future events in an unstable country, he should be able to specify the major " branch points" of future contingencies and to provide personal probabilities conditionally with respect to these. Thus, for example, while it would be unreasonable to expect an expert on the American economy to predict with precision the duration of a particular phase of an economic cycle (e.g., a recession), it is entirely plausible to ask him to specify the major potential "turning points" in the cycle (e.g., increased steel production at a certain juncture) and to indicate the probable courses of development ensuing on each of the specified alternatives.

Such differences in predictability among diverse subject-matter fields lead to important consequences for the proper utilization of experts. One obvious implication is that it may clearly be more profitable to concentrate limited resources of predictive expertise on those portions of a broader domain that are inherently more amenable to prediction. For example, in a study of long-range political developments in a particular geographic area, it might in some cases be preferable to focus on demographic developments rather than the evolution of programs and platforms of political parties.

However, the most important consideration is that even in subject-matter fields in which the possibility of prediction is very limited, the exercise of expertise, instead of being applied to the determination of *absolute* personal probabilities with respect to certain hypotheses, ought rather more profitably to be concentrated on the identification of the relevant branch points and the associated problem of the *relative* personal probabilities for the hypothesis in question, that is, relative with regard to the alternatives arising at these branch points.

Even in predictively very "difficult" fields—such as the question of the future foreign policy of an "unstable" country—the major branch points of future contingencies are frequently few enough for actual enumeration, and although outright prediction cannot be expected, relative predictions hinging on these principal alternative contingencies can in many instances serve the same purposes for which absolute predictions are ordinarily employed. For example, it would be possible for a neighboring state, in formulating its own policy toward this country, to plan not for "the" (one and only) probable course of developments but to design several policies, one for each of the major contingencies, or perhaps even a single policy that could deal effectively with all the alternatives.

6.13 Predictive Consensus Techniques

The predictive use of an expert takes place within a rationale that, on the basis of our earlier discussion, can be characterized as follows: We wish to investigate the predictive hypothesis H; with the expert's assistance, we fix on the major items of the body of explicit evidence E that is relevant to this hypothesis; we then use the expert's personal probability valuation of H, given E, as *our* estimate of the probability of H on the basis of E.

This straightforward procedure, however, is no longer adequate in those cases in which several experts are available. For here we have not the single probability valuation of only one expert, but an entire series of valuations, one for each of the experts. The problem arises: How is the best joint use of these various expert valuations to be made? (Compare Kaplan et al., 1950.)

Many possible procedures for effecting a combination among such diverse probability estimates are available. One possibility, and no doubt the simplest, is to select one "favored" expert and to accept his sole judgment. We might, for example, compare the past predictive performance of the various experts and select that one whose record has been the most successful.

Another simple procedure is to pool the various expert valuations into an average of some sort, possibly the median, or a mean weighted so as to reflect past predictive success.

Again, the several experts might be made to act as a single group, pooling their knowledge in round-table discussion, if possible eliminating discrepancies in debate, and the group might then—on the basis of its corporate knowledge—be asked to arrive at one generally agreeable corporate "personal" probability as its consensus, which would now serve as our own estimate. (One weakness in this otherwise very plausible-sounding procedure is that the consensus valuation might unduly reflect the views of the most respected member of the group, or of the most persuasive.)

One variant of this consensus procedure is to require that the experts, after pooling their knowledge in discussion and perhaps after debating the issues, set down their separate "second-guess" personal probabilities, revising their initial independent valuations in the light of the group work. These separate values are then combined by some sort of averaging process to provide a single value. The advantage of such a combination of independent values over the use of a single generally acceptable group value is that it tends to diminish the influence of the most vociferous or influential group member. Incidentally, in any consensus method of this kind in which separate expert valuations are combined, we can introduce the refinement of weighting an expert's judgment so as to reflect his past performance.

Another consensus procedure, sometimes called the "Delphi technique", eliminates committee activity altogether, thus further reducing the influence of certain psychological factors, such as persuasion, the unwillingness to abandon publicly expressed opinions, and the bandwagon effect of majority opinion. This technique replaces direct debate by a carefully designed program of sequential individual interrogations (best conducted by questionnaires) interspersed with information and opinion feedback derived by computed consensus from the earlier parts of the program. Some of the questions directed to the respondents may, for instance, inquire into the "reasons" for previously expressed opinions, and a collection of such reasons may then be presented to each respondent in the group, together with an invitation to reconsider and possibly revise his earlier estimates. Both the inquiry into the reasons and subsequent feedback of the reasons adduced by others may serve to stimulate the experts into taking into due account considerations they might through inadvertence have neglected, and to give due weight to factors they were inclined to dismiss on first thought as unimportant.

We have done no more here than to indicate some examples from the spectrum of alternative consensus methods. Clearly there can be no one universally "best" method. The efficacy of such methods is very obviously dependent on the nature of the particular subject matter and may even hinge on the idiosyncrasies and personalities of the specific experts (on their ability to work as a group, for example). Indeed this question of the relative effectiveness of the various predictive consensus techniques is almost entirely an open problem for empirical research, and it is strongly to be hoped that more experimental investigation will be undertaken in this important field.

6.14 Simulation and Pseudo-Experimentation

We have thus far, in discussing the intrinsic use of experts or of groups of experts, described their function as being simply to predict, in the light of their personal probabilities, the correctness or incorrectness of proposed hypotheses. This description, while apt both in principle and often in practice, may in some instances be overly simplified.

For one thing, in situations concerned with complicated practical problems, no clear-cut hypothesis to which probability values could be meaningfully attached may be immediately discernible. For another, several kinds of expertise, all interacting with one another, may have to be brought to bear simultaneously in anything but a straightforward manner. Examples of such cases are provided by such questions as: "How can tension in the Middle East be relieved?" "What legislation is needed to reduce juvenile delinquency?" "How can America's schools improve science instruction?" Here, before even a single predictive expert can be used intrinsically, some at least rudimentary theoretical framework must be constructed within which predictive hypotheses can be stated. This, of course, calls for expertise of the extrinsic kind. Generally, the process involved is about as follows. The situation at hand (say, current crime patterns) is analyzed, that is, stated in terms of certain specific and, it is hoped, well-defined concepts; this step usually involves a certain amount of abstraction, in that some aspects of the situation that are judged irrelevant are deliberately omitted from the description. Then either some specific action is proposed and a hypothesis stated as to its consequences on the situation in question, or, more typically, a law or quasi-law is formulated, stating that in situations of the kind at hand actions of a certain kind will have such and such consequences.

A variant of this is of considerable epistemological significance. Instead of describing the situation directly, a *model* of it is constructed, which may be either mathematical or physical, in which each element of the real situation is simulated by a mathematical or physical object, and its relevant properties and relations to other elements are mirrored by corresponding simulative properties and relations. For example, any geographical map may be considered a (physical) model of some sector of the world; the planetary system can be simulated mathematically by a set of mass points moving according to Kepler's laws; a city's traffic system can be simulated by setting up a miniature model of its road net, traffic signals, and vehicles; and so on. Now, instead of formulating hypotheses and predictions directly about the real world, it is possible instead to do the same thing about the model. Any results obtained from an analysis of the model, to the extent that it truly simulates the real world, can then later be translated back into the corresponding statements about the latter. This injection of a model has the advantage that it admits of what may be called *pseudo-experimentation* ("pseudo" because the experiments are carried out in the model, not in reality). For example, in the case of the analysis of the traffic system, pseudo-experimentation may produce reliable predictions as to what changes in the time sequence of traffic signals will ease the flow of traffic through the city.

Pseudo-experimentation is nothing but the systematic use of the classical idea of a hypothetical experiment; it is applied when true experimentation is too costly or physically or morally impossible or—as we shall discuss next—when the real-world situation is too complex to permit the intrinsic use of experts. [For a classical example of pseudo-experimentation, see Section 5.]

The application of simulation techniques is a promising approach, whose fruitfulness has only begun to be demonstrated in documented experiments. [See, for instance, Kennedy and Chapman, 1956.]

It is particularly promising when it is desirable to employ intrinsically several experts with varying specialties in a context in which their forecasts cannot be entered independently but where they are likely to interact with one another. Here a model furnishes the experts with an artificial, simulated environment, within which they can jointly and simultaneously experiment, responding to the changes in the environment induced by their actions and acquiring through feedback the insights necessary to make successful predictions within the model and thus indirectly about the real world.

This technique lends itself particularly to predictions regarding the behavior of human organizations, inasmuch as the latter can be simulated most effectively by having the experts play the roles of certain members of such organizations and act out what in their judgment would be the actions, in the situation simulated, of their real-life counterparts (American Management Association, 1957). Generally it may be said that in many cases judicious pseudo-experimentation may effectively annul the oft-regretted infeasibility of carrying out experiments proper in the social sciences, for it provides an acceptable substitute, which has been tried and proved in the applied physical sciences.

6.15 Operational Gaming

A particular case of simulation involving role playing by the intrinsic experts is known as *operational gaming,* especially war gaming. A simulation model may properly be said to be gaming a real-life situation if the latter concerns decision makers in a context involving conflicting interests. In operational gaming, the simulated environment is particularly effective in reminding the expert, in his role as a player, to take *all* the factors into account in making predictions that are potentially relevant; for if he does not, and chooses a tactic or strategy that overlooks an essential factor, an astute "opponent" will soon enough teach him not to make such an omission again.

Aside from the obvious application of gaming to the analysis of military conflict, of which there are numerous examples, ranging from crude map exercises to sophisticated enterprises requiring the aid of high-speed computing equipment, gaming has been used to gain insights into the nature of political and economic conflict. In the political field, cold-war situations have been explored in this manner, and in the economic field inroads have been made into an analysis of bargaining and of industrial competition. (See Thomas and Deemer, 1957; Mood and Specht, 1954; Cushen, 1956; Bellman et al., 1957.)

We note in passing that operational games differ greatly in the completeness of their rules. These may be complete enough so that at each stage the strategic options at the players' disposal are wholly specified, and also that the consequences resulting from the joint exercise of these options are entirely determined; this would mean that the model represents a complete theory of the phenomena simulated in the game. On the other hand, neither of these factors may be completely determined by the rules, in which case it is up to an umpiring staff to allow or disallow proposed strategies and to assess their consequences. Clearly, umpiring in this sense represents yet another important device for the use of expertise intrinsically within the framework of a scientific theory (viz., the model in question).

6.16 Review of the Main Theses

Before proceeding to a consideration of certain recommendations, which seem to us to emerge as conclusions from the analysis that has been presented, it is appropriate to pause briefly for a review of the main points of the foregoing discussion. Our starting point has been the distinction between the "exact" and the "inexact" areas of science. It is our contention that this distinction is far more important and fundamental from the standpoint of a correct view of scientific method than is the case with superficially more pronounced distinctions based on subject-matter diversities, especially that between the social and the physical sciences. Some branches of the social sciences (e.g., certain parts of demography), which are usually characterized by the presence of a formalized mathematical theory, are methodologically analogous to the exact parts of physics. By contrast, the applied, inexact branches of physical science—for instance, certain areas of engineering under "extreme" conditions—are in many basic respects markedly similar to the social sciences.

This applies both to methods of explanation and to methods of prediction. Partly because of the absence of mathematically formalized theories, explanations throughout the area of inexact sciences—within the physical and the social science settings alike—are apt to be given by means of the restricted generalizations we have called quasi-laws. The presence of such less-than-universal principles in the inexact sciences creates an asymmetry between the methods of explanation and those of prediction in these fields. This suggests the desirability of developing the specifically predictive instrumentalities of these fields, for once the common belief in the identity of predictive and explanatory scientific procedures is seen to be incorrect, it is clearly appropriate to consider the nature and potentialities of predictive procedures distinct from those used for explanation. As for predictions in the inexact sciences (physical as well as social), these can be pragmatically acceptable (that is, as a basis for actions) when based on even less methodologically sophisticated grounds than are explanations, such as expert judgment.

These general considerations regarding the methodology of the inexact sciences hold particularly intriguing implications for the possibility of methodological innovation in the social sciences. Here the possible existence of methods that are unorthodox in the present state of social-science practices merits the closest examination. This is particularly true with respect to the pragmatic applications of the social sciences (e.g., in support of decision-making), in which the predictive element is preponderant over the explanatory.

One consideration of this sort revolves about the general question of the utilization of expertise. We have stressed the importance in the social sciences of limited generalizations (quasi-laws), which cannot necessarily be used in a simple and mechanical way, but whose very application requires the exercise of expert judgment. More generally, when interested in prediction in this field (especially for decision-making purposes), we are dependent on the experts' personal probability valuations for our guidance. A systematic investigation of the effective use of experts represents a means by which new and powerful instruments for the investigation of social-science problems might be forged.

Further, the use in social-science contexts of a variety of techniques borrowed from other, applied, sciences that are also inexact (e.g., engineering applications, military and industrial operations research) deserves the most serious consideration, for there are numerous possibilities for deriving leads as to methods which are potentially useful in the social sciences also—in particular, the use of simulation as a basis for conducting pseudo-experiments comes to mind. Finally, there is the important possibility of combining simulation with the intrinsic use of expertise, especially by means of the technique of operational gaming. This prospect constitutes a method whose potential for social-science research has hitherto gone virtually wholly unexplored, and it is our hope that this neglect will soon be remedied.

6.17 Some Tasks for Methodological Research

The thoughts we have set down in this chapter are intended to represent a challenge to those who would like to see the applied social sciences narrow the gap that has been created between them and the applied physical sciences by the explosive progress of technology in the first half of this century. A particularly promising prospect, it seems to us, is a pragmatic reorientation of social-science methodology along some of the lines that have proved successful in their fellow inexact sciences in the applied physical field.

In order to achieve this, much work has yet to be done. Aside from the need for further conceptual analysis, especially with regard to the status of quasi-laws in theory construction and the expansion of the degree-of-confirmation concept to languages containing relations and functions, there are numerous empirical studies that are suggested by the approach we are recommending.

The following is a list of areas of such research. It is intended to be suggestive, rather than exhaustive, of the type of effort required to implement this new approach.

(1) *Methodology of expertise:*
  - (a) Performance of the individual expert: e.g., selection and training of experts, aids to their performance, scoring systems for predictions.
  - (b) Performance of groups of experts: e.g., methods of consensus formation, Delphi techniques of interrogation with feedback, investigation of other multi expert structures.
  - (c) Psychological problems in the use of expert groups: e.g., reduction of respondents' bias in conference situations and as game players, simulation of motivation in pseudo-experiments requiring role playing, person-machine interaction.

(2) *Methodology of pseudo-experimentation:*
  (Here our suggestions are, on the whole, only obliquely methodological, since—in our opinion—a firm methodology will evolve gradually from a process of prolonged trial and error.)
  - (a) Simulation techniques in the social sciences: e.g., simulation of industrial or business processes or of the operation of some sector of the national economy, or of some governmental activity.
  - (b) Gaming techniques in the social sciences: e.g., gaming of industrial competition, cold-war games, foreign-trade and investment gaming.
  - (c) Problems inherent in pseudo-experimentation: e.g., the question of "controlled" experiments, problems of scaling arising in the translation of results from a simulation model to the real world.

In all of these areas some preliminary studies have been carried out, which—while insufficient in themselves—lend great promise to more extensive efforts. Along such lines, it seems to us, there lie valuable and as yet only fragmentarily exploited hopes of augmenting the range of the methodological instrumentalities of the applied inexact and, in particular, the applied social sciences. ■

The analysis, presented in the foregoing essay, of methods appropriate for the inexact sciences, especially in regard to prediction, sets the stage for a new approach to the social sciences that might result in their more effective application to the social problems of the real world. Indeed, following up on some of the recommendations set down in Section 6.16, we might aim for the creation of what may be called "social technology". In analogy to ordinary physical technology, which attempts to translate the knowledge provided by the hard sciences into practical improvements in our way of life, social technology would seek to exploit the greater understanding achieved by the social sciences to improve the human condition in our real world. This is the subject of the following essay.

7 *SOCIAL TECHNOLOGY*[3]

7.1 *Introduction*

This section is concerned with a reappraisal of methodology in the social sciences. It not only attempts to establish the need for such a reappraisal, but offers specific proposals for modifying social-science methods and procedures. The practical implementation of these proposals is illustrated by examples.

It has been remarked that many of the difficulties that beset our world today can be explained by the fact that progress in the social-science domain has lagged far behind that in the physical sciences. Moreover, if we contemplate the continuing explosion of knowledge of our physical surroundings—a knowledge that will soon open up to us vast new techniques ranging from molecular to planetary engineering, with eerie implications for human society—we may well take a dire view of the future, unless we assume that the gap between the social and the physical sciences will not persist.

The disasters that may befall us if we fail to narrow this gap are many. Even if international relations do not deteriorate to the point of nuclear war, the despair of economically underprivileged nations and of underprivileged classes within nations may assume such proportions as to make the world a very tense and unpleasant place in which to live. Specifically, the disparity between economically lagging and advanced countries seems to be increasing rather than diminishing at the moment, and, consequently, an explosive situation is developing. Within prosperous countries, such as the United States, there is a distinct and growing threat that increased automation, coupled with an obsolete and aimless system of education, will lead to a restratification of society in which a large middle class may find itself without suitable employment and without adequate means of filling its leisure time enjoyably and constructively.

There are numerous other developments on the horizon, interacting with

3. From *Social Technology*, by Olaf Helmer, Copyright © 1966 by Olaf Helmer. Reprinted by permission of Basic Books, Inc., Publishers, New York.

those already mentioned, that carry seeds of possibly ominous implications. Three are singularly thought-provoking: the restructuring of our cities entailed by automation, new materials, new modes of transportation, and, above all, vastly enhanced means of communication; the trend toward widespread acceptance and use of personality-control drugs; and, somewhat but not much further in the future, the possibility of eugenic control through molecular engineering. Each of these developments is likely to have a far-reaching effect on our way of life, necessitating profound adjustments in social stratification and personal relationships. Whether our society will be able to undergo these modifications without severe disruptions will depend greatly on the wisdom and effectiveness of our social planners.

Thus, just as in physics and biology, so are we in the social sciences faced with an abundance of challenges: how to keep the peace, how to alleviate the hardships of social change, how to provide food and comfort for the inaffluent, how to improve the social institutions and the values of the affluent, how to cope with revolutionary innovations, and so on. But, unlike the physical sciences, where failures normally mean mere delays, the social sciences cannot afford to fail in their major aspirations; to do so could have a direct and catastrophic impact on society.

In the face of these tasks and these costs of failure and considering the lag of the social behind the physical sciences, it is easy to give in to a feeling of frustration and adopt an attitude of defeatism.

My thesis is that such a pessimistic outlook is unwarranted. The argument to support this thesis consists of two points. In the first place, the comparison of the social with the physical sciences is a spurious one, based on an epistemological misconception regarding the nature and purpose of scientific activity. Second—and this is the crucial point—there is every reason to believe that, by effecting specific changes in attitudes and procedures, we can substantially narrow the gap between physical technology and sociopolitical progress.

7.2 *Science, Technology, and Operations Research*

The purpose of scientific endeavor is to achieve a better understanding of the world and, thus, to develop valid theories concerning observable phenomena. Such theories are then used to predict future events and, in particular, to make conditional predictions of the consequences of alternative courses of action. The ability to make contingency predictions of this kind gives us a measure of control over the future which is then put to use in such applied fields as engineering and medicine.

This sequence of understanding, prediction, and ability to control (aspired to by the pure scientist) followed by actual control (exercised by the applied scientist or technologist) is not always observed neatly. Even in the physical sciences, where the tradition has been to defer applications until a theory was well confirmed through controlled experiments, deviations from this scheme are indulged in at times.

In the social sciences, the attempt to emulate this ideal pattern which is assumed to be characteristic of progress in the physical sciences has led to unnecessary frustration. By being able to point to the comparative vagueness of their concepts, to the comparative inexactness of their derivations, and to the comparative unreliability of their forecasts, many social scientists have rationalized their procrastination and accepted a stagnation of progress in their field that is quite incompatible with the tremendous strides toward an enriched understanding of human interactions that have actually occurred not only in economics and psychology, but to an almost equal degree in sociology and political science.

It should be noted that, in the applications of the physical sciences, too, it was only under duress that a perfectionist image of required scientific procedure was reluctantly abandoned. The exigencies of military combat during World War II brought on an effort, known as operations research, that has continued to develop and has become a widely accepted tool not only in the peacetime management of military affairs, but throughout commerce and industry as well.

Compared to a traditional scientific investigator, there is a crucial difference in emphasis on the part of an operations analyst, who is, of necessity, a pragmatist, interested primarily in effective control of his surroundings and only secondarily in detailed understanding of all the underlying phenomena. Thus, both the exact scientist and the operations analyst tend to make use of what is called a "mathematical model" of the subject matter; but, though in the case of the exact scientist such a model is apt to be part of a body of well-confirmed scientific knowledge, an operations-research model is usually of a much more tentative character. In other words, even if the current status of science provides no well-established theory for the phenomena to be dealt with by the operations analyst, he must nevertheless construct a model as best he can, where both the structure of the model and its numerical inputs have an *ad hoc* quality, representing merely the best insight and information that the analyst happens to have available. As further insights accrue and more experimental data become available, the operations analyst has to be prepared to discard his first model and replace it with an improved one. This tentative procedure, dictated by pragmatic considerations, is thus essentially one of successive approximation.

As mentioned before, this method was born out of necessity. It has been adopted by industry as an aid in coping with the demands of economic competition. The results, owing in part to the concurrent development of electronic computers, have been spectacular, as evidenced by improved manufacturing processes, new materials, better market forecasts, and so on.

It cannot be urged too strongly that the social scientists explore the possibilities that the operations-research approach has to offer. Although it would indeed be gratifying to have, say, political theories comparable in elegance, in logical persuasiveness, and in predictive reliability to physical theories, we cannot count on this to come about. In any case, the dangers that society faces are so great and the needs for rapid progress so evident that we cannot afford to wait—perhaps for a generation or more—until satisfactory, well-tested theories of human relations are available. The time has come to emulate not physical science, but physical technology.

The potential reward from a reorientation of some of the effort in the social-science area toward social technology, employing operations-research techniques, is considerable; it may even equal or exceed in importance that of the achievements credited to the technologies arising out of the physical sciences.

The methodological implications of such a reorientation can be summarized simply under the headings of "operational model-building" and "systematic use of expertise".

7.3 Operational Model-Building

The scientist, particularly when dealing with a complicated system, often finds it convenient or even necessary to construct a scientific model of it. If the model involves a representation by mathematical equations, it is called a mathematical model; but, of course, not every scientific model is a mathematical one.

The purpose in constructing a model of a given situation is to select certain elements as being relevant to the problem under consideration, to make explicit certain functional relationships among these elements, and to formulate hypotheses regarding the nature of their relationships. (It is these functional relations that are often most conveniently expressed in mathematical form.)

A characteristic feature in the construction of a model is abstraction; certain elements of the situation may be deliberately omitted because they are judged irrelevant, and the resulting simplification in the description of the situation may be helpful in analyzing and understanding it. In addition to abstraction, model-building sometimes involves a conceptual transference. Instead of describing the situation directly, it may be the case that "each element of the real situation is simulated by a mathematical or physical object, and its relevant properties and relations to other elements are mirrored by corresponding simulative properties and relations" [cf. Section 6.14]. A model involving such transference, in addition to abstraction, is called a "simulation model".

When an operations analyst constructs a model, simulative or not, he usually does so in order to determine the most appropriate action to take in the face of a given situation. His function is, after all, to give operational advice to a decision maker. Often, he may find himself at the frontier of the state of the art, and he may have to rely heavily on whatever expert judgment may be available, rather than on a solid (nonexistent) theory. His model is therefore apt to be *ad hoc*, tentative (that is, subject to modification and improvement), future-directed, and policy-oriented. Frequently, the reliability of such a model may leave much to be desired; yet its justification should derive from the fact that recommended actions based on it have a good chance of being more appropriate than actions selected without use of the model.

In recommending, as I do, that the social scientists divert some of their effort from the pursuit of pure science to problems of craftsmanship in social technology, I am advocating, among other things, the deliberate and systematic use of models of the operations-analytical type, including in particular both mathematical and simulation models.

The employment of formal models in social theory traditionally meets a certain amount of understandable, though not always justified, reluctance. It is to be hoped that such qualms will disappear when the pragmatic step is taken from the perfectionist demands of pure theory to the more modest reliability requirements of practical technology.

The advantage of employing a scientific model lies in forcing the analyst to make explicit which elements of a situation he is taking into consideration and in imposing on him the discipline of clarifying the concepts he is using. The model thus serves the important purpose of establishing unambiguous intersubjective communication about the subject at hand. Whatever intrinsic uncertainties may becloud the area of investigation, they are thus less likely to be further compounded by uncertainties owing to disparate subjective interpretations.

It should be pointed out in this connection that frequently the use of numerical parameters and thus of a mathematical model is an expedient device for conceptual clarification. Precise numbers are, it may be objected, an inappropriately rigid means of rendering concepts that are, of necessity, vague and possibly full of implied but unarticulated meaning. Yet consider, for example, the case where a political forecaster is questioned as to whether President Johnson will be reelected in 1968. He may feel more comfortable replying "very probably" rather than "with 80 percent probability"; but the questioner might well prefer to have him express the degree of his uncertainty by adding "plus or minus 10 percent" to the numerical probability statement, rather than have the onus of interpreting "very probably" according to his own subjective assessment of what that phrase may mean. (An interesting device for improving the logical consistency of a subject's personal probability estimates is discussed by de Finetti, 1962, pp. 357ff.).

A type of model, referred to before, that should prove of special importance in social technology is the simulation model. Here, instead of formulating hypotheses and predictions directly about the real world, it is possible to make such statements about the simulative entities of the model.

The importance of such models, especially when applied in the field of social technology, lies in the fact pointed out before [see Section 6.14] that they permit what I referred to as "pseudo-experimentation": "Pseudo-experimentation is nothing but the systematic use of the classical idea of a hypothetical experiment; it is applied when true experimentation is too costly or physically or morally impossible".

A classic example of such pseudo-experimentation is found in military operations analysis, where the evaluation of the relative effectiveness of alternative weapon systems, which clearly cannot be fully tested directly, is carried out via simulation. Since actual social experimentation is, similarly, almost always a virtual impossibility, pseudo-experimentation in a simulative model world is evidently a substitute worth examining.

Incidentally, among the simulation models are a number of varieties. There are paper-and-pencil models, usually involving sets of mathematical equations. These can be analyzed by standard mathematical techniques, or, if their complexity precludes this, their implications can be explored with electronic computers for any number of input parameter values. Then, there are such physical simulation models as might be used in the study of urban redevelopment, where the projected stages of transformation of a city may be displayed with the aid of a miniature mock-up. Another type of physical simulation model is represented by pilot and astronaut trainers, which are used for personnel training as well as for performance analysis. A particularly useful kind of physical simulation is that of operational gaming, about which more will be said later. It involves role-playing by human subjects in a laboratory situation in which the participants simulate real-world decision makers in a conflict-of-interest context. Since all of the social sciences deal with human interactions, this type of simulation is naturally of special interest to the social technologist.

I would, finally, like to mention at this point a technique that has become known in operations research as "scenario-writing". Though this is not in itself a form of model-building, it is a closely related activity. Scenario-writing involves a constructive use of the imagination. It aims at describing some aspect of the future; but, instead of building up a picture of unrestrained fiction or even of constructing a utopian invention that the author considers highly desirable, an operations-analytical scenario starts with the present state of the world and shows how, step by step, a future state might evolve in a plausible fashion out of the present one. Thus, though the purpose of such a scenario is not to predict the future, it nevertheless sets out to demonstrate the possibility of a certain future state of affairs by exhibiting a reasonable chain of events that might lead to it.

Scenario-writing has been applied, in particular, to the exploration of potential military or diplomatic crises, but it is a technique that promises to have useful applications in a wider field. By providing a sample of future contingencies, a set of scenarios may serve to warn of dangers ahead, it may afford an insight into the sensitivity with which future trends depend on factors under our control, and thereby it may enhance our awareness of available policy options.

The connection with model-building is at least threefold. First, the process of writing a scenario may be looked on as a primitive, one-person mode of simulation, inasmuch as the author forces himself to go through the thought experiment of examining a plausible developmental chain of events. Second, a useful heuristic device in setting up a formal model concerning a future situation may be to begin by writing several scenarios leading up to it. These can be of great help in discerning the decisive relationships among the elements of the situation and in eliminating negligible irrelevancies. Third, once a simulation model has been constructed, whether a gaming model or not and whether a computing model or not, the records of repeated runs of the model constitute a systematic source of scenarios and thus afford a methodical sampling of contingencies.

7.4 The Systematic Use of Expertise

While model-building is an extremely systematic expedient to promote the understanding and control of our environment, reliance on the use of expert judgment, though often unsystematic, is more than an expedient: it is an absolute necessity. Expert opinion must be called on whenever it becomes necessary to choose among several alternative courses of action in the absence of an accepted body of theoretical knowledge that would clearly single out one course as the preferred alternative. It should be noted here, incidentally, that an inability to determine a preferred alternative on theoretical grounds may have one or both of two essentially distinct reasons: either there may be a factual uncertainty as to the real consequences of the proposed courses of action, or, even if the consequences are relatively predictable, there may be a moral uncertainty as to which of the consequent states of the world would be preferable. The latter kind of doubt often arises even when there is a clear-cut basic ethical code, because the multiple moral implications of a complex change in the environment may not be directly assessable in terms of the basic code. The following examples illustrate these points: the design of a vehicle for landing on Mars is subject to the first-mentioned, factual uncertainty; the question of whether or not the workweek should be shortened to below forty hours involves real uncertainty as to which corresponding state of the world would be preferable; in weighing the pros and cons of permitting birth control, the Ecumenical Council must be gravely disturbed over the conflicting moral consequences of such a policy that are implied by their seemingly unambiguous basic moral maxims.

In the absence of a theoretically convincing reason for selecting a particular action or a particular policy for action, we turn for advice to experts. The degree of expertise displayed in their predictions or recommendations will be revealed in the relative frequency with which their pronouncements are eventually confirmed by later events. The handling of a particular problem usually calls for the judgment of several kinds of experts who may be regarded as belonging to one of two general categories: specialists or generalists. The former provide substantive information or predictions; the latter, problem-formulation, model-structuring, or preference-evaluation among predicted alternatives.

Fortunately, in the social sciences we are able to call on a vast reservoir of expertise of many kinds, both among substantive specialists and among generalists. While in some cases the expert judgment that is available may be derived from explicit application of existing theories, more often it may be highly intuitive in character and based on insights that, although no less reliable, may have thus far defied articulation within a theoretical framework. Much of this potential expertise now remains untapped in practical policy considerations. It could be put to much greater use if there were a recognized field of social technology that would have the task of regularly and systematically exploring and collating experts' opinions on the future, so that their latest findings would be available at such time as they might be needed by decision-making authorities. [Bertrand de Jouvenel, research director of the Futuribles group, has suggested that we go even further. He recommends that the activity of exploring possible futures, "futuribles", be institutionalized by providing a forum for regular public discussion of pending governmental policy decisions regarding the future. See de Jouvenel, 1967, especially Part 5, as well as the end of Section 7.7.5 below.]

It should be clear from what has just been said that there is no intention of proposing a replacement of traditional social-science endeavors by social-technology pursuits. On the contrary, I am suggesting that social science proper and social technology complement each other. The insights gained by the pure social scientist form the foundation on which social technology must build, regardless of whether they are expressed on a formal-theory or on an intuitive, pre-theory level. Conversely, being able to influence practical policy decisions through technological applications, the theoretician has an outlet for his ideas that provides both focus and incentive.

Wise political decision makers have, of course, always drawn on expert advice as an aid in crystallizing their own judgments. The recognition of social technology as an intellectual discipline in its own right, as is suggested here, would be a big step toward substituting for haphazard consultation of specialists the systematic use of systematically elicited expert judgment.

Let us thus turn now to the specific question of systematicity, in the sense of an orderly, planned, methodical procedure, in the elicitation and use of expert opinions. It should be very clearly understood that there is no single, elusive, optimal way to use expertise. What is called for is a conscious and deliberate broad-front attack on the entire problem of enhancing and articulating the enormous expertise potential that is now available in the social sciences and of bringing it to bear on the urgent needs of our society. This task should not proceed in the abstract; there is no time to perfect methods before applying them. Like the physical engineer, the social engineer, too, has to do much of his learning "on the job" and arrives at a safe building code through a gradual process of trial and error. While I cannot attempt here to outline a complete blueprint for such a program, I shall discuss some of the areas in which a concerted search for better methods is both needed and promising.

7.5 *Discussion of Methods*

The methods that we may want to employ in order to put the available expertise potential to the best practical use fall into three classes: methods for selecting experts, methods for aiding the performance of an expert, and methods for using groups of experts.

7.5.1 Selecting Experts

The selection of experts for consultation is usually made on the basis of what may vaguely be called their reputations. This process of selection, which in itself requires a certain amount of expertise, breaks down logically into two parts: the determination of which categories of expertise are needed, and the determination of who among the available persons is most expert in each such category.

Although the specification of the type of expertness may often be obvious, this is not always the case. What is sometimes overlooked by those seeking counsel is that a first-rate specialist may not always be good at taking a sufficiently general "systems" view in formulating the problem, whereas a generalist with a flair for model-building may lack either specialized information or a sense for the ethical implications of alternative courses of action. Also, it may require a certain amount of preliminary analysis of the problem area to ascertain precisely what specialists have to be enlisted. For example, a common failing in carrying out analyses of national economies aimed at long-range forecasting of such indices as the GNP is the neglect to consult sociological area experts in addition to economic specialists.

Regarding the second part of the selection process, the actual choice of individual experts, we have an opportunity for numerous empirical studies that may be highly rewarding. There is, first of all, the question of determining expertness on the basis of past performance (a problem of considerable logical intricacy) and of studying stability in personal expertise, i.e., the correlation between future and past performance as an expert. [As for scoring an expert's performance in terms of reliability and accuracy, see Section 6.11.]

Aside from such *a posteriori* assessment of performance, there is the question of *a priori* recognition of a person's qualification in terms of performance other than specific expert pronouncements, such as years of professional experience, number of publications, and status among his peers. The relationship between such objective indexes and the ability to make reliable predictions is clearly susceptible to empirical investigation. A recent experiment has suggested the tentative conclusion that an expert's self-appraisal of his relative competence in different areas of inquiry may be well enough correlated with his actual relative performance in these areas to be of significant aid in selecting experts for specific tasks. A report on the outcome of this experiment is given toward the end of Section 24.

7.5.2 Aiding the Performance of an Expert

If an expert who is primarily a generalist is asked for advice, his contribution may be, or should be encouraged to be, in the form of constructing a model. Even if such a model is tentative, which is particularly likely when a firm theoretical foundation is still absent, it may serve to clarify concepts and aid communication. If a generalist's opinion is sought when a preliminary model is already in existence, it is of the utmost importance to assure him of the desirability of any modifications of the model that he regards as imperative, lest the entire effort be devoted to "the wrong problem."

With regard to the proper employment of an expert specialist, he can be very effectively aided by facilitating communication. First of all, the prior formulation of an appropriate model serves both to communicate the problem to him with clarity and to receive his answer without risk of misinterpretation. Second, the expert is greatly aided in his performance if he has ready access to relevant information that may exist elsewhere; in this regard, rapid progress in data-processing may open up new possibilities by which the present swamping with irrelevancies will be eventually replaced through automated libraries with push-button availability of pertinent data. Third, in order to provide access to intuitive knowledge as yet unrecorded, an expert's performance can be enhanced most significantly by placing him in a situation where he may profitably interact with other experts in the same field or in different fields related to other aspects of the same problem. Traditionally, a simple mode of this type of communication has been in the form of round-table discussions; other modes, possibly more systematic, will be discussed below.

7.5.3 Utilizing Groups of Experts

In discussing methods of utilizing the services of more than one expert on the same problem, it is convenient to distinguish between two cases, although in practice they are liable to overlap. One is a situation in which the opinions of several experts on the same question or questions are solicited; the other is one in which experts with separate specialties are asked to comment on distinct aspects of a problem. Let us call these the symmetric case and the asymmetric case respectively, since the experts are employed symmetrically in one and asymmetrically in the other. It will be evident that methods specifically designed to meet one of these two cases can be modified to have applications to the other.

Symmetric Use of Panels. The traditional, straightforward way of using a panel of experts symmetrically has been to assemble them in one place, let them discuss the problem freely, and require that they arrive at a joint answer representing their consensus in response to the questions addressed to them. The statement of a dissenting minority opinion often is considered an additional option. Variants of this procedure have been tried and found promising, but carefully controlled experimentation designed to ascertain optimal techniques still remains to be performed.

Among the variants referred to are the so-called Delphi technique [referred to in Section 6.13 and to be taken up in some detail in a later chapter], which has the virtue of not requiring face-to-face confrontation, and the method of substituting a computed consensus for an agreed-on majority position. The Delphi technique has been used recently [i.e., in 1963] in a large-scale experiment in which several international panels of respondents were enlisted in an effort to arrive at long-range contingency forecasts of the state of the world twenty-five to fifty years hence. [A full report on this study is included in Section 45, Chapter VIII.]

A convenient consensus formula, applicable whenever the solicited judgments can be cast in numerical form (or even if they can merely be linearly ordered), is to use the median. Aside from being independent of a particular metric, it has the intuitively appealing quality that it can be viewed as the outcome of a democratic voting procedure, in the sense that half the panel considers the correct answer to be less than or equal to the median, while the other half considers it to be greater than or equal to the median. An obvious variant of the simple median is a weighted median, giving more than one vote to the opinions of experts whose judgment objectively deserves preferential treatment. For example, even self-assigned competence scores may justify such differential weights. If, in addition to a consensus, it is desirable to have an indication of the spread of opinions among the experts, that is, of the amount of their "dissensus", it may be expedient to state the interquartile range of their responses (which is the interval containing the middle 50 percent of them).

Asymmetric Use of Panels. When dealing with a multifaceted problem with the aid of a variety of experts of different backgrounds, perhaps the most important requirement in the interest of an efficient use of these experts is to provide an effective means of communication among them. Since each of the participating experts is likely to have his own specialized terminology, a conceptual alignment and a real agreement as to the identity of the problem may not be easy to achieve, and it becomes almost imperative to construct a common frame of reference in order to promote a unified collaborative effort.

One way to enforce a common interexpert usage and understanding of concepts is to present the problem in terms of an abstract model constructed in advance. Even more effective, and not excluding this approach, is a laboratory arrangement in which the experts are brought together to collaborate on a joint intellectual enterprise.

A specific device facilitating such cooperation, which had its first major application in a Peruvian anthropological experiment in 1955, is a contextual map:

> As an interdisciplinary team of planners faced with the complexities of a large interacting cultural system and its own problems of internal communication, we needed a method for systematically utilizing the special talents and experiences of the planners despite the frustrations of having to establish a common vocabulary, an agreed-upon ideology, a set of reasonable goals, a common context for symbols, and ways of translating ideas into actions. Our solution was to design and make up a "map room," whose walls contained a large matrix with time (in years) on the ordinate and the "variables" the group was interested in along the abscissa. This matrix was the "conceptual map" [Kennedy, 1956].

The cells of such a contextual map (perhaps "contextual matrix" would be a more apt term) are used to display goals, predictions, and actual achievements, thus furnishing each member of the team at all times with an up-to-date exhibit of the project status, in terms of accomplishments and residual desiderata.

The Peruvian case just cited is an atypical illustration because it involved actual experimentation in the field. Whenever a directly empirical procedure of this kind is not feasible, the mere use of such organizing aids as a contextual map may be insufficient, and serious consideration ought to be given to the possibility of pseudo-experimentation in the form of laboratory simulation.

Past experience with simulation models suggests that they can be highly instrumental in motivating the participating research personnel to communicate effectively with one another, to learn more about the subject matter by viewing it through the eyes of persons with backgrounds and skills different from their own, and thereby, above all, to acquire an integrated overview of the problem area. This catalytic effect of a simulation model is associated not only with the employment of the completed model, but equally with the process of constructing it. (In fact, the two activities usually go hand in hand. The application of the model almost invariably suggests amendments, so that it is not uncommon to have an alternation of construction and simulation.)

The heuristic effect of collaborating on the construction and use of a simulation model is particularly powerful when the simulation takes the form of an operational game where the participants act out the roles of decision- and policymaking entities (individuals or corporate institutions). By being exposed within a simulated environment to a conflict situation involving an intelligent opposition, the "player" is compelled, no matter how narrow his specialty, to consider many aspects of the scene that might not normally weigh heavily in his mind when he works in isolation. Thus the game laboratory induces an integrating effect comparable to what is known, in purely analytical studies, as a "systems analysis".

We note, in passing, that a player's assignment in an operational game may be either optimization or simulation. In the first case, he is to attempt, within the constraints of the game rules, to maximize a personal score (his "payoff" in game-theoretical terminology). This tends to put the verisimilitude of the game model, which after all is intended to be only an abstraction of the real world, to a severe test and to suggest amendments in the underlying assumptions. The second mode in which a player may function, namely as a simulant, is more likely to utilize his expertise properly, for in this role he is required to contribute constructively to the developing scenario by feeding in such simulated decisions which, in his estimate, would most faithfully reflect the decisions that his actual counterpart would make in the corresponding real situation.

Before leaving the subject of simulation—of the gaming or nongaming variety—a few words should be added on the role of the so-called computer models mentioned previously. One of the important early computer simulations was carried out in atomic physics, where the subject matter—as in the social sciences, but for wholly different reasons—does not lend itself very well to true experimentation. In the model, certain processes involving atomic and subatomic particles were represented by mathematical entities, the behavior of which was described by mathematical equations. Pseudo-experiments were then conducted, with random numbers used to represent collisions, deflections, and so on, in which the "paths" of these fictitious particles were observed. In this manner, it was possible to predict the behavior of thermonuclear devices because the mathematical model depicted the relevant features of the real world so accurately that the results obtained by putting the model through its paces on a computer could be directly applied to the analogous real-world circumstances.

In areas where such a complete theory of the underlying phenomena is absent, the predictive power of a computer model is, of necessity, comparatively limited, and its contribution to the control of our environment is, at best, indirect—namely, by enhancing the experts' intuitive understanding of the subject matter. The process by which this occurs is again twofold, just as in the case of noncomputer simulation—through model construction and model application.

Constructing a computer model puts explicitness to the most severe test. Since a computing machine cannot read between the lines, nothing may be left unsaid. The model constructor is forced, therefore, to build an entire theory, however tentative, of the elements and their interrelations that he wants to manipulate in the model. The discipline of such mandatory completeness may bring functional dependencies to his attention that would otherwise have remained unnoticed. Once a program has been written, the actual use of a computer model differs considerably from a manual laboratory simulation. While emphasis in the latter is on perception, understanding, and manipulation of the environment as one goes along, the computer requires "strategic" instructions that foresee contingencies and specify the alternative to be chosen for each branch point. Such specificity is often undesirable, because the researcher may not know in advance which alternative is the preferred one. To make up for this, a high-speed machine permits him to explore sequentially the consequences of selecting different alternatives at successive branch points.

In practice, it may often be expedient to start out with a preliminary manual simulation in which gradual adjustment of the initial assumptions and even of the model structure is comparatively easy and then, on the basis of insights gained through such manual operation, to proceed to the more formidable task of constructing a rigid computer program. Machine runs can then be used to explore in detail those regions of the "strategy space" that appeared most interesting from the previous manual examination. By proceeding thus in stages, the available expertise is likely to be used more effectively than if one requires the immediate formulation of a computerized model with its relative inflexibility and its demands for complete explicitness.

The foregoing discussion of various methods of utilizing experts and aiding their performance has, of necessity, been somewhat discursive and lacking in precise procedural prescriptions. The reason for this is that we are dealing with an area that is in a stage of considerable flux and development. Even in their application to physical technology, the techniques of operations research undergo constant augmentation, revision, and refinement; but, particularly when we turn to their extension to social technology, the field is wide open, as yet highly unsystematic, and greatly in need of careful experimentation.

In order to explicate the methodological suggestions made here, I shall attempt to indicate through examples how one might go about implementing these methods. A brief survey of the more challenging areas of research concerned with the future of human affairs yields numerous illustrations to this effect.

7.6 Illustrative Procedural Sketches

The purpose of this section is to provide not recipes but elucidation. It should be understood that there is no implied contention that the illustrative problems discussed below can be treated only in the manner outlined, or even that the suggested treatment is necessarily a good way of handling them.

Before presenting the following rather unsophisticated sketches, I want to reemphasize two points regarding them. One is that the approach illustrated by them is intended in no way to supplant traditional theoretical studies in the social sciences, but rather to supplement them by providing a pragmatic technology for implementing desiderata suggested by theory. No practical attack on any of the problem areas discussed below would make sense unless it were preceded by the most careful examination of the present state of the art and its deficiencies, in view of our social and political aspirations and the consequent needs of the future. Only the wisdom derived from both theoretical consideration of these issues and the practical experience of many experts in the field can possibly provide the right intellectual foundation for an appropriate technology.

The other point regarding the following sketches that must be borne in mind is that they *are*, indeed, nothing but the barest elucidatory sketches. Each of the five areas selected for illustration represents an important aspect of human affairs deserving of, and in fact receiving, the attention of countless scholars. Each area is, moreover, multifaceted, replete with subproblems and secondary implications, and frequently interacting with the others thus making it mere wishful thinking to presume that a simple grandiose scheme might exist that would somehow, with one stroke, transform a task of forbidding proportions into a manageable project. All I hope to accomplish by the following illustrations is to indicate some supplementary procedural devices that might aid in the translation of insights gained from theoretical considerations or practical experience into meaningful applications. All the hard problems remain; but the effort that must go into their solution needs the incentive provided by the prospect of applicability. The methodological suggestions given here are intended as a modest contribution toward enhancing that prospect.

We begin our examples with a problem area in which operations-analytical techniques have already been used extensively, probably because it required a combination of physical and social engineering.

7.6.1 Urban Redevelopment

In order to make long-range plans for the renewal of a city, it is necessary to have at one's disposal not only an extensive collection of data descriptive of the city's population, housing, industry, commerce, and transportation, but also a number of experts capable of interpreting trends in these variables and of making forecasts of future developments. Even if such forecasts are extrapolations based on simple mathematical models, they inevitably involve the experts' intuitive opinions (if only regarding the applicability of the model used for extrapolation). Hence the problem of making the best use of expert opinions and of reconciling possible differences among them has to be faced. This is where the Delphi approach, with its systematic procedure for arriving at a reasoned consensus, may come into play.

In order to cope not only with existing deficiencies (such as slums or an inadequate public-transportation system), but also with the anticipated long-range needs of the future implied by such forecasts as have just been discussed, it is necessary to examine the consequences of various zoning, fiscal, and investment policies. To facilitate such studies, a physical simulation model, at least in the form of a detailed map with overlays showing the present and anticipated geographical distributions of the variables mentioned above, is a prime requisite. Here, again, the employment of experts (on the growth and composition of the population, on industrial development, on final demands for goods and services, and on transportation technology) is indispensable. An effective way to make good use of a group of such experts might be to have them jointly go through a series of what may be called "developmental simulations". Using the physical mock-up as a convenient frame of reference, they would, within their respective areas of competence, predict what changes in the status variables of the city will be induced by a given policy within a year. These changes would be incorporated in the physical display, giving rise to a new initial status and thus setting the scene for another set of predictions to be solicited that advance the date another year, and so on, for as many years as would seem fruitful to consider. Carried out under laboratory conditions for a number of proposed policies, this activity would bring to light discrepancies among predicted trends and cause the participants to collate and reconcile their opinions. The result might well be a clear recognition of the superiority of one of the policies under consideration. If this is not the case at first, a postexperimental Delphi analysis of the participants' opinions might eventually lead to a consensus in this regard.

In addition to the physical display, and especially in the event that no consensus on an optimal policy has been attained by the experts, it may be desirable to lay out a contextual map, with time indicated along one axis and alternative policies contemplated on behalf of the city government along the other. Each cell on this map would give a summary of the expected effects of a particular policy at a particular date in the future. This exhibit would make it easier for those who actually have to make planning decisions for the city to give systematic consideration to the anticipated consequences of a variety of contemplated proposals.

7.6.2 *Educational Reform in the United States*

Since the main purpose of the primary- and secondary-school systems is to prepare children for adult life by providing them with necessary knowledge, skills, and values, there is a considerable time lag between the laying of plans for educational reform and the effects of such reform in terms of an increased ability to cope with the vicissitudes of adult life. The earliest time that one might hope to affect through current reform plans is a decade in the future, and the direct influence of any present reform may well still be felt through the first third of the twenty-first century. Any sensible approach that does not aim merely at correcting present or past ills must therefore include a survey of the expected needs of our society in the half century subsequent to the formulation of reform proposals. A careful solicitation and analysis of expert opinions in this regard might be the first step. Areas of expertise to be covered would have to include population statistics, economic conditions, sociological implications of economic changes, scientific and technological developments, effects of economic and technological changes on values, and so on. Some of these forecasts may be based on existing demographic and economic models, but intuitive judgment is likely to play a dominant role throughout, making something like a Delphi approach virtually mandatory. In particular, such a preliminary survey of expert opinion might seek to assess the relative probabilities of a teacher shortage (because of the expected increase in the ratio of youths to adults and the possibility of a shortened workweek, combined with a desire to continue education through life) and of a teacher surplus (because of the foreclosure of many other job opportunities by progressive automation).

Once a rough overall pattern of the future educational needs of our society has been established, one would have to turn to the question of devising appropriate educational innovations to meet those needs. These innovations might be of many kinds. They might be in the nature of administrative modifications, aimed at changing the incentive structure regarding teachers as well as students; they might involve changes in curricula or in teaching methods, possibly relying heavily on automated instruction; and they might even consist in the introduction of radically new educational institutions. Here again, the Delphi approach may prove expedient; it can be used, first, to solicit ideas for suitable educational innovations and, second, to appraise the efficacy of any such proposals that do not lend themselves easily to direct experimental evaluation. Along with this, it might be a useful aid to conceptual clarity to lay out a contextual map, with time indicated along one axis and proposed educational innovations along the other, filling in estimated marginal effects on educational output in the cells of the matrix. As for the testing of specific educational techniques, particularly automated teaching devices, it would seem that laboratory experiments (both simulated and actual) are clearly indicated.

7.6.3 Political Forecasting and Planning

Under this heading, which covers a broad area of concern, there are several subtopics that offer illustrations of the applicability of an operations-analytical approach. In the area of comparatively short-term forecasting and planning with respect to international affairs, some very rewarding operational work has already begun to be accomplished, namely with regard to the handling of international crises. Such crises are relatively predictable in the short run; that is, a survey of opinions among political analysts will easily produce a list of areas in which the occurrence of serious diplomatic disagreements within the next year or two may be anticipated with high probability. It is quite likely that such a list will, in retrospect, turn out to have been reasonably complete.

For those cases where a crisis is predicted with sufficiently high probability to arouse concern, the writing of several plausible scenarios may help to elucidate the points of contention and the mechanism by which diplomatic tension is likely to rise to the crisis level. Based on such a scenario, gaming by appropriate political and military experts may suggest the utility of various strategies (such as military or economic deterrence, accommodation, negotiation, declaratory policy statements, movement of military forces) for averting a crisis or for preventing a crisis from escalating into war. In such a game, the players (or playing teams) would play the role of the national security councils of the countries involved. In addition, a game at the level of national negotiators could simulate the conduct of international conferences and thus try to anticipate the special problems that might arise in their course. At yet a third level—namely, that of the persons who would be immediately involved in the management of operations accompanying an acute crisis (e.g., the president, the secretaries of state and defense, the chiefs of staff)—a simulation using true time (that is, an hour of game time per hour of simulated real time) and actual (or faithful replicas of actual) communication channels could pretest the smooth functioning of the top-level governmental decision-making apparatus. Simulation exercises of this kind, by discovering possible flaws in the governmental machinery and by focusing on those facets of the decision process where timing is apt to be most critical, may be of great importance in forestalling mutually unwanted escalation to war.

Our time horizon regarding crisis preparedness is of the order of months or, at most, a few years. When we try to extend our sights and inquire into the possible political structure of the world in the more distant future, specific prediction (and appropriate specific policy planning) becomes impossible. Yet, in order to engage in some general contingency planning, it would be desirable to form at least some approximate image of what the international scene, in terms of its military and economic power structure, might be like around the year 2000.

In order to obtain such an image, one might go through a two-stage process. One might begin by asking political experts to write plausible scenario sketches that start with the present and describe in broad outline a possible development of political world relations up to the year 2000; here, a scenario might be called "plausible" if, roughly speaking, it describes a chain of developments, each of which appears to be a reasonable alternative among the possible ones. Second, having obtained a set of representative scenarios of this kind, one might go through a Delphi analysis aimed at appraising these scenarios with regard to their relative plausibility. Of course, none would have a nonnegligible absolute probability of being a true prediction of things to come; but the subset of those having, by consensus, a comparatively high plausibility rating could well be considered to convey jointly the intended idea of the potential international situation in the year 2000.

That any contingency planning based on an image thus formed of the future would directly affect the probabilities of the alternatives of which that image is composed does not invalidate the suggested procedure but, in fact, demonstrates its usefulness; for it is precisely the foreboding content of unfavorable forecasts that might induce preventive action.

7.6.4 Measures Concerning Juvenile Delinquency

The problem of juvenile delinquency has a number of aspects, each requiring a different approach. There is the question of how to treat those juveniles who are now delinquents and of how to protect the rest of society from them. Then there is the question of how to detect the causes of delinquency and thereby to obtain a basis for predicting its occurrence. Last, but not least, there is the question of how to prevent juvenile delinquency in the future.

With regard to the first subproblem, the inmates of juvenile-correction institutions represent a literally captive audience for interrogation and experimentation, and, in fact, many such empirical studies are already being conducted. In order to provide proper guidance for such data collection (whether by interview or by observation of the effects of various detention treatments on postdetention recidivism), it is almost essential to have one or more mathematical models hypothesizing the dependence of delinquent behavior on specific measurable factors. A survey of the opinions and publications of experts (psychologists, social workers, correction-agency officers, and so forth) would, no doubt, produce numerous testable hypotheses of this kind that could be expressed in the form of numerical relationships. If such a survey were to produce more hypotheses than can reasonably be examined, then a consensus would first have to be obtained as to which among them are the most promising. For each hypothesis to be tested, there would be a definite requirement either to solicit certain information from the subjects or to carry out a controlled experiment with regard to certain variables. Standard statistical techniques should then be adequate to confirm or reject the hypothesis.

As for the second subproblem, that of isolating the causes of delinquency and, consequently, achieving some degree of predictability, past research has already yielded considerable success in the sense that future delinquency of small children has been found to be predictable with extremely high reliability. Such forecasts have been made on the basis of mathematical models relating the probability of future delinquency to several simply observable aspects of the child's home environment. Further refinements of the models used would have to aim not so much at raising the reliability of prediction (which already is very high), but at tracing the measured manifestations of the causes of delinquency back to underlying sociological factors.

The third subproblem concerns action, through legislation or other means, for dealing with the prevention of juvenile delinquency in the long run. Decisions in this area will certainly be strongly influenced by the empirical findings discussed above, regarding the effects of home surroundings and, in the case of prior offenders, detention treatment on subsequent delinquent behavior. This case is of particular methodological interest because it is typical of many investigations whose objective consists in recommendations for legislative action. A possible mode of procedure here may be somewhat as follows: (1) Collect and collate proposals for legislation from a group of appropriately chosen experts; if necessary, use a consensus technique to eliminate all but a few proposals that seem to offer some promise to the majority of experts consulted. (If, in addition to Proposal A and Proposal B, it is reasonable to give consideration to the joint proposal of both A and B, then list A + B separately.) (2) Solicit from each expert participating in the analysis for each proposal on the list an estimate of its probability p of passage, its effectiveness e if enacted, and the cost c of implementing it. Also obtain an estimate of the cost C to the nation if no measure is passed (to combat juvenile delinquency, in our present illustration). Here, "effectiveness" should be defined as the fraction by which C is expected to be reduced as a consequence of passing the proposed legislation (so that $e = 0$ corresponds to total ineffectiveness and $e = 1$ to total effectiveness). If estimates of these quantities were indeed obtainable, then it might be reasonable to measure each proposal's expected cost benefit to the nation by the product

$$p \cdot (eC - c)$$

so that the proposal for which this quantity is maximal would emerge as the respondent's preferred measure. (3) Conduct a Delphi study to arrive at a consensus regarding the quantities involved and thereby regarding the preference-ranking of the alternatives under consideration.

Unquestionably the approach to the general problem of policy recommendations that has just been sketched is inadequate as it stands. The definitions of the quantities required to be estimated involve some conceptual obstacles that need to be overcome. For instance, the notion of cost may involve nonmonetary and possibly even quite intangible resources (such as human happiness); also the overall desirability of a proposed measure is affected by the indirect costs or benefits of new legislation derived from side effects not directly related to the main issue, and the assessment of these must somehow be subsumed under the measure's cost-effectiveness estimate. Another point to be mentioned is that the probability p of passage should not be treated as statically as the above sketch may seem to imply; after all, the climate of opinion may be subject to change, and suitable steps may affect the value of p as time passes.

On the other hand, in spite of these conceptual difficulties and the virtual impossibility of assigning precise values to any of the quantities asked for, it may often appear that the ranking of the alternatives is highly insensitive to changes in the estimates over considerable ranges, so that a reasonably unambiguous ranking may emerge despite the undeniable degree of underlying vagueness.

7.6.5 Long-Range Economic Forecasting

While short-range forecasts (one to at most five years) concerning national economic indices have almost become a matter of routine, long-range pronouncements (ten to twenty-five years) on economic developments tend to be of a proscriptive rather than predictive nature. Thus the models on which such statements are based provide, at best, yardsticks in terms of potential progress against which actual progress might be measured. As in the case of long-range political forecasts, precise prediction is, of course, unattainable. Yet contingency planning in many areas (education among them) depends on having some idea, however imprecise, of future economic conditions, and it would therefore seem prudent to seek methods that might provide some indications of what to expect in this regard. In essence, the problem is the same, regardless of whether our concern is with the economy of a developing nation or of one that is already highly industrialized. Both cases will be discussed briefly.

The possibility has been suggested before that manual operational gaming might be applied to the study of suitable policies for aiding the development of an economically backward nation. [See the article written jointly by E. S. Quade and myself that is reproduced in Section 55, Chapter X]. This example of a highly complicated and, as yet, poorly understood problem situation in social technology illustrates well the variety of ways in which expert judgment might be utilized. The gaming approach would involve the following steps: (1) First of all, a game model has to be constructed in which certain economic decision-making processes are made explicit. The selection of the decision-making "nodes" in the nation's economic network that are to be represented in the model requires in itself a good deal of expertise and an intuitive grasp of the type of decisions on which the economy's welfare and growth depend most critically. In particular, since presumably the deliberate reactions of certain aggregates of the economy to changes in the environment must be studied, it is necessary to settle, at least tentatively at this stage, what degree of industrial and governmental aggregation is to be used in modeling the economy.

Having chosen the decision nodes (in gaming terminology, the roles of the "players"), it is necessary (2) to specify exactly what options are available at given stages of the game. For instance, the players representing the goods-producing sectors of the economy might be allowed, within stated constraints, to shut down or expand or modernize manufacturing facilities; to change the raw material and labor inputs; to vary the prices of their products; and so on. The governmental players might be permitted to introduce various fiscal or monetary policies and regulations (on taxes, subsidies, interest rates, tariffs, rationing, price floors and ceilings, minimum wage laws, and the like), as well as social and political innovations, with only indirect economic implications (social security, protection of minorities, raising of ethical standards, education, appeal to patriotism, expropriations, and so forth). Here again, in laying down the rules of the game governing the players' options and constraints, expert judgment is an essential ingredient, and clearly, in addition to economic experts, political and sociological specialists may have to be consulted.

Next, the game rules have to describe the consequences arising from the exercise of the options available to the players. Perhaps the most important aspect of this part of the model is the specification of the so-called production functions of the economic sectors, from which the effects on output of marginal changes in input, labor, investment, and manufacturing procedures can be determined. While it would be desirable to have these production functions stated in advance in the form of mathematical equations, this may be possible only through some rather arbitrary stipulations; and it may be more expedient to have specialists estimate changes in production as the game proceeds (taking into account such intangibles as the effect of education, of propaganda, of improved manufacturing processes, and so on) and only attempt gradually, after building up an inventory of such assessments, to generalize these casuistic determinations into mathematical formulas.

In (3) the playing of the completed game, the participants—whose skills should, if possible, include those of regional sociologists and political experts in addition to industrial, agricultural, and monetary economists—should act as simulators rather than (sectorial) optimizers. Early runs of the game would serve mainly to refine the underlying model and to permit the players to gain some insight into the sensitivity of the behavior of the economy to various assumptions and manipulations. Later, after a sufficient amount of synthetic experience has been accumulated and the model has been made to perform in a manner intuitively acceptable to the participating experts, the game may be used to explore the gross consequences of various alternative economic policies.

Needless to say, there is no guarantee that economic projections obtained in this manner would be highly reliable. But a great deal would already be gained if the reliability is not quite so low as that of less systematically obtained forecasts. Moreover, if the trend of events in the real world should disconfirm part of the developmental pattern predicted by the simulation, it should be easy to trace the disagreement to its source and amend the model accordingly for future use.

The intuitive judgment appealed to at several stages of the approach described above would undoubtedly be aided considerably by various analytical techniques. So-called no-change projections would establish reasonable bounds for projections based on postulated changes. Specific measures having empirically well-established consequences (e.g., the rise in soil productivity resulting from the application of fertilizer) could be taken into account systematically in estimating economic progress. Also, by now, there may be enough historical data on distinct methods of furnishing economic aid to underdeveloped countries by the United States and other economically advanced nations to discriminate in a statistically significant manner between their relative efficacies (the definition of "efficacy" admittedly offering some conceptual difficulties that may reintroduce a judgmental element at a higher level).

A study of long-range trends in the American economy could be structured formally very similarly to the study of the economy of a developing country. In substantive detail there would, of course, be considerable differences.

First of all, a comparatively vast amount of data are available in the form of economic and demographic time series regarding just about every conceivable aspect of economic life. A second substantive difference would lie, presumably, in the objective of the inquiry. Although in the case of an emerging nation our primary concern would be with finding ways of stimulating the economy, possibly through external aid, to make a smooth and rapid transition to a modern industrialized society, current interest in the case of the United States might tend to focus on the long-range implications of progressive automation and on the long-range requirements and effects of the so-called war on poverty.

A simulation model appropriate for the study of these problems would probably have to differentiate a somewhat larger number of economic sectors than may be needed for a newly developing country, and it would have to be geared to a longer time period (twenty years or more). Also, if one wished to examine, in particular, the sociological implications of automation, it would be necessary to construct a model sufficiently sophisticated to accommodate explicit consideration of various sectors of American society that are distinct with regard to income, education, race, or ethnic background. Nevertheless, in spite of these substantive specifics and the implied demands for appropriately specialized expertise, the approach on the whole could be essentially the same as that described in the preceding subsection.

7.7 The Society of the Future

Each of the foregoing examples concerns some aspect of the future of our society. Let us consider briefly the prospects of a comprehensive and systematic attack on this subject.

If, with Bertrand de Jouvenel, we refuse to succumb to what he calls "the new fatalism" of passively accepting new social institutions thrust upon us by an uncontrolled technological explosion, then surely it follows that we must search for a constructive approach that will ensure to us some measure of control over the future of our society.

7.7.1 *Structure of the Problem*

The search for such an approach, of necessity, has a predictive side as well as a normative one. That is, we have to ask ourselves, on the one hand, what trend forecasts can be made with regard to the social and political institutions of the future—in particular, what form our society would be likely to assume if we were to sit by inactively and what marginal changes are likely to be accessible to us if we so desire; and, on the other hand, we have to inquire which of these possible changes we should in fact seek to implement. This latter question, in turn, has two parts: How do we each individually decide, on the basis of our personal utility preferences, which among several possible alternative worlds we prefer; and, in a democratic society, how do we go about arriving at possibly far-reaching decisions affecting our future way of life on the basis of the individual citizen's preferences?

We thus have conceptually three subproblems, concerned respectively with prediction, with individual preference, and with a democratic choice mechanism for expressing social preference.

7.7.2 *Prediction and Uncertainty*

The predictive segment of the problem is that of forecasting possible major alterations in social and political institutions, ranging from shifts in established customs to changes in formalized procedures. We might ask, for instance, whether the age of conformity will give way to a new rise of individualism; what effects automation will have on social stratification; in what respects our daily way of life will be most profoundly affected by technological innovations; to what extent, and in what form, centralized governmental planning will affect individual enterprise in a capitalistic society; what aspects of national sovereignty are likely to be surrendered within the next generation; and so on.

Meaningful forecasts obtained in response to such questions, of course, will rarely be precise, because of the uncertainties owing to the fundamental complexities, both factual and conceptual, inherent in the social domain. The necessary lack of precision, however, by no means precludes the usefulness of no-change projections and, in particular, of an assessment of the degree of uncertainty associated with such trend extrapolations. Thus in forecasting the value of a quantity q at some future date, it is a valuable planning aid to have some estimate of the range R within which q is likely to lie (Figure 1).

In addition to giving ourselves an accounting of the nature and degree of uncertainties regarding future developments, it is of special importance to the social technologist to differentiate as far as possible between factual uncertainty in general, as illustrated by R in Figure 1, and what may more specifically be called "strategic uncertainty". That is, among the uncertain facts and events that give rise in our minds to the interval R (rather than a point projection) are deliberate future decisions by policymakers. For a particular policy P, the range of uncertainty R_P, while not reduced to a single point, may well be substantially smaller than R (see Figure 2). The range R_P may be said to represent the residual factual uncertainty after the uncertainty regarding policy P has been removed. Strategic uncertainty, thus, is the uncertainty as to what social policies will be adopted in the future. Therefore—to express it positively—the area within which we have strategic uncertainty is precisely that within which control can potentially be applied—that is, within which the social engineer must operate.

When the nature of the subject matter permits—and it often does—this analysis of uncertainty can be raised to a slightly more sophisticated level and, in that case, may elucidate more clearly the effects of alternative

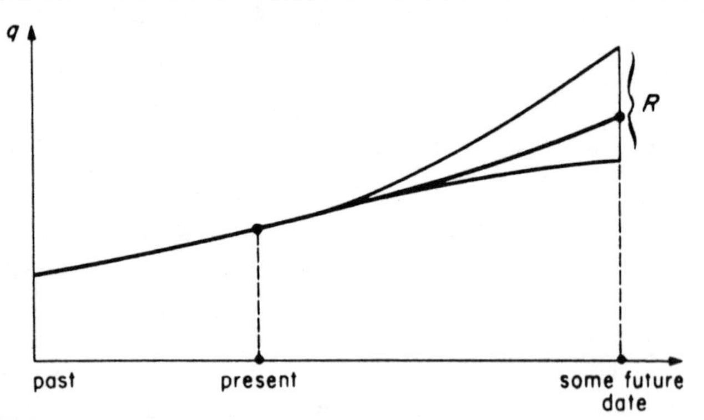

FIGURE 1

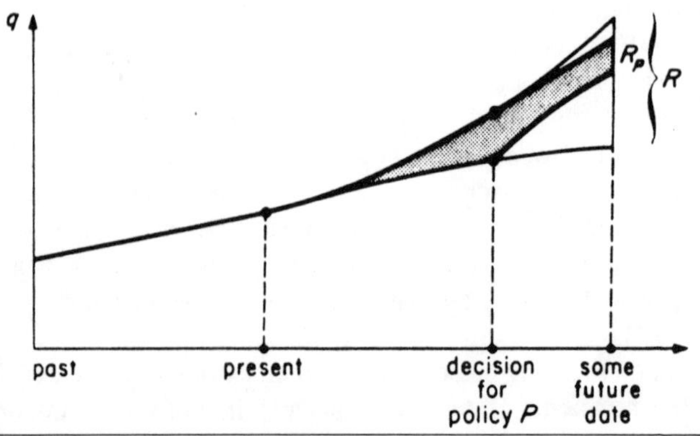

FIGURE 2

actions. I am referring to the possibility of meaningfully associating varying probabilities with the points of the range R (Figures 1 and 2). Often the central points of the range are considered more probable, while the probability diminishes to zero as we move toward the extremes of R. The resulting probability distribution, often bell-shaped, is shown in Figure 3, using a third dimension to display it.

For concreteness, let us imagine that q denotes the size of the world population, and R the range of estimates of q for the year 2000. Now consider the policy P of launching a multibillion-dollar worldwide educational campaign for birth control. The enactment of P would shift the probability distribution toward the lower end of R, whereas the opposite policy, non-P, of not conducting such a campaign, would shift it upward (Figure 4). (If these probability distributions were obtained on the basis of an analysis of expert opinions, a further and perhaps even more significant impression of the relative effects of P and non-P could be gained from a consideration of the probability distributions of the differences in q as a result of P compared to non-P.)

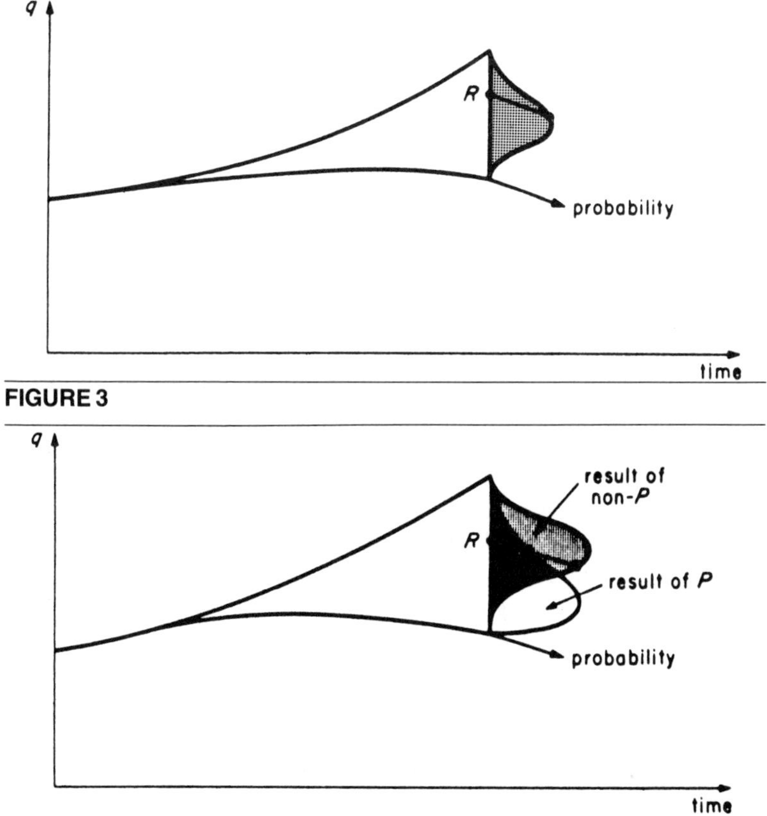

FIGURE 3

FIGURE 4

Returning now to the specific subject of the future of our social institutions, a good start in arriving at a survey of institutional changes that may be in the offing can no doubt be made by scanning the recent literature; this could be augmented by consultation with experts in such fields as social psychology, economic trends, and public affairs. [Some such forecasts are contained in Chapters VIII and IX.] Having obtained a list of institutional innovations considered more than remote possibilities, one could then proceed to subject the items on such a list to scrutiny by a panel of experts and attempt, by applying the Delphi technique of opinion extraction, to obtain a consensus as to the more likely contingencies among them and of the ranges of factual uncertainty associated with these contingencies. The outcome of such a preliminary survey would be twofold: It would reveal general "inevitable" trends, and it would provide warning signals of potential dangers to our society that, by virtue of falling within the domain of strategic uncertainty, might be avoidable through judicious social-engineering work.

7.7.3 Futuribles

The more or less routine forecasts of such a trend survey would have to be augmented by more imaginative surmises of possible futures (to use the Futuribles terminology), comprising among others social and political inventions specifically designed to circumvent some of the undesirable features inherent in the basic trend, if left undisturbed. To generate such constructive surmises requires a departure from the traditional mode of utopian literature, in which a supposedly better (or even ideal) world is created by the imagination and presented as a vision dissociated from reality, with no indication as to feasibility or even internal consistency.

If the social engineer wishes to approach this inventive task constructively, he will have to engage in what may perhaps be described as dynamic utopian planning. This process should consist in a systems synthesis, showing how a desired future state of our society can be evolved from the present one through a series of feasible steps. As a beginning, one might resort to the method of writing plausible scenarios (always taking the present time as the starting point). However, this would have to be followed by a developmental laboratory simulation based on expert opinions (much as in the special case of urban redevelopment). Together with the less sophisticated trend forecasts previously derived, such inventive scenarios reinforced by pseudo-experimental laboratory developments would constitute some of the sociopolitical alternatives from which we must select those we regard worth pursuing.

7.7.4 Preference Determination and Politics

The actual preference determination among these possible futures is a borderline topic between social technology and politics. Although the invention of social alternatives and a comparative analysis of them that might enlighten the individual as to his personal preferences belong within the domain of social technology as an unbiased discipline, any scheme of aggregating individual into collective preferences is a political device. As soon as we argue for or against such a scheme, we thereby enter the political arena.

The problems of fair voting procedures, even given the best democratic intentions, are well known; outstanding among them are the difficulties of avoiding the voting paradox (a group can appear among three alternatives to prefer A to B, B to C, and yet C to A), of protecting minorities against majority decisions, and of assigning equitable voting strengths to parliamentary representatives of groups of different sizes (e.g., delegates to the United Nations). The analysis and clarification of difficulties of this nature can and should be carried out dispassionately and objectively (as has been done, for instance, by Arrow, 1951, and by Shapley, 1962); yet the resolution of these difficulties requires political meta-choices—that is, decisions on the constitutional level. This places a singular moral obligation of political restraint on the analyst.

7.7.5 Institutionalization of the Futuribles Concept

Bertrand de Jouvenel, in his book *The Art of Conjecture,* has advocated that the systematic search for futuribles and the democratic choice among them be institutionalized. A concern with the future has, of course, always been implicit in any scientific undertaking and, thus, is as old as science itself. It is the systems-mindedness of our present day, supported by a growing computer-mindedness, that has suddenly made de Jouvenel's recommendation of a systems-synthetic attack on the problems of the future of our society appear not only feasible, but natural. The support for this new approach is growing so fast, in fact, that full-scale attempts at its realization may well be imminent.

To implement this idea would require setting up an institute specifically devoted to social planning. The obligation of such an organization would be rather clearly divided into three separate, though interrelated, functions: a predictive, a moral, and a catalytic one. The predictive function consists in carrying out the sociotechnological research needed to isolate the probably attainable among the logically possible futures for our society and to ascertain likely means of implementation. The moral function consists, on the one hand, in performing a logical analysis of equitable voting procedures for the determination of group preferences and, on the other, in elucidating the degree to which a particular possible future would in fact comply with a given set of basic (individual or group) preferences. Finally, the catalytic function which de Jouvenel in fact regards as the preponderant one, is that of enhancing the process of democratic choice vis-à-vis the available action alternatives and their probable consequences for the individual citizen. To fulfill this function, the envisaged institute may have to prepare detailed descriptions of the implications of each alternative in terms, not only of the overall social fabric, but of the daily life of the individual; in addition, and most important, it would have to provide a public forum where the advantages and disadvantages of attainable alternative futures could be discussed.

In comparing the operation of such a "Futuribles Institute", that is, of an organization that would promote a rational approach to the resolution of the problems of the future of a democratic society, with that of other research institutions directed toward the future, it is well to keep clearly in mind that it would have one outstanding distinct characteristic—namely, its obligation to conduct a continual analysis of moral values. This ethical mandate has two implications. First, in examining the possibilities of the future, it requires that its analysts proceed with exquisite intellectual integrity as they combine imagination and rational discretion, lest they appear to have convincingly eliminated every alternative but one, when, in fact, the choice has not been so uniquely narrowed. Second, no matter how successfully objectivity was preserved in the institute's pronouncements, political implications of the latter would impart to the institute the potentiality of becoming a factor of considerable political influence on the national scene.

The creation of an organization of this kind, that is, some form of institutionalization of the futuribles concept, seems not only highly desirable but eventually inevitable. Yet, in view of its moral and therefore political aspect, the utmost caution and a great deal of wisdom must be exercised in choosing the organizational format, as well as in selecting the personnel for such an institution. Too much is at stake to ignore the risk that the basic concept could easily be subverted, either passively through lack of imaginative boldness or actively through deliberate machinations of vested interests. In implementing the futuribles concept, there could be no place for people who are afraid either of their own shadows or of the shadows of things to come. A Futuribles Institute would have to be singularly reasonable without being "reasonable" in the sense of timidity and entirely above politics in order to take its place as a truly political institution that might "invent the future" by providing responsible and enlightened guidance in our ever more rapidly changing society. ■

Chapter III

The Role of Operations Research

8 CONCEPTUAL REALIGNMENT VIS-À-VIS THE FUTURE

During the decades following the end of World War II, a number of factors came together to create an intellectual climate that encouraged and, one might even say, necessitated a new attitude toward the future.

First, the problems with which society saw itself confronted were becoming more complex. Instead of being able to confine our planning to local concerns with such matters as school curricula, traffic congestion, water rights, land use, and the control of street crime, it became increasingly clear that there were also some larger issues on a national or even global scale that were of immense societal importance and might begin to yield to rational treatment if attacked boldly and farsightedly. These more-than-local issues turned out to have two aspects of unusual complexity: their sheer size and their interconnectedness. Their size called for a systems approach (urban systems, transportation systems, health-care delivery systems, energy systems, farm price support systems, space exploration systems, and so on); and their interconnectedness ("everything depends on everything else") implied that none of them could be studied and planned for in isolation from the rest.

Second, the rate at which our technological and social environment was changing was much greater than it had been in the past and was expected to increase. (This observation later became the main theme of Alvin Toffler's *Future Shock*; see Toffler, 1970.) Thus the prospect that the conditions of existence during a person's lifetime would remain essentially constant—an assumption quite proper in previous generations—no longer applied. The future, now expected to be substantially different from the past, began to be regarded with both curious and fearful anticipation.

There were many dramatic changes taking place in those years—television's appearance on the scene, the introduction of jet aircraft, the beginnings of space exploration, the so-called Green Revolution, the use of nuclear power for energy and weapons production, and so on—all with far-reaching social and political consequences. In addition, there were harbingers, some ominous and some promising, of further profound changes to come in the future. The immense effects on everybody's life of future developments in the computer field were beginning to be anticipated, as were—perhaps less obviously—the implications of the tremendous strides being taken in biochemistry and genetics.

While these two factors, complexity and rapid rate of change, produced conditions under which a closer examination of the future appeared desirable, a third factor brought about a real change in intellectual attitude toward the future. This was the recognition that the environment within which society has to function need not be accepted as a given condition to which to respond but that, through proper planning, something constructive might be done about the future. That is, aside from the near-term planning by individuals and corporate entities and local communities, the future operating environment for our national and global society might be amenable to the influence of beneficial interventive action.

9 TWO REVOLUTIONARY DEVELOPMENTS[1]

Grounds for this new optimism, which eventually led to the emergence of the field of futures research, may be seen in two revolutionary developments that were beginning to unfold during the 1950s and 1960s. One was the computer revolution already alluded to above, which began with the computer growing from a mere bookkeeping device to a highly versatile data processor and research tool; and it continued, and is still continuing—through time-sharing, the automation of computer programming, and computer conferencing—in the direction of establishing a true symbiosis between human and machine, where in a very real sense human intelligence will be enhanced through collaboration with a computer.

The other revolution in the making, which eventually is likely to add to our control over the future, was of a very different kind, being both more subtle and potentially even more influential. I am referring to the reorientation taking place within the so-called soft sciences, a reorientation discussed in some detail in the preceding chapter. The traditional methods of the social sciences are proving inadequate to the task of dealing effectively with the ever-growing complexity of forecasting the consequences of alternative policies and thus furnishing useful planning aid to high-level decision makers in the public and private sectors. This lack of policy orientation was beginning and is continuing to be effectively overcome. Rather than continue the futile attempt to emulate the physical sciences, researchers in the social-science area are realizing that the time has come to emulate physical technology instead. They are beginning to do this by seeking an interdisciplinary systems approach to the solution of sociopolitical problems. They will accom-

1. This section and the following one, with minor changes, represent a portion of my Rand paper P-3576, "New Developments in Early Forecasting of Public Problems: A New Intellectual Climate" (1967).

plish this by transferring the methods of operations research from the area of physical technology to that of social technology.

The potential reward from this evolving reorientation of some of the effort in the social-science area toward social technology, employing operations-analytical techniques, is considerable; it may even equal or exceed in importance that of the achievements credited to the technologies arising out of the physical sciences.

10 TECHNIQUES OF OPERATIONS RESEARCH

Operations research was first brought into being through the exigencies of World War II; it has since continued to develop and become a widely accepted tool, not only in the peacetime management of military affairs, but throughout the operations of commerce and industry (and in that case is often referred to as "management science").

Among the principal operations-research techniques that have proven themselves in these areas and that show great promise of being transferable to social technology are the construction of mathematical models, simulation procedures, and a systematic approach to the utilization of expert opinions. All of these techniques (it is almost needless to say) are greatly aided and continually refined by the computer, and the most recent phase of the computer revolution mentioned earlier may well add another order of magnitude to their potency. In particular, automated access to central data banks and, through computer conferencing, to fellow researchers will, in conjunction with appropriate socioeconomic models, provide the soft sciences with the same kind of massive data-processing and interpreting capability that, in the physical sciences, created the breakthrough that led to the development of atomic fission. ■

11 THE SCIENTIFIC STATUS OF OPERATIONS RESEARCH[2]

There has been a long-standing controversy about whether operations research may be regarded as a wholly scientific activity. It is my contention that the answer to this question is a qualified yes. There are two qualifications, one of purpose and one of method.

In comparing a scientific investigation with an operational analysis, we note, first of all, a difference in emphasis: Pure scientists are concerned primarily with the pursuit of truth and thus with a better understanding of the world in which we live; any application to coping with the real world, which may flow from such increased understanding, assumes secondary importance. Operations analysts, on the other hand, are pragmatists; their primary

2. This section is based on material taken from my Rand paper P-2795, "The Systematic Use of Expert Judgment in Operations Research" (1963).

concern is with the more effective handling of the real world, even if this may have to be accomplished without the desirable degree of understanding of all the underlying phenomena.

This difference in purpose between the purist striving for understanding and the pragmatist striving for control of his surroundings brings with it a methodological difference, which is the second qualification to which I referred above. Both the exact scientist and the operations analyst frequently utilize what is sometimes called a mathematical model of the subject matter. In the case of the scientist, such a model is apt to be part of the well-confirmed body of scientific theory, whereas an operations-research model is of a more tentative, *ad hoc*, character. In other words, even if the current status of science provides no well-established theory for the phenomena to be dealt with by the operations analyst, a preliminary model must nevertheless be constructed, where both the structure of that model and its numerical inputs may be based merely on intuitive insight and limited practical experience by the analyst or by whatever expert advisers on the subject matter may be available. As further insights accrue and more experimental data become available, the operations analyst has to be ready to discard the first model and replace it with an improved one. This tentative procedure, dictated by pragmatic considerations, is thus essentially one of successive approximation. In this regard, operations research has a status similar to that of the so-called inexact sciences, of which medicine, engineering, and most of the social sciences are examples. Applying the reasoning presented in the section on the epistemology of the inexact sciences in the preceding chapter, we may say that, in comparing operations research with an exact science, it is with regard to exactness that operations research falls short, but not necessarily with regard to the scientific character of its methods. The methods of the inexact sciences (including operations research), despite their reliance on less-than-universal laws and on intuitive judgment, can be just as "scientific" as those of the exact sciences, as long as certain standards of objectivity in confirming predictions are observed. With particular reference to the all-important reliance on expert judgment in operations research, it seems to me that the operations analyst, far from denying the need for intuitive expertise, should consciously acknowledge its use and indeed make the most of it. Only by replacing the surreptitious utilization of expertise by the explicit and systematic application of it can operations research hope to acquire the status of a science, albeit an inexact one.

As we discussed in the earlier epistemology section, the first question that must be raised is how objectivity can in fact be safeguarded if direct empirical evidence is replaced, even in part, by opinion, however expert. The justification for such a procedure may be seen in looking on the expert as an objective indicator, comparable to a measuring instrument. That is, the expert's predictive pronouncements have to be treated as an integral, intrinsic part of the subject matter, in the sense that information on his or her reliability—as evidenced by past predictive performance—must be added to our knowledge about the field in question. By incorporating in our model the performance of this instrument for measuring probabilities (i.e., the predictive expert), our data are supplemented by the expert's pronouncements and our theory is supplemented by objectively confirmable hypotheses on the expert's reliability.

The often unavoidable reliance on expert judgment in operations research therefore does not necessarily imply that objectivity is being thrown to the winds. However, in order to raise the level of objectivity and to utilize expert judgment most effectively when available, an effort has to be made to develop scientific techniques for identifying expert performance and for processing data consisting of expert pronouncements into predictions of the greatest possible reliability. ■

12 THE RELATIONSHIP OF OPERATIONS RESEARCH TO SYSTEMS ANALYSIS, TECHNOLOGY ASSESSMENT, AND FUTURES RESEARCH

My reason for dwelling at length on the role and scientific status of operations research is that most of futures research may be regarded as a subfield of operations research. In my opinion there is, in fact, a clear line of progression, which starts with operations research, goes from there to systems analysis, includes futures research, and continues to what has become known as technology assessment, each of these four fields being somewhat more specialized than the preceding one, as shown in Figure 5. (For those who prefer to define futures research less narrowly than I am inclined to do, so as to include speculative considerations of the futures synthesis type—such as scenario invention and utopian propositions—the domain of futures research would more properly be indicated by the larger, dotted-line rectangle shown in the figure.)

Operations research, also known as management science (particularly when applied to business and industrial problems), concerns itself with the efficient operation of parts of a given organization; for instance, military and industrial logistics are typical examples of operations-research topics.

Part of operations research is called systems analysis, namely, that portion seeking to optimize the operation of part of an organization by considering the overall needs of the whole organization rather than suboptimizing for the specific part. This criterion, of wishing to maximize the efficiency of the whole organization, has two important implications: It imposes an interdisciplinary approach, so as to take the many facets of the entire organization into proper consideration; and it almost invariably requires that some thought be given not only to present operations but also to the future of the organization.

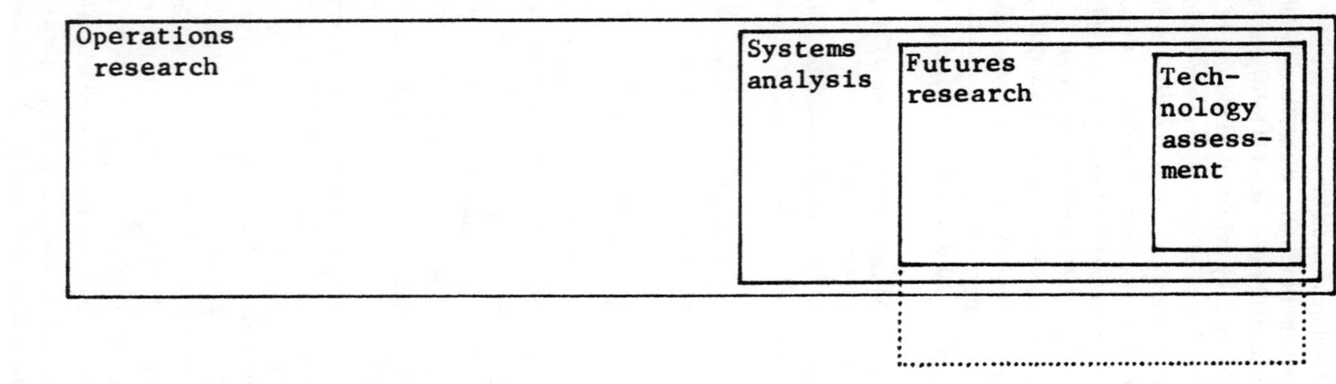
Operations research
Systems analysis
Futures research
Tech-
nology
assess-
ment

FIGURE 5

This is where futures research enters the picture: Whenever, in a systems-analytical context, the time horizon is sufficiently far in the future, so that the operating environment by that time will be substantially different from what it is at present, we are, by definition, in the area of futures research. While probably less than half of all operations research can rightfully be classified as systems analysis, most of systems analysis—in my judgment, something like 75 percent—is in fact identical with futures research.

As for technology assessment, finally, it is a small but highly important part of futures research. It considers the effects on an organization, which may well be society as a whole, of the prospective introduction of some new technology as well as the measures that might be taken to protect the organization against deleterious effects of the new technology or to enhance the benefits that the organization might derive from it.

13 THE INDISPENSABILITY OF EXPERT JUDGMENT[3]

Systems analysis, of which futures research, as explained earlier, constitutes the major part, can profit from the use of expert judgment in all phases of its work. Moreover there are compelling reasons why it must rely on it: One is the fact that systems analysis is an interdisciplinary activity; another, that it is future-directed.

13.1 The Interdisciplinarity of Systems Analysis

The main purpose of systems analysis is to provide an integrated approach to the study and planned manipulation of complex systems. Such systems almost invariably possess certain societal features, as in the case of a firm, a city, a transportation system, a nation. But even if they do not, as illustrated by a totally inanimate object such as a machine tool, there are inevitably certain social considerations involved in deciding how such a system ought to be designed and in judging how well it is performing. In fact, the features of the system itself and the aspirations and values of the system's users are generally so intricately interwoven that the systems analyst needs to include the users as part of the overall system he is investigating. Thus the very distinction between social and nonsocial systems becomes extremely tenuous.

Systems analysis, therefore, inevitably involves interdisciplinary considerations. Often numerous disciplines come into play, such as physics, chemistry, engineering, economics, sociology, political science, human values, ecology. In particular, it should be noted, the relevant disciplines always include some that belong in the realm of the social sciences.

3. The next three sections, with minor adaptations, are the first half of an essay entitled "Role-Playing and Other Judgmental Techniques", written in 1978 for the International Institute for Applied Systems Analysis and to be published soon as a chapter in a handbook on systems analysis.

13.2 The Future-Directedness of Systems Analysis

Any activity involving a planning effort is, by definition, future-directed. This clearly applies to systems analysis.

It is, however, useful to distinguish two kinds of planning activities: those based on the assumption that the operating conditions at the time the plans might be implemented will be essentially the same as those presently prevailing, and those where the operating conditions are expected to be substantially different from the conditions existing at the time the plans are being made. The former case, in which the relevant features of the world are assumed invariant over time, is only nominally future-directed; it is as though plans were being made for the present. The latter case, on the other hand, where no such invariance is implied, may properly be called future-directed; it requires forecasts of future operating conditions as a prerequisite of adequate planning. The relatively new field of futures research, which has come into being in recognition of the importance of future-oriented planning, concerns itself with the development and application of methods of forecasting and of utilizing such forecasts for improved planning.

For some systems-analytical work it is reasonable that it be only nominally future-directed; yet there are a few cases in which this is justified. Only in the hard sciences do we have the luxury of having at our disposal time-invariant laws (the laws of thermodynamics, for instance, applying equally in the twenty-first century as in the nineteenth). In systems analysis, because it transcends the hard sciences, when the assumption of time-invariance is made, it must be recognized as a simplifying stipulation requiring justification.

Such justification is harder and harder to attain as the maturation of systems analysis continues. The reason for this is twofold. First, many of the problems addressed by systems analysis concern increasingly complex situations, where the time horizon is farther in the future, as illustrated by current efforts to solve the energy crisis, to plan new cities, or to develop underdeveloped countries. Second, even in the case of studies having a short time horizon, the systems analyst cannot afford to forget that we live in an age of ubiquitous future shock, in which changes in our environment occur with ever-increasing rapidity, due mostly to technological advances and their societal implications. The time is past when such changes, even from one generation to the next, were barely noticeable and, consequently, planning "for the present" was entirely proper. Now, even in the short run, the hypothesis of environmental time-invariance as a basis for systems planning is usually found to be unwarranted.

Thus it is evident that systems analysis generally is in an essential way, rather than merely nominally, future-directed.

13.3 Implications for the Use of Judgment

The interdisciplinary and future-directed character of systems analysis makes some reliance on judgment indispensable. To see that this is so, it is only necessary to reflect on the conditions under which judgment-free conclusions, applicable to real-world planning, could be drawn. They include the presence of data derived from observations; the existence of a coherent, well-confirmed, and objectively (i.e., intersubjectively) testable theory establishing correlational and, if possible, causal connections among the observed phenomena; and the application, through extrapolation, of such a theory to the future consequences of contemplated actions. This is the pattern followed, by and large, in the case of straightforward engineering applications of the laws of physics.

These conditions are not satisfiable in the context of a typical systems analysis. First of all, well-confirmed theories are not currently available in any of the social sciences, and all we have are, at best, mildly confirmed, *ceteris paribus* regularities. While these are an enormously valuable substitute for the kind of well-confirmed theories to which the hard-sciences tradition has accustomed us [see Section 6, on epistemology, in Chapter II], they are generally strictly unidisciplinary; and established regularities connecting several disciplines—especially the all-important case of a social-science discipline and engineering technology—are virtually absent. Second, even if such well-confirmed interdisciplinary theories were available, their applicability to determining the future consequences of planned actions would be questionable because the *ceteris paribus* condition (the invariance of the operating environment) would generally be violated.

Consider, for example, the case of the government of a poverty-stricken nation contemplating measures intended to curb the future growth of its population. (Such measures might include birth-control propaganda or tax incentives encouraging smaller families.) The obstacles to an objective, preferably theory-based, approach would be formidable. The first thing the planner would need, and could not obtain by extrapolation from past time series, would be a baseline in the form of a population forecast on the assumption of no government intervention. Past observations would, no doubt, imply something close to an exponential growth pattern; but since common sense suggests that this could not continue indefinitely, the population projection would have to reflect influences that did not exist in the past, such as changes in people's values, general economic conditions, possibly even unprecedented famine. Moreover, the effectiveness of governmental intervention, even if it could be foreseen clearly under *ceteris paribus* conditions, would be altered by future changes in the operating environment, such as (again) the economy and, especially, technological advances and institutional modifications in regard to birth control.

This example illustrates the futility of trying to proceed in a complex planning context by formal theoretical means; but it also points the way to the solution. The answer, of course, lies in the proper utilization of expert judgment. Fortunately, in the social sciences we are able to call on a vast reservoir of expertise of many kinds. While in some cases the expert judgment that is available may be derived from the explicit application of rudimentary (and almost invariably intradisciplinary) theories, more often it may be highly intuitive in character and based on insights that, although no less reliable, may thus far have defied articulation within a theoretical framework.

For instance, in the population policy example, trained demographers would, on the basis of a mixture of theoretical considerations and intuitive insights, be quite capable of correcting naive exponential extrapolations and of thereby providing a reliable baseline forecast. Similarly, specialists in the disciplines relevant to birth-control techniques (social psychology, biomedicine, pharmaceutical manufacturing methods, and so on) could supply estimates of the time of occurrence of certain technological advances in this area and thereby provide inputs valuable in assessing the effects of governmental birth-control propaganda. The combined result of utilizing such cross-disciplinary expertise, while of course falling far short of the comparative certainty associated with hard-science predictions, is nevertheless likely to impart to forecasts a considerable improvement in reliability over those made without the benefit of such consultation.

Emphasis on the intuitive character of much of expert judgment is not intended to imply that all judgment of this kind is necessarily purely subjective and unsupportable by objective fact or intersubjectively accepted theory. Very often an expert serves primarily as an efficient transmitter of knowledge commonly accepted within the scientific community. But the point to be borne in mind is that an expert, through extensive experience within his field of specialization, often will be able to augment his objectively based information by purely intuitive, hence subjective, insights that will render his pronouncements that much more useful.

Experience clearly supports the view that in general the quality of decisions based on intuitive forecasts improves with the reliability of such forecasts, and that this reliability, in turn, depends greatly on the level of expertise of the forecasters. Therefore the need for care in selecting forecasters and eliciting and utilizing forecasts cannot be overemphasized.

13.4 Justification of the Use of Expertise

The admission of intuitive expert judgment, however indispensable, as a source of information represents a replacement of objective procedures with subjective ones, and the question may well be raised as to the epistemological justification of such an abandonment of standard scientific principles. The answer, briefly, may be given by pointing out that (i) systems analysis is, after all, outside the realm of science in the narrow sense, and (ii) the use of subjective judgment is, in fact, capable of some measure of objectivization. Both of these statements require some elaboration.

With regard to the first, systems analysis is a branch of operations research. As such its principal function is not to gain scientific insights but to provide assistance to planners and decision makers. This does not mean that the value of scientific insights is questioned or unappreciated or that systems analysis is an "art", implying total disregard for objectivity. Perhaps the designation of a "craft" might be more appropriate, where the quality of the results—i.e., of the advice it is able to offer decision makers—is capable of objective evaluation, regardless of whether the source of the results is objective or subjective. [The section in Chapter II on social technology states the difference between a traditional scientific investigator and an operations analyst—hence also a systems analyst—in some detail.] The pragmatic spirit in which a systems analyst has to operate may compel him to abandon purist scientific principles and accept a certain amount of subjective insight in order to fulfill his primary, advisory mission.

Concerning the second statement, the prescientific status of systems analysis may thus sanction the admission of subjective factors in the form of judgmental input data. However, an objective basis for its output, while not always attainable, remains desirable. In the case of using the subjective opinions of experts, it is conceptually possible [as explained in the epistemology section of Chapter II] to introduce some objectivity at a higher level by thinking of the experts as equivalents of measuring instruments. The use of expertise thus need not amount to a retreat from objectivity—that is, provided one is prepared to take that step to a metalevel where the experts can be treated as part of the subject matter under consideration. This step would involve a broad effort to establish a theoretical structure in that part of applied psychology that deals with the articulation and utilization of the existing expertise potential.

At the moment we still are in the same position with regard to this metadiscipline in which we find ourselves in relation to most of the social sciences; that is, we rely largely on mere intuitive insight rather than on well-confirmed theory when we believe that expert opinions can make a significant contribution to improved planning, especially when such opinions are articulated and utilized through systematic methods such as Delphi and gaming, to be discussed presently.

14 SPECIFIC OBJECTIVES IN USING EXPERT JUDGMENT

Expert opinions are of potential utility to many aspects of systems analysis. The most important forms in which expertise enters into the analytical process can perhaps be subsumed under the following four headings: conceptual inventiveness, factual estimation, factual forecasts, and normative forecasts.

14.1 Conceptual Inventiveness

It should go almost without saying that progress in any kind of intellectual pursuit—be it a strictly scientific activity or a prescientific enterprise such as a systems analysis—relies heavily on the occasional intuitive spark of an imaginative mind. New discoveries or new insights into relationships between observed phenomena usually come about as the result of some person's conceptual inventiveness.

There are many types of such inventiveness. Leaving aside strictly technological inventions, they include innovative concepts, such as the differential quotient or the social indicator; novel experiments, such as a test of the improved learning ability of worms after having eaten some of their own previously trained colleagues; and new strategies, such as the creation of an international food bank to stabilize agricultural prices and reduce the risk of famine.

The influx of intuition, in the form of such inventiveness, does not, incidentally, represent an ascension of subjective versus objective influences. Clearly even mathematics, the most "objective" of the sciences [as was pointed out once before, in Section 6], needs as much as any discipline an occasional brilliant inspiration to arrive at new discoveries. However, once a new fact or a new idea has been conjectured, no matter on how intuitive a foundation, it must be capable of objective test and confirmation by anyone. Thus the standards of scientific objectivity are not in any way put in question by the use of intuition in this form.

Novel ideas are a valuable but rare commodity. No methods for their mass production are available. It may be worthwhile, however, to give some thought to systematic ways and means of encouraging their invention. Sometimes informal brainstorming sessions have proven to be productive in this regard. Among the more structured procedures of using groups of experts, both operational gaming and Delphi inquiries, since they have some of the stimulative characteristics of brainstorming, are expedient tools for this purpose. The subsequent discussion of these techniques will further elucidate this point.

14.2 Factual Estimation

The informational starting point for a systems analysis is generally a description of the current status of the subject matter plus past time series of relevant indicators. This assumes that such data are readily available from reliable sources. In practice this is often not the case, either because adequate statistical information has not been recorded (as in the case of the per-capita income in a particular developing country) or because the desired information (say, the quality of a certain educational system) is too vaguely identified to permit anything but subjective evaluation.

In such cases, the systems analyst all too often makes the mistake of restricting himself to using whatever hard data are accessible, ignoring judgmental information, however potentially important it might be to the analysis.

Instead of thus omitting vital factors from the analysis, the analyst would generally do far better to obtain judgmental inputs from qualified experts. In the examples cited, an area specialist is likely to supply estimates of per-capita income which, while probably imprecise, would be accurate enough for most applications; similarly, an educational expert, given a suitable evaluation scale, could give useful comparative estimates of the quality of the educational system in question, either for the same system at different times or for different systems at the same time.

Thus, in the absence of hard data, expert opinion can have an important role in supplying "soft" judgmental inputs.

14.3 Factual Forecasts

In practice, the explicit resort to the use of expertise occurs most frequently in connection with factual forecasting. A reason for this [as pointed out in Section 13.3] is that extrapolation from past observations is generally insufficient to establish a theoretical foundation for valid forecasts and that it needs to be supplemented with the intuitive, not yet theoretically articulated, insights and interpretations of appropriate specialists.

Factual forecasts fall into two important subcategories: absolute and conditional forecasts. Both are properly made in probabilistic terms.

There have been many instances in recent years of absolute forecasts, particularly of technological, but also including societal, developments. Such forecasts, stating that the occurrence of some development by a certain date has such and such a probability, serve to establish the likely operating environment, or the range of likely scenarios, on which a planner will have to set his sights. They thus fulfill the indispensable function of providing the all-important background information without which a plan might be inappropriate or obsolete before it is considered for implementation.

By contrast, conditional forecasts state that if some condition were to arise, specifically if some action were taken, then the occurrence of a particular development by a certain date would have such and such a probability. A conditional forecast may have one of two significantly different purposes. One is the case in which an absolute forecast, say of an event E, is to be made, but the forecaster knows, or senses, that the probability of E's occurrence is quite different depending on whether some condition C does or does not prevail. In this situation, conditional forecasts of E, given either C or non-C, can be combined into an absolute forecast of E, provided an absolute forecast of C is available. Typically, in such a case, the conditional forecasts of E and the absolute forecast of C are made by different experts, because event E and condition C may well belong to different disciplines (as in the case of forecasting the state of the economy, depending on whether or not a technological breakthrough regarding a new source of energy will occur).

The other application of a conditional forecast is concerned directly with the planning process. A planner may wish to know about the consequences of a contemplated action, A. If B is one of the potential consequences, the decision on whether or not to carry out A may depend on the conditional forecasts of B, given either A or non-A. More generally, if a decision maker is faced with a choice among actions $A_1, A_2, \ldots A_n$ (where doing nothing may be one of the options), the conditional probabilities of various potential consequences $B_1, B_2 \ldots B_m$, given either A_1 or A_2 or . . . or A_n, may have a bearing on the decision and thus may have to be estimated.

It is worth noting that conditional forecasts often represent the first step toward theory formation. In the simplest case, if A and B are properties attributable to objects i, j, . . ., then a series of conditional forecasts—such as "if A(i) then B(i), with probability p_i", "if A(j) then B(j), with probability p_j", and so on—may lead to a general hypothesis of the form, "whenever A(x) then B(x), with probability p(x)", where p(x) is a function obtained by curve-fitting from the original values $p_1, p_2, \ldots$.

Tentative mathematical models built by systems analysts (and, more generally, by operations analysts) are not uncommonly put together on the basis of experts' casuistic estimates of the kind just described. The resulting "theories" are rarely intended to be more than first approximations of reality, to be discarded when new insights provide better approximations.

14.4 Normative Forecasts

Ordinary forecasts, whether absolute or conditional, represent estimates of what the future will, in fact, be like. At times they are, for emphasis, called "factual forecasts".

Normative forecasts, by contrast, are concerned with what the forecaster thinks the future ought to be like. They are thus related directly to the goal- and objectives-setting part of the planning process. It is in this area that the virtually total absence of a comprehensive theoretical approach is felt keenly, and reliance on expert opinion is here even more indispensable than in the case of factual forecasting.

There are as many aspects to normative forecasting as there are to the planning process; in fact, there is little difference between the two, except perhaps that the term "planning" sometimes implies an operationally systematic and practical procedure, whereas what is designated as "normative forecasting" is less impeded by considerations of feasibility and resource constraints.

A planning process generally involves a number of logically distinct steps, which, however, are not always clearly separated from one another in practice. They are the following.

14.4.1 Assessing the Future Operating Environment

This amounts to estimating the characteristics of the so-called exogenous changes that will have taken place in technology and society by the time any plans are expected to be implemented—exogenous in the sense that they are not under the planner's or decision maker's control. [The potential role of the expert in this context was covered in Section 14.3.]

14.4.2 The Setting of Overall Goals

Such goals are usually stated in very general terms, such as "enhancement of the welfare" of the organization (the nation, the city, the firm, the educational system, and so forth) for which plans are being made. The expert's task here is primarily one of interpreting what in essence is already fixed and casting vaguely expressed desires in a form such that it becomes possible to argue meaningfully whether the attainment of specific objectives would indeed, in view of the expected future environment, contribute to reaching the stated goals. Usually what is at first expressed vaguely as "welfare" turns out to be a multidimensional utility, and an important part of normative forecasting consists in assigning preferred weights to the individual components of that utility. Since it is rare that explicit and universally agreed-upon exchange ratios among the components can be defined, the intuitive insight of experts may be required to estimate how different attainment mixtures with respect to the overall utility's components would compare in the eyes of various stakeholder groups, taking into account future changes in the operating environment. It should be mentioned in passing that the utility dimensions include not only substantive differentiations (such as health, education, income, and security in the case of national planning, or market share and return on investment in the case of corporate planning), but also matters of preference between lower risk and higher expectations and between short-term and long-term gain.

14.4.3 The Specification of Objectives

Once the goals have been clearly identified, objectives may sometimes be specifiable in terms of the degree to which one ought to strive to attain the various goal dimensions—that is, if these are in fact measurable, so that a quantitative objective can thus be stated. Otherwise it is necessary first to define appropriate numerical indicators ("social indicators" in the case of societal planning), in terms of which objectives can then be formulated. (Examples of such objectives are the raising of the literacy level to 98 percent, the lowering of unemployment to 4 percent, or the expansion of production facilities by 20 percent. The specification of objectives may be relatively straightforward, except that both the choice of appropriate indicators and the selection of objectives that are likely to be feasible may require an understanding of the subtleties of the subject matter not available to anyone except a highly trained expert.

14.4.4 The Formulation of Action Programs

The translation of objectives into action programs, under budgetary and other resource constraints, is seldom a routine matter leading to a unique prescription. To arrive at an efficient recommendation generally takes a great deal of ingenuity and imagination, as well as cognizance of likely changes in operating conditions. Here, again, the role of intuitive judgment on the part of trained specialists is evident.

14.4.5 The Comparative Evaluation of Alternative Programs

The choice between two or more proposed action programs requires some form of cost-effectiveness analysis of the candidate programs, where both cost and effectiveness are apt to be multidimensional, affecting the degree to which various stated objectives may be expected to be met. Such assessments involve all of the difficulties mentioned under Section 14.4.2, such as the exchange ratios among utility components and—in view of the uncertainties regarding exogenous environmental changes—the risk-versus-expectation contraposition. While standard decision-theoretical analyses may be of assistance in making such a choice, there are inevitably so many intangible aspects present as to make some resort to intuitive insight virtually unavoidable.

In summary then, the need for intuitive judgmental inputs is evident and multifold throughout many aspects of systems analysis. Indeed, in practice, whether we look upon it approvingly or with a jaundiced eye, the informal use of intuition on the part of experts is already implicit in many activities in this field. The questions remain whether anything can be gained by giving explicit recognition to the role of expertise and whether systematic methods are in existence, or can be invented, providing experts with enhanced effectiveness in contributing their intuitive insight to systems analysis. The answer to the second question, I contend, is in the affirmative, and therefore, by implication, so is that to the first.

15 METHODS OF USING EXPERT JUDGMENT

As we have seen, expert judgment enters the systems-analytical process in many forms. It plays an essential role in

- inventing new concepts;
- designing the structure of models, including the modification of existing but inadequate models;
- supplying judgmental input data, especially in the form of forecasts;

- identifying the specific components of stated goals and providing the moral perception necessary to apportion weights of emphasis to these components; and
- offering normative visions of the future and inventing strategies for their attainment.

Once the fact has been accepted that the use of intuitive judgment in systems analysis is not a temporary expedient but a permanent and integral part of its normal procedures, it becomes imperative that orderly methods be employed by which judgmental contributions are utilized as effectively as possible.

In discussing such methods, it is useful to distinguish between those relating to individual experts and those concerned with the employment of groups of experts.

15.1 Individual Experts

If an analysis relies in part on judgmental inputs, the quality of its results clearly depends significantly on the quality of those inputs. Therefore it is important that the persons selected to supply such judgments be highly qualified experts and that the condition under which their expert opinions are solicited be as conducive as possible to their proficient performance.

[The matter of selecting appropriate experts has already been dealt with at some length in Section 7.5.1; so has the question of how to enhance an expert's performance, in Section 7.5.2.]

15.2 Groups of Experts

In a context such as a systems analysis, where some reliance on intuitive judgment is unavoidable, there are several reasons it may be preferable to employ more than one expert.

First of all, intuition is not infallible; it merely leads, statistically speaking, to significant improvement. Hence there is some justification in applying a principle enunciated by Norman Dalkey that "n heads are better than one". Applied, in particular, to numerical estimations—which include current-status assessments as well as probabilistic forecasts—the median of n estimates of a value can be seen to compare favorably with at least half and often substantially more than half of the individual estimates.

Second, whenever the use of the imagination is called on, the sheer increase in volume of ideas that may be expected from several as compared to one respondent affords a better chance that a really good idea will not be omitted from consideration. Such ideas may concern the pertinence of past observations, the design of experiments, the structure of models to be built, the description of desirable futures, and the invention of strategies and instrumentalities for their attainment.

These two reasons for the use of groups of experts, rather than individual ones, apply even in cases in which the required idea or information is strictly within a single intellectual discipline. A third reason is due to the multidisciplinary nature of systems analysis, which makes it difficult if not impossible for the intuitive insights of a single person to do justice to all relevant aspects of such an inquiry. Hence it is important to place proper emphasis on the need not only to be prepared to have to tap the expertise of a number of specialists from different disciplines, but to seek suitable methods involving interdisciplinary communication that permit the meshing of contributions from different fields of specialization that normally do not effectively interact with one another.

The traditional and simplest mode of drawing out a group of experts is, of course, that of a round-table discussion in which they can freely exchange ideas with one another. The stimulus of open conversation is particularly helpful when the objective of such an effort is to generate innovative concepts, and this effect can be enhanced by explicitly declaring the conference a brainstorming session, in which criticism of even far-out ideas is, at least initially, suppressed.

On the other hand, if the objective is factual—such as assessing the current situation, making conditional forecasts, or evaluating the feasibility of proposed action plans—then a free, face-to-face discussion may not be the optimal mode of operation, and a more structured procedure is generally preferable.

There are numerous reasons for this. In an open discussion of ideas among several persons, the noise level (both in the literal sense and, even more so, in the intellectual sense) may outweigh the actual information passed along, particularly in view of the known difficulties of cross-disciplinary communication, and there are likely to be all kinds of psychological undercurrents that may affect the quality of the end-product. Among these may be the undue influence of a dominant personality, the deference to authority (real or supposed), the reluctance to contradict opinions voiced by persons of higher status (because of age or organizational rank), the bandwagon effect of majority opinion, and, conversely, an unwillingness to abandon one's previously taken public stand on some issue.

Taken together, these potentially detrimental effects of an unstructured meeting may negate the undoubted assets of the intellectual stimulation it provides. ■

Two methodological approaches that seek to find a way out of this dilemma are operational gaming and the Delphi technique. Both replace open discussion with a controlled form of dialogue, both discourage the kind of psychological undercurrents just enumerated, and both lend themselves well to interdisciplinary discourse. [More will be said about these two approaches in Chapters V-VII.]

16 CONTROLLED EXPERIMENTS VS. INTUITIVE EXPERIMENTATION

Experimentation can take many forms, ranging from intuitive trial-and-error procedures ("If one thing doesn't work, let's try something else") to controlled laboratory experiments aimed at establishing a cause-and-effect relationship by varying one independent variable at a time and, in parallel, observing a control case in which that variable is left unchanged. Between these two extremes we have experiments with less than full control over environmental variables, which permit comparisons of different treatments yet may not yield conclusive evidence on why one treatment is better than another. In addition to such true experiments, there are the so-called pseudo-experiments, discussed earlier in some detail, in which experimentation takes place not in the real world under study, but in a model of the real world. Resorting to such pseudo-experimentation may be necessary [as pointed out in Section 6.15, on epistemology, in Chapter II] because true experimentation may be too costly or impossible for physical reasons (e.g., in atomic physics) or moral reasons (e.g., in contemplated social reforms).

Operations research—hence, by implication, systems analysis and futures research as well—because of its pragmatic orientation emphasized before, is not bent primarily, in contradistinction to pure science, on establishing "the truth" in some absolute sense but sees its mission as transmitting to decision makers the best possible advice to date, even at the risk that such advice, in hindsight, may later turn out to have been mistaken. A good operations analyst, needless to say, will hope, and even be justified in being quite confident, that serious errors of this kind will occur rarely and that, at worst, hindsight will merely show that his advice, while not perfect, might have been even better than it was.

In view of this tentative character of operations research, experimentation in this area tends to be of the less than fully controlled variety or, if true experimentation is not in the offing, of the pseudo-experimental kind. In either case, there is a presumption (often warranted but sometimes not) that the analyst's intuitive expertise will permit him to derive valid conclusions from the observed outcome of the experiments.

It should be recognized that in the hard sciences, too, noncontrolled experiments play an important role, in that they almost invariably represent the starting point from which the scientist, using his intuition, proceeds to formulate hypotheses that lend themselves to subsequent tests through controlled experimentation.. An operations analyst, because of time limits within which his advice is required, omits this last step (of controlled experimentation) and leaves it to the pure scientist to verify (or falsify, as the case may be) at his leisure the operations analyst's tentative conclusions.

To return once more to the matter of pseudo-experimentation, it should be pointed out that here, too, as in the case of true experimentation, we may distinguish between intuitive and controlled experiments. If the model in which such experiments are carried out affords only a poor representation of reality, then there would be little point in controlled experimentation, since, at best, the purpose could only be to provide intuitive suggestions toward the understanding of reality. On the other hand, if there is reason to believe that the model faithfully mirrors the essential features of the real world, then controlled experimentation in the model would lend high confidence in the expectation of the experimental results being transferable to explaining (and predicting) the corresponding real-world phenomena. Little, if any, controlled pseudo-experimentation has ever been carried out, but its promise should perhaps not be overlooked.

Chapter IV

Futures Research

17 THE ROLE OF FUTURES RESEARCH[1]

Futures research, as we have seen, constitutes a large part of systems analysis, which, in turn, is subsumed under operations research. The general purpose of futures research is to be an aid in long-range planning. To understand the special place of futures research in today's world one has to appreciate the increased need in this century for new ways of exploring the opportunities and perils of the future and to recognize the difference in approach, compared to traditional planning, through which futures research is expected to satisfy this need.

To put the subject of futures research in the right perspective, let me first of all attempt to clarify what futures research is expected to add to the traditional planning process. A planner, by definition, is trying to do something about the future. His business is to design a program of action that he hopes will lead to a future state of affairs that is better than what would take place if a different course of action were chosen, or better than that which would obtain by default if no action were taken. Thus, part of the planning process inevitably involves forecasts of the likely consequences of alternative courses of action. This is true regardless of whether we are concerned with planning in the private or in the public sector. When planning to manufacture a new product, it is up to the market researcher to predict the likely reception of contemplated variants of the new product. Similarly, when, say, alternative reform measures in the area of criminal law enforcement are under consideration, forecasts have to be made of the expected effect of each alternative measure on the incidence of criminal acts.

Since people have engaged in deliberate planning for thousands of years, and since planning always involves some measure of forecasting the future, what then is there that is novel about the present situation that has led to the development of the new discipline of futures research? The answer is that two things have happened.

First, planners these days are apt to tackle projects of greater complexity than used to be the case, as a consequence of which the lead times in many

1. This section is based on notes prepared for a business executives' seminar offered by the University of Southern California's Center for Futures Research in 1976.

cases have lengthened, so that the planning horizon often has to be not a year or two, but a decade or two in the future. For example, a new power plant, or a supersonic airliner, or a new hospital all require this kind of long-range planning. Second, the world around us is changing ever more rapidly, so that the environment within which whatever we are planning has to function will be quite different from the present; and the world twenty years from now will differ far more from the present than the present does from the world of twenty years ago. This increasing pace of change and its psychological and operational effects, as was mentioned once before, have been described most eloquently in Alvin Toffler's *Future Shock*.

These two phenomena, the longer lead times associated with greater complexity and the accelerated change in our surroundings, have had a profound effect on the planning process and have, in fact, created an entirely new attitude about the future. It used to be the case that it was quite reasonable to assume that, when planning some innovation, the rest of the world would remain essentially as we observe it to be at the time such plans are being made. That is, the planner's attitude was that of a short-term market analyst, who merely has to ask himself how a contemplated new product would do in the current market place. Such an attitude was quite proper even in areas where the consequences of one's actions might endure over a long period. For example, even a hundred years ago the pattern of society changed so little from one generation to the next that, say, an educational planner might quite validly have confined himself to considering the inadequacies of the educational system he himself had experienced and thereupon have proposed reform measures that would promise to ameliorate these shortcomings. Today, the situation has changed radically in this respect. A present-day educational reformer would have to realize that, at best, his reform ideas would not be implemented until some years down the line, and the students who would then begin to be exposed to that reformed system would spend a large portion of their lives during the first half of the twenty-first century. Hence, for the educational reforms to make any real sense, plans for such reforms would have to be based on whatever expectations we may have regarding the social and technological environments that will emerge for teaching, say, five to ten years in the future and, more important, for living in the early decades of the twenty-first century.

The difference, therefore, between traditional planning and the kind of planning that is now called for in many instances is that the latter must take into account not only the impact of proposed innovations on the world as we know it but also on the possibly profoundly changed circumstances within the operating environment for which such innovations have been designed.

Only in exceptional cases, when the time horizon is so near that even in today's climate of rapid change the external conditions may be expected to remain constant, can we resort to the traditional mode of forecasting the merely marginal effects of an innovative act. As a rule, though, the forecasting effort on which a sound plan must be based has to include, first of all, a comprehensive picture of all relevant facets of the future world at large and only secondarily a prediction of the marginal effect on that changed world of the introduction of the innovative measure under consideration.

This, then, is where futures research enters the scene. Its novel approach to planning is characterized, primarily, by an insistence that proper attention be paid to likely changes in the operating environment; along with that, because the relevant environmental features involve disciplines other than or in addition to the area of immediate concern to the planner, its procedures are of necessity multidisciplinary.

While, for a specific planning endeavor, not every aspect of the surrounding world of the future is of importance or even relevance, futures researchers, in order to be prepared for any planning assignment that may come along, are well advised to cast a wide net in seeking forecasts of future developments that will affect a potential operating environment. What is more, not only has it become mandatory that any specific long-range planning be preceded by an accounting of what our society as a whole is apt to be like at the target time of that planning process, but the future of that society itself has come under closer scrutiny, and futures research is taking a comprehensive and integrative view of the options that may be at our disposal with regard to shaping that society to our liking.

Among the profound changes in our society that the next few decades may bring and the possibility of which a long-range planner ought to be well aware are these:

- continuing pervasive advances, of which even today only the barest beginning is being experienced, in the computer and communications area;
- revolutionary developments in the field of plant, animal, and human genetics;
- further, far-reaching changes in societal values, manifesting themselves in new lifestyles and family patterns and in new goals for corporate management;
- the obsolescence of large-scale war and its replacement by terrorist acts on an unprecedented scale;
- devastating famines, affecting hundreds of millions of people, in the underdeveloped countries;
- the resumption of space exploration; and
- the replacement of the United States' world leadership by that of Japan and, later, China.

Note that I am not saying that these developments will definitely occur but merely that the possibility of their occurrence must be borne in mind in our long-range planning. This attitude of awareness has both a passive and an active component: Passively, our plans, if they are to be rational, must be made to fit our expectations regarding the changed environment of the future; actively, we may want to influence that future while there is yet time. ■

I now turn, first, to a brief survey of the accomplishments of futures research achieved by the early 1970s and its prospects as seen at that time, and, second, to a suggested research agenda for this field that I ventured to compose in 1975.

18 ACCOMPLISHMENTS AND PROSPECTS OF FUTURES RESEARCH[2]

18.1 Introduction

Futures research has emerged during the last ten years [the period referred to is that from 1963 to 1973] as a new field of great promise. Its accomplishments to date are far from world-shaking, but they are sufficient, I believe, to support that claim of future promise and to justify the expenditure of greater effort on its pursuit.

In discussing some of the accomplishments of futures research and some of the possibilities of its future direction, I shall not attempt to be comprehensive but shall confine myself to those aspects of its past with which I have been personally involved and to those aspects of its future that I am prepared to advocate.

18.2 Accomplishments

The scientific analysis of the future is concerned, not with predictions, but with forecasts and with the application of such forecasts to long-range planning. While a prediction asserts some future event with certainty ("The electoral system will be abandoned by the time of the next presidential election"), a forecast is a probabilistic statement ("There is a 5:1 chance that the electoral system will be abandoned by that time"). Forecasts, moreover, in view of their intended application to planning, are frequently cast in conditional form ("If the Democrats increase the number of their Senate seats in the next mid-term election, there is a 10:1 chance that . . ."), for the planner is particularly interested in the utilization of causal connections between potential future developments.

Futures research may be thought of as consisting of two parts: the development and refinement of methods of futures analysis, and the application of such methods to substantive forecasting studies and to long-range planning efforts. "Long-range" in this context, by the way, should be interpreted as referring to the period from about five to about thirty years in the future. Planning for shorter periods than five years usually can be based on reasonably straightforward extrapolation from the past, whereas diminishing mar-

2. This section, in essence, is a reprint of my 1973 contribution under the same title to the final report of the Commission on the Year 2000, edited by Daniel Bell but never published. The part dealing with cross-impact analysis, however, has been shortened considerably, since that topic will be taken up later in this volume in some detail (see Chapter VI).

ginal returns tend to nullify the value of extending the planning interval beyond thirty years. There are, of course, exceptions to this rule, depending on subject matter, but they are not too frequent.

In discussing the accomplishments of futures research, I shall dwell first on some of its methodological aspects and then turn briefly to a few of its substantive applications.

In the so-called exact sciences, forecasts (and even predictions) can generally be derived from well-confirmed, time-independent theorems. The majority of forecasts, however, in which we might be interested for planning purposes are in the realm of the inexact sciences: engineering, medicine, and the like, and the entire area of the social sciences.

A formal theoretical structure does not exist here. Admittedly, in disciplines such as behavioral psychology or economics, which are conceptually contiguous to the exact natural sciences, sets of reasonably well-established hypotheses are available that cover numerous but isolated aspects of these fields. But even there, the theoretical information generally permits only the derivation of forecasts concerning "pure" cases, that is, psychological experiments under controlled laboratory conditions or economic situations in which the influence of exogenous, noneconomic factors may be considered negligible.

In view of this situation, which exists despite the fact that a vast body of insights has been accumulated in the inexact sciences, methods other than derivation from theory have to be found to tap the available expertise and bring it to bear on the production of forecasts needed for planning purposes. As I stated in my essay on social technology [in Chapter II] in "soft" areas lacking a logically complete theoretical foundation, we may have to turn to the techniques of operations analysis and begin—regretfully, perhaps, but more realistically—to emulate physical technology rather than "hard" physical science.

For the rigorous scientist, the best often is not good enough, nor should it be. The operations analyst, by contrast, has an obligation to deliver to decision makers the best possible advice that can be obtained on the basis of existing insights, even if such information is not as reliable as a scientific purist would require. The reason, of course, is that decisions often cannot wait, and even a slight improvement in the information base, though it be far from perfect, may raise the quality of the decisions significantly. Thus, the pragmatic aspect of timeliness may have to take precedence over the intellectual desire for a more complete theoretical understanding of all the underlying factors.

The principal procedures available to the operations analyst for accomplishing his task are the construction of operational models and the systematic use of intuitive expert judgment. These two approaches are intimately related, and both play an important role in analyses of the future.

Expert judgment plays a dual function: It enters into the construction of a model, and it provides "soft" (i.e., judgmental) data as inputs into the model whenever hard data are unavailable. For instance, if it were a question of forecasting and planning the future of a developing country, a socioeconometric model would be constructed, using expert judgment to determine just what factors are important enough to be included in the model. Then, in the likely absence of firm information on many of the included factors, judgmental data would be solicited from the appropriate area experts in order to obtain the necessary inputs for the application of the model.

As an aside, it may be noted here that in cases of the kind illustrated by this example, social scientists sometimes appear to show little hesitation in constructing "soft models" but draw the line at the utilization of "soft data". However, it is probably a fair statement that the outcome resulting from the operation of such a model often is far less sensitive to the precise numerical inputs than to the inclusion or omission of various factors in the model and to the structure relating the factors to one another.

Once one has recognized the unpalatable inevitability of having to rely on expert opinions in analyzing the potentialities of the future, it becomes a matter of eliciting and utilizing expertise in an orderly and expeditious manner. Indeed the deliberate systematic use of unsystematized pretheoretical knowledge in the form of intuitive expertise has become a cornerstone of futures analysis.

The employment of expert judgment requires several separate, though closely related, tasks: (i) the identification of experts and assessment of their expertise; (ii) the provision of aids for improving the experts' performance; and (iii) the design of methods for using and collating the opinions of a group of experts.

Methods for accomplishing the first of these, in particular, still leave much to be desired. The recent past has brought about noticeable improvements among responsible practitioners in the use of experts in the selection of respondents and in the assessment of their capabilities. On the other hand, the proliferation of forecasting efforts has inevitably produced studies of varying quality, some of which have employed respondents of dubious claim to expertise in the area of inquiry. Also, there is a school of thought which insists that respondents for such inquiries be chosen by statistical sampling procedures appropriate for opinion surveys among a given population. In response to this view it should be pointed out that the notion of an expert, after all, is not an absolute but a relative one; that is to say, there is no well-defined uniform population of experts on a particular subject from among whom a representative sample could reasonably be drawn, but one might think, rather, of the experts as constituting an ordered set ranked according to their degree of expertise. Thus, a "sample" of three near the top may well be the equivalent of a sample of ten somewhat lower down on the ladder, and superior to any set, no matter how large, farther down in degree of expertise.

Another controversial notion regarding the selection of experts rears its ugly head when the subject of inquiry concerns the future of some societal group, say, a racial minority or the elderly or a group of political radicals. In such a case, it is claimed by some, care must be taken to have members of that group properly (and perhaps predominantly) included as respondents on the grounds that they are "the experts" with respect to that group. The error in this argument is that, while members of a group certainly are experts on the group's present dissatisfactions and future aspirations, their emotional involvement is likely to bias their view of the future and cause them to substitute wishful thinking for objective forecasts. More reliable forecasting judgments are obtainable in this case from experts "once removed", that is, from social psychologists and other specialists who have made a detailed study of the circumstances, the aspirations, and the promise of the group in question.

Turning now to item ii among the tasks enumerated in connection with the employment of expert judgment, which has to do with aiding the experts' performance in crystallizing their opinions, there are several requirements that should be listed under this heading. Two of these are rather obvious: Any relevant data should be made easily accessible, and the questions put to the expert should be carefully formulated, so as to be unambiguous and to avoid leading the respondent. In addition, it may be helpful to pose questions to the expert within the framework of a preformulated model, because this will provide a context that serves to communicate the problem to him with clarity and to receive his answer without risk of misinterpretation. Finally, perhaps the greatest assistance that may be rendered to an expert is to provide him with an appropriate simulated environment, that is, a mock-up of the real situation about which his judgment is being sought, in which he, and perhaps fellow experts, can carry out pseudo-experiments to help them clarify their conceptions about the real world that is being simulated. This device, as was pointed out earlier, is particularly important in situations, such as the planning of societal reforms, in which real experimentation is not feasible. [A particular type of simulation, also referred to earlier, namely, simulation gaming, will be taken up again in Chapter VII.] With regard to none of the aspects listed here of providing aid to the expert do any generally accepted recipes exist, but it is fair to say that considerable refinements in all of these respects have resulted from the numerous surveys of expert opinions conducted in recent years.

Methods of utilizing the opinions of groups of experts (item iii in the foregoing list) include, in particular, the Delphi technique, which seeks to avoid the psychological pitfalls of face-to-face discussions among the experts by employing sequential interrogations (by questionnaire or interview), in which the respondents, at each stage, are provided with a feedback of the panel's distribution of opinions obtained at the previous stage of inquiry. In the area of forecasting studies, the most promising advance beyond

Delphi may be seen in the development of the cross-impact technique, although here, even more than in the case of Delphi, a sound theoretical base is still lacking. Both the Delphi and the cross-impact techniques will be discussed in detail in Chapters V and VI, respectively.

Let me now turn very briefly to some of the substantive accomplishments of futures research, in addition to those already implied in the discussion of methods.

Generally speaking, the endeavors of futures researchers have had a very noticeable and, I think, beneficial influence on the outlook of planners in many segments of society. It was the efforts of futurists in the mid-1960s that caused the Office of Education to set up two educational policy research centers (at the Stanford Research Institute and Syracuse University). Some of the thinking of planners at the National Science Foundation seems very clearly to have been influenced by futures research. The Office of Technology Assessment may be considered an intellectual offspring of the futures movement, most particularly of the cross-impact-type of approach, in view of the emphasis in technology-assessment studies on secondary and tertiary effects of technological innovations.

While a number of agencies of the U.S. government have availed themselves of the Delphi method and related techniques for forecasting and planning purposes, futures research has also been given official recognition by foreign government organizations. In France, five-year plans have been prepared under the auspices of the Délégation à l'Aménagement du Territoire et à l'Action Régionale (DATAR); the West German government in the early 1970s set up a futures research department in the Office of the Chancellor; in Czechoslovakia, a large number of panels of experts officially prepare forecasts regularly in different societal sectors, and the interrelations among these forecasts are examined by means of a large-scale cross-impact effort; and in the Soviet Union the Delphi method has been given the honor of being referred to as the "Glushkov-Delphi method".

In the private sector, futures methods have proliferated equally. Particular interest has been shown in such countries as Canada, Denmark, England, France, Germany, Japan, Sweden, and Switzerland. In the United States, where hundreds of firms have commissioned a variety of futures studies, several companies—notably TRW and Monsanto—as well as the Conference Board are known to have taken the initiative in developing special-purpose techniques of futures analysis for undertaking large-scale forecasting and planning studies under their own direction.

As for the substantive areas to which futures analysis methods have been applied, let me enumerate some of those that have come to my attention; they have concerned the future of:

business and society	communications
civil defense	computers

- Connecticut
- economic indicators
- electronics industry
- employee benefits
- energy
- foundation-supported research
- global resources
- Hawaii
- higher education
- high school education
- highway transportation
- housing
- information-processing
- insurance
- marine transportation
- medical care
- newsprint
- plastics
- real estate
- retail trade
- science policy
- societal developments
- space exploration
- the state of the Union
- scientific breakthroughs
- technology and society
- telephone industry
- weapons development

While the reliability of the results obtained by the techniques of futures analysis has varied in their application to the subjects just enumerated, it is fair to say that in all cases they have, at the very least, contributed to a clearer understanding of the problem situation. A clearer formulation of a problem often is the most important step toward its resolution.

18.3 Desiderata

On the whole, the practitioners of futures research appear to be well aware of the present limitations of their field, regarding both the unproven reliability of its methods and the consequent lack of universal acceptance. However, there seems to be a general expectation that, in time, the hypotheses on the validity of the procedures will come to be based on experimental confirmation rather than faith and intuition, and that, along with the establishment of a more solid foundation, futures research will be able to make a substantial contribution to scientific progress and, with it, to the betterment of society.

Let me mention a few of the things that need to be done in order to achieve that higher plateau of acceptability, and then conclude with a statement of the long-term prospects for futures research that would then be entailed.

First of all, numerous experiments related to Delphi need to be carried out concerning the psychology of group interaction, the reaction of group members to the introduction of various forms of opinion feedback and other types of information, the comparison of self-, peer, and "objective" ratings of expertise, the correlation of expert performance regarding forecasts and retrocasts, the size, composition, and structure of Delphi panels, and presumably many other facets of the utilization of expertise. Such an experimental program, conducted, whenever possible, with real experts as experimental subjects and under carefully controlled laboratory conditions, could be expected to do a great deal not only toward establishing the reliability of present methods but also toward introducing procedural improvements that might raise the efficiency and the reliability of this approach by an order of magnitude.

The situation with respect to the cross-impact technique is somewhat different. [Cross-impact analysis concerns itself with the mutual interactions among future developments—in particular, with the effect of the future occurrence of an event on the probability of occurrence of other potential events. Details of cross-impact analysis will be examined in Chapter VI.] Since most of the inputs into a cross-impact matrix will have to be derived on the basis of expert judgment, no new questions arise here beyond those enumerated with reference to Delphi that call for experimental investigation, except possibly for the problem of how best to deal with the sheer quantity of judgmental data that have to be elicited. There are, on the other hand, a number of conceptual problems related to cross-impacts that should be explored. Let me mention a few of these to convey the flavor of the research that must be done: (i) In making cross-impact estimates, how does one avoid double-accounting, which might arise when a development D_1 has both a direct effect on D_2 and an indirect effect via its direct effect on some other development D_3? (ii) By what means can one make sure that a cross-impact matrix is balanced; that is, that, in a long series of trial runs, an event occurs with a relative frequency approximately equal to its predicted probability, and the average value of a trend similarly approximates its predicted value? (iii) In a cross-impact context, we are not just interested in the correlation between two events A and B, which is dealt with in standard probability calculus by considering the relative frequencies of A.B, $A.\overline{B}$, $\overline{A}.B$, and $\overline{A}.\overline{B}$, but rather with causal relations, where the time sequence is relevant and, consequently, the case of "A.B" has to be subdivided into "A before B" and "B before A". In order to deal with the resulting five cases (instead of four), is it necessary (or, at least, convenient) to develop a new, causal-probability calculus? (iv) When using a cross-impact matrix to test alternative policies, it is generally assumed that only the input event probabilities and trend values are affected by such a policy and the cross-impacts remain unchanged. Is this assumption justified, or how should it be modified? (5) In present cross-impact approaches, only pairs of developments are examined. In reality, it is often the joint influence of two or more developments that affect the probability of some other occurrence. How can such multidimensional cross-impacts be accommodated?

The answers to these questions would help place the cross-impact procedure on a sound theoretical footing and, by implication, increase the validity of the gaming applications of this approach to long-range planning. [Since the days when this was written, I believe to have succeeded in coping with some of the conceptual issues raised here regarding cross-impact analysis. See Section 35 of Chapter VII.]

It is to be hoped that, with an increased respectability of the theoretical foundation of these methods, they, together with other operations-analytical techniques, will become accepted as an integral and highly useful part of the methodological kit at the disposal of planners in all areas, including that of long-range corporate planning and the entire field of social technology.

With regard to the latter, in particular, the incorporation of such methods could be considered symptomatic of an overdue reorientation within the social-science domain toward a more active concern with the future of our society. There are other operations-research approaches not explicitly mentioned above—such as decision theory and game theory—which could be helpful in this transition toward sociotechnological applications, especially if an effort were made to stress and refine the pragmatic aspects of these disciplines. A literal softening-up of the social-indicator movement, in the sense of admitting soft, judgmental data, might profitably accompany such a trend.

One nondesideratum might as well also be mentioned in this context, namely, the politicization of futures research advocated in some quarters, especially in its application to societal problems. Futurists, without question, have the right, and perhaps even a moral obligation, to engage in so-called normative societal forecasting, that is, in advocating among the possible futures for our society those that they find desirable. But it is essential to keep the political act of advocation separate from the exploratory act of forecasting, lest the latter become biased by wishful thinking and hence scientifically worthless. This separation, admittedly, is not always easy to maintain, because there is a subtle feedback mechanism at work: The sequence of thought processes that are involved does not inevitably start with a given set of possible futures, follow with an examination of their desirability, and conclude with the selection of a subset for advocation; sometimes, the act of normative forecasting, conversely, leads to the invention of strategies that make futures possible that did not obviously appear to be so prior to such invention. It is this intermingling of invention, normative advocation, and factual forecasting that places a special obligation on the futures analyst not to allow his political conviction to override his scientific objectivity.

18.4 Prospects

Once futures research emerges from its prolonged infancy, its roles in the supporting cast of scientific endeavor will be manifold. Let me conclude this section by making some forecasts of what these roles will be. Having just inveighed against the danger of polluting objective forecasting efforts with wishful thinking, let me label the following statements as "normative forecasts" in order to give explicit recognition to my unquestionable bias.

Private Sector. The acceptance level of futures research in the private sector is already far from negligible, and with refined methods of proven reliability it is likely to increase by leaps and bounds. Even smaller firms, which cannot afford to maintain long-range planning sections of their own or to hire futures consultants, will avail themselves of forecasts and planning simulation models produced routinely for industry associations.

Public Sector. Integrated long-range planning in the public sector is generally somewhat harder to accomplish than in the private sector, partly because government tends to be too compartmentalized to permit a really integrated systems approach to planning and partly because plans tend to be time-phased in accordance with the short-term cycles of budgets and public appointees. But here, too, some strides are being taken, and futures research methods are being gradually accepted in specific areas such as education, health care delivery, and defense. The application of futures research to interdisciplinary and interdepartmental socioeconomic planning, on the other hand, will probably not come about on a sizable scale until the 1980s. [Remember that this was written in 1973.]

Social Technology. Gradual acceptance by the social-science community of methods for utilizing expert opinion, including applications of cross-impact analysis and simulated-planning models, will be slow but steady. The eventual effect will be, on the one hand, to produce a more coherent, theory-like structure and, on the other, to bring social scientists closer to the operational needs of real-world decision makers and thus, through social-engineering studies, to increase enormously their influence on the future shape of our society.

National Goals. Part of an integrated social-engineering effort will be an analysis of the goals of various sectors of society, of the implications of these goals, and of their mutual compatibility. This will involve an approach to social indicators that avails itself of judgmental, in addition to objective, measures of performance, and it will utilize simulation gaming, partly as a research tool but also in order to give representatives of societal groups an opportunity to explore firsthand, through pseudo-experimentation, the implications of their stated goals and the realism of their aspirations.

Future State of the Union. Systematic efforts at forecasting social and environmental trends as well as technological and political events, together with an analysis of national goals, will lead to a comprehensive examination of possible futures for our society, their relative merits from the viewpoints of special interest groups, and the implications of various political ideologies and platforms. Interdisciplinary simulation aimed at such exploration will be included in the curricula of many universities and possibly some high schools, contributing to a higher level of political sophistication among future graduates. [A modest first step in this direction was taken in the author's *On the future state of the Union,* excerpts from which are included in Chapter IX of this volume.]

World Resources. The dire forecasts regarding global food, energy, and mineral resources made by Dennis and Donella Meadows and others associated with the Club of Rome will have to be reexamined, as proposed earlier [in Section 18.2 above]. The results of further analysis, it is to be hoped, will suggest timely and realistic countermeasures in the form of governmental regulations and research-and-development efforts that may be less drastic than those mentioned in *Limits to Growth.*

Technology Assessment. The area of technology assessment, as indicated earlier, is "a natural" for futures research. Cross-impact analysis, in particular, seems to be tailor-made to its needs, and the government's effort, through the continuing work of the Office of Technology Assessment, will undoubtedly have an increasingly beneficial effect by foreseeing and forestalling some of the potential side effects of prospective technological innovations.

Adversary Process. Important governmental interventions in the form of legislation or regulatory measures are routinely based on the results of adversary hearings, which could be much improved by the introduction of techniques associated with futures research. A modified form of a Delphi inquiry, with its opportunity for responding to anonymous, adverse positions, may well be helpful here. Also, the affinity to technology assessment is evident, suggesting the possible utilization of cross-impact techniques, again modified to fit the format of an adversary inquiry. Some such reforms of the adversary process have a good chance of taking place in the near future, with likely benefits to resulting governmental interventions.

D-Net. Experiments are well under way with the use of experts responding via a computer-monitored network of electronic terminals (also known as a D-net). It may be expected that large-scale networks of this kind will come into wide use in the very near future, affording decision makers easy access to the so-called advice community. The mode of operation may be a type of Delphi inquiry, but may also assume more sophisticated forms of remote conferencing. D-nets will eventually constitute a new form of public utility, which may be established under public or private auspices. Their use in some of the activities outlined earlier (private and public planning, national goals analysis, technology assessment, adversary processes) is obvious.

International Cooperation. When planning for the more distant future, say, for a period of twenty to thirty years from the present, the clash between immediate interests and diverse ideologies is much less severe than when pursuing more immediate objectives. This suggests a "rapprochement via the future", which in fact has been noticeable at some recent international conferences and will play a more important role in the future. The creation of the International Institute for Applied Systems Analysis may be seen as a step in this direction. Joint futures research, devoted to the common problems of society regardless of political ideology, may make an important contribution to international understanding.

Others, no doubt, would wish to augment the foregoing list of ten items or give higher priority to items not listed. But the intent, in any case, was not to present an exhaustive compilation of future areas of application but to convey a flavor of the potentialities and prospects of futures research. ■

19 THE INSTITUTE FOR THE FUTURE

The first independent research organization devoted exclusively to futures research was the Institute for the Future, founded in 1968. Its organizing committee, whose efforts brought it into existence, consisted of Marvin Adelson, Paul Armer, Paul Baran, West Churchman, Henry David, Theodore Gordon, Olaf Helmer, Arnold Kramish, George Mandanis, and M. E. Maron. Its first president was Frank Davidson, succeeded by the present author, who in turn was succeeded by the current president, Roy Amara.

The Institute was first set up in Middletown, Connecticut, and later moved to Menlo Park, California.

The following are excerpts from the Institute's first prospectus, which I am including here for their value in further delineating the new field of futures research:

> Our time has been called variously the atomic age, the age of automation, the space age, and the age of anxiety. Undoubtedly it is all of these, for we live in a period of rapid and vast change. As change quickens in tempo and widens in sweep, the risks and opportunities that confront us call increasingly for expanded efforts to lead the course of events, rather than be led by them. An awareness of the future has thus become more important to the present than ever before, and the responsibility of those in private or public life who hold the public trust has now grown to include an obligation to shape their decisions as fully as possible by such an awareness. This is the premise that underlies the creation and research efforts of the Institute for the Future.
>
> The Institute for the Future is an independent research organization, founded as a nonprofit corporation for work solely in the public interest. It is the only organization in the United States dedicated exclusively to systematic and comprehensive studies of the long-range future. The Institute's primary aims . . . are fourfold: to enlarge existing understanding concerning technological, environmental, and societal changes and their long-range consequences; to develop new methodology to carry on such tasks; to make available without discrimination the results of such research and scientific advances to the public;

and to serve as an educational and training center for selected persons from business, government, foundations, and universities with respect to such research activities.

Like other concerned individuals, the members of the organizing committee found much evidence, some alarming, of the growing disparity between society's propensity to generate forces of change and its ability to control them. The committee questioned the notion that traditional means would be equal to the task of reducing this disparity or of accommodating its social consequences. To be sure, policymakers at all levels, public and private, were beginning to recognize the costs and limitations of piecemeal, improvised responses to events and to acknowledge the serious threats created by "backing into the future". And they could see that more effective planning a generation ago might well have helped to attenuate some of today's acute problems: air and water pollution, ecological mismanagement, the deterioration of the core city, the transportation overload, inadequate training for the disadvantaged, and so on. Yet when confronted with the increased pace and magnitude of today's change, and thus with a new urgency to take timely anticipatory action, policymakers found a lack of adequate research support. While excellent insights into many aspects of the problems they faced were available from many sources, a sufficiently concentrated and interdisciplinary research activity focusing on the future and having the necessary skills, scope, and freedom did not appear to exist, and consequently adequate contingency forecasts on which national policy decisions could be based were lacking. The impossibility of acting responsibly under these circumstances was central to the committee's conclusion that the time was indeed propitious to form a new institute organized solely to analyze the future.

The Institute's research program has two major components: development of forecasting methods for the analysis and synthesis of potential futures, and the application of such methods to the problems of society. . . . All of the Institute's efforts, including the programs of social and technological forecasting, are ultimately intended to aid current planning and decision-making. There is no single, inevitable, predestined future to be predicted and prepared for; instead there are countless possible futures—some desirable, toward realization of which we may choose to devote present energies, and some undesirable, which we may work to avoid. Illuminating the range of possible future alternatives, identifying the linkages from them to present decisions, and assisting in the formulation of appropriate policies—all these are essential to the Institute's research.

The idea for the Institute arises from a change in attitude toward the future. The fatalistic view that it is unforeseeable and inevitable is being abandoned. It is being recognized that there are a multitude of possible futures and that appropriate intervention can make a difference in their probabilities. This raises the exploration of the future, and the search for ways to influence its direction, to activities of great social responsibility. This responsibility is not just an academic one, and to discharge it more than perfunctorily we must cease to be mere spectators in our own ongoing history and participate with determination in molding the future. It will take wisdom, courage, and sensitivity to human values to shape a better world. But the time is short, for events move ever more rapidly. Now is the time to commit ourselves fully to the problems of the future of our society. ■

The establishment of the Institute for the Future was followed by that of other, similar research organizations both here and abroad. By the mid-1970s, I felt that there was a need to reassess the status of futures research and to try to set down some recommendations for future directions in this field:

20 AN AGENDA FOR FUTURES RESEARCH[3]

20.1 Review of What Futures Research Is About

Futures research, as an organized activity, is barely a decade old. [Note that this essay was originally published in 1975.] This is a very short time in the development of any intellectual movement. Not only has there been insufficient time to place the discipline of futures research on a solid conceptual foundation, but the pursuit of this desideratum—though well recognized by some—has been encumbered simply because demands for pragmatic results have had priority over a solidification of the foundation and because the rapidly increasing number of practitioners has of necessity included some charlatans and incompetents along with serious researchers.

The time has come, therefore, to reflect on what futures research is all about, what genuine promise it offers, what can be done to improve its intellectual basis, and what priorities should be assigned to its applications.

Futures research is a branch of operations research. Its function, like that of traditional operations research, is to provide decision makers with operationally meaningful assistance in the form of information and analysis.

The main characteristic that differentiates futures research from standard operations research is that its objective is to improve decision-making in the case of long-range plans. Here "long-range", in contrast to "short-range", clearly means that the operational conditions at the time of implementation are expected to differ substantially from those prevailing at the time of planning.

We note in passing that more and more of the important decisions are moving from the short-range into the long-range category. The reason for this is twofold. First, many of our decisions concern increasingly complex situations, where the time horizon is farther in the future, as illustrated by our attempts to solve the energy crisis, to plan a new city, or to develop an underdeveloped country. Second, as we all know, we live in an age of ubiquitous future shock, in which changes in our living environment occur with ever-increasing rapidity, due mostly to technological advances and their soci-

3. This essay was published in *Futures*, vol. 7 (February 1975).

etal implications. Together these two trends, by mutual reinforcement, have given futures research the premature prominence we observe today.

Once we recognize that futures research is indeed a branch of operations research, and specifically that branch concerned with plans that are to be implemented in a changed environment, a number of points become evident.

Because of the pragmatic nature of futures research, its function is primarily predictive rather than explanatory. By forecasting the environment and the consequences of alternative plans for coping with it, futures research attempts to improve the decision-making process. Often its findings may merely be based on observed correlations between phenomena or on the intuitive, pretheoretical judgment of experts, falling far short of a causal explanation for the expected consequences of proposed actions. While a fuller understanding of the underlying causes would surely always be welcomed, the success of futures research has to be measured in terms of the quality of the decisions it makes possible rather than its explanatory force.

Like operations research generally, futures research is prescientific in nature. The urgency of the task—be it the conduct of military operations (the context that gave rise to operations research) or the management of a crisis or the search for cures of social ills—is so great that there is no time to wait for the construction of neat scientific theories that would, by logical derivation, permit the identification of the optimal plan of action to be followed. Instead, in the tradition of operations research, the futures researcher constructs *ad hoc* models as best he can, well knowing that they may be imperfect and in need of later correction and improvement as more data are obtained and more experience is accumulated.

No claim is made that such imperfect models produce perfect foresight. That the resulting decisions are often nonoptimal should be no reason to reject the futures-research effort. Its aim is to produce the best practically attainable decisions, even if not necessarily the theoretically best decisions. Considering the often enormous payoff attached to decisions regarding the long-range future, even a small improvement in the quality of such decisions may yield appreciable returns.

20.2 Scientific Approach

A rigorous scientific approach involves three interactive elements: theory construction, collection of empirical data, and controlled experimentation. I have already pointed out that the model-building endeavor of operations research, and hence of futures research, falls short of the rigor demanded of scientific theory construction. Not only are its models comparatively "soft"; so, at times, are its data and its experimental procedures. There are, in fact, no hard data about the future; the futures analyst has to rely on soft, judgmental data instead. That is, he must use probabilistic pronouncements by experts about the future operating environment as a substitute for firm, observational data.

Any real experimentation is often replaced by pseudo-experimentation, using a simulation model in which players, acting the parts of decision makers in the real world, test the implications of alternative decisions in the model, in the hope that the simulation has sufficient verisimilitude to permit a transfer of the model results to the real world.

Reliance on the intuitive judgment of experts is thus not just a temporary expedient but a necessary ingredient of futures research, for such experts are needed in all phases of the effort. They are called upon (i) to supply judgmental data about the future, based on their intuitive, though often theoretically unstructured, insights into real-world phenomena; (ii) to construct *ad hoc* models or to judge the suitability of existing models; (iii) to apply their expertise as role players in simulation games; and (iv) to use their imagination and inventiveness to design the instrumentalities and long-range strategies that result in appropriate action programs for dealing with the problems of the future.

Despite its relative softness compared to a hard, scientific approach and, in particular, its inevitable reliance on expert judgment, futures research aspires to be objective. This looks, at first glance, like a contradiction in terms, since objectivity of a discipline can almost be defined as "the intersubjectivity of its findings independent of any one person's intuitive judgment" [see the section on epistemology in Chapter II]. To preserve the claim to objectivity, it is necessary for the futures researcher to dissociate himself logically from the experts, in the sense of regarding himself as an experimenter who uses the experts as measuring instruments of reality, whose pronouncements about the future world are taken in the same spirit as, say, the readings on a measuring device are taken as an indication of some property of the present world. The experts, therefore, are viewed as black boxes that receive questions as inputs and produce answers as outputs. Different experimenters, using different but comparable sets of such black boxes, should be expected to arrive at comparable results. This places a special obligation on the discipline of futures research to devise suitable measures for the degree of reliability of these instruments and to seek ways and means of improving their quality (i.e., of helping the experts increase the reliability of their performance).

Another point to be made is that, since futures research is concerned with the planning of human activities, it is, of necessity, multidisciplinary. Even if the planning objective itself is unidisciplinary (which is seldom the case), attention must be given to the technological, socioeconomic, cultural, and physical environmental circumstances, in consideration of which plans have to be made, as well as to the psychology of the decision makers. Usually, the more important a planning decision is, the more complex is the area to be surveyed and the more intricately interwoven are the considerations that different disciplines have to contribute. In planning a transportation system, a reform of the educational or the health care delivery systems, or a new city, there is hardly a single discipline that will not be required to supply specialized inputs into the planning process in the form of assessments by experts of probable future developments. Futures analysis, therefore, has to develop effective and efficient means of facilitating cross-disciplinary cooperation toward developing common planning objectives.

Finally, to fulfill its purpose of improving the decision-making process regarding long-range plans, futures research has to address itself explicitly to the criteria problem. There are several aspects of this. First, there is the question of identifying the planning criteria, that is—technically speaking—the payoff function or functions or the utility vector to be maximized. This involves several extremely difficult subproblems—specifically, that of exchange ratios in the case of multidimensional utilities, that of relative weights in the case of a multiplicity of beneficiaries who need to be satisfied, and that of changing value systems, which may cause future criteria of optimization to be different from present such criteria. Second, given a set of criteria, there is a question of determining the comparative degree to which alternative action programs can be expected to satisfy these criteria. All these tasks are analytical in nature, require cost-effectiveness and systems analyses, and must be clearly distinguished from the normative problems of what ought to be done about the future. [There is a large faction among futures researchers that wishes to emphasize this normative aspect of its work. In contradistinction to futures analysis, this segment of futures research, which is devoted to what is sometimes called "normative forecasting", might perhaps best be described as "futures synthesis". To date, this portion of futures research, which covers the spectrum from abstract utopian writing to belligerent demagogic activism, is poorly organized and badly in need of conceptual systematization.]

These features constitute a methodological approach for which there is a great, pragmatic need in our society. In the following attempt to outline an agenda for some of the specific research tasks that lie ahead, I shall list some of the areas that seem to me to be particularly in need of such attention.

20.3 Data Collection

All our knowledge about the future is ultimately derived by some form of extrapolation, however subtle, from the past. The kind of empirical data on which such extrapolations might be based are no different from the data that provide us with whatever insight into our present world we have, and their collection is the task of individual scientific disciplines, such as psychology, demography, or meteorology. Leaving aside whatever standard difficulties there may be in amassing such basic empirical information, the analysis of the future requires as inputs another kind of quasi-data in the form of judgmental estimates about future operating conditions. While these judgments are formed by experts through some implicit process of extrapolation from the past, this process is rarely based on a well-articulated theoretical procedure but more often is intuitive and pretheoretical in nature. Epistemologically, their function is comparable to that of measuring instruments.

This whole area of collection of judgmental data is in considerable need of further exploration, suggesting the following specific research items:

20.3.1 *Rating and Improving the Performance of Individual Experts as Forecasters*

How can the performance of an expert be calibrated? How do self- and peer ratings compare with one another and with other, more "objective", rating systems? How can an expert's performance be enhanced? What data, data-processing facilities, models, simulations, or communication devices would be most helpful to him?

20.3.2 *Using Groups of Experts*

If two or more experts supply probability distributions over time for the occurrence of some potential future event, what is the appropriate mode of combining their individual estimates into a joint probability distribution? What use can here be made of any available performance calibrations or information about systematic bias of the experts? How can the judgments of experts belonging to different fields of specialization best be combined into an interdisciplinary estimate? How do the anonymity and feedback features of Delphi compare with other modes of using experts, such as polling, face-to-face discussion, or other conventional conference procedures?

20.3.3 *Improvements in the Delphi Technique*

What degree of anonymity is most helpful to the performance of a Delphi panel? What influence does the wording of questions have? How should the entire questioning process be structured? If the subject of inquiry is multidisciplinary and if differential calibrations of the experts with regard to each discipline are available, how can the best use be made of this information? How does a hierarchical panel structure compare with a homogeneous one? How stable is a panel's judgment over time? What is the optimal panel size? Is a panel of two or three top-notch experts preferable to a panel of a dozen reasonably good experts?

All these questions call for extensive experimentation. There is an obvious obstacle to carrying out such experiments, because good experts are too rare a commodity and their time is too precious for them to be readily available as experimental laboratory subjects. Some of the indicated experiments have indeed been carried out, notably by Norman Dalkey, but using graduate students as surrogate experts. There remains a gnawing doubt whether all the results obtained in this manner carry over to the case of real experts, and at least some careful experimentation is mandatory to establish this crucial point. [Parenthetically, the kind of spectacular convergence of opinions obtained by Dalkey and myself in our first Delphi experiment in 1953 in connection with a military problem (see the report on that experiment included in Section 22) has rarely been repeated in subsequent applications. My intuition tells me that the technique's success in this regard at the time was due to a fortunate combination of circumstances, namely, the discriminate use of specialists in several relevant disciplines and the availability of at least a crude model structure that facilitated interaction of the panelists' inputs. Many of the later applications and experimental explorations of Delphi have, by contrast, been much more simplistic, prohibiting the subtle kind of interplay that contributed to the success of that first Delphi study, and a return to a more sophisticated approach may well be worthwhile.]

20.4 Model Construction

Futures-analytical models, as I indicated before, tend to be more tentative than rigorous scientific models. Because of their soft, *ad hoc* character, their quality—like that of soft data—depends greatly on the good sense of their constructors. The question arises whether, as in the case of collection of judgmental data, a group effort might be superior to an individual effort in selecting or inventing a model. This suggests the following research area.

20.4.1 Application of Delphi to Model Construction

How should a Delphi inquiry be structured, if its aim is to produce a model for a specific forecasting or decision-making purpose? In particular, how can the facility of a remote-conferencing network best be used toward this end?

The construction of models of any kind is not an easy undertaking when they are intended to cope with a subject matter within the general domain of the social sciences, and hardly any futures-analytical topics are devoid of aspects of social science. In this context, it would be helpful to have a simple, general-purpose model kit that would permit the construction of at least a rudimentary model, whatever the subject matter. One such kit, however inadequate in some respects, in fact exists in the form of the cross-impact approach. Its prescription is very simple: If your concern is with the future of topic X, make a list of potential future developments whose occurrence or nonoccurrence would either make a decisive difference in the future of X or would be a significant indicator of X's future status. Make probability estimates for the occurrence of these developments. Then look at them in pairs, and estimate how much the occurrence of each would affect the probability of occurrence of the other. Finally, use a Monte Carlo process to decide for each development whether it does or does not occur, making prescribed adjustments in the probabilities of the others as you go along. The result, in effect, is a modeling process that produces scenarios of the future, incorporating all important aspects relevant to the phenomena that were intended to be explored.

There are numerous open problems in connection with this handy-dandy tool for the future-oriented social scientist. Nevertheless, its promise seems far from negligible, and a pursuit of improvements in this technique is well worthwhile. [See Chapter VI for further details.] Specifically, this suggests the following item of study.

20.4.2 Basic Cross-Impact Concept

How can double-accounting in a cross-impact matrix be properly avoided? That is, if event A has a direct impact on event C but also has an indirect impact on it via another event, B, how can we make sure that this indirect impact is not also reflected in the direct impact of A on C and thus counted twice? How can multidimensional aspects be handled where two or more occurrences jointly affect the probability of another event?

Since the cross-impact approach attempts to deal with causal rather than merely correlative effects, the traditional case distinction for two attributes A and B into

$$A.B,\ A.\overline{B},\ \overline{A}.B,\ \overline{A}.\overline{B}$$

needs to be replaced, in the case of two events A and B, by

$$A.B,\ B.A,\ A.\overline{B},\ \overline{A}.B,\ \overline{A}.\overline{B}$$

where the first two instances differ in that either the occurrence of A precedes that of B, or vice versa. Hence the following item.

20.4.3 Causal Probabilities

Is there a need for a special "causal probability" calculus, or is the traditional, correlational probability calculus adequate for causal cross-impact applications?

The original approach to cross-impact dealt with the events only, that is, with occurrences at specific points in time. In considering potential future developments it is important, however, to give some attention also to trends, that is, to gradual fluctuations over time. In fact, most of the traditional econometric models, and similarly the system-dynamics approach, go in just the opposite direction by examining interrelations between trends only and neglecting point events altogether. In the cross-impact approach, it is conceptually easy (though troublesome in detail) to adjoin the consideration of trends to that of events. In fact, in the case of a trend, the equivalent of an "event", for cross-impact purposes, is a deviation of the trend value from its anticipated course. Some of the problems arising in this context are the following:

20.4.4 *Trend-Enriched Cross-Impact Concept*

Since the impact of a trend, T (on either an event or another trend), depends on the amount, ΔT, by which it deviates from its anticipated value, should the effect be considered a linear function of ΔT, or what other functional form is appropriate? Does an impact on a trend cause a persistent shift in its future course, a gradually declining shift, or merely a momentary blip? How does one decide which of these, in a particular case, is the most appropriate form of the impact? Can the separate, independent impacts caused by two or more developments be considered additive?

20.4.5 *Production of Cross-Impact Inputs*

What efficient procedures are there for eliciting large numbers of entries into a cross-impact matrix from a panel of experts? How can this process be expedited with the help of a network of computer terminals?

20.4.6 *Continuous Cross-Impacts*

How can the present cross-impact format, where an occurrence in one time period has an effect in the next or some later time period, be made continuous, so that occurrences can take place at any time and their impacts be registered at any time thereafter?

20.5 *Experimentation*

In the absence of a time machine, true experimentation about the future is a logical impossibility. Data obtained from an experiment are always data about the past, and statements about the future can be derived from them only by extrapolation. Hence we have to resort to pseudo-experimentation, which means the construction of a simulation model about the future and experimentation within that model in the hope that results thus obtained carry over to the real world of the future. There are some obvious questions in this connection.

20.5.1 *Validity of Pseudo-Experimentation*

How can the validity of results obtained by pseudo-experimentation be checked or measured? By what means can at least the relative validity be enhanced? How can the effectiveness of simulation gaming as an aid to the forecasting performance of an expert be increased?

Let me turn now specifically to a particular form of simulation gaming, namely, cross-impact gaming. Just as the basic cross-impact approach is a (perhaps somewhat simplistic) general-purpose type of modeling, cross-impact gaming similarly is a general-purpose mode of simulation. A cross-impact model of the future of topic X is turned into a simulation game by introducing one or more players into the model and giving them the option of intervening in the normal course of developments by interjecting an action program. The effects of such actions are handled in the model just as are those of any other events in that their impacts on the events and trends represented in the model are estimated and superimposed on the cross-impacts already present in the model. Perhaps the most important application of this idea is to planning situations, where a single player, the planner, intervenes in the normal course of events by trying out alternative action programs. But there is no reason why the simulation model cannot also be used by several players, representing different interests, who can use the model to study the interactions of their separate interventions. Some of the questions to be answered in this context are summarized in the following item.

20.5.2 Cross-Impact Gaming

How can the realism of cross-impact gaming be increased? How can it best be used to aid the forecasting and planning performance of the participating players? Can it be an effective stimulant to the invention of new strategies for meeting future contingencies? Can the simulation be used, by having the players observe the intuitive acceptability of the results of their actions, to correct and thereby improve the probability and cross-impact estimates on which the cross-impact model is based? What would be the legitimacy of such a self-correcting procedure? In the multiplayer case, can effective use be made of a network of computer terminals for processing the interactions of the various players' interventions?

20.6 Systems Analysis

The application of futures research to long-range planning involves the choice of policies and the design of action programs. These, in turn, if they are intended to be rational and practical rather than mere exercises of the imagination, have to take into account both the resource constraints on the actions and the expected payoff in terms of improved conditions at some future time. Thus cost-effectiveness considerations enter into the picture and, with them, all the problems of systems analysis.

20.6.1 Systems Costs

How can nonmonetary social costs be appropriately related to monetary costs so that overall systems costs can be meaningfully estimated? How can future costs be reliably estimated? What discount rate is appropriate, considering present interest rates, uncertainties regarding future costs and benefits, and our diminishing concern over the future as a function of the time horizon? Hence, how should future costs be compared to present costs? How should expenditures in the private sector be compared with those in the public sector?

How should outright expenditures be compared with investments made in the expectation of future repayment? Since future costs depend on future contingencies, is it possible to design a cost cross-impact model, in which the impacts of events and trend changes on costs are systematically analyzed?

20.6.2 *Systems Benefits*

Given a topic X, whose future is to be planned, what is an appropriate set of social or other indicators in terms of which a future condition of X can be described and different future conditions can be compared? What are the interest groups whose differential desires regarding the future condition of X must be considered? What rational methods are there for assigning weights to different interest groups? What are the dimensions of satisfaction in terms of which gratification with the future condition of X can be measured? How can such multidimensional utilities be combined, and what are their exchange ratios? What is the appropriate discount rate for future benefits, again considering increasing uncertainties of, and decreasing concern over, the future as the time horizon recedes? In the absence of a single payoff function, how can the overall degree be measured to which a given action program can be expected to comply with a variety of goal criteria? Can the kind of cost cross-impact model mentioned under the preceding item (systems costs) be extended to include benefit cross-impacts, reflecting diminished or enhanced benefits associated with substitutabilities and complementarities among proposed actions?

20.6.3 *Representative Scenarios*

Considering the usually vast number of possible scenarios of the future, no specific one of which has a more than negligible chance of occurring, is it possible to single out a small, manageable set of "representative" scenarios, in the sense that any scenario is sufficiently similar, for planning purposes, to one of the representative scenarios, so that a planner can confine himself to planning an action program against the contingencies depicted in the representative scenarios and still be confident that his program will stand up to every possible contingency? How can the scenario-generating mechanism of the cross-impact approach best be utilized in this context?

20.7 Substantive Applications: Exploratory

The research agenda outlined thus far has been concerned with methodology. Turning now to substantive applications (bearing in mind mostly the U.S. scene), I will confine myself to listing only some of those areas that seem to me both to be of outstanding importance and to have a specific requirement for the long-range aspects of futures research, in the sense that the operating environment at the time when the effects of any reform plans might be felt are expected to differ substantially from present operating conditions. Thus, for example, the subject of a reform of our criminal justice and health care delivery systems, while of unquestioned importance, will not be listed, for future changes in technology and in our value systems, which may indeed affect these societal institutions, will do so in only a minor way, considering the very major deficiences that are already in evidence.

This listing is broken down into four subcategories:

20.7.1 Public-Sector Applications

How should the educational system at all levels be reformed, utilizing new technologies now available or on the horizon, so that to those being educated the results will be meaningful during the rest of their lifetimes—much of which may be in the first half of the twenty-first century? What should be done to regulate and to preclude mismanagement of our anticipated ability to intervene in the human genetic structure through molecular engineering? In what direction should we concentrate our efforts to open up new sources of energy? What economic controls should be applied to cushion our society against the effects of a severe crisis in the supply of energy and other resources, and, conversely, against the effects of an eventual abundant supply of such resources? What provisions should be made through the planning of new cities for an increase in the U.S. population by another 50 million within the next generation? What measures should be taken to reduce all forms of pollution in the long run to acceptable or even comfortable levels? What transportation and communication networks should be planned for the future? How can governmental inefficiencies be reduced without endangering our democratic institutions?

20.7.2 Private-Sector Applications

What major R&D efforts should be supported? What power plants should be built? In what direction should the automobile industry move? What forms of collaboration with the public sector should be sought to facilitate the building of new cities and of new transportation networks? What are the potentialities of the still-exploding communication and computer industries? What will be the potentialities of space exploration, if and when it is resumed on a full scale?

20.7.3 Technology Assessment

What will be the direct and, particularly, the indirect effects on our society of anticipated developments in the communications area, such as the general availability of portable telephones and the ability to dial anyone in the world at negligible cost, the installation of automated libraries and of national data banks, the availability in most homes of two-way television terminals, and the introduction of a national computer utility? What will be the societal consequences of possible technology-induced crises, such as a severe energy or raw materials shortage, the necessity to ban automobiles from the city centers, or a radioactive or biological-warfare mishap that kills more than a million people? What would be the indirect and unexpected implication of certain measures of social engineering, such as the introduction of a negative income tax, major penal reforms, or the abandonment of the congressional seniority system? What would be the social consequences of certain major technological breakthroughs, such as genetic intervention, fusion power generators, artificial protein, or the commercial feasibility of transmuting chemical elements into one another?

20.7.4 International Applications

What are the global prospects regarding energy and raw materials resources (the Club of Rome problem), and what can be done to avert a catastrophic crisis? What reasonable international agreements can be made to reduce the pollution of the oceans? Similarly, what reasonable international agreements can be made to extend national control to larger areas of the oceans than is currently the case? What would be the implications of adopting a single world currency? What can be done to effect an orderly development of the underdeveloped countries? What is the future of arms control and disarmament? What would be the implications of a large-scale joint effort at space exploration? What would be the long-run effect of the introduction of an international system of social welfare? What are the exchange ratios, in terms of expected long-term benefits to the United States, of federal expenditures in areas related to foreign affairs, such as defense, espionage, diplomacy, international development, cultural exchange, and joint ventures?

20.8 Substantive Applications: Normative

There are those in the futures movement who consider social reform as the overriding objective of futures research. While I thoroughly sympathize with their motivations, there is a deplorable and self-defeating righteousness about their position, which seems to imply a resentment against any attempts at an objective exploration of what the future has to offer.

Futures research, in my opinion, can well make a profound contribution to social reform, and indeed it may rightly be considered to have an obligation to do so. But as a research activity it has to remain as objective as possible, drawing a clear line between analytical exploration and political activism. A political activist, in fact, if he wishes to be constructive rather than merely destructive, will derive all the more guidance and support from futures research, the more objectively such research clarifies the distinction between real potentialities and merely wishful thinking.

Aside from activist reformers, there are others, whose concern for the future takes a different form. They are the utopians and antiutopians, who describe fictitious future states of the world that they regard as desirable or detestable, and the inventors, who use their imagination to design specific social innovations intended to change our society for the better. None of these, either, can be considered futures researchers as such, but futures research is very relevant to their interests, as it is to those of the activist social reformers. Specifically, we can note the following topics that bear on the normative aspects of exploring the future.

20.8.1 Critique of Present Conditions

What are the dimensions of the quality of life (the "satisfaction indices") in terms of which satisfactions and dissatisfactions with the state of the world can be measured? With regard to which of these dimensions are dissatisfactions particularly strong, and among which segments of the public? What are the great issues of our time, and what are the anticipated issues of the future? What proposals for their resolution have been made, how feasible are these proposals, and what would be their side effects? What social inventions are needed to help resolve some of these issues?

20.8.2 Criteria for Social Reform

What planning criteria in the form of ethical standards, political platforms, social goals, societal movements, or utopian ideals have been proposed? How internally consistent and technologically feasible are they? What priorities and exchange ratios do they imply among the quality-of-life components? How would the attainment of such goals differentially affect different segments of the public?

20.8.3 Scenarios and Utopias

Given a utopian description and interpreting it as a fictitious future state of the world that can be approximated but never fully attained, what realistic, or at least plausible, scenarios are there that could lead constructively from the present state of the world to an increasingly closer approximation of the utopian state? What are the relative satisfactions felt by different segments of the public during the transitional stages presented by such a scenario? What implementation strategies and social inventions are required to bring such a scenario about? In other words, what are its political and sociotechnological prerequisites?

These, then, are some of the questions to which futures research might address itself. The list, I am sure, is incomplete, and others may place the emphasis differently. But I hope that the compendium I have presented is representative, in the sense of illustrating the large variety of topics that need and deserve to be probed and with which researchers in this field might profitably concern themselves. ■

Much of the criticism of futures research in recent years has been directed at its supposed failure to arrive at accurate predictions of things to come. In view of this it is legitimate to ask ourselves what the real merits of any forecasting efforts are. Let us take a brief look at this question next.

21 THE UTILITY OF LONG-TERM FORECASTING[4]

21.1 Futures Research and Long-Term Forecasting

Futures research as an identifiable intellectual activity received much of its early impetus from the long-range forecasting studies conducted under Rand and TRW auspices in the mid-1960s and their subsequent emulations by numerous other organizations. Recently a slight disenchantment with long-range forecasting seems to have set in in some circles, probably caused largely by the realization that predictions about the future more than a few years hence have been quite inaccurate. This inaccuracy may have been caused either by altogether wrong prophecies, especially in economics, or by a failure to foresee important developments, for example, the OPEC oil embargo, which triggered a sudden awareness of the energy crisis among the oil-importing countries. This disenchantment may be based on some misconceptions, having to do largely with the role of uncertainty. While the task of the forecaster surely includes the removal of as much uncertainty about the future as can legitimately be accomplished, it is equally important to bring genuine uncertainty, caused by deficiencies in currently available information, to the attention of planners. Futures research, and long-range forecasting in particular, should not be judged by the degree of uncertainty it conveys but by the degree to which it is capable of differentiating between unnecessary and unavoidable uncertainty.

Futures research may be defined as that part of operations research concerned with the support of planning activities relating to a future sufficiently far distant that the operating environment at the time the plans are implemented differs substantially from the operating environment at the time the plans are being made. An essential part of futures research, therefore, is the forecasting (not the prediction!) of such changes in operating conditions. (In the terminology generally accepted by now, forecasts as distinct from predictions are stated in probabilistic terms.)

For example, someone preparing to publish a new newspaper may safely rely on a survey of present preferences among the newspaper-reading public in order to decide what emphasis to give to various features. The operating environment is not likely to change very fast, and no futures research is re-

4. What follows is a paper written for *TIMS Studies in the Management Sciences,* vol. 12 (New York: Elsevier, 1979).

quired. On the other hand, someone growing trees for profit and having to decide between lumber, wood pulp, and other uses of his product decades hence must be concerned over the continuing demand for wooden houses and newsprint at that time. Here, futures research may be of help, both by deriving relevant probabilistic forecasts and by establishing planning procedures that properly account for the expected changes and the uncertainties implied by such forecasts.

21.2 *The Role of Conditional Forecasts*

In addition to providing nonconditional forecasts of exogenous developments that will constitute the setting against which plans for the long-term future have to be made, it is equally important, if not more so, for futures research to furnish certain conditional forecasts, specifically, estimates of the probable implications of various alternative policies and of alternative action programs for implementing a given policy; furthermore, these conditional forecasts should take into consideration the previously established forecasts of external operating conditions. Such conditional forecasts are clearly needed when the planner operates in what is called the exploratory mode—that is, when a selective decision among competing policies or action programs has to be made—for it is by their implications that they will be judged. Conditional forecasts also play a role, though a somewhat different one, in the so-called normative planning mode. Here the planner operates in reverse: He starts with what he considers a preferred end condition and then, if indeed he acts as a planner and not just a utopian dreamer, searches for ways and means of implementing the "policy" of attaining the wished-for state. In this case, a conditional forecasting analysis will serve to ascertain which implementation plan may be expected to come closest to achieving the desired end.

21.3 *Intuitive and Theory-Based Forecasts*

Thus, from a planner's point of view, the desirability of having both absolute and conditional long-term forecasts seems to be quite evident and, if none is supplied, it is inevitable that, in fact, the planner merely relies on his own, perhaps not even articulated, forecasts. One should note in passing that even forecasts based merely on purely intuitive insight rather than on established theory are of some value here, provided there is reason to have some trust in their reliability. If a forecast does happen to be theory-based, in the sense of being an instance of a general law that derives explanatory force from being part of a coherent theory of the phenomena in question, that will be of additional utility to the planner; it will not only enable him to choose the best among given alternative strategies but, because of its explanatory character, it will help him design strategies that are apt to influence the future in a desired direction. Since forecasts frequently fail to be explanatory in this sense, the burden of constructing candidate strategies tends to fall on the inventive imagination of the planner—a creative aspect of planning that is often given inadequate attention.

In view of the planner's need for forecasts and their added utility to him when they incorporate explanations, the two principal questions that remain are (i) whether it is possible to obtain forecasts of sufficient reliability and precision to improve the planning process over what it would be if the planner were left to rely solely on his own intuitive expectations, and (ii) whether, in addition, such forecasts can be made within the framework of an explanatory theory.

21.4 Reliability and Precision of Forecasts

With regard to the first question, a number of comments are appropriate. First of all, it is important to keep in mind that perfection in planning, while a laudable ideal, is not a necessary criterion of the utility of forecasts to the planning process. Even if, statistically speaking, the systematic use of forecasts produces only a slight improvement in the expected results of planning, such forecasts may well be worthwhile.

Second, experience has shown that long-range forecasts obtained from professional experts can in fact be quite accurate. A survey conducted at the Institute for the Future a few years ago (R. Ament, 1970) examined Delphi-generated forecasts made years earlier. The survey showed that of the events that had been given a probability, say, of 60 percent of occurring by the time the survey was made, about 60 percent had in fact occurred by that time.

Third, it may be objected by some that, even if exactly 60 percent of all events forecasted with a probability of 60 percent to occur by a certain date did occur by that date, the uncertainty implied by this information would still be so great as to render the forecast useless to the planner. In response to this objection it must be pointed out that it would be a delusion to think that planning does not proceed in an atmosphere of uncertainty. A probabilistic forecast, as opposed to a precise prediction, imposes a realistic awareness of the uncertainty of the future. This awareness compels the planner to incorporate provisions for contingencies in his plans; without such provisions he might be courting disaster.

Fourth, and finally, it has been said quite correctly that it is the mark of a good executive to display sufficient acumen in discerning likely future contingencies to be able to make the right decisions without having to resort to outside advice in the form of forecasts. However, this phenomenon does not testify to the existence of some form of divination but more likely points to the presence of a relatively superior intelligence that enables the executive to judge the reliability of all sorts of signals he receives from the environment and thereby to form, implicitly or explicitly, his own set of forecasts. He is, in other words, himself the kind of professional expert whose forecasting talents one might wish to use beyond his own decision-making sphere.

21.5 Availability of an Explanatory Theory

Let us now consider the second question raised earlier, which concerns the feasibility of making forecasts that are supported by the explanatory framework of a coherent theory. The ideal case here is represented by astronomical forecasts—which virtually amount to prediction—such as that of the next appearance of Halley's comet. What makes this such a high-probability forecast is its being based on well-understood and well-confirmed physical laws, plus the fact that deliberate intervention in the occurrence of this event is not a practical possibility. Most of our planning, of course, takes place in a sphere that lacks this high degree of certainty, and the kind of long-range forecasts on which we would like to rely inevitably involve some aspect of human affairs, either in the sense that the subject matter itself is societal in nature or that the probability of occurrence of the event being forecasted is affected by the degree of human intervention. [This point was emphasized once before, in Chapter III in dealing with the indispensability of expert judgment.]

Typical examples are economic and technological forecasts. The occurrence, say, of another worldwide economic depression clearly concerns, and is affected by, human events. And even a purely technical forecast, say, of a breakthrough in solar-to-electric energy conversion obviously is influenced by the amount of research and development effort devoted to it. In cases of these kinds, the theoretical structures on which the forecasts are based are neither well understood nor well confirmed, which is typical of a context that is multidisciplinary and lies at least partly within the social sciences [see the epistemology discussion in Chapter II]. Intuitive insight therefore plays at least as large a part as reasoned arguments in obtaining such forecasts.

Thus the answer to the question under discussion cannot be wholly in the affirmative: Not all forecasts of interest in typical planning situations may be expected to occur within the explanatory framework of a coherent theory. However, while the reasons for a long-range forecast containing societal elements are apt to be largely intuitive, there are generally some law-like regularities, having a limited but nonnegligible degree of confirmation, which at least lend some support to purely intuitive insight. Thus there tends to be an explanatory element present that may carry enough weight to permit the planner to identify measures that have more than a random chance of influencing events in the desired direction. For example, a government planner, wishing to bring about a reduction in the consumption of motor fuel, may propose a doubling of the gasoline tax, in the expectation that the demand, being somewhat elastic, would respond to the resultant price rise. The implied forecast here is based on a law of economics that, though known to have exceptions, provides a certain amount of guidance for economic behavior.

Moreover, reliance on past time series, in this case, will furnish some clues as to how much of a reduction in gasoline demand might be expected as a result of the proposed tax increase.

While in the field of economics such mildly confirmed regularities abound, often even in quantified form, that is rarely the case in other social sciences and occurs even less often in multidisciplinary situations. It is here that the cross-impact approach offers, if not a complete remedy, at least a better-than-nothing substitute for law-like regularities.

21.6 Cross-Impact Analysis as a Theory Substitute

The cross-impact concept was invented in the first place to enrich the results of sets of intuitive forecasts, such as a series of technological forecasts that might be obtained through a Delphi survey of expert opinions. Instead of merely requiring estimates of the probabilities of occurrence of potential future events considered in isolation from one another, a cross-impact analysis also inquires into the effects the occurrence of any one of the events included in the survey would have on the probability of occurrence of the remaining events. Intuitive numerical estimates of these effects, called cross-impacts, are recorded in a square matrix, (x_{ij}), where x_{ij} is a measure of the impact that the occurrence of the ith event, E_i, has on the probability of occurrence of the jth event, E_j. Thus, the cross-impact matrix represents a set of estimates of the causal relationships among the events under consideration. The quantities x_{ij} as a rule have to be obtained through intuitive estimation by experts and do not in themselves convey any information that would explain the reasons for the causal relationships they indicate. However, if the x_{ij} are generated through some kind of Delphi procedure, the respondents, in justifying a nonzero assignment to a particular x_{ij}, may provide an intuitive argument for, and thus a possible explanation of, the claimed causal relationship. Moreover, while the x_{ij} individually and aside from any incidental explication given by their estimators are not explanatory in nature, the matrix (x_{ij}) as a whole represents a coherent pattern of causality assertions and may be regarded as the next best thing to a theory of the phenomena under consideration.

Possible scenarios of the future, which a planner may be considering, are formulated in terms not only of events—such as technological breakthroughs, acts of legislation, earthquakes, and elections—that take place at specific times, but also of trends representing gradual developments—such as population growth, GNP, and degree of pollution. Cross-impact analysis has been extended to include trends as well as events, essentially by interpreting as an event a trend's deviation from its anticipated value [the details of which will be discussed later, in Chapter VI]. The estimation of causal connections, or cross-impacts, can thus be extended to all of the elements that make up a scenario of the future.

21.7 Application to Multidisciplinary Planning

The utility, to a planner, of a long-range forecasting study augmented by a cross-impact analysis, becomes very apparent when the subject area in which plans are to be made is essentially multidisciplinary, because conventional extrapolative analyses almost certainly will fail to provide the kind of explanatory information from which a sound strategy can be constructed. A good example is a recently conducted study in the area of long-range transportation planning [see Section 50 of Chapter IX]. Here the planning agency was confronted with the need to forecast not only developments in transportation technology but also in its future operating environment, that is, in communication technology, demography, economic conditions, land-use policies, energy availability, people's changing values, and so on. In a planning situation of this kind where there are no well-confirmed regularities covering the different areas of concern and, especially, their interconnections, the planner can attempt to put together his own surrogate theory in the form of a cross-impact analysis. Thus he can build a foundation upon which to design strategies that have at least a slightly better chance of coping with future contingencies than those arrived at without the benefit of this kind of systematic underpinning.

The procedural steps he would have to follow in such an undertaking might be described briefly as follows:

Step 1: Identify potential future developments, either events or trends, whose occurrence or whose deviation from expected values would have a significant effect on the future operating environment of the planner's subject area.

Step 2: Obtain forecasts, through Delphi or other methods, regarding these developments.

Step 3: Estimate the cross-impacts among these developments.

Step 4: Use cross-impact analysis [see Chapter VI for details] to establish the relative sensitivity of the developments to one another.

Step 5: Estimate the degree to which the event probabilities or the trend values can be influenced by deliberate intervention on the part of the decision-maker or decision-making agency on whose behalf plans are being made. In doing so, separate the developments that are not influenced easily from those that are. The former establish the spectrum of exogenous, uncontrollable characteristics of the future environment for which plans are being made. The latter are the operative developments through the manipulation of which the planner can hope to influence the course of future events in a desired direction.

Step 6: Establish the resource constraints that prospective plans must be designed to accommodate.

Step 7: Using the sensitivities ascertained earlier and the developments identified as operative, select or invent alternative action programs within the stated resource constraints that seem to be promising candidates for attaining desired objectives.

Step 8: Use cross-impact analysis to determine the relative merits of these alternative action programs in terms of expected results and their dispersion, and thus select one or several of the most promising alternatives.

For many obvious reasons—the surrogate character of the cross-impact analysis as a theory substitute; the possibly inadequate selection of developments for inclusion in the analysis; the relative unreliability of the forecasts as well as the cross-impact estimates, even if obtained from experts; the possibly incomplete selection of action programs included in the comparative analysis—the outcome of this approach may not, in fact, be the optimal strategy. However, the procedure represents a selection process that, if carried out judiciously and conscientiously, may yield a set of strategies from which, through a process of further analysis, a satisfactory close-to-optimal strategy can be distilled.

21.8 Summary

The points made here may be summarized as follows:

Forecasts, whether explicit or merely implicit, are an essential ingredient of the planning process. In the case of long-range planning, the planner needs two kinds of long-range forecasts: those concerning the expected, changed operating environment and those concerning the consequences of contemplated policies. The utility of such forecasts depends on their precision and reliability and is further enhanced if they are developed within an explanatory setting that enables the planner to understand any causal relationships and to use them to design appropriate strategies. Forecasts are rarely very precise, especially if they concern societal and multidisciplinary matters, but their precision as well as their reliability can be at least slightly enhanced if they are obtained through a systematic solicitation of expert opinions, such as might be provided by a Delphi survey. An explanatory setting for forecasts in the form of a well-confirmed theory is generally absent; however, a substitute having some, though limited, utility can be constructed through the vehicle of a cross-impact analysis. ■

Chapter V

The Delphi Technique

The Delphi technique of extracting opinions from a panel of experts has already frequently been alluded to. Its intended purpose is to make the best use of a group of experts in obtaining answers to questions requiring reliance, at least in part, on the informed intuitive opinions of specialists in the area of inquiry. (The indispensability, on occasion, of such expert judgment has already been discussed in detail in Section 13.) The Delphi technique was designed to accomplish this with a minimum of interference from the kind of psychological distractions that usually attend open-forum discussions among panels of experts, and to achieve as close a consensus as possible compatible with individual divergencies from the central tendency of the panel's opinions. In addition, the reasons for any residual dissensus were to be exhibited clearly, so as to enable a subsequent analysis of the findings of a Delphi survey to ascertain whether such judgmental discrepancies were due to factual differences, semantic interpretations, or theoretical disagreements.

The Delphi technique—it should be clearly understood—is not a polling procedure, since the selection of the experts to be consulted is not an integral part of the method. It merely addresses the question, once a panel of experts has been chosen, as to how to set up an efficient and effective communication process through which to survey the group's opinions. This does not mean that the selection process is not important; this, however, presents a separate problem (already discussed at some length in Chapter III).

The Delphi method was first invented in 1953 by the author in conjunction with Norman Dalkey in order to address a specific military problem. Both the project itself and the report on it were originally classified as secret. After this classification was dropped, we were able to publish the following summary of the procedure and its findings.

22 AN EXPERIMENTAL APPLICATION OF THE DELPHI METHOD TO THE USE OF EXPERTS[1]

22.1 Introduction

"Project Delphi" is the name for a study of the use of expert opinion that has been intermittently conducted at the Rand Corporation. The technique

1. This essay, by Norman Dalkey and myself, was first published under the same title in 1963. It is reprinted here by permission of The Institute of Management Sciences from *Management Science,* vol. 9, no. 3 (April 1963), copyright 1963.

employed is called the Delphi method. Its object is to obtain the most reliable consensus of opinion of a group of experts. It attempts to achieve this by a series of intensive questionnaires interspersed with controlled opinion feedback.

The present paper gives an account of an experiment conducted about ten years ago. The content of the paper has, for security reasons, only now [i.e., in 1963] been released for open publication.

The experiment was designed to apply expert opinion to the selection, from the viewpoint of a Soviet strategic planner, of an optimal U.S. industrial target system and to the estimation of the number of A-bombs required to reduce the munitions output by a prescribed amount.

The technique employed involves the repeated individual questioning of the experts (by interview or questionnaire) and avoids direct confrontation of the experts with one another.

The questions, which are all centered around some central problem (in our present case, an estimate of bombing requirements), are designed to bring out the respondent's reasoning that went into his reply to the primary question, the factors he considers relevant to the problem, his own estimate of these factors, and information as to the kind of data that he feels would enable him to arrive at a better appraisal of these factors and, thereby, at a more confident answer to the primary question. The information fed to the experts between rounds of questioning is generally of two kinds: It consists either of available data previously requested by some one of the experts (e.g., output statistics for steel mills), or of factors and considerations suggested as potentially relevant by one or another respondent (e.g., the extent to which power transmission facilities permit reallocation of electric power). With respect to the latter type of information, an attempt was made (not always successfully) to conceal the actual opinion of other respondents and merely to present the factor for consideration without introducing unnecessary bias.

This mode of controlled interaction among the respondents represents a deliberate attempt to avoid the disadvantages associated with more conventional uses of experts, such as round-table discussions or other milder forms of confrontation with opposing views. The method employed in the experiment appears to be more conducive to independent thought on the part of the experts and to aid them in the gradual formation of a considered opinion. Direct confrontation, on the other hand, all too often induces the hasty formulation of preconceived notions, an inclination to close one's mind to novel ideas, a tendency to defend a stand once taken or, alternatively and sometimes alternately, a predisposition to be swayed by persuasively stated opinions of others.

By systematically exploring the factors that influence the judgment of the individual expert, it becomes possible to correct any misconceptions that he may have harbored regarding empirical factors or theoretical assumptions underlying those factors, and to draw his attention to other factors which he may have overlooked in his first analysis of the situation. Needless to say, considerable discretion has to be exercised by the experimenters in any efforts designed to make an expert change his mind, in order to obtain results which are free of any bias on the experimenter's part. A device for helping to assure this is to feed in only such data as have been asked for by at least one respondent and are obtainable from reliable sources, and to suggest only such theoretical assumptions as seem to represent a consensus of a majority of respondents.

If the purpose of the experiment is the estimation of a numerical quantity (in our case the number of bombs required to do a certain job), it may be expected that, even if the views expressed initially are widely divergent, the individual estimates will show a tendency to converge as the experiment continues. This is almost inevitable in view of the progressively more penetrating analysis of the problem, achieved partly by means of the procedural feedback described above.

On the other hand, it cannot even ideally be expected that the final responses will coincide, since the uncertainties of the future call for intuitive probability estimates on the part of each respondent. To some extent this terminal disagreement can sometimes be decreased by applying justifiable corrections to the final answers. Such corrections are in fact an integral part of the procedure; they must, however, be based on a careful analysis of the responses, taking into account whatever can be learned regarding (i) a consensus as to basic assumptions, (ii) the sensitivity of the individuals' responses to changes in these basic assumptions, and (iii) their estimates of functional dependencies rather than mere point estimates. Essentially, the resulting corrections amount to a replacement of the individual expert's estimates concerning some of the components of the main problem by a consensus of estimates by all the experts. For example, in the experiment mentioned in this report, the problem of estimating the total number of bombs was factorable into that of determining, for each of several industries, what percentage of each industry must be destroyed and the average number of bombs per plant needed to do so. Each respondent made estimates of both these quantities. For the first, which involved the selection of the industries to be bombed, the choices made were too divergent to permit the taking of a consensus. The second estimate, however, was a perfect example of a case wherein a consensus would seem to yield more reliable results; accordingly we corrected the respondents' final answers by replacing their own numbers for bombs per plant by the median of all (seven) estimates. Table 1 reflects the resulting trend. It will be noted that the ratio between the largest and smallest responses, which was initially 100 to 1, dropped finally to about 3 to 1, and upon correction was ultimately reduced to only 2 to 1.

TABLE 1 Estimated Number of Bombs

		Answer	
Response	*Smallest*	*Median*	*Largest*
Initial	50	200	5000
Final	159	255	494
Corrected final	167	276	360

22.2 Description of the Experiment

The experiment was conducted with a panel of seven experts. Four of these were economists, one was a physical-vulnerability specialist, one a systems analyst, and one an electronics engineer.

There were altogether five questionnaires, submitted at approximately weekly intervals. The first and third of these were followed up by interviews with each of the respondents. We present here a condensed log of the proceedings.

Questionnaire 1

This is part of a continuing study to arrive at improved methods of making use of the opinions of experts regarding uncertain events.

The particular problem to be studied in this experiment is concerned with the effects of strategic bombing of industrial targets in the U.S. . . .

Please do not discuss this study with others while this experiment is in progress, especially not with the other subject experts. You are at liberty, though, to consult whatever data you feel might help you in forming an opinion.

The problem with which we will be concerned is the following:

Let us assume that a war between the U.S. and the S.U. breaks out on 1 July 1953. Assume also that the rate of our total military production (defined as munitions output plus investment) at that time is 100 billion dollars and that, on the assumption of no damage to our industry, under mobilization it would rise to 150 billion dollars by 1 July 1954 and to 200 billion dollars by 1 July 1955, resulting in a cumulative production over that two-year period of 300 billion dollars. Now assume further that the enemy during the first month of the war (and only during that period) carries out a strategic atomic bombing campaign against U.S. industrial targets, employing 20-kiloton bombs. Within each industry selected by the enemy for bombardment, assume that the bombs delivered on target succeed in hitting always the most important targets in that industry. What is the least number of bombs that will have to be delivered on target for which you would estimate the chances to be even that the cumulative munitions output (exclusive of investment) during the two-year period under consideration would be held to no more than one quarter of what it otherwise would have been?

TABLE 2 Confidence-of-Destruction Estimates

	Respondent						
Response	*1*	*2*	*3*	*4*	*5*	*6*	*7*
Primary (50% confidence)	125	50	150	300	200	1000	5000
10% and 90% confidence	75-200	25-150	100-175	250-800	70-500	—	2500-10000

This question will be referred to below as the "primary question".

In a follow-up interview to the first questionnaire, each respondent was asked to provide a breakdown by industries of the number of bombs specified by him and to reproduce some of the reasoning that went into his estimate. He was further asked to estimate the number of bombs needed to do the job with 10 percent and with 90 percent confidence of success, and to indicate what kind of data he would consider most helpful in arriving at a better appraisal.

The total number of bombs were estimated as shown in Table 2. (The respondents have been ordered according to the numerical order of their corrected final responses.) The choices of target systems were quite distinct, the only common feature being the inclusion of the steel industry in each.

Questionnaire 2

As the result of the first round of interviews, it appears that the problem for which we are trying with your help to arrive at an estimated answer breaks down in the following manner.

There seem to be four major items to be taken into consideration, namely:

(A) the vulnerability of various potential target systems,
(B) the recuperability of various industries and combinations of industries,
(C) the expected initial stockpiles and inventories, and
(D) complementarities among industries.

Taking all these into account, we have to

(1) determine the optimal target system for reducing munitions output . . . to one fourth . . . ,
(2) estimate for this target system the minimum number of bombs on target required to create 50 percent confidence of accomplishing that aim. . . .

We would like to establish the background material consisting of A, B, C, D more firmly. . . . With regard to A and B, the interviews have suggested the following tentative breakdown of possibly relevant factors: (Here, two lists of factors were given, related to vulnerability and recuperability respectively.)

Question 1. Does the preceding breakdown of the problem agree with your intuitive approach to a solution? If not, explain in detail; in particular, are there major items in addition to A, B, C, D which should be taken into consideration?

Question 2. What additional factors, if any, do you consider relevant to the problem of vulnerability? Which of the factors listed do you consider irrelevant?

Question 3. What additional factors, if any, do you consider relevant to the problem of recuperability? Which of the factors listed do you consider irrelevant?

Question 4. What factors should be taken into account for our problem in assessing the size and role of initial stockpiles?

Question 5. What factors should be taken into account in our problem as regards determining complementarities among industries?

Question 6. Are there any general comments you wish to make?

The response consisted of a large volume of informal comments. The most significant among these pointed out the difference between economic and physical vulnerability, the influence of the planned munitions product mix, the importance of substitutabilities of plants and materials, and the dependence of the lead times of components on the damage done to the industries producing these. Only some of this material was reflected in the later phases of the experiment.

Questionnaire 3

You are being asked today for a reconsideration of your original estimate. The question is restated below, together with a few explanatory comments. We are also listing a few facts and estimates, which you may wish to take into consideration in forming a revised opinion.

Restatement of primary question: . . .

Comments: (Clarification of the terms "industrial target" and "bomb on target" and of some assumptions to be made by the respondents in forming their estimates.)

Data on U.S. economy:

(a) Number of plants presently (i.e., in 1951) accounting for indicated percentages of various industries' outputs: . . .
(b) Percentages of metals output going into munitions, consumption, and gross investment: . . .
(c) Percentages of munitions value constituted by value of metals input: . . .

Data on structural vulnerability:

(d) Examples of damage with 20-KT bomb obtained from Japanese bombings: . . .
(e) Vulnerability estimates for specific industries: . . .

TABLE 3 Revised Estimates

	Respondent						
Response	*1*	*2*	*3*	*4*	*5*	*6*	*7*
To Question 1	158	89	200	250	256	800	450
To interview	158	106	184	250	256	525	450

Question 1. What is your revised answer to the primary question of Questionnaire 1?

Question 2. Do you consider the tabulation of industrial plants given under (a) above reasonably correct? (If not, please specify.)

Question 3. What changes, if any, in that tabulation do you expect by mid-1953?

Question 4. Do you roughly agree with the estimates of physical vulnerability expressed under (e) above? (If not, please specify.)

Question 5. For the following industries, how would you allot the minimum number of bombs on target called for in the primary question?

Steel
Petroleum refining
Aluminum
Copper
Power
Atomic bombs
Aircraft engines
Heavy steel fabrication
Machine tools
Electron tubes
Aviation fuel
Antifriction bearings
Other industries

The follow-up interviews served to clarify a few uncertainties and produced further minor revisions. The responses to the primary question are given in Table 3.

Questionnaire 4

The principal purpose of this questionnaire is again to obtain from you revised answers as to the numbers of bombs allotted to various industries—the revisions to be based on consideration of the information supplied below as well as any further thought you may have given to the matter. In addition you will be asked to make certain recuperation forecasts . . . and to make a critical comparison between your own bombing schedule and two others to be specified below. (These two bombing schedules, labeled A and B below, had been obtained as follows: The seven bombing schedules obtained previously were roughly ordered cyclically in such a manner that each was as similar as possible to its two neighboring schedules; according to the numbering of the respondents the following cyclical order was obtained: 1234765. Each expert was then confronted with the bombing schedules of his two neighbors in this ordering, e.g., 1 with 2 and 5.)

Additional information on the target system: . . .
Information on stockpiles: . . .
Information on the power system: . . .
Information on the uses of steel: . . .
Information on the bombing of Europe in World War II: . . .
Information on Japanese recuperation: . . .

Question 1. In the last column of the following table, indicate your revised bombing schedule:

Plants Producing			*Industry*	*Bombing Schedules*			
50%	*75%*	*100%*		*A*	*B*	*Your Former Figures*	*Your Revised Figures*
17	37	215	Steel				
25	85	437	Petroleum				
2	5	12	Aluminum				
4	6	12	Copper				
125	325	3700	Power				
		7	Atomic bombs				
4	8	21	A/C engines				
3	6	9	Steel fabric.				
20	55	316	Machine tools				
8	17	53	Electron tubes				
		14	Aviation fuel				
3	6	19	Ball bearings				
			Other				
			Total:				

Questions 2 and 3. Draw graphs indicating the estimated progress of steel and munitions output recuperation after bombing according to your revised schedule. (Coordinate systems were provided.)

Question 4. Compare your proposed bombing schedule with that given under A above. While you estimate your own schedule to reduce munitions output over two years to 25 percent, a reduction to how many percent do you expect from Schedule A? _____ Briefly, why is your proposal superior to Schedule A?

Question 5. The same for Schedule B.

The revised total numbers of bombs, obtained in response to Question 1, are shown in Table 4. The comparison with other bombing schedules brought out a number of interesting points, the most important of which were brought to the group's attention in the subsequent questionnaire.

TABLE 4 Revised Total Number of Bombs

	Respondent						
Response	*1*	2	3	4	5	6	7
No. of bombs	166	153	200	250	300	332	500

Questionnaire 5

In this final questionnaire you will have a last opportunity to revise once more your earlier estimates if you should feel so inclined. The possibility of such a further revision suggests itself in view of (i) a piece of information, given below, on World War II munitions expenditures . . . , (ii) certain considerations emphasized by the respondents themselves in their replies to the preceding questionnaire, and (iii) a possible discrepancy, in some cases, between the prescribed bombing goal and the accomplished munitions-output reduction as indicated by your graph (response to Question 3 of the preceding questionnaire).

Attached you will find your previous response sheet. On the graph that represents the answer to Question 3, the munitions output under normal wartime expansion without bombing has been indicated by a dotted line; this corresponds to the assumptions stated in our original formulation of the problem in the first questionnaire. Also indicated, in red, is the approximate munitions output, in percentage of the normal output, computed from your graph. If this number differs substantially from 25, this may of course be due to your having drawn the graph freehand, or to a difference of opinion as to the amount of munitions output under normal expansion. If, however, the difference is due to your having attempted to reduce munitions output to 25 percent of what it would have been without expansion, you have in fact overbombed and may wish to revise your estimates accordingly.

Distribution of munitions expenditures in 1944: . . .

Considerations emphasized by respondents in preceding questionnaire:

(1) the effect of industrial expansion on the number of plants producing 75 percent
(2) use of the principle of equal marginal utility in assigning bombs to industries
(3) observation of intraindustry complementarities (e.g., aluminum and alumina)
(4) observation of interindustry complementarities (e.g., aluminum and aircraft engines)
(5) the possibility that concentrating the attack allows concentration of the recuperation effort

Question. Please fill in the blank columns in the following table (here the table of the preceding questionnaire was reproduced, with the left-hand half as before, and the right-hand half replaced by columns with the following headings):

Estimate number of plants in mid-1953 producing.		*If this industry were to be bombed, estimate no. of bombs on target needed to destroy.*		*Give your finally revised bombing schedule.*
75%	*100%*	*75%*	*100%*	

TABLE 5 Final Bombing Estimates

	Respondent						
Response	*1*	*2*	*3*	*4*	*5*	*6*	*7*
No. of bombs	177	159	200	255	312	314	494

The respondents' final bombing estimates are shown in Table 5.

22.3 Correction of the Final Responses

As indicated at the end of Section 22.1, the final responses given above are capable of correction on the basis of replacing some of the individual component estimates by a consensus of estimates. Whenever this was done, the median of the responses was taken as the consensus. Our procedure was, first of all, to tabulate for each of the industries considered the medians of (i) the expected numbers of plants respectively producing 50 percent, 75 percent, and 100 percent of the total output in mid-1953, and (ii) the number of plants requiring two rather than one bomb on target for destruction.

We then listed (iii) the percentage of damage to each industry that each expert intended as indicated from the figure he gave for the numbers of plants in mid-1953, the number of bombs needed to destroy 75 percent and 100 percent, and the number of bombs to be allocated to each industry, and (iv) the corresponding numbers of bombs as computed with the aid of the tabulation obtained under item iii. The total of these latter numbers, for each respondent, was taken as his corrected final answer, as shown in Table 6.

The five successive sets of responses, plus the corrected totals, are shown in Figure 6, which brings out very clearly the gradual convergence of the an-

TABLE 6 Corrected Final Estimates

	Respondent						
Response	*1*	*2*	*3*	*4*	*5*	*6*	*7*
Final	177	159	200	255	312	314	494
Corrected final	167	179	206	276	292	349	360

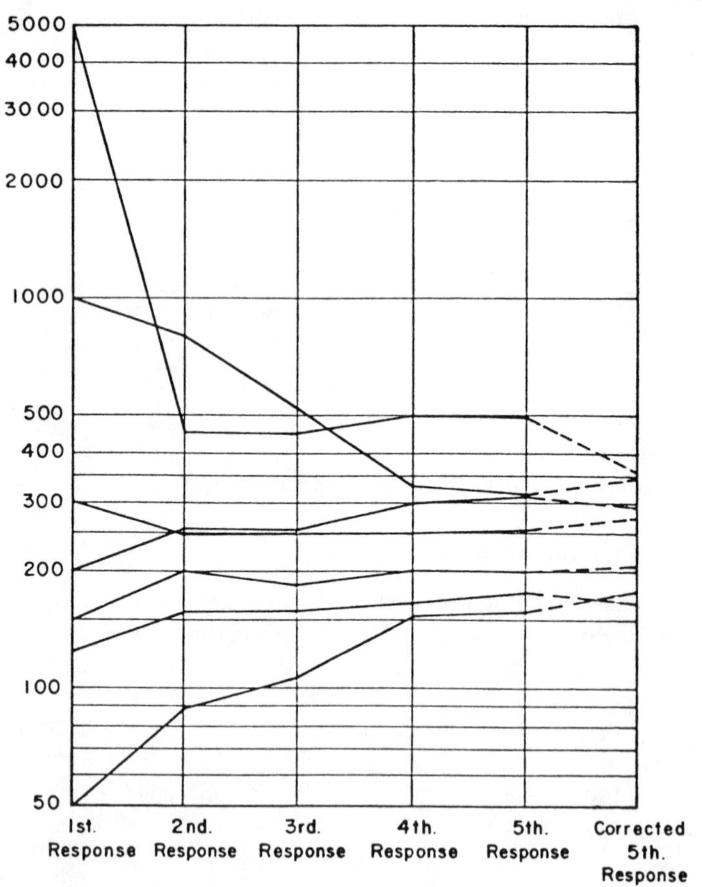

FIGURE 6

swers. The smallest answer is seen to have increased monotonically from 50 to 167, while the largest decreased from 5000 to 360. The median advanced slightly from 200 to 276. There are strong indications that, if the experiment had been continued through a few more rounds of questionnaires, the median would have shown a downward trend and the ratio of the largest to the smallest answer would have shrunk to 2 or less.

22.4 Critique of the Experimental Procedure

The following points represent a summary of the items for which the experimenters are conscious of the need for apology:

(i) The experts' responses were not strictly independent. Although the respondents on the whole complied with the initial cautioning not to discuss the experiment with one another while it was in progress, their other working assignments on related subjects required some contact among several of them.

(ii) At least one of the respondents was also used by the experimenters as a consultant on one aspect of the subject matter of the experiment.

(iii) Some "leading" by the experimenters inevitably resulted from the selection of information supplied by the experts.

(iv) The experiment was terminated prematurely, before it was possible to give as much emphasis to complementarities and recuperation as had been given, say, to vulnerability.

(v) The comparison of two "neighboring" bombing strategies, called for in Questionnaire 4, was a shortcut necessitated by the pressure of time; it was intended to throw some light on the sensitivity of the bombing figures given by each respondent. This purpose would have been served better by a less biased but more time-consuming approach.

(vi) Vague questions inviting general critical comment, such as were presented in Questionnaire 2, produce literary outpourings of little value for the analysis and should either be omitted or replaced by an interview.

(vii) The correction of the final responses, carried out above in view of certain median considerations, may seem plausible but nevertheless should be given a firmer theoretical foundation.

The authors are convinced that most of these shortcomings can gradually be eliminated by further experimentation in this area. Even as it stands, the method exemplified by the experiment reported here is highly conducive to producing preliminary insights into the subject matter at hand, on which a more effective research program may be based, even though the predictions obtained in the form of an opinion consensus may be lacking in reliability. But with further progress in the methodology of the efficient use of experts, it may be hoped that a carefully contrived consensus would often turn out to be an acceptable substitute for direct empirical evidence when the latter is unavailable. [For a further discussion of the methodology of the use of expert opinion, see the earlier section on epistemology in Chapter II. For reports on two experiments in the use of expert opinions regarding the qualitative ranking of given alternatives, see Thrall, Coombs, and Caldwell, 1958, and Caldwell, Coombs, Schoeffler, and Thrall, 1961. An earlier experiment in the use of an expert consensus for predictive purposes was reported by Kaplan, Skogstad, and Girshick, 1950.] ■

23 FURTHER EVOLUTION OF THE DELPHI TECHNIQUE

After its first application, described above, in 1953, the Delphi technique was in disuse until, a decade later, the idea came up that it might be a convenient vehicle for obtaining technological forecasts. An extensive long-range technological forecasting study using Delphi was conducted under Rand auspices by Ted Gordon and myself. [A report on this study, first published in 1964, is included in Chapter VIII of this book.] The substantive results of this study received a good deal of attention and, among other things, persuaded the firm of TRW to conduct a series of internal Delphi studies, which they named "Probes", aimed at identifying promising areas for future research and development by TRW. These surveys were considered quite successful by TRW's management, not least of all because the Delphi process of inquiry established a new, morale-building form of vertical communication among the participants on various levels within the firm. The reports at meetings of industrial planners on the practical utility of these exercises eventually brought on a flurry of all sorts of so-called Delphi surveys in the private and public sectors both here and abroad. During the decade from the mid-1960s to the mid-1970s, the interest in exploring future contingencies grew, for better or worse, into a full-fledged futures movement, with futures societies and futures research institutes and professional journals all over the world.

The numerous Delphi studies conducted since the mid-1960s rarely, to my knowledge, seem to have followed the pattern of the 1953 original, with its in-depth interviews of the participating experts and the attention to emerging sidelines to the inquiry whose pursuit promised to be helpful in answering the inquiry's primary questions. Instead, something almost like a "standard Delphi format" evolved, usually consisting of four rounds of inquiry administered through mailed questionnaires and well illustrated by the example contained in the following essay (an example, incidentally, from the 1964 technological forecasting study referred to above).

24 THE DELPHI METHOD FOR SYSTEMATIZING JUDGMENTS ABOUT THE FUTURE[2]

To talk about methodology before specifying a set of problems may seem like putting the cart before the horse. However, the particular method I want to discuss is applicable to a wide variety of problems with which we are confronted today; moreover, an advance awareness of the limitations of available methods may introduce a healthy element of realism into specification of areas most in need of attention.

2. Excerpted from a talk given at the University of California, Los Angeles, Institute of Government and Public Affairs and published by it under the above title as M-61 (1966), and from an internal Rand paper, P-3558, "Analysis of the Future: The Delphi Method" (1967).

The problems I am concerned with are typified by those we have to face in the area of public policy planning: for example, in planning the war on poverty or the war on crime; or in devising a public policy for the future of education; or in setting a long-range agricultural policy; or in deciding what form of aid to give to developing countries; or in laying down guidelines for a national science policy.

These problem areas have several characteristics in common: They are long-range, they are cross-disciplinary, they largely lack a theoretical foundation as a basis for attack, and they are urgent. Let me comment briefly on these four features.

By describing problems as long-range, I mean that it is necessary, in order to take a rational approach to their solution, to form first of all some rather definite image of what the world of the future will be like or, at least, what it might be like. It used to be the case that in many areas of public affairs, policies could be made without such explicit reference to the future. For example, an educational reform policy might have been formulated by merely examining the past and present failings of the educational system and seeking to eliminate these failings. Such an approach is justified as long as the general social environment can be expected to change slowly from one generation to the next. However, we have entered an era of such rapid technological change, with consequent socioeconomic change, that we can no longer afford this attitude of relative complacency; our plans would be obsolete before they were implemented. This need for basing policy decisions on an explicit consideration of our expectations for the future and our options for the future is currently being recognized ever more widely, both by government planning agencies and by private industry. The future, it might be said, has become respectable—it is "in".

The second point, that the problems cut across several disciplines, is only too obvious. The most clear-cut case is perhaps that of urban planning, where it is hard to think of a discipline that should not be represented. But even if one takes a field such as educational reform, thoughtful planning must of necessity involve not only all aspects of the area of education proper, including the technological prospects of programmed instruction, but also projections, for many decades ahead, of the socioeconomic environment for which the educational system is intended to prepare youngsters or retrain adults. An adequate attack on problems of this nature demands not only separate contributions from many different disciplines, but effective multidisciplinary collaboration as well. This is easier said than done, and I shall return to this desideratum later.

Third, it is important to realize that the projections into the future, on which public policy decisions must rely, are largely based on the personal expectations of individuals rather than on predictions derived from a well-established theory. Even when we have a formal mathematical model available—as is the case, for example, for various aspects of the national economy—the input assumptions, the range of applicability of the model, and the interpretation of the output all are subject to intuitive intervention by an individual who can bring the appropriate expertise to bear on the application of the model. In view of the absence of a proper theoretical foundation and the consequent inevitability of having, to some extent, to rely on intuitive expertise—a situation that is further compounded by its multidisciplinary characteristics—we are faced with two options: We can either throw up our hands in despair and wait until we have an adequate theory enabling us to deal with socioeconomic and political problems as confidently as we do with problems in physics and chemistry, or we can make the most of an admittedly unsatisfactory situation and try to obtain the relevant intuitive insights of experts and then use their judgments as systematically as possible.

This dilemma brings me to my fourth point, the matter of urgency. The current pace of change is so fast that the first alternative is not open to us. Public policy decisions must be made promptly, or they will be made by default. In dealing with problems of the future of our society, we find ourselves more and more under the same pressure of events that, during wartime, compelled military leaders to seek advice from operations analysts. Perhaps the terms "war on poverty", "war on crime", "war against discrimination", "war against disease", and "war against pollution" have been aptly chosen; in these wars too we must accept guidance from operations research as long as a well-rounded and completely tested scientific theory is not available.

Social scientists should be urged to explore the possibilities the operations-research approach has to offer. While it would indeed be gratifying to have political theories comparable to physical theories in elegance, logical persuasiveness, and predictive reliability, we cannot count on this to come about. In any case, the dangers that society faces are so great and the needs for rapid progress so evident that we cannot afford to wait—perhaps for a generation or more—until satisfactory, well-tested theories of human relations are available. The time has come to emulate not physical science but physical technology. But how?

The best we can do, under the circumstances, when we do have to rely on expert judgment, is to make the most constructive and systematic use of such opinions. In dealing with experts, there are basically three rules that I think ought to be followed: (i) Select your experts wisely: (ii) create the proper conditions under which they can perform most ably; (iii) if you have several experts on a particular issue available, use considerable caution in deriving from their various opinions a single combined position. The so-called Delphi technique deals with this last point. [For a discussion of the first two points, see Chapter III.]

The Delphi approach has to do with the problem of combining the opinions of the members of a panel of experts into a single position. Perhaps the traditional and in many ways the simplest method of achieving a consensus has been to conduct a round-table discussion among the experts and to have them arrive at an agreed-upon group position. This procedure is open to a number of objections. In particular, the outcome is apt to be a compromise between divergent views, arrived at all too often under the undue influence of certain psychological factors, such as specious persuasion by the member with the greatest supposed authority or merely the loudest voice, the unwillingness to abandon publicly expressed opinions, and the bandwagon effect of majority opinion.

In recent years we have been experimenting with a new approach to overcome these difficulties, which has become known as the Delphi technique. The Delphi technique, in its simplest form, eliminates committee activity among the experts altogether and replaces it with a carefully designed program of sequential individual interrogations (usually best conducted by questionnaires) interspersed with information and opinion feedback.

It may be easier to describe the principles involved in this procedure by reference to a particular example. When inquiring into the future of automation, each member of a panel of experts in this field was asked to estimate the year when a machine would become available that would comprehend standard IQ tests and score above 150 (where "comprehend" was interpreted behavioristically as the ability to respond to questions printed in English and possibly accompanied by diagrams). The initial responses consisted in a set of estimates spread over a sizable time interval, from 1980 to never. A follow-up questionnaire fed back to the respondents a summary of the distribution of these responses by stating the median and—as an indication of the spread of opinions—the interquartile range (that is, the interval containing the middle 50 per cent of the responses). Each respondent was then asked to reconsider his previous answer and revise it if he desired. If his new response lay outside the interquartile range, he was asked to state his reason for thinking that the answer should be that much lower, or that much higher, than the majority judgment of the group.

Placing the onus of justifying relatively extreme responses on the respondents had the effect of causing those without strong convictions to move their estimates closer to the median, while those who felt they had a good argument for a "deviationist" opinion tended to retain their original estimates and defend them.

In the next round, responses (now showing a smaller interquartile range) were again summarized, and the respondents were given a concise summary of reasons presented in support of extreme positions. They were then asked to revise their second-round responses, taking the proffered reasons into consideration and giving them whatever weight they thought was justified. A respondent whose answer remained outside the (new) interquartile range was required to state why he was unpersuaded by the opposing argument. In a fourth, and final, round these criticisms of the reasons previously offered were resubmitted to the respondents, and they were given a last chance to revise their estimates. The median of these final responses could then be taken as representing the nearest thing to a group consensus. In the case of the high-IQ machine, this median turned out to be the year 1990, with a final interquartile range from 1984 to 2000. The procedure thus caused the median to move to a much earlier date and the interquartile range to shrink considerably, presumably influenced by convincing arguments.

Figure 7 presents a record of the round-by-round estimates; the larger dots indicate the positions of the quartiles.

This convergence of opinions has been observed in the majority of cases in which the Delphi approach has been used. In a few of the cases in which no convergence toward a relatively narrow interval of values took place, opinions began to polarize around two distinct values, so that two schools of thought regarding a particular issue seemed to emerge; this may have been an indication that opinions were based on different sets of data or on different interpretations of the same data. In such cases, it is conceivable that a continuation of the Delphi process through several more rounds of anonymous debate-by-questionnaire might eventually have tracked down and eliminated that basic cause of disagreement and thus have led to a true consensus. But even if this did not happen, or if the process were terminated before it had a chance to happen, it should be realized that the Delphi technique would have served the purpose of crystallizing the reasoning process that might lead to one or several positions on an issue and thus help to clarify the issue even in the absence of a group consensus.

The foregoing illustration is intended to describe the basic essentials of the Delphi technique. Refinements are made to fit each particular case; two of them are discussed below.

One is that of introducing weighted opinions. If it were easy to measure the relative reliability of different experts objectively, we would obviously give greatest, if not exclusive, weight to the opinions of those who are most reliable. In view of the absence of such measurements, we have experimented with the idea of relying to some extent on the experts' self-appraisal of their relative competence in making a reliable estimate. We found the results to be quite promising. This device was used in November 1965, when twenty members of the faculty of the Graduate School of Business Administration at the University of California (Los Angeles) made forecasts of ten economic and business indices for the last quarter of 1965 and for the entire year 1966 (twenty answers altogether). The procedure was as follows: In addition to going through four rounds of Delphi arguments, the respondents were asked to rank their relative competence with regard to the estimation of each of the ten indices. Then, instead of using for each index the median of all twenty final responses as the group consensus, and thus as the group's prediction for 1966, we took only the responses of those individuals who had ranked themselves relatively most highly competent for that particular index

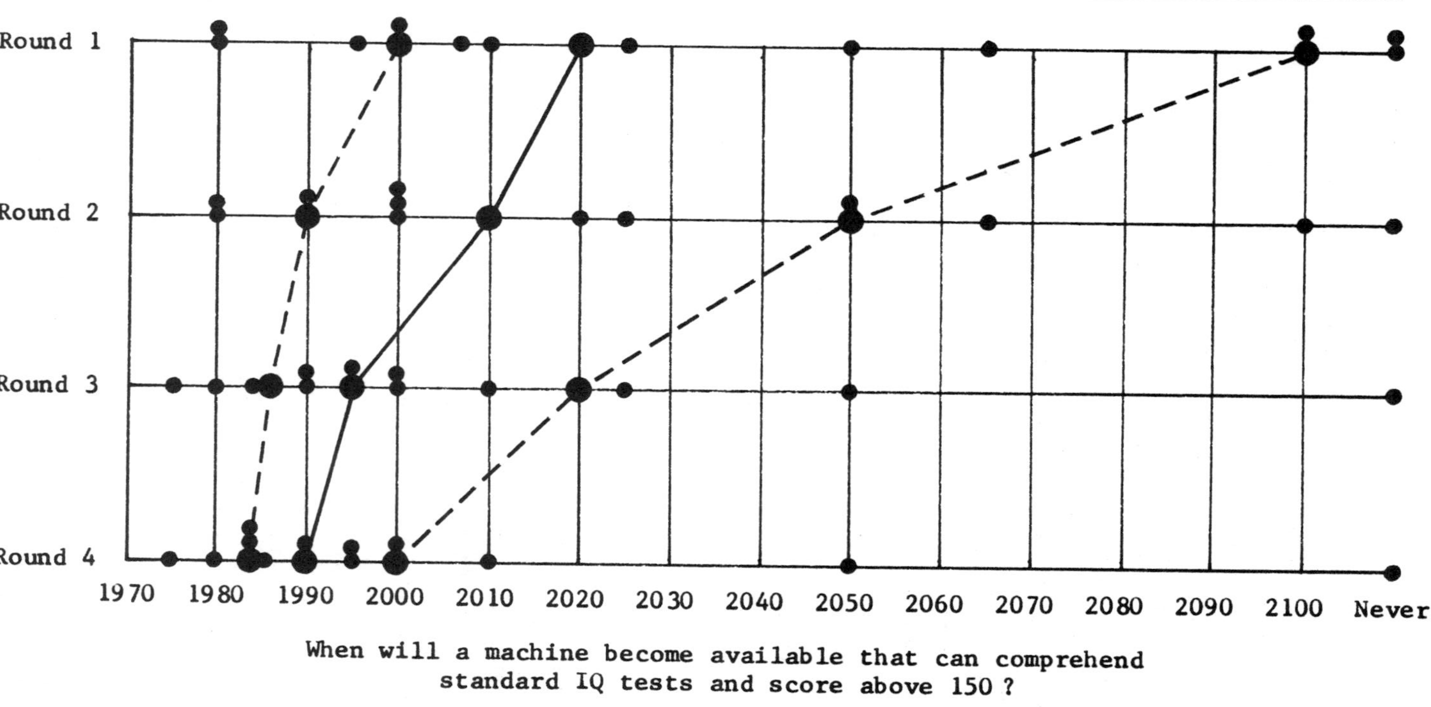
Round 1
Round 2
Round 3
Round 4
1970
1980
1990
2000
2010
2020
2030
2040
2050
2060
2070
2080
2090
2100
Never
When will a machine become available that can comprehend standard IQ tests and score above 150 ?

FIGURE 7

and then used the median of just these forecasts as the group consensus. It subsequently turned out that this select median, compared to the median of all responses, was closer to the true value in 13.5 out of 20 cases. [This was an experiment closely paralleling an earlier one conducted by Bernice Brown and myself at Rand in 1964, in which we had asked 20 almanac-type questions of a panel consisting of 23 Rand researchers. There, too, we had found that subgroups of respondents with a high self-ranking beat the entire group in two-thirds of the cases. See P-2986, Rand, 1964.]

Second, and finally, let me point out a slightly more sophisticated use of the Delphi approach, where it is used in conjunction with a simulated decision-making process. A typical situation to which this mode of using expertise is applicable is one in which budgetary decisions have to be made on the basis of cost-benefit estimates.

When costs and benefits are clearly measurable objective terms, there is no need to resort to the use of mere opinions. But in practice, benefits resulting from the choice of given policy alternatives are almost never capable of unambiguous measurement; even in the case of cost estimates it is usually only the dollar expenditures that are closely predictable, while social costs may be as elusive as the benefits. In such cases, a consensus of judgments made by experts may be helpful in obtaining an appraisal.

In a recent experiment conducted in the course of a project concerned with educational innovations, expert opinions were used in a context of this sort. Applying a Delphi process, we first obtained a list of potential educational innovations, together with rough cost estimates for each. We then asked the panel of experts to go through a simulated planning process by deciding how a given budget should be allocated to the educational innovations contained in the given list. In order to make these allocations rationally, the participants had to engage in an intuitive cost-benefit appraisal of each item on the list. The manner in which a group consensus of each such appraisal could best be obtained was by way of a Delphi synthesis of their individual opinions.

These examples are intended merely to illustrate the potentialities of the Delphi technique. Numerous further experiments need to be carried out to test the extent of its validity and to refine it to the point where it may be fully accepted as one of the standard tools for the analysis of the future and, in particular, for policy applications in the general area of social technology. ■

25 QUESTIONS OF VALIDITY

To be sure, a Delphi inquiry does not always yield the amount of opinion convergence shown in the instance of the question about a 150-IQ machine cited above. But by and large, statistically speaking, such a tendency has been well established. Even in cases in which the views of the experts do not converge but, as they sometimes do, cluster around two distinct values, the

Delphi inquiry serves the purpose of identifying the reasons why there is some disagreement among the experts and of ascertaining whether the nature of such disagreement is factual or purely semantic. (If it is the latter—that is, if a question had inadvertently been formulated so ambiguously as to allow different interpretations—then it behooves the conductor of the inquiry to amend the wording in subsequent rounds.)

It goes without saying that convergence per se, even when it occurs, is not sufficient to validate the method, because it is convergence toward the correct value that matters. A number of experiments have been conducted to establish that, on the average, such convergence in the right direction does indeed take place. The results have generally confirmed that this is the case, although admittedly the amount of such experimentation has to date been insufficient to satisfy the severest skeptics.

There are two reasons why relatively few experiments have been conducted to validate the predictive power of Delphi inquiries. One is that long-range forecasts cannot be verified until a sufficiently long time has elapsed, which may be on the order of ten or more years. The other is that Delphi is a method pertaining to the utilization of expert opinions; hence, to validate the method properly, experts would have to be used as laboratory subjects. But experts invariably are preoccupied with more pressing problems than making themselves available as guinea pigs for controlled laboratory experiments.

In view of this situation, experimenters have generally confined themselves to using as subjects surrogate experts in the form of graduate students and to replacing forecasting questions by retrospective "almanac-type" questions. The intuitive rationale for this procedure was that any results obtained thus would carry over to the case of forecasts derived by experts, because the basic thinking processes that are involved would not be all that different between (i) real experts and surrogate experts, and (ii) forecasts and retrocasts. (Personally, I share this confidence with regard to the second item; that is, the thinking process, say, on the part of an economist in predicting Japan's GNP for the year 2000 and retrospectively estimating Japan's GNP for the year 1950, is not likely to be too different. But I am somewhat skeptical with regard to the first item, since the anonymous debate generated by the Delphi procedure is likely to produce more convincing arguments when conducted among real experts than when conducted among would-be experts such as graduate students.)

As for the experiments that have been conducted, let me report briefly on a few. (1) Delphi experiments with student subjects, using almanac-type questions, which Norman Dalkey and I, and, later, Dalkey alone more extensively, conducted, have well confirmed that, statistically speaking, successive Delphi rounds tend to produce not only convergence but also convergence toward the true value. Most of such convergence, however, was observed between the first and second rounds, with later rounds adding little improvement—a fact that led me to the admittedly unproven contention expressed earlier that inexpert arguments among students are relatively unconvincing, whereas it might be expected that arguments among real experts would have been sufficiently convincing to produce further opinion convergence in later rounds. (2) At UCLA's business school, it has been the custom toward year's end to produce forecasts of economic and business indicators for the next year (such as GNP and automobile sales). On one such occasion, a doctoral student, Robert Campbell, used two classes of graduate business students to conduct a controlled experiment, in which he divided each class randomly into two halves, had one half produce forecasts by "conventional" methods (extrapolation, group discussion, and so on), and instructed the other half to use a four-round Delphi procedure. Verification, in this case, was available within one year, with the result that, in both experimental classes, the Delphi group won in two-thirds of the cases, in the sense of having produced a forecast that came closer to what later turned out to be the true value than did the control group. (3) As already mentioned in Section 21, an examination at the Institute for the Future of the validity of a substantial number of forecasts obtained earlier through Delphi inquiries showed, on the whole, encouragingly satisfactory results.

In addition to such explicit evidence of the validity of the Delphi technique in producing relatively reliable forecasts, there is, of course, a large body of intuitive confirmation obtained by hundreds of practitioners over the years.

However, there is no doubt that a good deal of further experimentation would be desirable, both to solidify claims to reliability or to superiority over other approaches and, perhaps even more important, to attain improvements in the technique that would raise its reliability. [Compare also what has been said earlier, in Section 20.3.3, as part of a proposed agenda for futures research.]

26 VARIANTS OF DELPHI

There is obviously nothing sacrosanct about the four-round Delphi procedure described earlier, and many variants have in fact been employed, ining the use of fewer or more than four rounds, changes in question format, and variations in panel structure.

Among the variants that may deserve special mention, aside from that using self-ratings, described above, I would like to list the following:

26.1 An Extra, Preliminary Round

The usual first round sometimes needs to be preceded by an open-ended initial round intended to help delineate the subject matter of the inquiry. Thus there might be an opening "Round 0" asking for entries to be considered in subsequent rounds. For instance, a technological forecasting study, instead of immediately inquiring into the probability of the occurrence of certain technological breakthroughs by some given date, might first invite the respondents to list potential breakthroughs that, in their opinion, ought to be included in the subsequent probability estimation procedure. Hence the preparatory Round 0 may not require numerical answers, which, for the ensuing regular rounds, is mandatory in order to make it possible to arrange the responses in linear order and compute the quartiles of their distribution.

26.2 Mini-Delphi

Mini-Delphi is an abbreviated procedure that is particularly efficient both in group decision-making situations and in cases in which mere order-of-magnitude estimates are called for. In a mini-Delphi inquiry, part (but not all) of the anonymity of the regular Delphi process is abandoned and the participants are together in the same room. The procedure in estimating (or deciding on) a specific quantity is as follows:

Step 1: Each panelist independently and secretly writes down his estimate of the quantity. The responses are collated by a nonpanelist, and their distribution is displayed before the group, without identifying specific responses by respondent.

Step 2: A brief debate takes place, in which participants have an opportunity to defend relatively low or relatively high values.

Step 3: Each panelist once more votes independently and secretly. The responses are collated, and their median is accepted as the group's consensus.

The efficiency of this procedure, say at gatherings such as board meetings, derives both from the elimination of lengthy debates over issues on which the first vote reveals essential unanimity, and from the guarantee of anonymity of the second vote taken after all had a chance to listen to arguments brought up in the discussion.

26.3 Ranking by Delphi

Occasionally the task before a group may be to rank a number of objects according to, say, preference. Here, although the responses are numerical, there is a slight problem in how to feed back the distribution of responses and, eventually, to obtain a group ranking. This requires the construction of a master ranking based on the individual respondents' rankings. There is no unique "correct" way of doing this, but I have found the following procedure convenient and fair: Establish, for each item, its median rank as well as its mean rank; order all items according to their median ranks and, in case of ties, use the mean rank to break the tie. If ties remain, revert to the group and, applying mini-Delphi to the tied items, establish their desired ranking.

26.4 Budget Allocation by Delphi

A similar problem, although slightly more intricate, arises when a group is to arrive through a Delphi process at the allocation of a given budget over a number of expenditure items. Again, there is the question of feeding back, and eventually adopting as the group's consensus, a master allocation derived from the individual allocations supplied by the participants. One possibility would be to allocate to each budget item the average amount allocated to it by the group members. This has the disadvantage of giving relatively too much weight to "extremists". For example, if among ten voters all but one wish to allocate zero to an item while the remaining one wishes to allocate 100 per cent of the budget to it, the average allocation would amount to 10 per cent, which would overrule the vast majority. Clearly, as is generally the case in Delphi-derived choices, the median (which in this case is zero) would be a fairer allocation, in the sense of being more democratic. However, the median allocations to a set of items do not generally add up to the given budget and, in fact, more often than not tend to underspend the available funds. This has led me to the following, median-based algorithm for obtaining an allocation that maximizes voter satisfaction; it is best explained by an example: Assume that ten voters, A through J, are to allocate a budget of 100 points over eight items, and suppose that their individual allocations are as shown in this tabulation:

	A	B	C	D	E	F	G	H	I	J
Item 1	10	30	5	10	25	10	0	10	0	20
Item 2	10	0	10	20	0	10	15	0	0	10
Item 3	20	0	40	20	25	10	10	20	40	10
Item 4	0	10	5	0	10	10	25	30	40	0
Item 5	10	30	5	10	15	20	10	10	5	15
Item 6	30	30	10	20	0	10	10	10	5	15
Item 7	10	0	25	5	25	20	15	20	5	30
Item 8	10	0	0	15	0	10	15	0	5	0

Now rearrange the allocations to each item in ascending order:

											M
Item 1	0	0	5	10	10	10	10	20	25	30	10
Item 2	0	0	0	0	10	10	10	10	15	20	10
Item 3	0	10	10	10	20	20	20	25	40	40	20
Item 4	0	0	0	5	10	10	10	25	30	40	10
Item 5	5	5	10	10	10	10	15	15	20	30	15
Item 6	0	5	10	10	10	10	15	20	30	30	10
Item 7	0	5	5	10	15	20	20	25	25	30	20
Item 8	0	0	0	0	0	5	10	10	15	15	5
	5	25	40	55	85	95	110	150	200	235	100

Add up each column (as shown) and determine which is the last one not exceeding the budget of 100. This is the sixth one, whose sum is 95. (Note, incidentally, that the medians, represented by the average of Columns 5 and 6, in this example add up to 90.) If we were to make the allocations indicated by column 6, we would in fact satisfy all the votes to the left of the dotted line—"satisfy" in the sense that at least the number of points desired by the voter has been allocated to an item. Having five more points to spend, we can seek to "capture" as many additional points as possible, in our example by adding five points either to Item 5 or to Item 7 or to Item 8, each of which choices would satisfy two additional votes. The choice between these options could easily be settled by majority vote or else by mini-Delphi. Suppose the choice fell on Item 5; then the final allocation would be that shown in the column headed M (for master allocation), which satisfies all the votes to the left of the solid line (56 out of 80, or 70 per cent).

26.5 Automated Delphi

Finally, reference ought to be made to recent experiments in automating part of the Delphi procedure. A four-round Delphi inquiry, if conducted via mailed questionnaires, is apt to take many months. To reduce the time required it is possible to make use of a computer network, have each respondent sit at a terminal, feed questionnaires to him in the form of a computer printout, have him respond by typing his answers, have the computer collate all responses and automatically produce the next questionnaire, and so on. In this mode of application, the total time required to run a Delphi inquiry may be reduced to a few hours or, even if time is allowed between rounds to think things over and to consult reference materials, to a few days. This type of "D-net" operation, as it has been called, has been successfully tried on several occasions, and it is safe to predict that, in the not-so-distant future, national (or even international) D-nets with large multidisciplinary rosters of experts will be at the disposal of decision makers in both the public and private sectors, constituting what might be considered a new form of public utility, which may well supersede the present, rather disorganized, utilization of the so-called advice community.

27 SUMMARY

By way of a summary it may be said that Delphi is a frequently used technique for eliciting a group opinion from a panel of experts, a technique that seems to have some advantage in reliability and possibly even in expeditiousness over more conventional methods of utilizing such a panel. There are many variants of the technique in existence, and further experimentation is needed to decide just which variant, under given circumstances, is optimal. Possible applications include the following:

- assessment of present conditions and issues;
- market forecasts;
- long-term technological and societal forecasts regarding a corporation's or a public institution's future operating environments;
- normative forecasts, i.e., the formulation of corporate or governmental goals and policies;
- the identification, including possibly the invention, of potential measures for implementing a given policy;
- the comparative evaluation of alternative action programs (including their interaction with the operating environment, a subject that may also involve cross-impact analysis); and
- management decision-making in the public and private sectors.

Chapter VI

Cross-Impact Analysis

28 ORIGIN OF THE CROSS-IMPACT CONCEPT

The cross-impact concept, already briefly mentioned in Section 21.6, was first thought of in recognition of the fact that forecasts of future events, when made in isolation from one another, fail to take their mutual effects into systematic consideration and thus lack a degree of refinement whose addition, it was felt, might well increase their reliability. Cross-impact analysis, I believe, has indeed made a contribution to this effect. Moreover, it has turned out, in the difficult context of multidisciplinary considerations, to serve as an aid in model-building and thus in the first step toward theory construction.

The original impetus for translating the germ of the cross-impact idea into a practical device arose in the context of a parlor game called Future, which Ted Gordon and I had been commissioned in 1966 to design for Kaiser Aluminum as a promotional idea. That game dealt with the construction of a future world twenty years hence in which some or all of sixty potential events (technological breakthroughs, legislative measures, natural occurrences, international treaties, and the like) might have taken place. Each of these had initially set probabilities of occurrence (taken in part from our own long-range forecasting study; see Chapter 8). These probabilities, however, underwent changes as the play of the game progressed, partly due to the influence of player actions and partly—this is where the cross-impact notion came in—because a given event's probability of occurrence was assumed to be influenced by the prior occurrence or nonoccurrence of some of the other events in the set.

29 THE FUTURE OF X

The crude model underlying the game just described was subsequently refined to make it suitable for scientific applications to the study of the future.

Suppose we were interested in the future of subject matter X, possibly because we are, in fact, planning the future of X. For example, X might be a particular business firm, or higher education in the United States, or a certain city's transportation system, or the global food supply. Our first step might be to set an appropriate time horizon, which might be a year or a decade from now or even farther in the future. Next we might ask ourselves in what ways the operating environment for X is likely to change between the present and that time horizon; that is, what events might take place that (a) have a reasonable chance of occurring and (b) if they occurred would have an important impact on the future of X and, therefore, on whatever plans we may be formulating regarding the future of X.

Let a list of such events be $E_1, E_2, \ldots, E_m$. These events may be of such a kind that we have no control at all over their occurrence (e.g., natural or even man-made catastrophes), and thus may represent completely external determinants of our planning environment. They may also include events that, while beyond our full control, can be influenced by us, in the sense that our actions may affect the probability of their occurrence (e.g., technological breakthroughs and acts of legislation, which can be made more likely by R & D expenditures and lobbying efforts, respectively). Events completely under our control, that is, potential actions that we can choose to undertake as part of the implementation of a planning effort, should not be included among the Es but reserved for separate consideration.

In a practical planning context, if the number m of events originally selected for inclusion is unmanageably large, the planning team may find it advisable to conduct a mini-Delphi among themselves, rank-ordering the suggested events by importance and then dropping off (at least temporarily) those that fall below some reasonable cutoff point in that ranking.

In a straightforward Delphi-type forecasting effort, the next task would appropriately consist in an estimation of the probability, over time, of the occurrence of each of the selected events. When conducting a cross-impact analysis, this process is indispensable, too, but it would be regarded as merely the first step, namely, as the estimation of the *ceteris paribus* probability of each event, to be amended later due to the mutual effects, or "cross-impacts", of the occurrence or nonoccurrence of some of the other events.

In reflecting how best to undertake a study of the future of X or, more properly, of the potential futures of X, it soon became apparent that the developments relevant to such an investigation, in addition to events, which are occurrences at some point in time, should include trends, that is, gradual developments best described by time series. Examples of such trends are population, GNP, rainfall, profits, crime rates, and energy consumption.

Thus, in addition to selecting events $E_1, E_2, \ldots, E_m$, we should ask ourselves, in setting out to study the future of X, what trends are relevant to X, relevant in the sense that either (a) they are important indicators of how well X is doing, or (b) they are such that unexpected changes in them would (like the occurrence of an event E_i) have a noticeable impact on the future of X and, by implication, on plans relating to that future. Let $T_1, T_2, \ldots, T_n$ be the trends selected for this purpose. (Again, as in the case of events, if their number initially is unmanageably large, they may have to be pared down, possibly through the convenient device of a mini-Delphi.)

In analogy to estimating the probability of occurrence of each E_i, we would next seek some *ceteris paribus* estimates of the future course of each T_j, between the present and the chosen time horizon. Again, a Delphi procedure may be the appropriate vehicle. Once this has been accomplished, we can address the question of the mutual influences of event occurrences and trend fluctuations; this is done by setting up a cross-impact matrix.

30 CROSS-IMPACT MATRICES

Let us refer to events and trends jointly as "developments". If k of these are under consideration (in the above example: $k = m+n$), they might be designated by $D_1, D_2, D_3, \ldots, D_k$. The corresponding "cross-impact matrix" is a two-entry table, as shown in Figure 8.

Each cell in this matrix will eventually carry some cross-impact information. For instance, the cell where the D_2 row intersects the D_3 column, indicated by a dot, will carry information about the extent to which D_2 will affect D_3 (note the direction of the arrow). Here, if D_2 is an event, it will be its occurrence or nonoccurrence that will cause the effect; if D_2 is a trend, it will be the size and direction of the deviation from its predicted course that will cause the effect. The effect on D_3, in turn, depends on whether D_3 is an event or a trend. If it is an event, the effect will be a raising or lowering of its probability of occurrence; if it is a trend, the effect will be an upward or downward fluctuation and thus a deviation from its predicted course.

We note immediately—and this will be an important aspect of cross-impact analysis—that a development, if it suffers an impact, may in turn

↗	D_1	D_2	D_3	. . .	D_k
D_1					
D_2			o		
D_3					
.					
.					
.					
D_k					

FIGURE 8

exert impacts on other developments, and so on, so that we will be able to observe a rippling, or ricochet, effect. This will have significant implications for the planning process, especially in the context of so-called technology assessment (to be discussed in a later chapter).

In practice, it may be expedient to reintroduce explicitly the distinction between events and trends. The cross-impact matrix then assumes the more complex format shown in Figure 9.

A convenient procedure preparatory to constructing a quantitative cross-impact matrix is to set up, first, a "qualitative cross-impact matrix", such as shown in the example of Figure 10. Here, a + indicates a noticeable effect in the same direction (e.g., occurrence of E_2 raises the probability of E_3 and

	E_1 E_2 ... E_m	T_1 T_2 ... T_n
E_1 E_2 ⋮ E_m		
T_1 T_2 ⋮ T_n		

FIGURE 9

	E_1	E_2	E_3	T_1	T_2
E_1		+			--
E_2	-		+		+
E_3	+				
T_1		+			
T_2		++		-	

FIGURE 10

raises the level of T_2). A − indicates an effect in the opposite direction (e.g., E_2's occurrence lowers the probability of E_1, and a rise or fall in T_2 lowers or raises T_1, respectively). A double symbol, ++ or −−, indicates a particularly strong impact. The absence of any symbol shows that the impact, if any, is negligibly small. Here again, a practical way of constructing a qualitative cross-impact matrix of this kind is through a mini-Delphi.

There have been a number of different suggestions for converting a qualitative into a quantitative cross-impact matrix (including several by myself). Before presenting, at least in outline, my current thinking on this issue, I would like to make some general remarks on the cross-impact approach which are independent of the particular numerical procedure that is adopted for dealing quantitatively with cross-impacts.

31 INTERDISCIPLINARY MODELING[1]

Traditional social modeling, which originally got under way largely in the field of economics and has since spread to many other societal areas, tends to exhibit certain deficiencies that detract from the verisimilitude of the models and hence from their predictive capability. This becomes particularly noticeable when such models are intended to be applied to highly complex systems.

Econometric models of national economic trends, for example, while of great value in displaying certain relationships between economic variables, generally fail to yield accurate forecasts for the national economic system as a whole. This has been seen very clearly in the attempts to use such models for guidance in the management of the Indian economy; and more recently, in the United States, we have observed the failure to halt inflationary tendencies despite the application of the monetary and fiscal policies suggested by traditional economic models. [Since this was written, the rate of inflation in the United States, after a further sizable increase, has decreased substantially, though perhaps as an inadvertent side effect of other economic measures.] Similarly, with regard to the system-dynamics approach applied by Forrester and Meadows to the problem of global resources and reported in *Limits to Growth,* there is a widespread belief that even that model, though more sophisticated than traditional ones in some respects, is not fully successful in the manner in which it attempts to represent real-world relationships. The reason for the inadequacy of these models is that they have at least one, and sometimes all, of the following shortcomings:

(i) they are unidisciplinary rather than multidisciplinary;
(ii) they reflect correlations only, rather than causalities;
(iii) they exhibit trends only rather than events as well as trends;

1. This section is taken from the opening pages of "Interdisciplinary Modeling", a chapter I contributed to *World Modeling,* edited by C. W. Churchman and R. O. Mason (New York: Elsevier, 1976).

(iv) they contain no explicit feedback loops; and
(v) they are deterministic rather than probabilistic.

These failings, or their positive counterparts (multidisciplinarity, attention to causal effects, inclusion of events, allowance for feedback, and consideration of probabilistic uncertainty), are not entirely independent attributes. For example, an econometric model of a national economy, typically consisting of a set of simultaneous equations (both algebraic and ordinary differential equations), which under "normal" conditions works well and may quite adequately reflect the operation of the real economy, may experience a "system break" caused by an external occurrence that can only be handled within the model by abruptly switching to a different set of input parameters. [For a discussion of system breaks see, for example, Winthrop, 1972.] Such a discontinuity is usually traceable to a noneconomic source (see item i above), it represents a causal effect rather than a correlation (item ii), and more often than not is brought about not by a gradual development (a trend, such as rising expectations) but a point event in time (such as a technological breakthrough, a natural catastrophe, a legislative act; see item iii). Moreover, the reaction of the economic system to such exogenous influences generally has reverse repercussions on the external system, which, in turn, may produce subsequent shocks to the economy. But the model offers no means of reflecting such (positive or negative) feedback (item iv), nor can it take into account the uncertainty attaching to exogenous interventions by assigning appropriate probabilities to their occurrence (item v).

In order to deal with matters of causality, it is necessary to introduce an explicit time direction and go beyond the simultaneous, merely correlative, interaction of trends. In a model consisting of a set of simultaneous equations, this means that some of these would have to be difference equations or differential difference equations, so as to be capable of relating occurrences at one time to other, "causal", occurrences at an earlier time. This feature, incidentally, is present in the system-dynamics approach, and it permits the introduction of feedback loops, where, say, a rise in trend A causes a subsequent decline in trend B, which in turn may cause a further rise in trend A at a later time. (Thus, feedback loops—item v—presuppose the ability to handle causal effects—item ii.) The system-dynamics model also is multidisciplinary (item i) but is deficient in items iii (inclusion of events) and v (probability). Of these, the noninclusion of events is likely to be the more significant omission, while the ability to handle probabilistic uncertainty is merely a related, convenient expedient for modeling the occurrence of relevant events.

At present, there does not seem to be a wholly satisfactory method of modeling intricate social systems in such a way as to utilize the powerful traditional simultaneous-equations approach and at the same time include all of the characteristics enumerated here as desirable. However, I do not regard this problem as insurmountable, and in fact there is a new approach being developed that seems to go in the right direction. It offers enough promise to deserve the attention of others interested in modeling complex social interactions, and the purpose of this essay is to present for wider consideration the potential merits of this new approach.

We note, first of all, that the system-dynamics model can easily be extended to accommodate probabilistic features. This means that only one of the five deficiencies mentioned earlier would still apply, namely, the noninclusion of "events", that is, occurrences at a certain point in time that cannot conveniently, or even logically, be handled as mere trend fluctuations.

The problem, then, is one of devising a method of modeling the possible occurrence of potential events and of doing so in a manner that permits the adjoining of such an events model, in a natural way, to a traditional trends model of the econometric or system-dynamics type.

The approach to the solution of this problem I want to present here . . . ■ (as will be obvious to the reader) is that of cross-impact analysis, which puts us in a position to look for systematic relationships between potential developments (events as well as trends) and thus provides us a way to pursue what had been thought of by many as a lost cause, namely, a theoretical approach to law-like regularities in the inexact sciences.

Once we shall have succeeded in converting a qualitative cross-impact matrix constructed to study the future of X into a quantitative matrix by filling its cells with numerical coefficients telling us just how each development D_i affects each other development D_j, we will have a powerful planning tool at our disposal. Suppose that D_j is a desirable development that we wish to promote (either an event to be brought about or a trend to be enhanced). Then we can examine alternative action plans that are feasible, consider how they would affect not only D_j directly but any other development D_i that, in turn, will affect D_j as specified by the cross-impact coefficients, and then attempt to optimize among these choices.

Actions proposed by a planner and enacted by a decision maker are also, of course, events of a kind; but conceptually they must be clearly distinguished from the events considered as cross-impact entries, their occurrence being subject to deliberate decision rather than pure probability. However, an action (an "enacted event"), while not subject to cross-impact-induced probability fluctuations, has impacts on other developments not unlike those caused by the occurrence of stochastic events included in the cross-impact model. These impacts and the chains of cross-impacts triggered by them can, and should, be taken into consideration by the planner, lest he overlook possibly deleterious side effects of his proposed action plan.

An action, or a set of actions, may serve to pursue several goals simultaneously (the enhancement of several D_j, in cross-impact terminology). In that case, as is often true in a planning situation, the selection of one out of several possible plans of action may require the prior construction of indifference curves regarding the outcome in terms of expected enhancements of D_js. Moreover, since different actions generally have different costs associated with them, such indifference curves may have to take into account, in addition to the effect on the D_js, the cost of the actions.

No amount of analysis, even if the input figures could be trusted completely, can ever remove a residue of uncertainty; nor should it, since the future is not predictable but only forecastable in probabilistic terms. In cross-impact analysis, uncertainty appears explicitly in the form of the events included in the model whose occurrences are subject to estimated probability distributions over time.

Needless to say, the inputs into a cross-impact model carry with them additional uncertainties, since they have to be derived largely if not wholly from intuitive expert estimates. These "judgmental data" include the *ceteris paribus* event probabilities and trend values over the time interval from the present to the chosen time horizon, as well as the cross-impact coefficients (yet to be specified). In applications of a cross-impact model to a planning effort, these judgmental inputs have to be further augmented by cost and benefit estimates, each of which is apt to be multidimensional, since generally social costs and benefits may have to be considered in addition to monetary ones.

In practice it has been found that a complex area of inquiry may require a sizable cross-impact matrix for realistic study. An example to be presented later will involve a 20×20 matrix (9 events and 11 trends), but often substantially larger matrices may be called for. The sheer volume of judgmental inputs needed and the repeated running of a model involving all these inputs make it mandatory to have highly efficient methods of extracting estimates from appropriately chosen experts (mini-Delphi turns out to be handy for this purpose) and to have an interactive computer program, interactive in the sense that displays of intermediate results will enable planners to interject actions on a trial-and-error basis. This latter mode of operation, it should be noted, is a special form of simulation gaming, to which we return later.

32 CONSTRUCTION OF A CROSS-IMPACT MODEL

The cross-impact concept has been in a state of evolution since its inception some fifteen years ago. Early versions, my own as well as those proposed by others, have proved to be unsatisfactory in some regards, although that has not detracted particularly from their applicability. I have developed a revised approach (to be presented later in this chapter), but the detailed example to be reproduced presently is of an earlier version, because documentation for it is readily available and, moreover, the conceptual apparatus is somewhat more transparent than is the case for the latest variant.

The steps required to set up a cross-impact model for studying the future of X are as described below; they are, incidentally, largely independent of the particular variant of cross-impact analysis that is employed. Each step will be illustrated with an example representing a twenty-development application to the global-resources problem which is the subject matter of *Limits to Growth* (Meadows et al., 1972). Much of this material is taken from an earlier study of mine undertaken under the auspices of IIASA,[2] where a computer program for this model was written by Günther Fischer.

Step 1: Choice of the subject matter X.

Example: Global resources.

Step 2: Choice of the time horizon.

Example: Fifty years hence, i.e., 2027 (since the study was conducted in 1977).

Step 3: Stipulation of the temporal "resolution", i.e., the fineness of the temporal grid.

Example: Five years. In other words, the entire fifty-year period from 1977 to 2027 is broken down into ten "scenes" of five years each; that is, the changing condition of the world is examined once every five years.

Step 4: Identification of the decision makers; they are the "players" of the cross-impact game, i.e., of the cross-impact model being constructed when it is used as a simulation game.

Example: For illustrative purposes, we have chosen three players: (a) the United Nations, (b) the United States, (c) OPEC.

Step 5: Selection of the potential future events that have a nonnegligible chance of occurring and that would, if they occurred, have a profound effect on the future of X.

Example: Nine events were selected.

E_1: breeder reactor (the placing into operation of the first breeder reactor with a capacity of at least 500,000 kw)

E_2: solar power plant (the placing into operation of the first solar power plant with a capacity of at least 500,000 kw)

E_3: fusion power plant (the placing into operation of the first fusion power plant with a capacity of at least 500,000 kw)

E_4: storage battery (a technological breakthrough making it economically feasible to store large quantities of electricity)

*E_5: mineral extraction (a technological breakthrough in mineral extraction—including, for example, ocean mining and the use of satellites for detection of

2. Olaf Helmer, *Cross-Impact Gaming Applied to Global Resources,* RM-78-4 (Schloss Laxenburg, Austria: International Institute for Applied Systems Analysis, 1978).

ore deposits—making it possible to extract minerals at less than half of the previous cost)

*E_6: depollution (a technological breakthrough in depollution, making it possible to achieve depollution at less than half of the previous cost)

*E_7: nonagricultural food (a technological breakthrough in nonagricultural food production, such as aquaculture or manufacture of artificial protein, making it economically feasible to increase the previous world food production by at least 20 percent)

E_8: weather control (a technological breakthrough making it economically feasible to bring about substantial regional weather changes)

E_9: transmutation (a breakthrough in physics making it economically feasible to manufacture many chemical elements from subatomic building blocks and thus to convert abundantly available low-grade substances into high-grade raw materials)

(Note that none of these events can be brought about directly by player decisions; most of them, if not all, however, can be affected by such decisions.) Some events, annotated with asterisks, are potentially recurrent; the remainder may occur only once.

Step 6: Selection of the trends that ought to be monitored, either because they are important indicators of how well X is faring or because unexpected deviations of their values from their anticipated courses would profoundly affect the future of X.

Example: Eleven trends were selected.

T_1 : world population (in billions)

T_2 : food per capita (using an index value of 100 for 1977)

T_3 : pollution (an overall index of pollution, on a scale from 0 [= no pollution] to 100 [= all life extinct], with the 1977 level set arbitrarily at 25)

T_4 : raw materials (the known reserves of nonrenewable raw materials, other than fuel, that are economically exploitable by existing extraction methods, using an index value of 100 for 1977)

T_5 : industrial output per capita (using an index value of 100 for 1977)

T_6 : birth-control acceptance (the percentage of the world's population who in principle have accepted the idea of birth control)

T_7 : acreage productivity (a world average, using an index value of 100 for 1977)

T_8 : energy production (the total production of all forms of energy, using an index value of 100 for 1977)

T_9 : investment fraction (the amount of investment in capital goods, expressed as the percentage of the sum of such investment and personal-consumption expenditures)

T_{10}: harvest conditions (the average harvest conditions, as determined by weather, pests, diseases, and natural catastrophes, measured on a scale from 0 to 100, with the 1977 level set arbitrarily at 50)

T_{11}: quality of life (a world average, measured on a scale from 0 to 100, with the 1977 level set arbitrarily at 50)

(We note that the first five of these are identical with the five principal trends whose interactions were investigated in the *Limits to Growth* study.)

Step 7: Description of the actions that the players may take.

Example: Among the many that might have been chosen, the following were selected to illustrate the potentials of a gaming application. The parenthetical letters refer to the players:

A_1 : ban of fission reactors (a,b)
A_2 : depollution treaty (a)
A_3 : establishment of a world food bank (a)
A_4 : global agritechnology transfer (a, b)
A_5 : oil supply disruption (c)
A_6 : law discouraging energy waste (b)
A_7 : global birth-control propaganda (a, b)
A_8-A_{16}: R&D to promote E_1-E_9 respectively (b)
A_{17}: R&D to promote T_5 (b)
A_{18}: R&D to promote T_{10} (a, b)

Step 8: Determination of a budget for each player and each scene, as well as price tags for the actions.

Example: The details in this regard will not be included here.

Having thus chosen the elements to be represented in the model, the next steps are to provide some numerical estimates for the input data. Except for the (then) present, 1977, situation (the initial status of Scene 1), all of the inputs refer to the future; hence, by their nature, they can at best be based on extrapolations from the past but in all cases require some expert judgment. To obtain such judgmental data, a method such as Delphi recommends itself.

Step 9: Estimation of event probabilities.

Example: The following probabilities of occurrence of the events, by scene, are illustrative only; they are intended to be accurate only in their order of magnitude.

Scene	*1*	*2*	*3*	*4*	*5*	*6*	*7*	*8*	*9*	*10*
E_1	0.04	0.12	0.20	0.24	0.22	0.14	0.09	0.07	0.06	0.05
E_2	0.02	0.10	0.35	0.50	0.60	0.65	0.70	0.75	0.80	0.85
E_3	0.00	0.00	0.02	0.06	0.15	0.30	0.40	0.44	0.43	0.40
E_4	0.10	0.25	0.35	0.40	0.40	0.35	0.30	0.25	0.20	0.15
E_5	0.10	0.19	0.27	0.34	0.40	0.45	0.49	0.52	0.54	0.55
E_6	0.05	0.07	0.10	0.15	0.20	0.25	0.29	0.32	0.34	0.35
E_7	0.01	0.02	0.04	0.06	0.09	0.12	0.16	0.20	0.25	0.30
E_8	0.01	0.02	0.04	0.06	0.09	0.12	0.16	0.20	0.25	0.30
E_9	0.00	0.00	0.01	0.01	0.02	0.02	0.03	0.03	0.04	0.04

Step 10: Estimation of anticipated trend values.

Example: The following are illustrative estimates of the trend values at the beginning of each scene. (The value at the beginning of Scene 11, of course, represents the terminal value for Scene 10.)

Scene	*1*	*2*	*3*	*4*	*5*	*6*	*7*	*8*	*9*	*10*	*11*
T_1	3.9	4.3	4.7	5.0	5.3	5.6	5.9	6.1	6.3	6.5	6.7
T_2	100	96	93	92	92	93	94	95	97	100	102
T_3	25	30	34	37	39	40	40	36	31	26	20
T_4	100	95	90	95	91	78	81	85	90	96	103
T_5	100	101	103	106	110	115	121	128	136	145	155
T_6	20	24	28	32	36	40	44	48	52	56	60
T_7	100	101	103	106	110	115	121	128	136	145	155
T_8	100	110	120	132	145	160	178	197	217	240	264
T_9	20	21	22	23	24	25	26	27	28	29	30
T_{10}	50	51	52	53	54	55	56	57	58	59	60
T_{11}	50	48	45	42	40	41	42	44	48	53	60

Step 11: Estimation of the "volatility" of each trend. Each trend, T_j, aside from being thrown off course by cross-impacts, is assumed to sustain random fluctuations in each scene (due, as it were, to unspecified impacts from causes not explicitly included in the model). The distribution of these fluctuations is assumed to be normal, with quartiles at $t_j \pm v_j$, where t_j is the expected trend value one scene hence and v_j is the trend's volatility.

Example: For simplicity, the volatilities of each trend have been assumed to be constant for all scenes, as follows:

T	T_1	T_2	T_3	T_4	T_5	T_6	T_7	T_8	T_9	T_{10}	T_{11}
v	.05	2	1.5	2.5	4	3	3	5	.5	5	2.5

If, for instance, the value of T_1 at the beginning of Scene 5 should, indeed, turn out to be 5.3 as indicated in Step 10, the forecast for the beginning of Scene 6 (shown as 5.6) should be interpreted as being a value drawn from a normal distribution about 5.6 whose quartiles are at $5.6 \pm .05$ (i.e., at 5.55 and 5.65). The randomization introduced in this manner simulates exogenous sources of uncertainty with which a planner would be faced in the real world.

Step 12: Laying out the qualitative cross-impact matrix. This intermediate step toward constructing the quantitative cross-impact matrix is helpful since it settles the question of which of the matrix cells require the numerical estimation of cross-impact coefficients. (Often, in practice, only one-quarter to one-third of all cells have nonzero entries.) In deciding where there are (nonzero) impacts, it is important to avoid double counting. If a development A has an impact on B, and B on C, then A has an indirect impact on C, which must be distinguished from any additional direct impact on C that A may or may not have. Only if it does should such an impact be noted as a nonzero entry.

Example:

	E_1	E_2	E_3	E_4	E_5	E_6	E_7	E_8	E_9	T_1	T_2	T_3	T_4	T_5	T_6	T_7	T_8	T_9	T_{10}	T_{11}
E_1		-	-						+			--					++			-
E_2	-		-	+								--					++			
E_3	--	-							+			--					++			
E_4		++										--				+				+
E_5									-				++							
E_6	-	-	-									--								+
E_7								-			++					-		+		
E_8												-							+	+
E_9	+		+		-								++					+		
T_1		+	+				+			+	-	+		-	+	+		-		
T_2							-			+	+		+							+
T_3	+	+	+			+				-		+							-	-
T_4					-			-					+	+						
T_5												+	-		+	+		-		+
T_6										-					+					
T_7							-				++					+				
T_8	-	-	-										+	+		+	+	+		
T_9	+	+	+	+	+	+	+	+	+					++		+	+	+		-
T_{10}							-				++									
T_{11}																		+		

Step 13: Construction of the quantitative cross-impact matrix; i.e., estimation of the numerical cross-impact coefficients to take the place of the symbols used in the qualitative matrix. This, of course, requires a definition of just what each coefficient is to indicate. Since a model somewhat different from this one will be presented later, the definition applicable to the current case will not be included at this point. I will merely mention that, in describing the cross-impact from one trend to another, say from T_1 to T_2, both the triggering deviation (of T_1 from its anticipated value) and the induced deviation (of T_2) are measured in units of the volatilities v_1 and v_2, respectively. If d_1 and d_2 are the deviations thus measured and c_{12} is the cross-impact coefficient, then essentially $d_2 = c_{12}d_1$ (except for a scale transformation, which serves to assure that the trend values remain within a prescribed interval from a minimal to a maximal value, e.g., between 0 and 100 if the trend represents a percentage). The volatility may be considered a natural choice for the unit of measurement, because by using it we compare the size of a trend fluctuation with that of a normal background fluctuation sustained due to external (unspecified) causes.

Example: The entire quantitative cross-impact matrix will not be reproduced here, but a few examples of cross-impact coefficients may serve as illustrations: (i) The effect of investment on industrial output: the cross-impact from T_9 to T_5 is 1.5; hence if T_9 in Scene 6 is not 25 but, say, 26, which is two units larger since the unit v_9=.5, it follows that the value of T_5 in the next scene (i.e., Scene 7) will be approximately 1.5×2, or three units larger than it would have been without this impact (approximately only, because of the aforementioned scale transformation, which introduces a slight distortion); since v_5=4, this means that T_5 will be increased by 12. (ii) The effect of weather control on pollution: the cross-impact from E_8 on T_3 is −1; hence the occurrence of E_8 causes the value of T_3 to be lowered by approximately −1×1.5, or −1.5. (iii) Self-impact of the population: if T_1, for whatever reason, deviates from its anticipated value, this deviation will largely carry over to the next scene, and in fact the cross-impact coefficient from T_1 to T_1 itself is assumed in this model to be .95.

Step 14: Determination of the impacts of any actions. This requires the construction of an impact matrix such as that shown in Figure 11, in which the impact of each action on each development contained in the model is indicated.

Example: As in Step 8, the details in this regard will not be included here.

	D_1 D_2 D_3 . . .
A_1	
A_2	
A_3	
⋮	

FIGURE 11

The model should now be ready to run. While, in principle, it can be run by hand, using paper and pencil and a table of random numbers, if the model is at all sizable (such as the 20 × 20 illustrative example we have been using), the use of a computer program is virtually indispensable.

33 *RUNNING A CROSS-IMPACT MODEL*

To begin with, to check the proper performance of the model, it is best to conduct a number of "basic runs", in which no interventive actions are taken. A single such run proceeds as follows:

In Scene 1, "decide" by a standard Monte Carlo drawing of random numbers which of the events occur. This standard procedure consists in comparing each event's probability p of occurring in Scene 1 with a randomly drawn two-place number r between .00 and .99; if $r < p$, the event is assumed to occur, otherwise not. Next, in accordance with these occurrences and nonoccurrences (the latter induce balancing deviations in the opposite direction from those induced by the former), adjust the event probabilities and trend values for Scene 2 as prescribed by the cross-impact matrix.

Then proceed to Scene 2, having adjusted the trend values further by adding random volatility deviates. Again decide which events are now occurring, and also observe the deviations of trend values from their anticipated values as of the beginning of Scene 2. Adjust the event probabilities and trend values for Scene 3 according to the cross-impacts caused by event occurrences (or nonoccurrences) and trend value deviations. Repeat the procedure for all remaining scenes (Scenes 3 through 10, in our example). The result will be a "scenario" of event occurrences, by scenes, and of trend value adjustments.

A basic run might result in the following typical scenario:

Event occurrences:

Scene	*1*	*2*	*3*	*4*	*5*	*6*	*7*	*8*	*9*	*10*
E_1				1						
E_2					1					
E_3									1	
E_4				1						
E_5		1					1			
E_6					1					
E_7										1
E_8								1		
E_9							1			

Trend values:

Scene	*1*	*2*	*3*	*4*	*5*	*6*	*7*	*8*	*9*	*10*	*11*
T_1	3.9	4.2	4.4	4.5	4.4	4.5	4.7	5.0	5.5	5.8	6.2
T_2	99	88	81	78	79	96	113	114	118	120	127
T_3	26	33	32	38	37	28	23	25	20	14	12
T_4	98	92	100	90	80	85	109	117	130	142	148
T_5	99	86	96	126	133	111	154	184	193	198	204
T_6	23	31	32	28	32	40	42	45	60	73	72
T_7	95	90	95	100	106	122	129	145	164	187	188
T_8	105	113	119	130	150	173	212	234	283	304	345
T_9	19	20	24	24	22	24	27	29	29	31	31
T_{10}	49	52	45	45	56	61	64	57	65	71	65
T_{11}	50	49	37	32	34	39	49	59	57	68	66

Two basic runs will yield different scenarios because of the random effects that are present. A large number of runs should produce average trend values close to the input values and frequencies of event occurrences in each scene that closely reflect the input probabilities.

We note for future reference that the particular basic run exhibited above happens to have produced the following noteworthy features: A very low level of harvest conditions (T_{10}) in Scenes 3 and 4 causes per-capita food (T_2) to be very low in Scenes 4 and 5, in turn causing population (T_1) to be 3 to 6 percent lower than expected thereafter. The occurrence of the first breeder reactor (E_1) and the first solar power plant (E_2) in Scenes 4 and 5 causes energy production (T_8) to rise substantially above the anticipated values. The (unusual) occurrence of transmutation of elements (E_9) in Scene 7 causes raw materials (T_4) to rise sharply toward the end.

Next, after one or, preferably, several basic runs, some sensitivity runs might be conducted, aimed at ascertaining how sensitively the outcome depends on some of the inputs or on some of the random occurrences. For instance, one might ask how different the results would be if the cross-impact from weather control (E_8) on pollution (T_3) were doubled, or if transmutation of elements (E_9) were achieved in Scene 1, or if birth-control acceptance (T_6) were 10 percent higher throughout. The results of such sensitivity tests are likely to give valuable clues to where policymakers, in deciding on an action plan, might best concentrate their leverage in order to achieve their goals.

To illustrate the idea of a sensitivity run, let me select just one such example: How would the basic scenario be affected if, in Scenes 1 and 2, a substantially lower per-capita food supply (T_2) were assumed? In order to be able to compare a new basic run, conducted with this change in inputs, directly with the basic run recorded earlier, it is essential to use the same random numbers at analogous decision points, so that we will be equally "lucky" or "unlucky" in both cases. The resulting scenario was as follows:

Event occurrences: No change from the original basic case, except that E_6 (depollution), which had occurred in Scene 5, did not occur at all.

Trend values:

Scene	*1*	*2*	*3*	*4*	*5*	*6*	*7*	*8*	*9*	*10*	*11*
T_1	3.9	4.1	4.1	4.3	4.4	4.6	4.7	5.0	5.5	5.8	6.2
T_2	93	80	82	84	84	97	112	113	117	119	127
T_3	26	33	31	36	36	34	28	30	25	17	13
T_4	98	92	101	90	76	81	106	118	131	142	149
T_5	99	85	98	133	139	113	151	183	192	197	203
T_6	23	31	32	28	33	42	44	45	60	73	72
T_7	95	90	94	99	105	123	129	145	164	186	188
T_8	105	113	119	130	149	173	211	233	283	303	345
T_9	19	20	23	23	22	24	27	29	29	30	31
T_{10}	49	52	45	45	57	61	62	55	64	70	65
T_{11}	50	45	31	34	40	44	48	58	55	67	66

We note that the effect of a lower per-capita food supply (T_2) in Scenes 1 and 2 is to lower the population (T_1) in Scenes 2 to 4 substantially; but the smaller population, in turn, causes T_2, and consequently T_1 itself, to rise again later, so that the final population figures toward the end are comparable to those of the basic case. These fluctuations also are reflected in the values of the quality of life (T_{11}). The nonoccurrence of progress in depollution (E_6) noted above can be traced to something of a fluke: The lowering in population size (T_1) caused pollution (T_3) to decline slightly, which in turn reduced the probability of E_6's occurrence; the value of the applicable random number must have been just below the probability of occurrence of E_6 in Scene 5 in the basic case but just above the new, slightly reduced probability in this new run. (The rationale for this reduction in probability, by the way, was that the effort to bring about E_6, with the decreased need for it, would itself decrease.)

Similar in nature to a sensitivity test, such as exemplified above, is the case of players' interventions. To illustrate a simple one-player intervention, we may examine the effect of an OPEC oil embargo in Scene 1. Again, to make direct comparisons with the basic case possible, the same random numbers were used at analogous points. The scenario resulting from Player c taking Action A_5 in Scene 1 was as follows:

Event occurrences: No change from the basic case, except that E_3 (fusion power), which had occurred in Scene 9, did not occur at all.

Trend values:

Scene	*1*	*2*	*3*	*4*	*5*	*6*	*7*	*8*	*9*	*10*	*11*
T_1	3.9	4.2	4.4	4.5	4.4	4.4	4.6	4.9	5.4	5.7	6.1
T_2	99	88	81	76	76	94	113	114	119	120	128
T_3	26	33	32	37	36	28	22	25	20	16	13
T_4	98	92	97	92	82	86	109	116	129	142	147
T_5	99	86	90	121	132	112	156	185	193	199	203
T_6	23	31	32	28	31	40	42	45	61	73	72
T_7	95	90	93	98	104	121	127	144	164	186	187
T_8	105	104	118	129	150	174	212	233	283	296	331
T_9	19	20	23	24	22	24	27	29	29	31	31
T_{10}	49	52	45	45	56	61	64	57	65	71	65
T_{11}	50	49	37	32	32	36	48	59	57	68	66

The oil embargo in Scene 1, except for its obvious immediate influence on energy (T_8) in Scene 2, has little lasting effect of any size. However, it is interesting to observe some of the minor repercussions, because they are typical of the kind of tertiary ricochet effects to which technology assessment investigations have drawn some attention. Thus, the decline in energy production (T_8) in Scene 2 causes raw materials (T_4) and industrial output (T_5) to be low in Scene 3. But while the deterioration of industrial output continues, reinforced by the decline in raw materials, that same trend causes the latter to recover in Scene 4. However, T_4's recovery, in turn, sets off a recovery of T_5, and so on, resulting in some slight oscillations of T_4 and T_5. The decline in energy production (T_8) also causes a reduction in acreage productivity (T_7), which is passed on via food supply (T_2) to population size (T_1). The reduced population pressure causes efforts toward fusion power (E_3) to decline, with the result that E_3 fails to take place, causing energy production (T_8) to be noticeably lower toward the end.

In the real world, an oil embargo, as illustrated in this example, would call forth reactive interventions by other countries. For instance, the United States (Player b) might, in Scene 2, enact a law against energy waste (A_6) and redouble efforts to achieve breakthroughs in obtaining energy from breeder reactors and solar power plants (A_8 and A_9). A numerical tabulation of the resulting scenario will be omitted here.

The point to be made by these examples of simulation gaming is that pseudo-experimentation of this kind can lead to important insights into future threats and opportunities and into the potentialities of alternative strategies for dealing with them. It should be remembered that the developments included in the model presented here and the numerical inputs into the model were chosen purely for illustrative purposes. Had they been determined on the basis of a more serious, substantive research effort, I have little doubt that the insights resulting from the construction of game-generated scenarios would provide highly realistic policy guidelines. This brings us back from merely using our 20 × 20 model as a convenient means of illustrating the method of cross-impact analysis to resuming briefly the discussion, begun in Section 31, of the implications of the *Limits to Growth* study.

34 *A SEQUEL TO* LIMITS TO GROWTH

The publication of the *Limits to Growth* study has had the immensely beneficial effect of alerting people throughout the world to the catastrophic implications within the twenty-first century of doing nothing to prevent a continuation of present trends in resource depletion and rising population levels. This warning having been effectively conveyed, however, it is imperative that a constructive approach be initiated in the form of a plan of action that will forestall the dire global consequences of inaction.

As conditions get worse—insufficient food per capita, inadequate energy supply, depleted mineral resources, an insufferably polluted environment—it is inconceivable that governments throughout the world will passively sit by and be content watching the demise of civilization. In fact, interventive events will inevitably take place, in the form of regulative, legislative, and diplomatic actions, as well as a reinforced endeavor to bring about the technological advances required to halt the observed trends toward disaster.

The system-dynamics approach to the global resources problem, used in the *Limits to Growth* study, has certain deficiencies, as I pointed out earlier, in that it represents a deterministic rather than a stochastic model and considers the interrelations among trends only instead of among events as well as trends. To cope with the development of global plans for moving in the direction of effective intervention while there is yet time, it is necessary to go about the construction of a new type of model in earnest—a model that is capable of handling the occurrence of interventive events and actions.

The model presented here, to be sure, is only a methodological prototype. The construction, in detail, of such a model, because of the obviously enormous complexity of the subject matter, requires considerable effort by a team at least comparable in size and in cross-disciplinary diversity to that of the Meadows team. I hope such an effort will be undertaken in the near future.

Even the relatively primitive and numerically unsubstantiated 20 × 20 model presented here allows us to see that the conclusions arrived at by this type of model may have a rather different flavor from those obtained in the *Limits to Growth* study. To this end, we note that our model contains certain stochastic events, E_1 to E_9, which are assumed to occur with preset positive probabilities. To approximate the *Limits to Growth* case, in which none of them is assumed to take place, we changed all their probabilities of occurrence to zero, with the following results:

Event occurrences: None.
Trend values:

Scene	*1*	*2*	*3*	*4*	*5*	*6*	*7*	*8*	*9*	*10*	*11*
T_1	3.9	4.2	4.4	4.5	4.4	4.4	4.5	4.7	5.1	5.3	5.8
T_2	99	88	81	78	79	93	108	103	99	100	114
T_3	26	33	32	38	44	50	43	43	39	31	23
T_4	98	92	93	78	66	67	84	75	72	77	79
T_5	99	86	96	126	132	100	121	153	153	150	149
T_6	23	31	32	28	32	40	41	39	52	65	65
T_7	95	90	95	100	104	115	111	111	121	139	143
T_8	105	113	119	130	141	144	163	163	195	199	234
T_9	19	20	24	24	22	24	27	28	28	29	30
T_{10}	49	52	45	45	56	58	55	50	55	61	57
T_{11}	50	49	37	32	35	36	36	50	46	55	59

Comparison with the basic-case tabulation at the beginning of Section 33 shows dramatic changes for the worse in all trends except birth-control acceptance (T_6) and capital investment (T_9). If the changes are not quite as drastic as the *Limits to Growth* study would have suggested, this may well be due to our relatively conservative assumptions on the effect of the occurrence of Events E_1 to E_9. The point is that, whatever assumptions one might wish to make regarding their influence, the type of model shown here makes it possible to examine how sensitively the outcome depends on the occurrence and interactions of the events in question and therefore, by implication, on interventive actions initiated to affect the likelihood of their occurrence.

To conclude this section, let me present one more case, which illustrates to what extent the scenario shown for the no-events case can be modified for the better through relatively modest interventions by the United Nations and the United States. Assuming the actions indicated below over the first twenty years (Scenes 1 to 4) of the half century spanned by the run of the model, and retaining the assumption of zero probability prior to the impact of those actions, for event occurrences, the following scenario was obtained:

Interventive actions:

Scene	*1*	*2*	*3*	*4*
Player a (U.N.)	A_2,A_3	A_4,A_7	A_7	A_7
Player b (U.S.)	A_6,A_8	A_8,A_{12}	A_{12},A_{17}	A_{18}

Event occurrences:

Scene	*1*	*2*	*3*	*4*	*5*	*6*	*7*	*8*	*9*	*10*
E_1				1						
E_5			1		1		1			

Trend values:

Scene	*1*	*2*	*3*	*4*	*5*	*6*	*7*	*8*	*9*	*10*	*11*
T_1	3.9	4.2	4.5	4.6	4.6	4.7	4.7	4.9	5.3	5.6	6.0
T_2	99	90	83	84	89	105	116	113	113	113	121
T_3	26	30	28	35	39	44	38	38	33	27	22
T_4	98	92	93	85	70	81	106	111	116	125	130
T_5	99	83	96	136	143	110	132	163	171	176	180
T_6	23	31	39	52	68	74	70	62	68	74	70
T_7	95	90	99	108	115	129	128	131	142	162	166
T_8	105	110	117	128	147	154	178	186	226	236	278
T_9	19	21	24	24	22	24	27	29	29	30	30
T_{10}	49	52	47	47	61	63	60	53	57	64	58
T_{11}	50	48	39	35	40	46	48	55	52	64	63

As can be seen, the counteractions taken during the first twenty years of the fifty-year period under consideration have the effect of improving all the indicators markedly, to the extent of even generally exceeding the levels attained in Scenes 3 to 6 in the basic case.

It may, of course, be objected that this result merely is a consequence of the input numbers chosen for our illustration. So it is; yet more carefully chosen, and thus presumably more realistic, numbers are unlikely to change the outcome by an order of magnitude. In any event, I do not wish to anticipate the substantive results of a more serious planning study along the lines suggested here; my intention, rather, is to show the potentialities of a new methodological approach that permits simulated reactions by decision-making agencies to unforeseen technological, environmental, or strategic contingencies.

In particular, the "only feasible solution", presented by Mesarovic and Pestel (1974), might be subjected to close reexamination by such an approach, not so much to test its validity but to determine whether its precariousness can be attenuated through the inclusion of model-endogenous interventive events.

35 A REVISED CROSS-IMPACT MODEL[3]

Cross-impact analysis, in any of its forms suggested to date, from the original version as employed by the author together with Ted Gordon in Kaiser Aluminum's Future game to the numerous derivatives introduced in the literature (see, among others, Gordon and Hayward, 1968; Helmer, 1972, 1977a, 1977b; Dalkey, 1972; Enzer, 1974; Duperrin and Godet, 1975) has certain defects, some minor, some more serious. I pointed out some of these (Helmer, 1977a); others were reviewed more recently by Alter (1979). Among the deficiencies are logical inaccuracies as well as factual inadequacies. The former include four cases:

(a) Impermissible probability values: In some models, there may be no guarantee that probability values, when modified through cross-impacts, remain in the interval from 0 to 1.
(b) Lack of commutativity: In the case of two simultaneous impacts, the combined impact may depend on the order in which the individual impacts are applied.
(c) Probabilistic imbalance: If the impact of the occurrence of an event of probability p on an event of probability q changes q to q' and the impact of the nonoccurrence of the former changes q to q'', then it may not be exactly but only approximately the case that $q = pq' + (1-p)q''$.
(d) Double counting: If A has an impact on B, and B on C, and also A on C, then it may be difficult, in estimating the direct impact of A on C, to keep this logically separate from its indirect impact via B.

While logical inaccuracies in principle are unacceptable, they have in practice interfered less with applicability than the factual inadequacies, because the logical discrepancies have tended to be quite minor when looked at in terms of numerical outcomes. The factual inadequacies, by comparison, in

3. This is an abbreviated version of my article, "Reassessment of Cross-Impact Analysis", *Futures*, vol. 13 (October 1981).

some cases have represented serious obstacles to realistic applicability of the models. These shortcomings of a factual kind include the following four:

(e) Mere correlations: Some models are based on an interpretation, not originally intended, of cross-impacts as correlations between potential occurrences rather than causal connections; while even the establishment of mere correlations can be helpful to the forecasting of future operating conditions, for planning purposes it is essential to have some insight into the cause-effect relationships between interventive actions and resultant changes.

(f) Events only: Potential occurrences, in some models, are limited to sudden developments, or events, taking place at a particular point in time, to the exclusion of gradual developments, or trends, which are appropriately described in terms of numerical time series.

(g) Linearity: In models where the effects of trend deviations are taken into account, the impact of such a deviation may be proportional to the size of that deviation—a simplistic assumption not always wholly realistic; moreover, impacts are generally assumed to be independent of the time at which they occur as well as of the size of the affected event probability or trend value.

(h) Two-dimensionality: Only pairs of occurrences are considered in cross-impact analysis, whereas in reality the effect of A on B often depends on other conditions, C; the usual *ceteris paribus* assumption in stating pairwise cross-impacts does not always give full justice to the true complexity of the situation.

35.1 Desiderata

Despite these shortcomings, it is important that futures researchers should not feel discouraged from making a serious effort to place cross-impact analysis, because of its special role pointed out earlier, on as sound a foundation as possible.

It clearly would be desirable to construct a cross-impact model that overcomes all eight of the above defects, and I shall make an effort in what follows to suggest a slightly new approach, which, when properly and fully implemented, may succeed in avoiding all of the deficiencies listed with which other models have been beset.

Of the eight potential objections, three—namely, a, e, and f—never did apply to my version of cross-impact analysis, and I do not intend to alter my approach in those regards. Let me take up the other five desiderata one at a time and discuss what can be done about them.

35.2 Lack of Commutativity

Instead of seeking to ensure commutativity, I propose to sidestep the issue altogether by never having more than one cross-impact impinge on a development at a time. To achieve this, two modifications will be introduced. First, the impacts of a trend on other developments will be handled via an "excess event" associated with the trend, which is assumed to occur with a probability that is the larger the more excessively the trend deviates from its forecasted values.

To illustrate the concept of an excess event, we may consider the case of a trend T measuring the supply of food to the population of a given country. If T falls slightly below the expected value, there may be no noticeable consequences. However, when such a shortfall becomes increasingly large, there is an increasing probability that an "excess event" takes place, that is, that the food supply shortage becomes unbearable and triggers other events (such as a popular uprising) or affects other trends (such as the labor productivity rate). Thus the other developments included in the model, while showing little sensitivity to small deviations, eventually (i.e., at some unpredictable, stochastic level) respond to excessive deviations.

Thus all cross-impacts appearing in the model will derive from the occurrence of some event—either one of the given ("ordinary") events or an excess event.

The second modification consists in the scenes no longer being of constant length (say, a year, as has been the case in many applications); instead they will be the intervals between event occurrences and thus of random length. One of the effects of this arrangement is that normally only one event will occur at the end of a scene; hence only its impacts will at that time be recorded. In the rare case that the model's randomization algorithm happens to select two or more events, signifying the end of a scene, to occur simultaneously, one will be drawn randomly, and only it will be assumed to occur at that time. This device prevents there ever being more than one impact on a development having to be accounted for at one time.

35.3 Probabilistic Imbalance

The new model will be a *ceteris paribus* rather than an expected-value model, in the following sense. While other models have taken the expected values (of trends and of event probabilities) as constituting the benchmark case [approximated, in the limit, by a large number of "basic runs"; see Section 33], and have described the marginal effects of cross-impacts as deviations from that basic situation, the proposed model uses as its benchmark the *ceteris paribus* case, defined as that situation which would be expected to obtain if no events were taking place. [Selwyn Enzer (1979) refers to this as the "baseline case". Compare the no-events case used as an illustration in Section 34.] Thus the probability of occurrence of an event, in the *ceteris paribus* case, is estimated on the assumption of no prior occurrence of either the event itself or any other event under consideration (whether ordinary or excess); the value of a trend at a given time is estimated on the assumption that no event (of either kind) has occurred up to that time; and, again, the marginal effects of cross-impacts are stated as deviations from that basic case.

The advantage of this approach is that we no longer have to be concerned over possible violations of the balancing law, c, since we no longer proceed in terms of deviations from expected values. Also, incidentally, in gaming applications of the model there is greater symmetry between events and actions: The nonoccurrence of an event, like the nontaking of an action, induces no deviations from the benchmark case.

35.4 Double Counting

The avoidance of double counting is a matter for which the cross-impact estimators are responsible, and, since their judgments are based to some extent on intuition, there can be no guarantee of error-free estimation. However, in a *ceteris paribus* model their intuition can be furnished with somewhat better guidance than would be the case in an expected-value model. In the simplest case—of A having an impact on B, and B on C, and A also having a direct impact on C—we note that this latter impact should be estimated on the assumption that no other event has taken place, hence in particular that the event B (if indeed B is an event) or the excess event associated with B (if B is a trend) has not taken place. If the model were of the expected-value type, the estimate of the direct impact of A on C would have to be made on the assumption that the direct impacts of A on B and of B on C were of expected size—an instruction of little intuitive appeal or utility, since it is virtually impossible to translate into a hard-and-fast operational rule. By comparison, the directive under our new approach is quite straightforward. Of course, as was said before, cross-impact estimators, relying on their intuition, may still commit errors; but at least the meaning of what they are supposed to estimate is unambiguous.

35.5 Linearity

The question of linear dependence on trend deviations no longer applies, because of the stipulation described under commutativity above, to the effect that impacts caused by a trend are introduced via an intervening excess event. As for the often assumed constancy with respect to time and with respect to the values of the affected probabilities or trends, this is only a matter of computational simplicity. If nonconstancy appears important, exceptions to this effect can always be made in the computational algorithms; I have in fact made use of that possibility myself in the past.

35.6 Two-Dimensionality

The same applies to the matter of two-dimensionality. If, in exceptional cases, it is important to allow for the dependence of an impact on the status of some third development in the model, this can be done, though at some cost in computational ease. Confining this provision to a few exceptional cases, instead of introducing three-dimensionality across the board, prevents the model from blowing up intolerably in size.

35.7 The Revised Cross-Impact Model

Let me now demonstrate how a model can actually be constructed along the lines suggested above. I propose to do so by once more going through the specific sequence of steps that a cross-impact model constructor would have to follow and illustrating each step this time by means of a very simple 4 × 4 (2 events and 2 trends) examples. (Needless to say, a realistic situation can rarely be expected to be captured in terms of so few developments.)

By way of a preface, let me point out that the construction of a new model proceeds from the assumption that events are conceptually easier to deal with than trends (an assumption that has been well recognized by, for example, Enzer, 1979; and Mitchell, Tydeman, and Georgiades, 1979). Consequently, changes in trend values and the impacts of trend value changes on other developments are handled through the device of trend-associated events. It has already been indicated, in Section 35.2, how cross-impacts of a trend change on other developments are to be effected via an excess event, associated with the trend, that occurs randomly with a probability that is an increasing function of the size of the trend's deviation from its anticipated value. In addition, it will be assumed that trends are subject to random fluctuations caused by occurrences not explicitly included in the model.

The mechanism for handling this will be the introduction, for each trend, of an exogenous random event (of otherwise unspecified identity) whose occurrence triggers a randomized fluctuation of that trend. The question is: How often does such random noise take place, and how large is its effect? The expected frequency of occurrence of the associated exogenous event will depend on the trend's "susceptibility" to exogenous conditions, and the expected size of the resulting fluctuation will depend on the trend's "volatility", both terms to be explicated below. (Random fluctuations of event probabilities might likewise be introduced; such a refinement, involving probabilities superimposed on probabilities, will for simplicity be omitted in the present model.)

The construction process involves the following steps:

Step 1. Choose the subject matter (the future of X), the time horizon, and the unit of time. The latter should conveniently be commensurate with the rapidity with which major changes in the status of the subject matter are expected to occur. Also identify the actors on whose behalf this planning model is being constructed. (The significance of identifying the actors lies in the fact that this affects the structure of the model. An impact of one event's occurrence on another event's probability of occurrence may take place through the deliberate intervention of an actor, or it may be an automatic, endogenous effect built into the model, depending on whether the appropriate actor is or is not assumed to be role-played in the gaming application of the model.)

Example: The future of energy in the United States; time horizon: twenty years; unit of time: four years; actors: the U.S. energy industry and the U.S. government.

Step 2. Identify the events, E_1, E_2, E_3 . . . , that have a nonnegligible chance of occurring during the time period under consideration (i.e., from the present to the time horizon) and whose occurrence would make a major difference to the future of X; specify which of these events are potentially recurrent. Similarly, identify the trends, T_1, T_2, T_3 . . . , that ought to be monitored over the time period of interest, either because they represent important indicators of how X is faring or because unexpected rises and falls in their values would make a major difference to the future of X.

Example: E_1 = a major technological breakthrough in solar energy (that would, within four years, make it possible to produce solar-generated energy on a large scale and economically competitive with other sources of energy). E_2 = a serious accident in a nuclear power plant (at least as serious as that at Three Mile Island). T_1 = the amount of nuclear-generated electricity produced annually in the U.S. (using an index value of 100 for 1980). T_2 = the amount of energy imported from abroad (in percentage of total energy consumed in the United States). Of the two events, E_1 may occur only once, while E_2 may recur any number of times.

Step 3. For each event, estimate its cumulative probability of occurrences as a function of time over the period under consideration. (In practice, the estimator here has the option of making his estimate in the form of a probability density function, if he finds this intuitively more appealing, from which the required cumulative probability can then be calculated.) The probabilities are to be estimated under the "null assumption" of no prior occurrence of any event (including the event itself, if it happens to be a potentially recurrent one, as well as any excess event triggered by a trend's unexpected deviation from its forecasted course) and no interventive action by any of the actors.

Similarly, for each trend, estimate its values during the period under consideration, again under the null assumption (which, in this case, includes the nonoccurrence of the exogenous event associated with the trend). To obtain these probability and trend-value estimates, the judgments of appropriate experts may have to be solicited, possibly through a Delphi inquiry.

Example: The cumulative probabilities of E_1 and E_2, by the years specified, are estimated to be as follows:

	1984	*1988*	*1992*	*1996*	*2000*
E_1	.40	.60	.72	.82	.90
E_2	.50	.75	.85	.91	.95

The values of the trends are estimated as follows:

	1980	*1984*	*1988*	*1992*	*1996*	*2000*
T_1	100	120	140	160	180	200
T_2	25	25	25	25	25	25

Intermediate values of probability and trend values are to be obtained by interpolation. (Reminder: the values shown here are for illustrative purposes only and carry no claim to be realistic.)

Before proceeding to Step 4, a few words need to be inserted on the scene structure of the model. Previous models (my own and others) have assumed a sequence of scenes of constant length. By contrast, as already indicated above, a scene in the present model will end when an event occurs and thus will be of random length. In this context, "events" will include "ordinary events" as introduced in Step 2, "excess events" associated with trends through which the latter's deviations from anticipated values exert an impact on other developments, and unspecified "exogenous events" whose impacts on trends account for their random fluctuations. The probabilities of occurrence of the ordinary events have been indicated in Step 3. What remains to be specified are the probabilities of the other two types of events, as well as the impacts of all of the events and the algorithms for processing these impacts.

When a scene ends, because of the occurrence of an event, then (i) the cumulative probabilities of all events are updated, and (ii) the impacts of the event that occurred are applied by adjusting the affected trends and (ordinary) event probabilities. In addition, if the scene-ending event was an excess event, then (iii) the anticipated course of the trend with which that event is associated gets updated. In particular, i, the updating of a cumulative event probability, c(t), is carried out by replacing c(t) by

$$c^*(t) = \frac{c(t) - c(t_o)}{1 - c(t_o)}$$

where t_o is the time at which the scene ended. If the event is potentially recurrent and has a constant probability density, α, then

$$c(t) = 1 - e^{-\alpha t}$$

and it can easily be verified that $c^*(t) = c(t - t_o)$. As for carrying out ii, the application of impacts, the details of this operation will be described below in connection with Step 5.

The updating of trends, iii, means that the trend deviation ΔT (= $T - T^A$, where T is the actual and T^A the anticipated trend value) is set back to 0, once the built-up effect of the trend's deviation has been discharged into the system via the impacts of the excess event. Computationally this means that, until an excess event takes place, a record has to be kept of the actual values of the trend (as determined by the modifications that the impacts from other developments and from exogenous events associated with the trend impose on it), as well as of its values as they would have been anticipated had no such intervening impacts occurred—the difference between the two being the trend's deviation, ΔT, from its anticipated course. Once an excess event associated with the trend takes place, the modified trend becomes the new anticipated referent, and ΔT therefore becomes 0 until fresh impacts produce further modifications.

Step 4. For each trend T, stipulate a lower bound L and an upper bound U. These should be chosen so that the attainment of these values in reality, while conceivable, is extremely unlikely and, in fact, would reflect such a far-out situation that the modeler would be willing to forego its inclusion within the range of investigation.

Next, again for each trend, estimate its "susceptibility" to exogenous influences, that is, to effects that are not explainable, or even expressible, in terms of the developments explicitly represented in the model, and thus—as far as the model is concerned—are put down to random noise. The susceptibility, s, of a trend may be explicated as the average frequency, per unit of time, of noticeable exogenous impacts of this kind on T; and it will, in fact, be assumed that the exogenous event associated with T occurs recurrently with a probability density s, hence a cumulative probability of $1 - e^{-st}$, where t is the time.

Finally, under Step 4, estimate the "volatility" v of T, which is a measure of the expected relative deviation, per unit of time, from its anticipated values, due to exogenous impacts sustained during that time interval. The phrase "relative deviation" here refers to the relative size of the deviation compared to the maximal deviation, which is $U - T$ if the deviation is positive, or $T - L$ if the deviation is negative. Thus the relative deviation of T from T^A is 1 for $T = U$, is -1 for $T = L$ and, of course, is 0 for $T = T^A$. Hence the relative deviation, δT, equals

$$\frac{\Delta T}{U - T^A} \text{ when } \Delta T \geqslant 0 \text{ and } \frac{\Delta T}{T^A - L} \text{ when } \Delta T < 0.$$

To define the volatility v, we now consider the combined impacts on T, per unit of time, from occurrences of the associated exogenous event. This v is the upper quartile of the distribution of the relative deviations produced by these combined impacts. (We note that, if single impacts from exogenous-event occurrences have a distribution with an upper quartile, say, of size w then, since the expected number of single such impacts per unit of time is s, we have, at least approximately, $v = w\sqrt{s}$.)

Example:

	L	U	s	v
T_1	0	400	1	.05
T_2	10	50	2	.14

We can now specify the probability of occurrence of the excess events. If the relative deviation is k × v (that is, if T differs from T^A by k times the typical deviation due to random noise), then the associated excess event is assigned a probability density of $k^2/(k^2 + 9)$ (which is 0 for k = 0 and .5 for k = 3). No justification, except intuitive appeal, is offered for the choice of this particular function. The corresponding cumulative probability (for constant k) is

$$1 - e^{-\frac{k^2}{k^2+9}t}$$

The next step will be concerned with the estimation of cross-impacts (including the impacts from exogenous events, whose manifestations are random trend fluctuations). All such impacts are of one of two types: Type I is a permanent impact, while Type II is a temporary blip (see Figure 12). Impacts on event probabilities are always assumed to be of Type I, whereas in the case of trends the impacts may be of either type, except that trend self-impacts must be of Type II in order to avoid an explosive propagation of any deviation.

Any impact will be expressed in terms of two parameters: the delay time, d, before the full effect of the impact is felt, and the effectiveness, e, of the impact, which is the fraction of the distance from the upper or lower bound by which the impact moves the original value in the direction of that upper or lower bound. (In the case of probabilities, the upper and lower bounds are always assumed to be 1 and 0, respectively.) Here, $d \geqslant 0$ (for Type II: $d > 0$) and $-1 \leqslant e \leqslant 1$. At time $t_o + d$ (where t_o is the time of occurrence of the impacting event), the original value V (of the trend or of the cumulative probability, as the case may be) is changed into $V + e(U - V)$ if $e > 0$, or into $V + e(V - L)$ if $e < 0$. Between t_o and $t_o + d$, the change will be linear.

For Type I the change described by this function persists from then on, whereas for Type II it decays linearly, and a reversion to the original value occurs after a time delay which, for simplicity, is assumed always to be equal to 1 (although a contrary assumption, requiring the estimation of yet a third parameter, could be just as easily accommodated).

In the case of the occurrence of an exogenous event, it will be assumed that the impact on the trend with which it is associated is always of Type II;

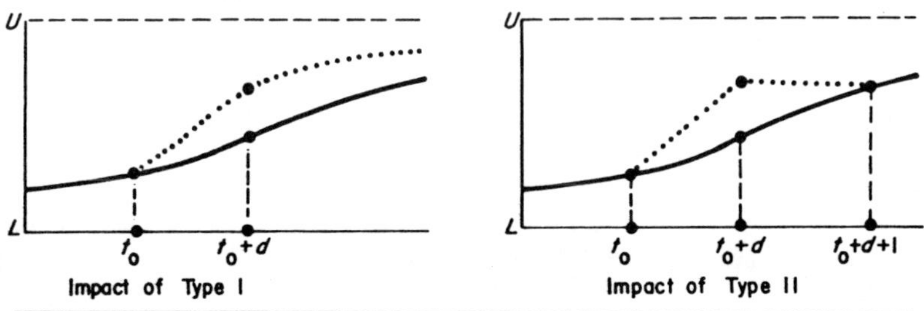

FIGURE 12

the rationale being that if the impact were permanent (i.e., of Type I), the modeler should have included such an event among the ordinary events explicitly represented in the model. Moreover, in contrast to the fixed impacts caused by ordinary or excess events, the impact of an exogenous event will be randomized. In fact, it will be drawn from a normal distribution having its quartiles at $\pm v$, which is $G_v(t) = F(.6745t/v)$, where F(t) is the cumulative normal distribution with a standard deviation of 1, that is,

$$F(t) = \frac{1}{\sqrt{2\pi}} \int_{-\infty}^{t} e^{-\frac{1}{2}x^2}\, dx$$

Note that F(.6745) = .75.

Step 5. For each event, whether ordinary or excess or exogenous, estimate its cross-impacts on ordinary events and on trends. In the case of an excess event, which may be the result of either an upward or a downward deviation, the impacts on other developments may be different depending on whether it is an upward or downward excess event.

In practice, it may be convenient first to construct a qualitative cross-impact matrix, showing just where (positive or negative) impacts occur.

Example:

	E_1	E_2	T_1	T_2
E_1	-			-
E_2	+	-	-	
T_1		+	+	-
T_2				
Exo			±	±

In this matrix, the entries in the Exo line are reminders that the occurrence of this exogenous event associated with a trend will cause that trend to undergo a random upward or downward fluctuation.

The qualitative entries in the above matrix, finally, have to be replaced by quantitative ones. Each nonzero cell will have to contain three numbers, indicating the type of impact (I or II), the delay time (d), and the effectiveness (e).

Example: The matrix entries, for convenience, are here listed consecutively rather than in the form of a two-dimensional display:

	Type	*d*	e
E_1 on E_1:	I	0	-1
E_1 on T_2:	II	1	$-.3$
E_2 on E_1:	I	.75	.4
E_2 on E_2:	I	.10	$-.2$
E_2 on T_1:	II	.05	$-.2$
T_1 on E_2:	I	$\begin{cases} 0 \\ .10 \end{cases}$	.3 if T_1 is high $-.2$ if T_1 is low
T_1 on T_1:	II	1	$.8 \cdot \delta T_1$ (i.e., 80% of any deviation may be self-perpetuating; here δT_1 is the relative deviation, as defined in Step 4)
T_1 on T_2:	II	$\begin{cases} .25 \\ .10 \end{cases}$	$-\delta T_1$ if T_1 is high $-.6\delta T_1$ if T_1 is low
Exo on T_1:	II	.50	$.074F^{-1}(r)$ } where r is random, $0 \leq r < 1$,
Exo on T_2:	II	.50	$.0208F^{-1}(r)$ } and F^{-1} is the inverse of F(t)

Note that, for exogenous events, we always assume, as stated before, that the type is II and the impact, in view of the definition of "volatility", should be drawn randomly from a normal distribution having its quartiles at $\pm$v; moreover, we shall uniformly assume that we always have d = .5.

35.8 Basic Run

The model is now ready for a "basic run", i.e., for a passive application involving no interventive actions.

For the 4 × 4 example introduced above, a single such basic run was carried out through hand calculations, using tabulated random numbers; the times of event occurrences were rounded up to the nearest multiple of .05. The resulting scene sequence that happened to emerge is shown in the following tabulation:

Scene Number	*Time of Scene End*	*End of Scene Triggered by*	*Scene Number*	*Time of Scene End*	*End of Scene Triggered by*
1	.60	Ex_2	10	3.10	Ex_2
2	.70	E_1	11	3.15	Ex_2
3	1.65	Ex_2	12	3.45	Ex_2
4	1.75	E_2	13	3.50	T_1
5	2.00	Ex_2	14	4.30	Ex_2
6	2.45	E_2	15	4.45	T_1
7	2.55	T_1	16	4.65	Ex_2
8	2.60	Ex_1	17	5.00	—
9	2.80	T_2			

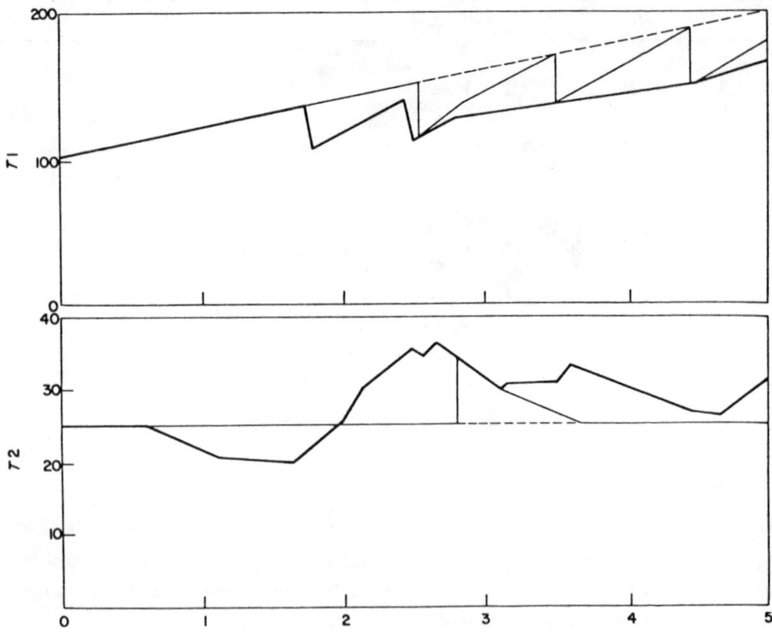

FIGURE 13

T_1 or T_2 indicates that the trend's deviation from anticipated values caused an associated excess event to occur (which terminated the scene), and Ex_1 and Ex_2 are the exogenous events related to T_1 and T_2.

We note that E_1, which was assumed to be nonrecurrent, did indeed occur once, namely, at the end of Scene 2, whereas E_2 occurred twice, at the ends of Scenes 4 and 6. The trends behaved as shown in Figure 13, where a dashed line shows the original forecast, a thin line shows the scene-by-scene anticipation, and a heavy line shows the actual trend values produced by this run.

35.9 Resumption of Model Construction

The model constructed thus far is adequate for a passive study of the future of a given subject area. But in order to have a useful planning instrument, it is necessary to incorporate a feature that permits active intervention. To have utility to the planner or decision maker, the model must have the form of an operational game, that is, it must be capable of accepting interventive actions and providing insight into the likely consequences of the superimposition of such decisional manipulation upon the "natural" course of events.

An action, conceptually, is like an event, except that its occurrence is not random but deliberate. To say that it is deliberate does not mean that it is not subject to possible constraints. These can be model-endogenous, such as the prior occurrence of some other event; or they can be exogenous, such as budgetary limitations.

From the model builder's point of view, we may distinguish two kinds of actions: preformulated and unpremeditated. If only preformulated actions are accommodated, this means that the planners, as players of the game, have the option, at any time of their choosing, of stopping the ongoing run of the model and making a game move by interjecting one or more of the listed actions at their disposal. Such an action generally will not take effect immediately but rather after a fixed or randomized delay. When it does take effect, it will generate impacts analogous to those of any other (nondeliberate) event.

In the real world, planners and decision makers often react to an unexpected exigency by inventing an appropriate counteraction. Such unpremeditated intervention can also be permitted in a gaming simulation, but only at the considerable cost of disrupting the run of the model sufficiently long until the new action has been clearly defined, costed out, and its impacts agreed upon. In practice, a better procedure in such simulation gaming may be merely to record ideas for new action types as they arise, to leave their incorporation in the model structure until the current run has been completed, and then, in subsequent runs, have the new actions available as additional preformulated options.

For the present, I shall restrict myself to this latter alternative and assume that all actions, technically, are preformulated. This then leads to the following additional steps in model construction:

Step 6. For each actor (as specified in Step 1), prescribe a (discretionary) budget within which he has to operate over the time period covered by a model run. Such budgetary constraints may be one-dimensional (e.g., fiscal) or multidimensional (e.g., involving fiscal, basic resources, and sociopolitical considerations). Also, they may be overall constraints for the entire period or serial constraints for subperiods, such as years. In the latter case, the rules have to state whether unspent amounts may be carried over to the next subperiod.

Example: Actor 1 (energy industry): $20 billion for the entire period (of twenty years); Actor 2 (U.S. government): $8 billion per time unit (of four years) for each of five units, with no carryover.

Step 7. For each actor, describe the actions he may take and the conditions under which they may be taken.

Example:
Actor 1: A_{11}: invest in solar-energy R & D (no condition)
A_{12}: build a solar-energy plant (only after E_1 has occurred)
Actor 2: A_{21}: same as A_{11}

A_{22}: strengthen and enforce safety regulations regarding nuclear plants (no condition)

A_{23}: limit the amount of energy imported from abroad (only if T_2 is above 30)

Step 8. For each action, specify its cost in terms of the budget (or the budgetary components) defined in Step 6. Where appropriate, the cost may have to be stated as a function of the intensity of the action (see example below).

Example:

A_{11}, A_{21}: \$100 million per "unit" of investment intensity.
A_{12}: \$1 billion per million kW output.
A_{22}: \$50 million per unit of time.
A_{23}: \$10 million per unit of time.

Step 9. For each action, state the time delay d (possibly stochastic) with which it will be realized, and its impacts (by type and effectiveness e) on the (ordinary) events and the trends of the system. Note that, when an action is taken, it will, like any other event, cause the current scene to be terminated.

Example:

Example:	*Action*	*Affected Development*	*Type of Impact*	*d*	*e*
	A_{11}	E_1	I	.1	$1 - .7^k$
	A_{12}	T_1	I	$2 \pm .5$	$-(1 - .9^k)$
		T_2	II	$2 \pm .7$	$-(1 - .8^k)$
	A_{21}	E_1	I	.2	$1 - .75^k$
	A_{22}	E_2	I	.1	$-.4$
	A_{23}	T_2	I	.25	$-.2$

(Here, k refers to the number of units invested, and the notation 'a ± b' designates a normal distribution with mean a and quartiles a ± b.)

This, in essence, completes the model construction, and a full run with player interventions could be carried out. While no example of such a run for our illustrative 4 × 4 case will be presented here, it should be pointed out that there are still a number of options left open regarding the information structure of the model. That is, stipulations need to be made regarding just what information an actor should have available concerning the exact state of his simulated world, including moves by other actors, when he contemplates introducing a move of his own. The quality of such information, incidentally, may well depend on "meta-moves" by the actor, consisting in expenditures on information-gathering activities that may include so-called library research, consultation of experts, and even—in the case of competitive games—industrial or military espionage. ■

The model described above may well not represent the last word in cross-impact analysis. But although it is conceptually somewhat more intricate than other, earlier models, it does seem to meet most of the objections that have been stated with regard to them. Its slightly greater complexity should not be a noticeable impediment, either in programming or in running time, to computerized application of the model.

Chapter VII

Feasible and Desirable Futures

36 *INGREDIENTS OF PLANNING*

Much has already been said in the preceding chapters of this book on various aspects of the planning process, and it is time to take a systematic look at where we stand. Let us, then, review briefly the main ingredients of planning and reexamine our ability to deal with them.

All planning is about the future, and there are no hard facts about the future. Although in some narrowly confined areas extrapolation from the past may yield reliable predictions about things to come, virtually all planning concerns complex affairs involving multidisciplinary considerations, including, in particular, matters belonging in the realm of the social sciences, and extrapolation in such cases is an uncertain guide. The need for reliance on expert judgment—at least additionally, and often exclusively—is inescapable. Such expertise, of course, is based on what has been learned in the past, but whatever extrapolation goes on in the expert's head is likely to be intuitive rather than the result of formal derivation.

The expert's role in planning is by no means confined to predicting what will happen in the future or even to helping us arrive at probabilistic forecasts in this regard. The planning process involves the discovery, if not the invention, of possible futures; the sifting of possible futures as to feasibility; and the examining of feasible futures as to desirability. All of these phases of the planning activity call for the insight and imagination of experts in the areas that are the subject of such planning.

There are, therefore, several ingredients of the planning process; "ingredients" being a better term than "phases" (which I have used) because they are not necessarily considered consecutively; rather, each may, by a process of elimination and suggestion, affect each of the others.

Planning usually has its origin in an element of a dissatisfaction with the present state of affairs or with the expected implications of present trends if left unaltered. The first ingredient of planning, therefore, is a critique of the present.

Recognizing what is wrong now may suggest areas of improvement and thus set a planning activity in motion. However, to go about this process systematically requires that we sort out both our goals for a better future and our abilities for achieving a better future.

Goals, of course, are very different, depending on whether we are planning in the private or in the public sector. The overriding consideration in private-sector planning is that of profit, and variations on this theme essentially amount to a relative emphasis on short-term or on long-term profit expectations. The desire to strengthen the viability of a firm is not really a separate goal; it is merely an affirmation that long-term profits should not be placed at risk for the sake of short-term advantages. To attain its goal, a firm will formulate certain objectives, such as attaining a specified share of the market or a certain capital-earnings ratio. These are examples of "business indicators", which measure the well-being of the firm. The dissatisfaction of the firm's managers with the present state of affairs will abate as the business indicators selected by them as measures of their objectives begin to rise toward their desired levels.

Goals in the public sector, by contrast, are tied to what is loosely called "the public interest", that is, to what the public—or that portion of the public that has control over the government—views as the "quality of life", taking that term in its widest sense. While a more detailed discussion of quality-of-life issues will be presented in a later chapter, let me now merely point out that the quality of life is a multidimensional entity, having as components the quality of health care, the quality of the physical environment, and so on; that dissatisfaction with any particular component, say with health care, will generate the goal of improving health care, which in turn will lead to the statement of specific objectives, such as a per-capita increase in hospital beds or a reduction in the death rate of infants. These yardsticks, indicating the success rate of an improvement program, are examples of "social indicators".

In order to attain desired objectives, be they improvements in business or in social indicators, the planner needs to propose measures whose enactment, by the appropriate decision-making agency, is likely to promote those objectives. (In practice, particularly in the operation of small business enterprises, the planner and the decision maker may well be identical. Otherwise, the planner merely acts as a simulator of, and staff adviser to, the actual decision maker.)

If the planning activity is short-range, it may be assumed that the operating environment at the time the plan is to be implemented will be essentially like the operating environment at the time the plan is being formulated. In this case, the nature of the dissatisfaction with present conditions provides appropriate guidance for improvements. Conversely, in long-range planning, when (by definition of "long-range") the operating environment at the plan's target time is expected to have changed substantially compared to present conditions, dissatisfaction with the present, while providing valuable clues to avenues of amelioration, needs to be supplemented with forecasts of just how that environment is likely to change and what consequences such change will have on the nature of dissatisfaction with prevailing circumstances and on our options for improvement.

While planning in the private sector may be short- or long-range, depending on the nature of the business and possibly on management's preference between quick profits and viability in the long run, public-sector planning is almost invariably of the long-range variety. The reasons are sluggishness and scale: It usually takes a long time for governmental decision-making processes to get things done; and the areas touched upon by public decisions tend to be so numerous that conditions are not likely to remain stationary in all of them between making and realizing plans for change.

Even when we compare the process of public planning with that of long-range corporate planning, there are notable differences between them. Although, in both cases, there is a presumption of substantial changes in the environment, calling for a forecasting effort as a precondition for planning, the corporate planner can generally assume that the future environment, though uncertain, is fixed, whereas the public planner is faced with the possibility that some aspects of the operating environment will be affected by the implementation of the very plans he is concocting. The added complexity of such feedback, while not totally absent in the private-sector case, cannot be ignored in the public sector, especially when plans are concerned with matters of far-reaching implications.

Another difference, which in this case weighs in on the side of greater complexity for the corporate planner, is in the competitive environment. How well a firm will be doing depends not only on its own actions and on the passive environment, but also on the behavior of its competitors in the marketplace. It is the outcome of this "game", in which they are all "players", that will determine the fate of each. This competitive ambience, except in the conduct of foreign affairs, is less obtrusive in the case of governmental operations. Admittedly, the governmental decision-making machinery tends to be more diffuse than that of the private sector, leaving room for some conflict between participating agencies, but the government's role, rather than being that of an adversary, more often is that of a conciliator among interest groups having conflicting preferences regarding pending decisions.

When deciding what strategy of action to propose as a means of furthering the organization's objectives, a planner needs to give due consideration to all of these aspects that are relevant to the case. Often it will be expedient to formulate several strategic options, along with estimates of each alternative's likely implications, leaving the ultimate choice to the person or agency responsible for the final decision.

To summarize, these are some of the ingredients of the planning process: the use of expert judgment, analysis of present causes of dissatisfaction, goal-setting, the determination of objectives in terms of business or social indicators, forecasting changes in the operating environment (if it is a matter of long- rather than short-range planning), the invention and selection of measures to be examined for inclusion in a possible action program, and finally the actual choice, among these strategic options, of a particular set of actions.

Let us now review very briefly the tools at our disposal for coping with each of these planning ingredients.

37 EXPERT JUDGMENT

Enough has already been said earlier on the topic of using expert judgment. Section 14, in particular, pointed out various ways in which expertise can be used. Among the methods of using groups of experts are the Delphi method and its variants (especially mini-Delphi), cross-impact analysis, and simulation gaming (cross-impact gaming as well as other forms of it).

38 SATISFACTION AND DISSATISFACTION

Dissatisfaction with the present, as has been said, gives rise to the desire for improvement and thus often is the beginning of a planning activity.

Deficiencies in present conditions generally are too obvious to require expert judgment. High unemployment, smog, high-school graduates' inability to do simple arithmetic, low profit levels all are plainly evident to the untutored layperson. In contrast to such observable facts, however, present trends are not always equally clear, because they involve a tacit element of judgmental forecasting. Will currently rising levels of unemployment, or of smog, and so on, continue at the same rate? Or are the rates with which these increases decelerate an indication that things will soon be getting better? In mathematical jargon, which derivative of the index in question is the most trustworthy predictor?

Another difficulty, more apparent in public than in corporate planning, is the multidimensionality of satisfaction. Whether we are concerned with the overall quality of life or with one of its components, such as the quality of health care, it may often be the case that in some respects our degree of satisfaction is high, or at least rising, whereas in other respects it is low, or at least dropping alarmingly. Here we may be able to improve one satisfaction aspect only at the price of worsening another, and we get inevitably involved in questions of exchange ratios between satisfaction components, which usually are moral issues (if a single individual is concerned) or even political issues (if the value preferences of different groups have to be reconciled). For example, how much real income are people prepared to give up for a lowering in pollution levels? What deterioration in civil liberties are they willing to accept in order to achieve a decrease in crimes of violence?

In situations of this sort, where we are dealing with trends, with a multiplicity of satisfaction dimensions, or with both, observations of the present must merely be taken for what they are: warnings of possible troubles ahead or of the forthcoming need to make moral or political choices between different satisfaction aspects. Decisions on what can and should be done depend on future analysis, that is, on a careful examination of feasible futures and their evaluation in terms of desirability—a subject to be resumed presently.

39 GOALS, OBJECTIVES, AND ACTION MEASURES

As these terms tend to be used, goals are more general than objectives. A goal consists in enhanced satisfaction in some particular respect (say, satisfaction with some aspect of the quality of life, or with profits), while an objective consists in a specific change that would bring one closer to goal fulfillment, such as raising a particular social or business indicator.

Goals and objectives, taken individually, rarely are controversial, except when they refer to the relatively distant future, in which case there may be differences of opinion concerning the effect of changes in people's value system on what is considered desirable. Sets of goals or objectives, considered jointly, by contrast, can be highly controversial, because the question arises at once as to what relative weight of effort should be given to each separate element in the set. A good example of this may be seen in opposing political platforms, whose individual planks often are supported by both parties, but the matter of relative emphasis (say, between defense and social security) may be a hot political issue.

↗	O_1	O_2	. . .
A_1		++	
A_2	−		
.			+
.			
.			

Neither statements of goals nor of objectives, in themselves, form a plan. A plan is a proposed program of action measures, to be taken in order to achieve given objectives. Since a particular measure may and often does affect more than one objective, the controversial character of sets of objectives immediately carries over to programs of action measures. In order to sort out the pros and cons of a proposed program of actions, A_1, A_2, . . . , it may be well to list also all the objectives under consideration, O_1, O_2, . . . , and construct a qualitative impact matrix, as shown, noting the actions' expected (strong or weak or even negative) effect on the various objectives. While such a matrix provides no conclusive verdict, it is a simple yet valuable aid in discussing the relative merits of alternative action programs either in open debate or in a mini-Delphi session.

In very intricate planning situations, this simpleminded approach may have to be augmented with the use of more sophisticated tools, to be considered next.

40 FUTURES ANALYSIS OF OPTIONS

For long-range planning in a multidisciplinary context, typical of most public-sector needs as well as those of large corporations, the approach described above represents merely a conceptual preliminary to a more systematic analysis.

At the very least, a survey of possible future changes in the operating environment, best conducted through a Delphi study, is indicated. This means (i) the selection of relevant events and trends whose occurrence or fluctuations, respectively, would affect the future operating environment in a nonnegligible way; and (ii) the estimation of the probabilities of their occurrence or of out-of-the-ordinary fluctuations.

From here, one might continue by conducting a full-fledged cross-impact analysis regarding these trends and events, thereby also laying the foundation for systematic scenario selection and simulated testing of alternative strategies.

But even without going to such lengths, that is, on the basis of a Delphi survey without attention to cross-impacts, the planning effort is likely to receive help and stimulation from a mere listing of relevant contingencies and the probabilities attached to them. A clearer conception of what is desirable will be obtained, ameliorative measures will suggest themselves, and intuition will be aided in the selection of a particular plan of action.

A more thorough planning effort might include some or all of the following tasks:

(1) Identification of separate interest groups ("stakeholders") and of the specific differences in their preferences for stated goals or proposed objectives. If this task is carried out by soliciting expert opinions, through Delphi or otherwise, it is less important to include members of such interest groups (who are likely to be highly prejudiced) than to consult experts about such groups, such as sociologists, psychologists, economists, and possibly social workers.

(2) Determination of the relative weights that should be given to these interest groups. This is an act not of exploration, but of policy-setting (or, in the futurists' jargon, of "normative forecasting").

(3) A passive cross-impact analysis of events and trends, passive in the sense that as yet no interventive actions are introduced. The purpose is to obtain a clearer understanding of how future contingencies interact with one another and thereby to get some clues for promising or needful interventions. Passive runs of a cross-impact model will, among other things, systematically produce a set of scenarios, from which a subset of "representative" scenarios (see Section 20.6.3 in Chapter IV, and Chapter X) may be selected. A representative set of scenarios affords the planner the possibility of testing a proposed action program against each member of that limited set and, if it does well in each case, of feeling reasonably well assured that the

program would perform well under any scenario that might transpire to be the actual one in the real world.

A representative set of scenarios for X (the subject domain of the planning effort), very briefly, can be constructed as follows: Examine the developments (events and trends) in the cross-impact matrix of X and select, in order, the most influential development, D_1, the next most influential development, D_2, and so on. Often a set of three, D_1, D_2, D_3, may suffice. Here "influential" is understood to mean that its occurrence (if it is an event) or its inordinate fluctuations (if it is a trend) will have a powerful influence on the future of X. Influentiality in this sense can best be determined intuitively with the aid of mini-Delphi, paying attention to the size of the cross-impacts generated by the developments (as indicated by the cross-impact coefficients). Then, if (say) D_1 is an event, divide all scenarios into two sets consisting of those in which, respectively, D_1 does or does not occur. Next, if (say) D_2 is a trend, subdivide each of these two sets of scenarios further into three each, assigning a scenario to the first if D_2 has relatively low values, to the second if D_2 has relatively high values, and to the third if neither of these is the case. These six scenario sets are then further subdivided into two or three each, depending on whether D_3 is an event or a trend, yielding a total of 12 or 18 sets of scenarios in this example. At what point to stop this process is a matter of judgment, depending on how many developments are regarded to be of crucial importance and how much time for analysis is available. Once these scenario sets are identified, a particular scenario is selected randomly from each to form the desired set of representative scenarios.

(4) The identification and possibly invention of interventive actions worthy of consideration. A Delphi survey can be very useful for this purpose; it stimulates the respondents to propose possible measures and, at the same time, acts as a filter to sift out the best from a larger total set of suggestions. (The function of Delphi here might be regarded as that of an anonymous brainstorming session.)

(5) Costing-out proposed action measures, both singly and, when necessary, in combination (to account for possible cost savings). This can be done by conventional costing methods when such are available. Often, at this stage, order-of-magnitude costing may suffice to eliminate many candidate measures, and such gross costing can often be conveniently accomplished by use of mini-Delphi.

(6) Comparative cross-impact analysis of alternative action programs, based on the previous selection of possible actions and the estimation of their associated costs. While, in theory, all possible combinations of actions could thus be considered in an effort at true optimization, this may not be practical, despite the speed of computerized simulation runs. A judicious selection of action programs by the planning team can usually be relied on to cut the task down to manageable proportions, especially since each simulation run will

provide fresh insights and help in the selection of further programs for testing. The result of such test runs will consist in cost-benefit appraisals of alternative programs, possibly differentiated according to the various stakeholder groups that are involved. The method for conducting such cross-impact simulation was demonstrated in the preceding chapter. Several further comments may here be appropriate.

First of all, because of the built-in random features, no two runs of a cross-impact model, even with identical interventions, will yield exactly the same scenario. Hence it is advisable to run the same case several and possibly a large number of times in order to obtain estimates of the average (or "expected") outcome as well as of the standard deviation. (When a decision maker is faced with the choice between two plans, one of which promises higher expectations but also a larger standard deviation and hence greater risk, he will have to make a policy decision dictated by his, or his organization's, preferences.)

Second, an interactive simulation run, where the planner interjects actions in response to the scenario as it unfolds, may be regarded as a one-person game against nature. Thus, instead of following a fixed plan of interventions, an opportunity is offered to test a general strategy that merely stipulates in advance how certain contingencies should be met if and when they are encountered in the course of a simulation run.

Third, the notion of a one-person game (against nature) can immediately be extended to encompass multiperson games, that is, situations in which several decision-making agencies intervene with actions in the course of developments as they observe their unfolding. The scenario then, of course, reflects the joint effects of such actions as well as of random occurrences. It should be noted that the application of the concept of multiperson gaming is appropriate not only when there are genuinely hostile opponents with incompatible preferences but also in cases where the interests of stakeholder groups with only slightly differing preferences must be accommodated or where, as is often the case in corporate or bureaucratic organizations, the decision-making process is diffuse enough to permit participation in it of different persons, each having his own, biased interpretation of what is best for the organization. (The relevance of both game theory and organization theory to this discussion has prompted me—or given me the excuse—to include sections on these topics later in this chapter.)

(7) Final choice of an action strategy, based on what has been learned from the preceding comparative cross-impact analysis. This choice may be the determination of a single action program, or it may be—in line with the definition of the term "strategy" as used in game theory—a contingent set of instructions for actions to be taken, depending on the observed features of the scenario as it develops. In a competitive context, selection of a "mere" strategy (as opposed to a fixed program) may be essential; but even in a one-person

"game against nature", allowance for strategic options may be a wise precaution—for example, when future prospects depend vitally on whether or not a particular technological breakthrough has occurred. While the choice of the strategy to be implemented may be obvious, for several reasons this is not always the case, and intuition, in the form of the decision maker's wisdom, may once more be called upon. Among the reasons for this necessity may be the requirement to balance expectation and risk, or monetary and social costs and rewards, or the advantages accruing to various stakeholder groups.

Intuition, in this ultimate decision task, may have to lean for valuable aid on what has become known as decision theory. Especially when the number of options to be compared is considerable and problems of multidimensionality (in terms of utilities, costs, and variety of stakeholders) have to be coped with, an analysis employing probabilistic decision trees, such as decision theory has to offer, may turn out to be indispensable. However, it must be remembered that decision theory, to be effectively applicable, must be supplied with numerous inputs, most of which are judgmental in character, in that they have to be obtained on the basis of informed estimation. These inputs include probabilities, payoffs (possibly to different interested parties and often multidimensional), and costs (often also multidimensional).

41 TECHNOLOGY ASSESSMENT

A particularly important class of planning tasks belongs in the area of what has become known as technology assessment.

Technology assessment may be defined as the systematic study of the effects on society that may occur when a technology is introduced, extended, or modified, with special emphasis on the impacts that are unintended, indirect, and delayed. It also involves the identification and analysis of interventive actions that may be taken to affect the impact of a technology on society.

From this definition it is evident that technology assessment can benefit from cross-impact analysis. Not only that but, historically speaking, there are some indications that the early thinking in cross-impact terms, with its stress on indirect causal links, contributed to kindling the idea of setting up the Office of Technology Assessment under congressional auspices.

The purpose of assessing a technology with regard to its societal implications is to provide aid to decision makers who have the responsibility of either promoting or retarding the development of the technology in question, of choosing the particular mode of its implementation, or of devising control measures to enhance its desirable or suppress its undesirable effects on society.

"Technologies" here comprise not only physical technologies in the usual sense but also social technologies. Thus technology assessment includes the analysis of the consequences (particularly the nonobvious ones) of proposed social-engineering efforts, such as may be represented by pending social legislation.

Technology assessment has to concern itself with questions such as these:

- What will be the societal, technological, and physical environment into which the new technology is to be introduced?
- What segments of society will be particularly affected by the implications of the new technology?
- What are the nonobvious, secondary, and tertiary effects of that technology?
- In terms of what indicators can the effects of the affected groups be measured?
- What measures can be taken with regard to the development of the new technology that may serve to enhance its beneficial and mitigate its detrimental features?
- What alternative technologies are available that may in some respects compare favorably with the technology under consideration?
- To what extent and in what particular form should the new technology be implemented?
- What control measures might be taken that would enhance or restrict application of the technology and thereby increase its benefits and diminish its drawbacks?

Since technology assessment exemplifies the kind of complex long-range planning discussed in the preceding section of this chapter, the methods of futures analysis itemized there apply to this case. This includes, in particular, the remarks concerning the multiplicity of interest groups, the multidimensionality of costs and benefits, and the pertinence of a gaming approach.

42 THE ROLE OF GAME THEORY IN LONG-RANGE PLANNING

There have been many references to gaming up to this point, and a few to game theory. Before ending this chapter on feasible and desirable futures, the determination of which is the essence of long-range planning, I would like to add some brief remarks on the potential role of game theory in planning and its relationship to gaming activities.

42.1 Game Theory and the Social Contract

Any form of social interaction, be it among persons or organizations or nations, can be viewed as a game that is being played, or rather a continuing series of games, in which the players in some sense strive to maximize their individual or corporate or national utilities. In a parlor game, such as poker or bridge, one side's losses are the other's gains. The game is what is called "zero-sum": No assets are created or destroyed; the total payoffs to the players add up to zero. This is not true of the social games we play, say, when we try to win friends and influence people, corner the market, or negotiate to curtail nuclear proliferation. Such games are not zero-sum, for the interests of the participants are not wholly opposed, and the outcome may benefit all if they act wisely or hurt them all if they do not.

		B 1	B 2
A	1	1,1	11,0
	2	0,11	10,10

A simple example of a non-zero-sum game between two players, of the so-called prisoner's dilemma type, is shown in the illustration: Player A has a choice between two strategies, labeled 1 and 2, and so does Player B. A's payoff is listed first, B's second. Thus, if A chooses Strategy 1 and B chooses Strategy 2, A will receive 11 points and B will receive 0 points. It is seen that, no matter what B does, A will receive 1 more point if he selects Strategy 1 rather than Strategy 2. The same holds for B. If A and B both choose these "optimal" strategies, they will each receive 1 point. Had they, on the other hand, each chosen their "nonoptimal" strategies (2), they would each have received 10 points.

The unfortunate truth with regard to such non-zero-sum games is that in order to arrive at a high payoff for all it is not sufficient simply to resolve to be both cooperative and rational. It takes the existence of a whole cultural environment, in which we can reasonably expect that cooperative moves on our part will find a cooperative response on the part of our opponents in the game. It is the existence of such patterns of expectation that does much to differentiate civilization from the jungle. To the extent that a tacit expectation of such reciprocation exists, it is referred to as "the social contract".

To achieve a modicum of a civilized culture, based on a social contract, requires patient effort over a long period of time and possibly considerable sacrifice. For in playing the games we do in an as yet relatively uncivilized environment, we are constantly confronted with the necessity of choosing between making the most of the current play of the game and selecting a tactic which, though nonoptimal in terms of immediate payoff, seeks by example to create a pattern for future mutual cooperation. In a way, the choice is the old familiar one between maximizing profits in the short run and maximizing them in the long run; except that here, if we opt for the long-run profit and are successful, we are apt to raise everybody's assets along with our own.

In ordinary human relations in our society, we have taken great strides in this direction away from the jungle. Through custom and law we have succeeded in creating a cultural pattern in which the majority expects crime and other antisocial behavior not to pay. What is more, quite aside from the avoidance of actionable behavior, we have acquired numerous standards in our daily lives that go under such labels as "courtesy", "consideration of others", and "charity"; by now we simply think of these as "right" out of habit and tend to forget that they are the result of a slowly evolving expectation of reciprocity.

A similar kind of evolution has taken place with regard to the behavioral patterns among business firms as well as between business firms and both labor and the general public. Nevertheless, there is much room for improvement here. Violations of the spirit, if not the letter, of antitrust legislation are cases in point; so are strikes, which are costly to management, labor, and the general public. In the public sector, relations between ethnic groups, while improving, still show a lack of satisfactory mutual accommodation, inflicting negative payoffs on all concerned.

The one area of human relations in which we are still relatively closest to the jungle and most greatly in need of more civilized patterns of expectation is that of international relations, where the threat of war, with its disastrously negative payoff to all, is still one of the realities of the present. One can only hope that here, too, during the next generation, we shall succeed in abandoning what has been referred to as the delicate balance of terror in favor of a more civilized pattern of behavior within the society of nations.

42.2 Game Theory and Gaming

Game theory is a mathematical theory dealing with abstract competitive situations involving players, moves, and payoffs. Given that certain fundamental conditions are met (essentially that the players have a utility preference scale that is linear in the payoff amounts and in the probabilities involved in probabilistic combinations of outcomes), the theory seeks to determine optimal strategies, that is, instructions on how to move in any situation that may be encountered in a given game, so as to maximize the expected payoff. To say that game theory is a mathematical rather than an empirical theory means that its results are based on logic rather than observation, and being incapable of empirical falsification, it has no predictive force regarding the behavior of players. All one can say is that rational players ought to play optimal strategies prescribed by game theory if they wish to be as satisfied as possible with the outcomes in the long run.

Supplying actual solutions to strategic problems has not been the most important accomplishment of game theory. Its strength and the importance of its role in discussions of conflict resolution have derived from its conceptual innovations. The notions of players and payoffs, applied to conflicts not previously viewed as games, have enriched the discourse in these areas. In economics and in military theory particularly, considerations of strategic uncertainty and the role of information in strategic planning, the distinction between cooperative and noncooperative modes of play, the very notion of a strategy as a set of instructions for selecting specific moves as a function of information acquired in the course of playing a game, and the role of coalitions among players—all of these have provided the basis for a more meaningful and systematic attack on the problems in these disciplines.

Gaming, in contrast to game theory, is a simulation activity. After constructing a model of reality (with all the abstractions usually involved in that process), gaming consists in what we have called "pseudo-experimentation" in the model. Its purpose is to observe how the entities represented in the model react to player interventions, in the hope that this empirical information about the model will give some clues as to how the real world is likely to react to similar interventions. The degree to which this transference from the model to reality is justified clearly depends on how faithfully the important features of reality are simulated by the model.

In principle, when we wish to study the future of some portion X of the real world and when we have a reasonably faithful model of X available, we might, instead of engaging in simulation gaming, look to game theory for guidance in selecting an optimal strategy. In practice, however, the utility of game theory is quite limited, for two reasons: Game theory to date can cope entirely satisfactorily only with zero-sum conflict situations, a type of conflict in which a planner is rarely, if ever, interested; and in the case of non-zero-sum games, the theory offers solution concepts such as that which, in our little 2×2 example in Section 42.1, provides a very unsatisfactory "optimal" strategy. To be sure, the payoff of one unit to each player furnished by that strategy is the most each player can guarantee for himself if the game is one of total noncooperation. But in the real world, the players' behavior will be modified either by the availability of negotiable cooperative ploys or by the expectation of some tacit cooperation based on a pattern of past accommodation. Thus the real world will be seen to have features that preclude the application of game theory in its present form.

42.3 Game Theory and Organization Theory

The members of an organization (e.g., a business firm or a government department) ostensibly pursue a common goal (the welfare of the organization), yet individually they are likely to pull in slightly different directions since their personal biases and preferences will be superimposed on the organization's overall utilities. Thus, in a sense, the members of an organization are players in a game.[1]

Organization theory and game theory both are concerned with the interactions of the decisions of a group of people acting under given constraints. It therefore is reasonable to expect the existence of an approach to organization theory via the theory of games. As it happens, it appears that the application of the game-theoretical apparatus to the study of organizations promises to be of substantial benefit to both parties concerned—to game theory as well

1. The following section, in essence, is identical with my article, "The Game-Theoretical Approach to Organization Theory", *Synthèse,* vol. 15 (1963).

as to organization theory. One can go even further, it seems to me, and in fact assert (i) that both game theory and organization theory are in real trouble today, (ii) that organization theory can be viewed as a very natural extension of game theory as far as applications are concerned, and (iii) that by giving proper recognition to this intimate relationship between the two fields, they are both likely to overcome their present difficulties.

These difficulties are of a very different nature in the two cases. The trouble with organization theory, briefly and bluntly, is its nonexistence. There has been a lot of talk about organization theory and there have been numerous sporadic studies in this general area (particularly those generally designated as case studies). But there has, as far as I can see, been no serious and successful attempt to build up an adequate conceptual framework within which to construct a unified theory of organizations. Even the basic concept of an organization, and hence of the subject matter of this supposed theory, is extremely vague. For this reason alone it would be most fortuitous if game theory had to offer a ready-made conceptual framework that might be exploited and expanded appropriately to establish a satisfactory conceptual basis for a theory of organizations.

The trouble with game theory is of a very different kind, since its concepts are exact enough to permit axiomatization. Despite considerable advances in the mathematical theory, especially regarding two-person zero-sum games, the theory of games, in my opinion, has reached a state of near stagnation with regard to its applicability to the real world. This is true not only of the non-zero-sum and n-person parts of the theory but applies equally to the zero-sum two-person case.

In order to establish a framework within which to discuss these matters, let me recall the epistemological apparatus for applying a mathematical theory to the real world. A mathematical theory of necessity takes as its starting point some basic assumptions (see Figure 14), which possibly may be a set

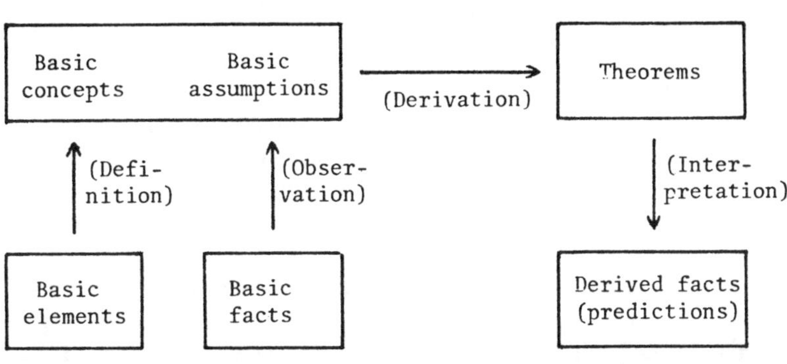

FIGURE 14

of formal axioms and which are formulated in terms of certain basic concepts. From this basis the theory will derive certain theorems. The application to reality takes place by establishing what are sometimes called correlative definitions, that is, by interpreting the basic concepts as standing for certain basic elements in the real world. This correlation associates certain basic facts with the basic assumptions, and if the basic facts have been established by observation, we may predict—as derived facts—the statements about the real world corresponding to the theorems of the theory.

Applied to two-person zero-sum games, the theory usually assumes merely that the players have a utility preference scale that is linear in the payoff amounts and in the probabilities involved in probabilistic combinations of outcomes.

Let us note in passing in what indirect sense we may speak of predictions in game theory: Usually the normative formulation is preferred, namely that, if a zero-sum game is played by two persons each having a linear utility scale with respect to the outcomes (let us call them briefly "linear players"), then each ought to play an optimal strategy as prescribed by game theory. But this is equivalent to predicting that each will on the average be most satisfied with the outcome if he plays an optimal strategy. A slightly different twist can be given to the predictive element by the following formulation: A linear player, if he is rational and if he assumes his opponent to be rational, will select an optimal strategy. By thus formally adding the player's rationality and his appraisal of the opponent's rationality to the basic assumptions, we can now shift from a prediction of the player's relative satisfaction with the outcome to a prediction of the player's behavior during the play of the game. This formulation will greatly facilitate the transition to predictions in organization theory.

Now, to defend my statement about the inadequacy of game theory in point of applicability, let us remember that the principal fields of application to date are economic, where the payoff is monetary, and military, where the payoff is in terms of some combat advantage. In the economic case, the assumption of linearity, as is well known, is usually absurd, especially when the amounts involved are sizable compared to the player's assets (to a very poor person, a thousand dollars may be worth almost as much as a million dollars); and by the time we go over from the ostensible monetary payoffs to linear utilities, the game almost invariably turns out to be non-zero-sum. As for the military applications, the situation is even worse: The payoff there is usually in terms of some vaguely conceived military advantage, and the mathematical model has to introduce some completely fictitious measurable utility in order to make the situation amenable to game-theoretical treatment. Take, for instance, the rather well-known Blotto-type game in which two opposing commanders commit their battalions to fight over the possession of several positions of military advantage. The customary payoff is the difference in the number of surviving battalions plus so many credit points for each position held. Even if such a scoring system were to reflect reasonably accurately the military utility of specific outcomes to one side, there is little reason to assume that this utility is linear with respect to probability combinations of such outcomes or that the military utility to the other side should be assessed by the same formula. (Parenthetically, in more serious situations, as when assessing nuclear parity, a naive assumption of linearity, here applied to a nuclear-weapons count, has led to erroneous conclusions as to the existence or absence of such parity.)

Thus, in order to do justice to the areas of application for which game theory was supposedly developed, it is necessary, first, to create an applicable theory of non-zero-sum games, and, second, to go rather thoroughly into an analysis of the sensitivity with which optimal strategies depend on the choice of a particular payoff function when no such specific function is unambiguously implied by the real situation.

The next thing to look at, then, is the status, with regard to applicability, of the non-zero-sum theory. Here, aside from rather inconclusive attempts to deal with special negotiatory situations, only the two extreme basic assumptions have been considered in great detail, namely complete cooperation and complete noncooperation, in each case coupled again with the assumption of linear utilities. The former, of course, is the original von Neumann-Morgenstern theory, the latter the equilibrium-point theory.

Among the two principal areas of application, the economic and the military, the von Neumann-Morgenstern theory may at best be applicable to the economic one, since the assumption of complete cooperation among military opponents is clearly absurd. In the economic case, we no longer are confronted with the difficulty of nonlinear utilities as in the zero-sum case, because—since the game is non-zero-sum anyway—we may as well assume that the ostensible monetary payoffs have for each player been replaced by linear utilities. But here a new difficulty arises: The linear utilities associated by the players with the monetary outcomes are no longer commensurable and transferable, and therefore the prescription, which the theory offers, of maximizing the expected return to the coalition of the players becomes meaningless.

The equilibrium-point theory, on the other hand, is not quite so badly off. It requires no commensurability of utilities and is at least in special cases able to predict the behavior of rational players. It does presuppose complete noncooperation, however, and for that reason is rarely applicable directly to real-life situations. Let us consider two trivial examples. The game with payoff matrix

	B	
A	1,1	11,0
	0,5	10,10

—where, as in the earlier example in Section 42.1, Player A chooses between rows, Player B between columns, and A's payoff is listed first, B's second—has a unique equilibrium point (first row, first column) with payoffs of 1 to each player. (An equilibrium point is a pair of strategies such that neither player would wish to change his strategy unless the other did.) Yet the mere agreement among the players to let Player A go first will cause both to switch to their second strategies and give each a tenfold return. Notice that in this case it is merely a question of whether the constraints of the situation permit transition to this slightly different game; if they do, a pair of rational players will automatically accept it. Next look at the game obtained from the previous example by changing 5 to 11:

	B	
A	1,1	11,0
	0,11	10,10

(which is our old friend from Section 42.1). The equilibrium point is the same as before, but the corresponding strategies are now "strongly dominant" (that is, each is preferred by its player, no matter what he knows of the opponent's choice of strategy); therefore under strict noncooperation the theory rightly recommends that the equilibrium point be played. Again, a small amount of cooperation (as we had noted earlier) would cause each player to switch to his second strategy, giving each a payoff of 10. But in this case more than just a transition to a slightly different game, acceptable to any rational player, is involved. The cooperation here presupposes a relationship between the players extraneous to the immediate game situation. This relationship may be one of several: They may be playing within a social environment having the institution of enforceable contracts and avail themselves of this opportunity; or there may be an attitude of mutual trust that would warrant the entering of a purely informal agreement; or, more specifically, there may be an experience pattern derived from a series of plays of the same or similar games against the same opponent, which will lead each to expect the other to play his second strategy.

The point I am hoping to make with these trivial examples is that the equilibrium-point theory often suggests what appears to be an unreasonable solution, in the sense that there may be a different outcome that is preferred by all players, and that this preferred solution can often be achieved by a rather minute and obvious amount of cooperation. What happens when such cooperation takes place may of course formally be interpreted as the embedding of the given game in a larger game, which can then be regarded as a strictly noncooperative game and for which the equilibrium-point solution is reasonable, in the sense that no other outcome is preferred by all players.

But this shows clearly the limits to which game theory as such can be expected to take us. Given rational players with known utility preferences, it can—at least in many cases—predict the players' behavior in a given noncooperative game. Moreover, given a game with certain cooperation options, it may tell us if that game can be embedded in a larger, noncooperative game having a reasonable equilibrium-point solution (in the earlier sense). But what it cannot generally do is to predict the behavior, even of rational players with known utility preferences, with regard to their cooperative options, insofar as these depend on the players' attitudes toward their fellow players and toward any behavior patterns they may have observed in past plays. At this precise point, therefore, in order to be in a position to predict decision-making behavior in cooperative situations of this kind, it becomes mandatory to go beyond the limits of game theory proper. It is in this context, I think, that organization theory appears as the natural extension of game theory.

Like game theory, organization theory is somehow concerned with an interacting group of people in a decision-making situation. But in two decisive respects it has to allow for greater sophistication than game theory: First, it must assume that the members of the group, in addition to certain utility preferences, have other recognizable characteristics of a psychological nature (such as attitudes toward fellow members and toward risk, and possibly learning ability); and second, instead of dealing with just one fixed competitive situation with well-determined outcome possibilities, it must be capable of handling a continual recurrence, a flux, of situations calling on the participants to make decisions in the light of their preferences, capabilities, and attitudes.

Applied to the simplest possible case of a two-person game, game theory should be able to predict, on the basis of rationality and the known utility preferences of the players, how the game will be played once noncooperatively. But if we wish to predict what would happen if this game were played repeatedly under certain cooperation options, we have to turn to organization theory—which, however, would require additional assumptions regarding the players' attitudes.

What I am saying does not amount to a definition of the subject matter of organization theory. I am merely trying to state, from the game-theoretical point of view, some minimum conditions concerning what real-life situations a theory of organizations should be capable of handling.

If the proposal of establishing organization theory as a natural extension of game theory should find acceptance, then this entails a whole program of research in this joint area of interest, which is the study of human interactions in decision-making situations under given constraints.

Let me then take a brief look at the prospects of such a joint enterprise—a theory of games directed somewhat more deliberately toward applicability, and a theory of organizations built on a game-theoretical foundation.

Conceptually, game theory would profit, because by relegating motivations other than utility preferences to organization theory, it would confine game theory to that area in which it can reasonably be expected to show results, and remove the uneasiness about why game theory seems to be unable to cope with cooperative games (in the sense of suggesting, or predicting, rational behavior). As for organization theory, the advantage of being able to latch on to the existing vocabulary of game theory, as I pointed out before, would be considerable. But it is also clear that an immediate effort would have to be made to introduce formally the additionally needed, typically organizational, concepts having to do with the players' attitudes of various kinds.

As for specific areas of research suggested by this approach, let me list a few, without the slightest attempt at completeness:

(1) An analysis of the sensitivity with which optimal strategies depend on slight changes in the payoff function, both for zero-sum and noncooperative non-zero-sum games. This is important when a conflict situation in which there is no obvious one-dimensional utility is modeled by a game having a one-dimensional linear payoff function.

(2) An examination, both analytical and experimental, of ostensibly zero-sum games, that is, of games with ostensible zero-sum monetary payoffs, which in fact are non-zero-sum when realistic utility preferences are introduced. In particular, it would be interesting to determine under what circumstances such an associated non-zero-sum game has a reasonable equilibrium-point solution.

(3) A complete theory of negotiation games under the assumption of the availability of enforceable contracts.

(4) A systematic examination of the following type of embeddability problem: Given a pair of payoff matrices for a non-zero-sum game, assume that the equilibrium-point theory has no reasonable solution to offer for noncooperative play. In that case, by what cooperative devices (such as passage of information, contractual agreements) could the given game be embedded in a larger game that both players would like to play at least as well as the given game and that does have a reasonable equilibrium-point solution?

(5) The isolation of suitable attitudinal predicates, in terms of which people can be characterized and their actions in competitive decision-making situations can be predicted. A first step in this direction might possibly be taken by subjecting subjects to a series of standardized non-zero-sum games and classifying them according to their choices of strategy.

(6) An analysis of the mutual-influence structure within a group as a function of the members' attitudes.

(7) An empirical study of the performance of small organized groups in playing games. Given n people (where n at first may well be 2 or 3) with certain utility preferences and attitudes, with a given communication structure and a preestablished mutual-influence structure, how well will each perform when the group is subjected to a suitable series of standardized test games?

I would like to finish with a plea regarding methodology. Several of the examples I just gave call for what is primarily psychological research. But it would be disastrous if the mathematicians used this to rationalize their doing nothing about it. Here if ever seems to me to be a clear-cut and perhaps even crucial case calling for the much-advertised application of mathematical methods to the social sciences. Paradoxically, psychology can possibly receive the greatest help by being steered away from its traditional method of carefully controlled series of laboratory experiments and toward what amounts to more of an engineering approach to its problems. That means the construction of possibly a multitude of tentative mathematical models, the evaluation of which need not be through detailed experimentation, since we are at this stage interested not so much in minute exactness but in gross workable ideas. There are in fact two devices we can use to trade unneeded overexactness for badly needed speed. One is a cautious use of expert judgment wherever it is available, the other an exploitation of high-speed computing facilities, which can be used in Monte Carlo fashion to examine the implications of mathematical models for a multitude of values of their input parameters. There may be some real hope that a concerted effort along these lines may help to produce within the foreseeable future the foundations of a highly applicable theory of organizations. ■

I have felt impelled to include this seeming digression into game theory and organization theory because to some planning activities concerned with sifting out feasible as well as desirable futures from the possible ones—though surely not to all—they are indeed relevant. I am thinking, in particular, on the one hand, of planning in a competitive context (such as market competition, military preparedness, or diplomatic maneuvers) and, on the other, of management planning within a large corporation or a major public-sector enterprise (such as secondary education or the criminal justice system). In the former case, while what is desirable may be clear, what is feasible will depend on the moves of other actors in the game; in the latter case, feasibility may have to be tempered by what the various members of the organization consider desirable. The capability of realistic long-range planning in these areas will no doubt be noticeably enhanced once game and organization theories and, especially, the neglected territory between them have been put on a satisfactory, applications-oriented foundation.

I would like to conclude this chapter with an example of a study in normative forecasting, namely, an application of the Delphi technique to the identification of research projects deserving of funding, carried out in 1970 at the request of the Kettering Foundation.

43 FUTURE OPPORTUNITIES FOR FOUNDATION SUPPORT[2]

The following brief account is based on excerpts from a report under this title.

The assignment required that the study address itself to two tasks: the nomination of candidate proposals and the selection of a program of projects from among the candidate proposals. The present report identifies a large

2. Olaf Helmer and Helen Helmer, Report R-11, Institute for the Future (1970).

number of potential areas of support and accompanies each proposal with an evaluation in terms of (i) its probability of success if adequately supported, (ii) its probable societal impact if successful, (iii) its estimated annual and total support requirements, and (iv) its cost-effectiveness.

The central device used in this study was a survey of expert opinions by the Delphi technique. As the experts we were fortunate enough to be able to use the following forty-three persons: Saul Alinsky, Richard de Bold, Philip Bondy, James Bonner, Kenneth Boulding, Harrison Brown, John Burlew, Ramsey Clark, James Comer, Norman Cousins, Charles Day, Richard Farson, Joseph Fisher, Andre Fontaine, George Gallup, Alfred Gellhorn, Bertrand Goldberg, William Golden, Pat Gunkel, Theodore Hesburgh, Marvin Hoffenberg, Frederick Hooven, Peter Hooven, Charles Kettering, John Kincaid, Willard Libby, Richard Lombard, George Mandanis, David Mathews, Andrew Morgan, Samuel Proctor, Nicholas Rescher, Henry Reuss, Walter O. Roberts, Olin Robison, Rudy Ruggles, Leonard J. Savage, Joseph Slater, Stewart Udall, Peter Van Vorhees, Phyllis Wallace, Christopher Wright, and Paul Ylvisaker. This group was augmented, in the first round only, by ten staff members each of the Kettering Foundation and of the Institute for the Future. (The reason for their exclusion from later rounds was that, while Round 1 merely asked for ideas, Rounds 2 and 3 were concerned with the evaluation of ideas resulting from Round 1, and the participation of the Foundation or Institute staff members might conceivably have introduced some bias into these evaluations.)

In the first Delphi round, the respondents were asked to give brief descriptions of research projects they wished to nominate for consideration. To assist them in this task, a taxonomy of sixty-four areas of potential interest was submitted to them; these areas were grouped under six headings: society, systems and institutions, environment, international affairs, values and mores, and science and technology. The response consisted of 189 entries, which the experimenters combined and reduced to 165.

The second round required an evaluation of these 165 items in five regards. The questionnaire instructions in fact read in part as follows:

(a) *The formulation of the proposal:* If you wish to suggest an amendment to the formulation, please do so on the back of the evaluation sheet. . . . If you have made an amendment, it will be assumed that your subsequent evaluation refers to the statement as amended by you.

(b) *The probability* that the proposed project, if adequately funded, will successfully accomplish its stated goal.

(c) *The importance* of the results of the proposed effort, if indeed it should be successful, in terms of their societal impact. Here, if you should judge the impact to be strong, it would be helpful if you could indicate in a word or two what type of impact you are envisaging. (The choice given the respondents was between four alternatives: virtually no impact = 1, slight impact only = 3, moderate impact = 5, strong impact = 7.)

(d) *The degree* to which support of the proposal would *fill a gap,* in the sense that support from other sources, to your knowledge, is nonexistent or insufficient. If you know of adequate other support, you are asked to state its source.

(e) *The required level of funding:* To support a given project below a certain minimum level would clearly be wasteful. On the other hand, support above a certain level would generally yield sharply diminishing marginal returns. Hence you are being asked to advise the Foundation, if it were to support the project at all, what you would consider reasonable minimum and maximum levels of funding.

The responses to Parts b, c, and e of Questionnaire 2 were collated, their medians were computed, and these medians were taken as numerical indicators of the panel's opinions as a group. Based on these assessments, more than half of the proposals under consideration were eliminated from the final round on one of three grounds; too low a probability of success; too small a societal impact even if successful; or outside the cost range (for reasonable minimum support) between $250,000 and $5,000,000 (which was stipulated as the Foundation's scope of interest).

The remaining 80 proposals formed the input into the final, third, round. The wording of a few was slightly revised, based on suggestions received from the respondents. It was thought that 80 was too large a number to require that each respondent examine each proposal. Consequently the list was divided into two sublists of 40 and each was submitted to one-half of the respondents, selected randomly. In the third round, then, each respondent received a list of the 40 proposals assigned to him for reevaluation, together with the median assessments derived from Round 2. Each panelist was asked to review those 10 (out of the 40) entries with regard to which he thought himself relatively most knowledgeable and to revise the assessments if he felt they needed it. In addition, he was to rank from 1 to 10 those proposals among the 40 he considered to be most appropriate for Foundation support.

A few of the Round 2 medians were thus revised in Round 3. Most of the revisions occurred with regard to probability and impact, since few respondents seemed to have strong opinions on funding levels.

In order to be able to present the results of this evaluation in some orderly fashion, it was thought desirable to combine the probability and impact ratings into a single effectiveness index. There are many ways this can be done, and the experimenters selected one that seemed intuitively acceptable. We assumed, in fact, that among the impact ratings of $I = 1, 3, 5, 7$ each corresponds to an effort, e, worth twice as much as the preceding one, expressed by the formula $e = 2^{½(I-1)}$. This leads to the "expected effectiveness", E, defined as $E = p \times e$, where p is the probability of success. (Thus, for example, a proposal with probability .6 and impact 5 has effectiveness $E = .6 \times 4 = 2.4$.)

Clearly, a proposal is most attractive if its effectiveness is high and its cost is low. According to this criterion, the "ten most wanted" studies turned out to be on the following subjects:

(1) human intelligence
(2) urban communications
(3) transportation and communication
(4) leadership regeneration
(5) the future of the corporation
(6) instinct toward violence
(7) U.S. population and environment
(8) acceptance of population control
(9) crowding
(10) medical care systems analysis

Just to convey the flavor of these proposals, I reproduce the full wording of the first three:

> *Human intelligence:* The classical notion of an intelligence quotient has been recognized by many researchers as having outworn its utility; yet its naive application is still widespread. What is needed is a new, comprehensive, up-to-date study of human intelligence, with its results published in a form that is useful and comprehensible to educators at all levels and does not lend itself to the traditional bureaucratic abuse to which the IQ concept has been subjected. Such a study should include a redefinition of "intelligence"; it should examine the merits and limitations of existing testing procedures and possibly devise new ones; and it should ascertain the dependence (or independence) of intelligence on cultural differences and on genetic factors. The study should further include experimental research concerned with methods of enhancing intelligence through, for example, very early education and/or sensory stimulation, the development of intelligence drugs, methods of improving the prenatal environment, and nutritional supplements.
>
> *Urban communications:* Intraurban communications ("the local loop") is in a state of emerging crisis. This is largely due to (i) unreliable and short-term-oriented demand forecasts and (ii) long amortization horizons for (obsolescing) common-carrier facilities. An integrative study program should forecast demands for communications services within and among highly urbanized areas in the United States over the next two decades. Sectors of demand to receive special attention could be industry, banking, municipal governments, publications, communications media, and educational institutions. Through cost-effectiveness and contingency analyses, such a study would determine the technological alternatives that best satisfy projected demand. The study would investigate, in particular, the joint impact of communications satellites, broadband coaxial cables, and advanced techniques for modulation and signal processing.
>
> *Transportation and communication:* How much of the displacement of people could be removed by sufficiently effective means of verbal and pictorial communication? Conferences and lectures could relatively easily be arranged by telecommunication with little radical equipment (in particular, without the luxury of television). Sufficiently advanced communication would permit very effective shopping by televisor at great savings in transportation and to the advantage of buyer and seller. With such communication techniques the present pressure to

concentrate offices and stores in big cities and to have clerical workers and administrators always physically present in the offices where they work could be largely obviated. While the communication industry presumably sees the advantage of expanding in the direction suggested, the question might be raised under foundation auspices whether the interests of the communication industry as now organized really are parallel to those of the public in this respect. A broad examination should be planned of the extent to which transportation of people will be replaced by communication.

Finally, some comments on the methodology used in this study:

We live in a time when societal emergencies are crowding in upon us with increasing urgency and when, consequently, the wise expenditure of philanthropic largesse has assumed greater importance than ever. Indeed, public clamor and specific legislation add weight to the foundations' own desire to act as true guardians of the public interest. It is not inappropriate, therefore, for foundations to look for new and more systematic approaches to determining the most worthwhile public causes to which they might give their attention and support.

The present study may be regarded as a first pilot effort in this direction, and it is hoped that, aside from its substantive content, its methodological approach might provide a modest contribution to the emerging debate on a possible reorientation of philanthropic programming methods.

The practice—not without exceptions, admittedly—has been for foundations to be approached with funding requests by individual proponents of ideas for supposedly worthwhile projects, and for foundation officials to award grants to some extent on the basis of their intuitive preferences and of the persuasiveness with which project proposals have been stated.

The approach used in the present study, while leaving the ultimate decision-making responsibility of foundation officials unimpaired, has been different in two major respects. It has appealed to a set of specialists in a broad variety of fields to formulate proposals for projects that might serve the public interest, and it has asked these same experts not just to appraise these proposals individually, but to evaluate them comparatively in the spirit of what amounts to a rudimentary systems-analytical approach.

The device used for this purpose has been a simplified version of the Delphi method, which typically addresses a series of inquiries to a panel of respondents, providing feedback between rounds on the responses received in the preceding round.

The merits of this approach, particularly when applied to an all-out effort rather than a mere pilot one, may be characterized as follows:

(i) Proposals are solicited on a systematic basis rather than received haphazardly.
(ii) Participants, by being asked to propose several projects in the public interest, are stimulated to think innovatively and not just to promote a single, favorite project.

(iii) Project proposals, by being edited into a format that is reasonably uniform, have a better chance of being judged on their comparative merits rather than on the basis of possibly speciously persuasive formulation.

(iv) Proposals are evaluated in the spirit of a systems-analytical approach, in the sense that (a) assessments are required of their cost, probability of success, and effectiveness (in terms of societal impact); and (b) each respondent is encouraged to simulate the eventual program selection process by stating which particular subset, out of the total set of proposals, he would most wish to advocate.

(v) Overspecification of the mode of execution of a proposed project is avoided, which on balance is advantageous (provided the formulation leaves no doubt as to the overall purpose of the project) because it facilitates the decision-making process and gives appropriate discretion to those who will eventually be charged with the execution of the project. ■

Chapter VIII

Long-Range Forecasts

44 REVIEW AND PREVIEW

Up to this point, the emphasis in this book has been on methodology, with occasional references to substantive applications. From here on, this orientation will be reversed; that is, attention will be centered on explorations of the future, with consideration of methods taking second place.

All planning derives its rationale from the fact that the future is at least partly subject to our choice and control. Forecasts enter the planning process in two respects: They are needed to establish the changed operating environment (absolute forecasts) and to assess the implications of alternative action plans (conditional forecasts).

If we could make forecasts of both kinds in the form of true predictions rather than merely probabilistic statements, the planning process would degenerate into one of simple optimization. It would amount to selecting the best, in an absolute sense, among all available courses of action. In reality, since all forecasts consist in probability estimates, the most we can hope for is to make such estimates with reasonable reliability and to select the relatively best, in an expected-value sense, among the possible sets of actions at our disposal.

In addition to the uncertainty implied by the need to rely on probability estimates, the planning process—as I have emphasized repeatedly—is further complicated by two factors: complexity and "theorylessness". Sheer complexity of most planning situations makes the planning task comparable to playing a game of chess; while, in principle, each move could be optimized (there are not even any probabilistic uncertainties present in this case), the number of possible moves and their consequences is too vast to permit a full comparative exploration. Because of the inevitable involvement, in planning, with social-science problems (economic, psychological, political aspects, and so on) as well as with multidisciplinary considerations (e.g., the psychological impact of economic changes), the planner is constantly faced with the regrettable absence of an adequate theoretical foundation on which to base predictions or, at least, forecasts. Thus the planner's life, for two reasons, is not an easy one.

The theme of this book has been to acknowledge this unsatisfactory state of affairs but to seek a positive approach rather than give in to despair. The prescription I have been trying to offer can perhaps best be summarized under three headings:

- *The use of expert judgment:* Even in the absence of a theoretical infrastructure, appropriately chosen experts are quite capable of arriving at probabilistic forecasts, both absolute and conditional, that are far more reliable than lay guesses, and the reliability of such estimates can be further enhanced by using groups of experts and applying the Delphi technique to them.
- *The use of cross-impact analysis as a surrogate for proper theory:* Through this approach it is possible to construct the next-best thing to a theory, permitting systematic consideration of law-like regularities, even in areas that span several of the conventional disciplines.
- *The use of pseudo-experimentation as a rehearsal for the future:* By applying simulation gaming—for instance (but not necessarily), with the help of a cross-impact model—alternative strategies for creating a desirable future can be pretested for feasibility and side effects.

The historically first systematic use of intuitive expert judgment for the purpose of making a series of forecasts in a variety of different fields took place in a Delphi study that I conducted together with Theodore Gordon under the auspices of the Rand Corporation in 1963. A part of the report on the outcome of this study is reprinted in what follows.

45 REPORT ON A LONG-RANGE FORECASTING STUDY[1]

45.1 Intent of This Study

This is a report on an experiment in forecasting that has been conducted during the past year. "Forecasting" is used here in the sense of mapping out possible futures, as distinguished from "predicting" a single future. The purpose of this undertaking was both substantive and methodological.

Substantively, our interests lay in assessing the direction of long-range trends, with special emphasis on science and technology, and their probable effects on our society and our world. Here, by "long-range" we had in mind something on the order of ten to fifty years. Our natural curiosity in this regard was enhanced by an awareness of the fact that the work at Rand is in many instances closely related to plans and policies affecting the rather distant future and that consequently the direction of our studies and the substance of whatever recommendations may result from them are inevitably influenced by our concept of the shape of things to come.

Methodologically, we found ourselves confronted by a near-vacuum as far as tested techniques of long-range forecasting are concerned. Here our hope

1. This is part of a report under the same title, by Theodore Gordon and myself, Rand paper P-2982 (1964), and subsequently published as an appendix to my book *Social Technology*, Copyright © 1966 by Olaf Helmer. Reprinted by permission of Basic Books, Inc., Publishers, New York.

was to sharpen the few systematic methods that are available and, through practical experience, to gain some insight into specific needs for further methodological research.

Depending on one's point of view, a project such as this may be considered predestined to failure because of its overambitious scope, or predestined to success because even very little progress in so important and neglected an area is bound to be of value in the design of long-range plans. Actually, the outcome of this experiment has in no way been spectacular. Nonetheless we hope that the reader of this report will agree with us that our undertaking has indeed been mildly successful, in the sense that our findings represent a beginning in the process of sifting the likely from the unlikely among the contingencies of the future, and that we have obtained some hints as to how such efforts can be conducted more effectively hereafter.

Future events can be considered as roughly belonging to one of two sets: the expected and the unexpected. A study such as this cannot hope to uncover the unexpected, spectacular, unanticipated breakthroughs; rather, it must concentrate on narrowing down the dates and circumstances of occurrences that can be extrapolated from the present. We recognize this as a shortcoming of our present study. Nevertheless, some of the substantive predictive material was, to the experimenters at least, unexpected. In that sense, the future may now hold fewer surprises for some of us.

45.2 Subject Matter

Among the many features of the world of the future that are competing for exploration, we had, for the sake of sheer manageability, to select only a few. Our choice, while somewhat arbitrary, was guided by the desire to have a collection of areas that in combination would provide broad (though not exhaustive) coverage of the most important determinants of the society of the future. We finally decided on the following six topics:

(1) scientific breakthroughs
(2) population control
(3) automation
(4) space progress
(5) war prevention
(6) weapon systems

[Of these, only the first five are included in this present excerpt. The reasons for omitting the portion on weapon systems are that most of the forecasts were relatively short-range and are now obsolete and that much of the material—included in the study because of the Rand sponsorship—is not likely to be of great interest to persons outside the community of military planners.]

In seeking out the future trends in these areas, we were of course well aware that we would not through some miracle be able to remove the veil of uncertainty from the future. This did not seem to us to imply, though, that it is altogether impossible to make meaningful assertions of substantive content about the future.

The reliability with which the future can be predicted is a matter of degree. In planning our daily lives, we are accustomed to predicting the immediate twenty-four-hour future with a reasonable degree of certainty. Plans as far as a year ahead—say, concerning the budget of a family, a firm, or the federal government—although afflicted with a noticeable degree of uncertainty, still are recognized and accepted as a highly reliable means of regulating our lives. Even if the planning horizon is five to ten years away, as it is with many major governmental decisions, standard trend projections, obtained by extrapolation from the recent past and from knowledge of current activities, usually provide fairly reliable results. Nevertheless, in employing past and present trends as indicators of the future, we begin to be strongly aware of the need for judicious intuitive assessment.

For the more distant future, as the uncertainties grow, increased reliance on intuitive (as opposed to theory-supported) contingency forecasts becomes inevitable. However, this does not deter us from planning ten to fifty years ahead, as evidenced by our public policies regarding such matters as educational institutions, urban renewal, aid to developing countries, procurement of military weapon systems, space exploration, and so on.

In view of such common practice of long-range planning, which both affects the ten- to fifty-year future and is itself influenced by our expectations regarding the world at that time, it seems reasonable to adopt a pragmatic attitude: Since the use of intuitive forecasting as a basis for long-range planning is unavoidable, we should at least make an effort to obtain this intuitive judgment as systematically as possible from persons who are recognized experts in the area of concern. Until a satisfactory predictive theory of the phenomena in question becomes available, it would seem that any improvement in reliability, however slight, that could be achieved by replacing casual guess with the controlled use of intuitive expertise would be desirable because of the benefits that long-range public policies might derive from it.

These potential benefits are likely to grow with each decade; because of the ever more explosive rapidity with which new technological developments are apt to take hold, it becomes increasingly important to foresee the advent of such impacts in order to prepare for their social consequences and to avert possible calamities.

It is this potentially large payoff from even minor advances in the reliability of trend forecasting—not to mention humanity's natural fascination with the idea of exploring the future regardless of any tangible returns (just like exploring the Moon)—that we offer as justification for the present effort.

Our procedure, if we are fortunate, might even succeed incidentally in crystallizing the nucleus of a predictive theory of the subject matter under inquiry, by goading the experts from whom we solicit opinions into formulating some of their perhaps hitherto unarticulated reasons for these opinions. Thus we hope that an effort such as ours may go beyond merely filling a temporary gap and set into motion analytical thought processes that eventually might lead to the formulation of a scientific theory regarding the phenomena in question.

45.3 Method

The method we have employed for the systematic solicitation of expert opinions is the so-called Delphi technique. Instead of using the traditional approach toward achieving a consensus through open discussion, this technique eliminates committee activity altogether. [For details, see Chapter V, especially Section 24.]

We selected six groups of experts, one each for the six areas to be surveyed. Of the approximately 150 persons approached, 82 responded to one or more questionnaires. Of these, 35 were members of Rand, 7 others were Rand consultants, and the remaining 40 were not connected with Rand; 6 of these 40 were European respondents. Some of the participants responded voluntarily also to questionnaires submitted to other panels. (It was our practice, in order to keep the participants informed of all phases of the experiment, to send copies of the questionnaires for all six panels to each respondent, distinguishing that addressed to his own panel by a special color of paper.)

Each panel of experts answered four sequential questionnaires, spaced approximately two months apart. The average number of filled-in questionnaires received from each panel per round was 14.5 (making a total of $6 \times 4 \times 14.5$, or 348).

45.4 Illustration of Procedure

To illustrate our procedure, we will give the details of a small segment of the inquiry conducted with the help of Panel 1 on Scientific Breakthroughs.

In the opening round we addressed the following question to the panel:

Questionnaire 1.1.

One of the major problems of conducting a predictive study which poses its questions on the basis of extrapolations of current technology is the almost unavoidable exclusion of discontinuous state-of-the-art advances.

In this current study a period of 50 years is being considered. It is possible that inventions and discoveries not yet visualized could have a major impact on our society during this interval. It is easy to observe that the pace of scientific and technological innovation has been steadily increasing and that the time between origination and application has been decreasing. Therefore we believe that many generations of inventions can find application during the period under study.

> Some insight even into discontinuous state-of-the-art advances might perhaps be gained by examining the world's need for such advances, in view of the old truism that necessity is the mother of invention. Therefore, you are asked to list below major inventions and scientific breakthroughs in areas of special concern to you which you regard as both urgently needed and feasible within the next 50 years.

Collation and paring of the responses led to a list of 49 items, which were presented to the panel in the next round (Questionnaire 1.2) with a request to indicate, for each item, the probability of actual implementation in each of the following time intervals:

1963-1965	1972-1978	1997-2013
1965-1968	1978-1986	Later than 2013
1968-1972	1986-1997	Never

Three examples of the 49 items were these: B1, chemical control over heredity—molecular biology; S8, popular use of personality-control drugs; and P10, reliable weather forecasts.

For each item, each respondent's probability distribution over time obtained from Questionnaire 1.2 was used to determine approximately the year by which the item, in his opinion, had a probability of 50 percent of being implemented. For the three illustrative items, these "50 percent years" had the following medians and quartiles:

	Median	Quartiles
B1	1993	1982-2033
S8	2050	1984-2050
P10	1975	1972-1988

In the case of P10, for instance, this means than one-quarter of the respondents thought that the date by which P10 had an even chance of occurring would be prior to 1972 (the lower quartile) and, similarly, that one-half thought it would be prior to 1975 (the median) and one-quarter that it would be later than 1988 (the upper quartile).

On the basis of findings such as these, it was judged that for 10 of the 49 items (Item P10 among them) there existed a reasonable consensus among the respondents. This consensus was announced to the respondents in Questionnaire 1.3, together with an invitation to take exception if they differed strongly from this majority consensus:

> P10 (reliable weather forecasts): Not within 5 but within 35 years.
>
> Do you, by and large, agree with the opinion represented by the consensus? If you disagree . . . , briefly state your reason for your differing opinion.

As for the remaining 39 items, on which an insufficient consensus had been observed, the experimenters at this point used their discretion in singling out a subset of 17 items that they thought to be deserving of further exploration. These were presented once more to the panel, together with an indication of the consensus status to date and a request for a statement of reasons for opinions differing from those of the majority. In some cases the item was reworded, because it was felt that the ambiguity of the original phrasing, rather than any factual disagreement among the participants, might have been partly responsible for the observed divergence of responses. (This contention was supported, in various instances, by explicit comments to this effect from the respondents.) In the case of our examples, B1 and S8, Questionnaire 1.3 followed up thus:

Description of Potential Breakthrough	*Consensus or Dissensus to Date*	*In your opinion, by what year does the probability of occurrence reach* 50%	90%	*If your 50% estimate falls within* ***either*** *the earlier* ***or*** *the later period indicated, briefly state your reason for this opinion*
B1 Feasibility of chemical control over hereditary defects through molecular engineering	Consensus that it will occur; disagreement as to when			Why before 1987 *or* after 2013?
S8 Widespread socially accepted use of nonnarcotic personality-control drugs producing specific psychological reactions	Divergent opinions, possibly due to differing interpretations of the original question			Why before 1987 *or* after 2013 or never?

The responses now had the following medians and quartile ranges:

	Median	Quartiles
B1	2000	1989–2015
S8	2000	1980–2033

We notice that in both cases the quartile range narrowed, while the median shifted to a somewhat later year for B1 and to a considerably earlier year for S8. Our sample was too small and unstable to permit us to trace such changes to specific causes. (The instability of the sample had two causes: the long interval between questionnaires, and changes in the composition of the panel.) We may merely conjecture that the sharpening in wording of the questions contributed to the narrowing of the quartile ranges; whether this also produced the shift in medians is even more uncertain.

The procedure for composing the last questionnaire in the series, 1.4, was similar to that used in the preceding cycle: elimination of a few additional items, announcement of a satisfactory consensus on some, and restatement (possibly again involving actual rewording) of the remainder. Both of our illustrative items were judged to need such reconsideration. In this case, the information given to the panel comprised both a statement of the majority opinion and an indication of the reasons for a deviating opinion on the part of a minority. As far as B1 and S8 were concerned, the questionnaire appeared as follows:

Description of Potential Breakthrough	*Majority Consensus to Date*	*Minority Opinion*	*50% Year*	*90% Year*
B1 Feasibility (not necessarily acceptance) of chemical control over some hereditary defects by modification of genes through molecular engineering	By 2000	Will take longer or occur never, because it would necessitate intervention during embryonic development, when the fetus is inaccessible; hence would require prior development of techniques of gestation in vitro		
S8 Widespread and socially widely accepted use of nonnarcotic drugs (other than alcohol) for the purpose of producing specific changes in personality characteristics	By 2000	Will take 50 years or more, because research on psycho-pharmaceuticals has barely begun, and negative social reaction will cause delays		

This time the outcome was as follows:

	Median	Quartiles
B1	2000	1990–2010
S8	1983	1980–2000

Thus, for B1 the median remained unchanged and the quartile range shrank a little further; in the case of S8, the median was now even earlier than before and the quartile range shrank considerably. In both cases we now had what may be considered a reasonably narrow consensus.

45.5 The Substantive Outcome: Introductory Remarks

Having illustrated our procedure through the cases of these three representative items, we now present the prima facie predictions by our panels and return later to a discussion and critique of the method. The reader is cautioned, however, to regard the data about to be listed with some reservation. They consist of summaries of considered opinions about the future by a small group of people, each an expert on some, but not necessarily all, of the subjects under inquiry. There is no question but that more reliable predictions could have been obtained with a greater effort and a wiser group of experimenters. We shall try to indicate later, through retrospective wisdom, how we believe that an effort such as this can be improved to the point where it might become a more reliable and valuable planning tool.

45.6 Predicted Scientific Breakthroughs

Panel 1's predictions of scientific breakthroughs are listed in Table 7. Throughout, the year given is in terms of the "break-even" date, that is, the date for which there is an equal expectation that the event in question will materialize before or after it. The events are ordered according to the median date.

TABLE 7

Scientific Breakthrough	*Median*	*Quartiles*
Economically useful desalination of sea water	1970	1964-1980
Effective fertility control by oral contraceptive or other simple and inexpensive means	1970	1970-1983
Development of new synthetic materials for ultra-light construction	1971	1970-1978
Automated language translators	1972	1968-1976
New organs through transplanting or prosthesis	1972	1968-1982
Reliable weather forecasts	1975	1972-1988
Operation of a central data storage facility with wide access for general or specialized information retrieval	1980	1971-1991
Reformation of physical theory, eliminating confusion in quantum relativity and simplifying particle theory	1980	1975-1993
Implanted artificial organs made of plastic and electronic components	1982	1975-1988
Widespread and socially widely accepted use of nonnarcotic drugs (other than alcohol) for the purpose of producing specific changes in personality characteristics	1983	1980-2000
Stimulated emission ("lasers") in X and Gamma ray region of the spectrum	1985	1978-1989
Controlled thermonuclear power	1986	1980-2000
Creation of a primitive form of artificial life (at least in the form of self-replicating molecules)	1989	1979-2000

(continued)

TABLE 7 (Continued)

Scientific Breakthrough	*Median*	*Quartiles*
Economically useful exploitation of the ocean bottom through mining (other than offshore oil drilling)	1989	1980-2000
Feasibility of limited weather control, in the sense of substantially affecting regional weather at acceptable cost	1990	1987-2000
Economic feasibility of commercial generation of synthetic protein for food	1990	1985-2003
Increase by an order of magnitude in the relative number of psychotic cases amenable to physical or chemical therapy	1992	1983-2017
Biochemical general immunization against bacterial and viral diseases	1994	1983-2000
Feasibility (not necessarily acceptance) of chemical control over some hereditary defects by modification of genes through molecular engineering	2000	1990-2010
Economically useful exploitation of the ocean through farming, with the effect of producing at least 20% of the world's food	2000	2000-2017
Biochemicals to stimulate growth of new organs and limbs	2007	1995-2040
Feasibility of using drugs to raise the level of intelligence (other than as dietary supplements and not in the sense of just temporarily raising the level of apperception)	2012	1984-2050
Human-machine symbiosis, enabling people to extend their intelligence by direct electromechanical interaction between the brain and a computing machine	2020	1990-never
Chemical control of the aging process, permitting extension of the life span by 50 years	2040	1995-2063
Breeding of intelligent animals (apes, cetaceans, and so on) for low-grade labor	2045	2020-never
Two-way communication with extraterrestrials	2063	2000-never
Economic feasibility of commercial manufacture of many chemical elements from subatomic building blocks	2100	2007-never
Control of gravity through some form of modification of the gravitational field	2100	2035-never
Feasibility of education by direct information recording on the brain	2600	1997-never
Long-duration coma to permit a form of time travel	never	2006-never
Use of telepathy and ESP in communications	never	2045-never

45.7 Predicted Population Trends

The questions addressed to Panel 2, on population control, were concerned with world population growth between now and the year 2050. The following graphs (Figures 15 and 16) exhibit the median and quartile curves derived from the panel's predictions for the birth rate, the death rate, the net growth rate (the birth rate minus the death rate), and the population size.

The population curves in Figure 16 were derived as follows: From the responses of each individual we determined approximately what, according to him, the population would be as a function of time; for each year t between the present and 2050, we then selected the median and quartiles of these predictions.

An obvious alternative method is to use the three net growth rate curves shown in Figure 15 and to compute the corresponding population curves; the result does not differ significantly from that in Figure 16.

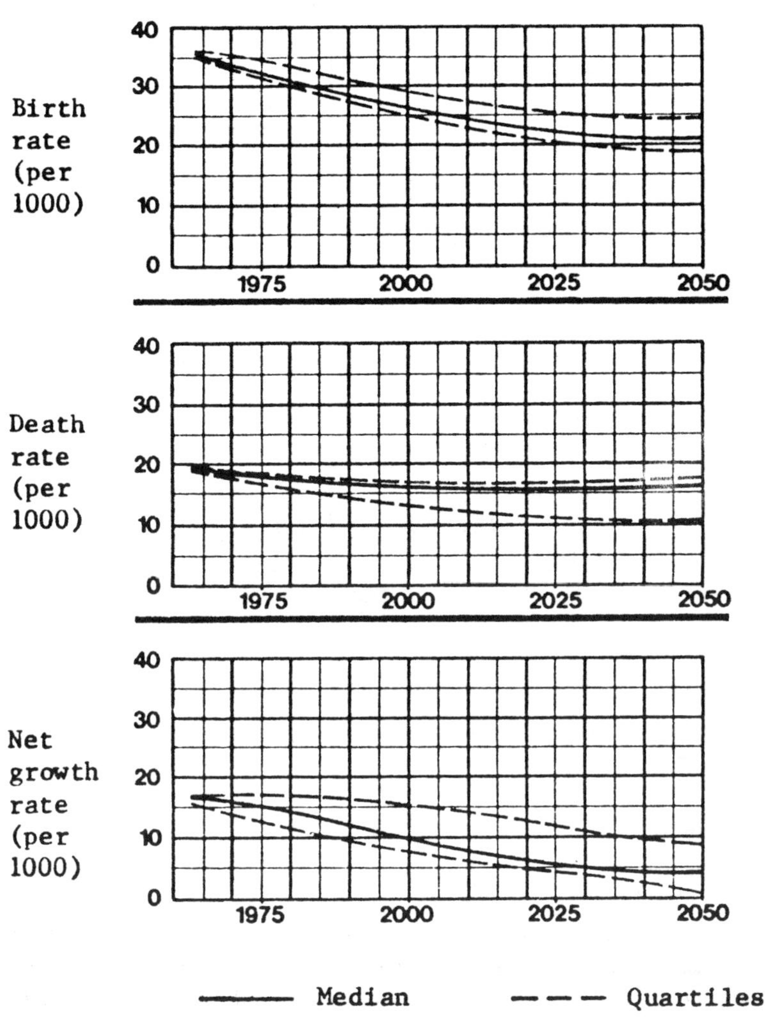

FIGURE 15

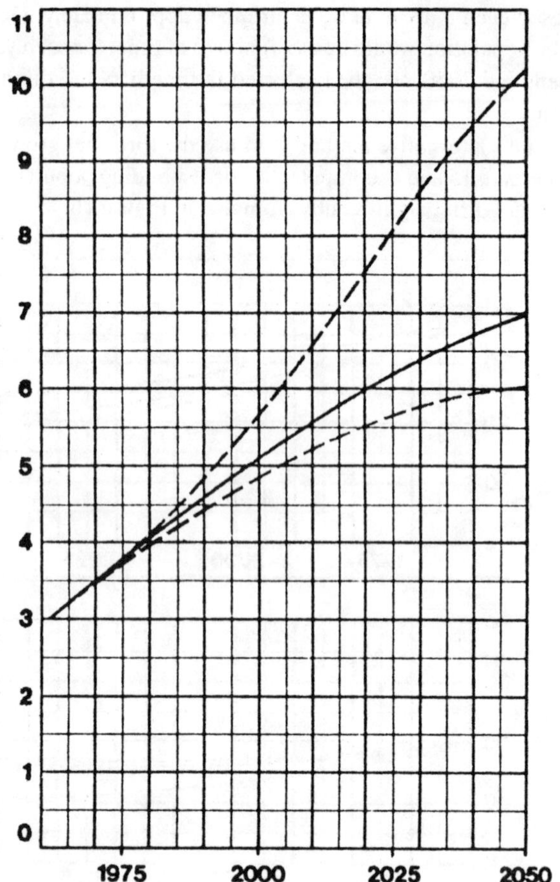

Population estimate (billions)

——— Median   – – – Quartiles

FIGURE 16

We note that the population trend forecast by our panel is considerably more conservative than estimates obtained by straightforward extrapolation from past population growth, as shown in Figure 17, where the shaded area, lying entirely below the projected curve, represents the quartile range of the panel's forecast over the next eighty-seven years.

We did inquire into the reasons for the opinions reflected in these relatively low population estimates.

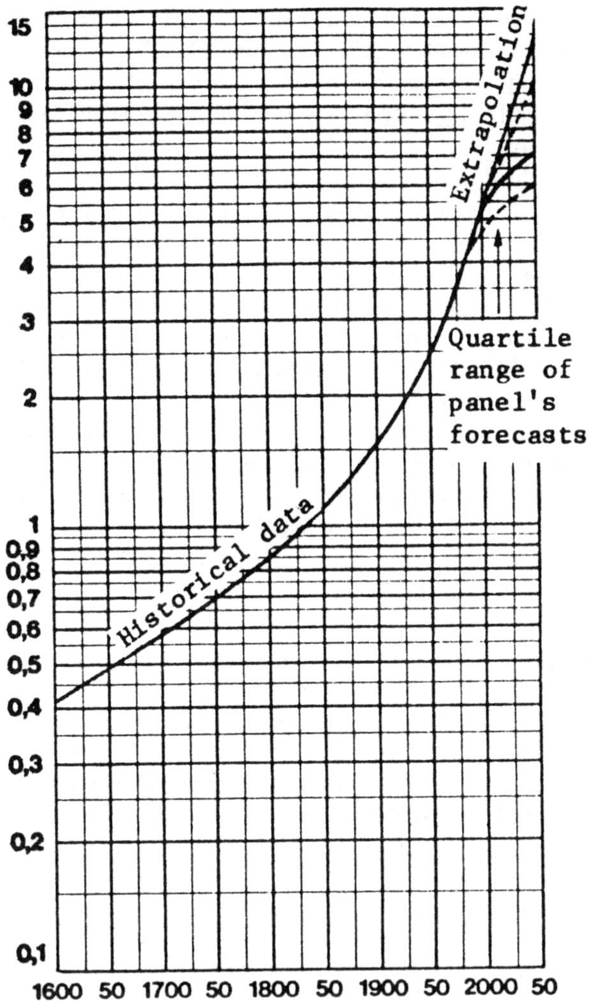

World population from 1600 to 2050 (billions)

FIGURE 17

Not surprisingly, the following three factors emerged as the principal ones affecting birth and death rates, and consequently population:

- the degree of acceptance of birth-control measures
- the rate of further medical progress
- advances in the production and distribution of food

Of these, judging by the variance of responses, the first seems to be the least predictable. There was much more of a consensus regarding predictions of the availability (as opposed to the acceptance) of birth-control measures. This, incidentally, was confirmed by the Science panel (Panel 1), which predicted the general availability prior to 1980 of simple and inexpensive means of fertility control.

Further medical advances were seemingly generally accepted as a matter of course. The consequent drop in the death rate will be attenuated, in the opinion of most respondents, by insufficient advances in the production and distribution of food. A minority even predicted famine conditions and a consequent eventual sharp rise in the death rate.

These misgivings regarding food production and distribution should perhaps be examined in the light of relevant forecasts made by the Science and Automation panels (1 and 3). According to Panel 1, commercially efficient production of synthetic food may be expected within forty years, to be augmented in the early part of the next century by large-scale ocean farming. In spite of this forecast of food abundance for even a much-enlarged world population, there may still be an ominous gap between potential and effective availability of food for all, because, according to the view expressed by Panel 3, an effective worldwide system of food distribution may not be implemented until later in the twenty-first century.

In view of such facts as the uncertainty regarding large-scale acceptance of birth-control measures, the comparative certainty of further medical progress, and the doubts about equitable food distribution, one cannot help but wonder whether the panel's forecasts (which in the median suggest a non-famine-induced leveling off of the population curve) would have remained quite so optimistic had the Delphi process of examining the reasons for proffered opinions been carried through another round or two.

45.8 Automation Predictions

The predictions by Panel 3 regarding major developments in the field of automation are summarized in Table 8. In addition to technological progress in automation, the panel was asked to give some thought to the problem of unemployment resulting from automation. Almost all respondents agreed that the problem is a very serious one. While one-third of the panel felt that social upheavals will accompany automation, the majority opinion indicated that suitable countermeasures, taken either preventively or at least therapeutically, will forestall severe social disruptions.

Ten countermeasures, proposed by the panel members themselves, were appraised by the panel with regard to potential effectiveness in reducing unemployment, overall desirability, and the probability of actual implementation. The averages of the appraisals concerning these three aspects turned out to be highly correlated, as shown by the results in Table 9, in which the measures at

TABLE 8

Development in the Field of Automation	*Median*	*Quartiles*
Increase by a factor of 10 in capital investment in computers used for automated process control	1973	1970-1975
Air traffic control—positive and predictive track on all aircraft	1974	1970-1977
Direct link from stores to banks to check credit and to record transactions	1974	1972-1980
Widespread use of simple teaching machines	1974	1971-1977
Automation of office work and services, leading to displacement of 25% of current work force	1975	1970-1975
Education becoming a respectable leisure pastime	1975	1972-1985
Widespread use of sophisticated teaching machines	1975	1975-1990
Automatic libraries, looking up and reproducing copy	1976	1971-1982
Automated looking up of legal information	1978	1971-1988
Automatic language translator—correct grammar	1978	1971-1996
Automated rapid transit	1979	1973-1985
Widespread use of automatic decision-making at management level for industrial and national planning	1979	1977-1997
Electronic prosthesis (radar for the blind, servomechanical limbs)	1985	1975-1990
Automated interpretation of medical symptoms	1985	1980-1990
Construction on a production line of computers with motivation by "education"	1986	1976-1991
Widespread use of robot services, for refuse collection, as household slaves, as sewer inspectors, and so on.	1988	1980-1996
Widespread use of computers in tax collection, with access to all business records—automatic single tax deductions	1989	1980-1996
Availability of a machine which comprehends standard IQ tests and scores above 150	1990	1984-2000
Evolution of a universal language from automated communication	2000	1980-never
Automated voting, in the sense of legislating through automated plebiscite	2000	1995-2300
Automated highways and adaptive automobile autopilots	2002	1995-2045
Remote facsimile newspapers and magazines, printed in home	2005	1992-2030
Human-machine symbiosis, enabling people to extend their intelligence by direct electromechanical interaction between the brain and a computing machine	2010	1985-2600
International agreements that guarantee certain economic minima to the world's population as a result of high production from automation	2025	2018-2100
Centralized (possibly random) wire tapping	never	2500-never

TABLE 9

Proposed Measure	*Average Effectiveness*	*Average Desirability*	*Average Probability*
Creation of new types of employment	mod/high	high	mod/high
Retraining of persons unemployed through automation	mod	mod/high	high
All-out vocational training program	min/mod	mod/high	mod/high
Education for better leisure-time enjoyment	min/mod	mod/high	mod/high
Massive aid to underdeveloped regions (including parts of the United States)	mod	mod	mod
Two years of compulsory post-high-school education	mod	mod	mod
Legislation shortening the work week by 20%	min/mod	neut/mod	mod/high
Massive WPA-type programs	min/mod	neut	mod
Legislation lowering the retirement age by 5 years	min/mod	neut	mod
Legislation protecting household and service jobs from automation	nil/min	neg	min

NOTE: The abbreviations used here are to be interpreted as follows: mod=moderate, min=minor, neut=neutral, neg=negative.

the top of the list are considered effective, desirable, and probable, while those at the bottom are considered ineffective, undesirable, and improbable.

45.9 Predicted Progress in Space

A summary of predicted progress in space is given in Table 10. We note that for events whose median break-even dates are within the next fifteen years, the quartile ranges are remarkably narrow, reflecting no doubt the rather firm timetable of near-future space achievements to which our space specialists expect to adhere.

45.10 Predictions Concerning War and Its Prevention

The members of Panel 5, on War Prevention, were asked both in the first questionnaire (June 1963) and the last questionnaire (January 1964) to give us their personal probability estimates of the occurrence of another major war within 10 and within 25 years. The responses were these:

	Median	*Quartiles*
June 1963		
Probability of war within 10 years	10%	3-33%
Probability of war within 25 years	24%	5-50%
January 1964		
Probability of war within 10 years	10%	1-20%
Probability of war within 25 years	20%	4-30%

TABLE 10

Development in Space Exploration	*Median*	*Quartiles*
S.U. orbital rendezvous	1964	1964-1966
U.S. orbital rendezvous	1967	1965-1967
Increased use of near-Earth satellites for weather prediction and control	1967	1967-1970
Unmanned inspection and capability for destruction of satellites	1967	1967-1970
S.U. manned lunar flyby	1967	1967-1970
Establishment of global satellite communication system	1968	1967-1970
U.S. manned lunar flyby	1970	1967-1970
Manned lunar landing and return	1970	1970-1970
Rescue of astronauts stranded in orbit	1970	1968-1975
Operational readiness of laser for space communications	1970	1968-1975
Manned co-orbital inspection of satellites	1970	1970-1974
Manned scientific orbital station (10 persons)	1970	1970-1975
Development of reusable booster launch vehicle	1975	1970-1975
Solid-core nuclear reactor propulsion	1975	1970-1975
Ionic propulsion (nuclear-generator powered)	1975	1972-1975
Temporary lunar base (2 persons, 1 month)	1975	1975-1975
Development of reusable maneuverable orbiting spacecraft	1975	1972-1979
Manned Mars and Venus flyby	1978	1975-1979
Reexecution of critical experiments in deep space (Michelson-Morley, speed of light, equality of gravitational and inertial mass and so on)	1981	1973-1995
Permanent base established on Moon (10 persons, indefinite stay)	1982	1982-1982
Manufacturing of atmospheres suitable for human beings on Moon or planets (no implication of surrounding entire Moon or planet with an atmosphere is intended)	1982	1980-1989
Deep-space laboratories and observatories for high-vacuum, zero-g, and space research	1982	1975-1994
Earth weather control, in the sense of having a highly reliable ability to cause precipitation from certain types of clouds	1982	1978-2002
Manned landing on Mars and return	1985	1980-1990
Probes (small instrumented unmanned payloads) out of the solar system	1986	1979-1994
Manufacturing of propellants and raw materials on the Moon	1990	1980-2020
Establishment of permanent research stations on near planets	1990	1990-2013
Commercial global ballistic transport (including boost-glide techniques)	2000	1985-never
Establishment of a permanent Mars base (10 persons, indefinite stay)	2006	1990-2040

(continued)

TABLE 10 (Continued)

Development in Space Exploration	*Median*	*Quartiles*
Manned landing on Jupiter's moons	2030	1994-2050
Pluto flyby	2050	2015-2050
Intergalactic communication	2050	2050-2050
Long-duration coma to permit a form of time travel	2050	2016-2800
Manned multigeneration mission to other solar systems	2050	2050-2800
Extraterrestrial farming	2050	2016-never
Regularly scheduled commercial traffic to lunar colony	2050	2050-never
Communication with extraterrestrials	2050	2050-never
Competition for planetary raw materials	2400	2050-never
Manned Venus landing	2400	2050-never

A significant decrease in the probabilities between the June and January responses is evident. Even in the case of the 10-year estimates, where the median remained at 10 percent, the shift of the quartile range as a whole is quite pronounced. While the identity of the panel membership was not stable enough to draw the conclusion directly from this summary evidence that events of the intervening seven months had caused most of the respondents to take a rosier view of the future, examination of the responses of those individuals who participated in both the first and fourth questionnaires did tend to confirm this hypothesis. For example, none of them raised the value given to the probability of war within 10 years, and the median reduction of probability was 20 percent of the value originally given.

The panel's view as to the manner in which a major war might break out, if at all, did not change significantly between June 1963 and January 1964. When we average the minor differences in responses between these dates, the panel's opinions on the relative probabilities of the modes of outbreak may be summarized as follows:

Inadvertence	11%
Escalation of a political crisis	45%
Escalation in the level of violence in an ongoing minor war	37%
Surprise attack at a time when there is no ostensible acute crisis	7%

We considered the main assignments of Panel 5 to be the proposal and appraisal of realistic and effective measures that might be undertaken in the future in order to reduce the overall probability of occurrence of another major war. Members of the panel submitted a total of forty-two distinct proposals for consideration. These were then resubmitted to the panel for appraisal.

Much of the response was in verbal rather than numerical form. Even numerical responses, such as effectiveness and probability-of-implementation ratings and desirability rankings, were subject to interpretation and relative weighting. Taking all these caveats into account, it appears that the picture which emerges can be described roughly as presented in Table 11, arranged in the approximate order of decreasing overall desirability, with "effectiveness" to be understood as referring specifically to the lowering of the probability of war. A boldface entry indicates a considerable consensus among the panel members:

TABLE 11

Proposed Measure	*Overall Desirability*	*Effectiveness if Implemented*	*Probability of Implementation*
Build-up of Western-bloc conventional forces	**high**	high	high
Increased security of command-and-control and retaliatory capability	**high**	high	**high**
Development on both sides of invulnerable delayed-response weapons that are incapable of surprise attack	high	high	**high**
Greater political and economic unity among free advanced democracies	**high**	**high**	medium
U.S.-S.U. political agreement to seek peace and restrain other nations from developing nuclear weapons	high	high	medium
Establishment of a standing worldwide U.N. police force, not subject to veto	high	**high**	**low**
Improved defensive warfare techniques to reduce probability of escalation in limited wars	high	**medium**	medium
U.N. economic and military aid to areas threatened by political upheaval	high	medium	low
Develoment of a code of international law and establishment of effective world courts of justice and a world supreme court	high	medium	**low**
U.S.-promoted rapid technological and economic development of underdeveloped nations	high	low	high
Strengthening of the U.N. with the objective of forming a world government	medium	**high**	**low**
Bilateral U.S.-S.U. arms control agreements	medium	**medium**	high
Studies by sociology, group psychology, and so on, seeking clues to war prevention	**medium**	medium	**high**
U.S.-S.U. political association against China or other third party	medium	medium	high

[This list, in the original, continued through twenty-eight additional items, with progressively less favorable evaluations. Table 11 suffices to convey the flavor of the unabridged tabulation.]

In order to obtain some idea of the potential impact of these measures, we concluded our inquiry by asking each respondent his opinion of how much the probability of a major war in the next 10 and the next 25 years would be reduced if the measures he favored were pursued vigorously. While the medians of the noninterventive estimates (January 1964; see the unnumbered table at the beginning of this section) had been 10 and 20 percent respectively, for the 10- and 25-year periods, these medians, with intervention, turned out to be 2.5 and 6 percent, which represents a lowering of the probability of war by 75 and 70 percent, respectively. We also examined the record to find each individual's reduction in these probabilities; the medians of these reductions turned out to be 25 and 33 percent, respectively, which—while not nearly so large—may still be considered strong evidence of the respondents' optimism regarding the possibility of reducing their own dire forecasts by taking appropriate preventive measures.

45.11 The World of 1984

If we abstract the most significant items from the forecasts of all six panels, the following picture emerges of the state of the world as of 1984:

The population of the world will have increased by about 40 percent from its present size to 4.3 billion—that is, provided no third world war will have taken place before then. There is an 80 to 85 percent probability that it will not, if present trends continue, but this probability can be raised to 95 percent by appropriate policy measures.

To provide the increased quantities of food needed, agriculture will be aided by automation and by the availability of desalinated seawater.

Effective fertility control will be practised, with the result that the birth rate will continue to drop.

In the field of medicine, transplantation of natural organs and implantation of artificial (plastic and electronic) organs will be common practice. The use of personality-control drugs will be widespread and widely accepted.

Sophisticated teaching machines will be in general use. Automated libraries that look up and reproduce relevant material will greatly aid research. Worldwide communication will be enhanced by a universal satellite relay system and by automatic translating machines. Automation will span the gamut from many service operations to some types of decision-making at the management level.

In space, a permanent lunar base will have been established. Manned Mars and Venus flybys will have been accomplished. Deep-space laboratories will be in operation. Propulsion by solid-core nuclear reactor and ionic engines will be becoming available.

In the military arena, ground warfare will be modified by rapid mobility and a highly automated tactical capability, aided by the availability of a large spectrum of weapons, ranging from nonlethal biological devices and lightweight rocket-type personnel armament to small tactical nuclear bombs and directed-energy weapons of various kinds. Ground-launched anti-ICBM missiles will have become quite effective. Antisubmarine warfare techniques will have advanced greatly, but improved, deep-diving, hard-to-detect submarines will present new problems.

45.12 The World of 2000

When we continue our projection to the year 2000, the following major additional features emerge as descriptive of the world at that time, judging from the forecasts of the six panels:

The population size will be up to about 5.1 billion (65 percent more than 1963).

New food sources will have been opened up through large-scale ocean farming and the fabrication of synthetic protein.

Controlled thermonuclear power will be a source of new energy. New mineral raw materials will be derived from the oceans. Regional weather control will be past the experimental stage.

General immunization against bacterial and viral diseases will be available. Primitive forms of artificial life will have been generated in the laboratory. The correction of hereditary defects through molecular engineering will be possible.

Automation will have advanced further, from many menial robot services to sophisticated high-IQ machines. A universal language will have evolved through automated communication.

On the Moon, mining and manufacture of propellant materials will be in progress. People will have landed on Mars, and permanent unmanned research stations will have been established there, while on Earth commercial global ballistic transport will have been instituted.

Weather manipulation for military purposes will be possible. Effective anti-ICBM defenses in the form of air-launched missiles and directed-energy beams will have been developed.

45.13 Conceivable Features of the World in the Year 2100

When we try to look as far ahead as to the year 2100, there can be no pretense regarding the existence of any consensus among our respondents. We record the following developments, for which there was a median forecast of no later than 2100, not as a prediction of the state of the world at that time but as an indication of what a number of thoughtful people regard as conceivable during the next few generations to come:

By the year 2100 the world population may be of the order of 8 billion.

Chemical control of the aging process may have been achieved, raising a person's life expectancy to over 100 years. The growth of new limbs and organs through biochemical stimulation may be possible. Person-machine symbiosis, enabling a person to raise his or her intelligence through direct electromechanical tie-in of the brain with a computing machine, is a distinct possibility. Automation, of course, will have taken further enormous strides, evidenced in all probability by such things as household robots, remote facsimile reproduction of newspapers and magazines in the home, and completely automated highway transportation.

The problem of adequately providing the necessities of life for all peoples of the earth will presumably have been solved by international agreements based on the abundance of new sources of energy and raw materials opened up in the twenty-first century. As for materials, it is even possible that elaborate differential mining processes will have been abandoned in favor of commercially efficient transmutation of elements.

Conceivably, revolutionary developments will have become feasible as a result of control of gravity through some form of modification of the gravitational field.

A permanent lunar colony may well have been established, with regularly scheduled commercial traffic between Earth and Moon. A permanent base on Mars, landings on Jupiter's moons, and manned flybys past Pluto are likely accomplishments. Even a multigeneration mission to other solar systems may be on its way, aided conceivably by artificially induced long-duration coma. Two-way communication with extraterrestrial intelligent beings is a definite possibility.

45.14 Editorial Comments on These Forecasts

Before leaving the substantive aspects of this report and proceeding to a discussion of method, we would like to interject a few remarks reflecting our own reaction to some of the panel forecasts.

First of all, we would like to register our surprise at some of the ideas that have been propounded. To other persons, of course, a different set of items might be the unexpected ones. These are among the ones we had failed to anticipate:

- The implication that the water-covered portions of the earth may become important enough to warrant national territorial claims.
- The possibility that continued developments in automation will result in serious social upheavals; the almost complete acceptance of the necessity of regulative legislation.
- The probability, in the relatively near future, of very widespread use of personality-control drugs.
- The notion of an actual symbiosis of human and machine.
- The use of computers as "colleagues" rather than servants or slaves.

- The fact that control of gravity was not rejected outright.
- The relative confidence that the population curve would begin to level off during the next generation.
- The strong likelihood of the emergence of weapons of a nonkilling, non-property-destroying nature, covert perhaps, attacking on the psychological or biological level.
- The idea of perishable counterinsurgent arms.
- The general disagreement with the concept of deep-space military applications, such as heliocentric strategic fleets.
- The anticipated relatively high probability of another major war.
- The absence, on the one hand, of significantly new ideas for the prevention of war, and the confidence, on the other, that the application of what may almost be called traditional proposals to this effect hold great promise for reducing the probability of war.

Second, we feel it incumbent on us to point out certain warnings that seem to be implied in the opinions of our respondents. Our motivation in doing so is not to prophesy doom but to indicate the areas, however obvious, in which a major effort will have to be concentrated in order to avoid future disaster. They can be subsumed under four headings:

45.14.1 War Prevention

While the odds are considered to be against another major war within the next generation, even a 20 percent chance of this (within twenty-five years), which is the War Prevention panel's median prediction, is clearly intolerable. The main danger appears to be in mutually undesired escalation and downright inadvertence; hence a major effort to seek improved ways of forestalling such disaster is mandatory.

45.14.2 Equitable Distribution of Resources

While there is a consensus that eventually there will be an abundance of resources in energy, food, and raw materials, it is not at all a foregone conclusion that they will be plentifully available in time to keep ahead of the increasing world population or, what is more, that effective means of an equitable world distribution of such assets will have been found and agreed upon. To solve these problems in time will clearly be a great contribution toward the prevention of (big or small) wars.

45.14.3 Social Reorganization

The anticipated explosive growth in the amount of automation is likely to reshape the societies of industrialized nations considerably, perhaps beyond recognition. While improved and highly automated methods of education will make the acquisition of technical skills available to a larger fraction of the population, only the very ablest people are likely to be needed to manage the new, automated, economy. Since robots are apt to take over many of the services, especially the more menial ones, large segments of the population may find themselves without suitable employment within an economy of potential abundance. Farsighted and profoundly revolutionary measures may have to be taken to cope with this situation and to create new patterns within which a democratic form of society can continue to flourish. "Earning" a livelihood may no longer be a necessity but a privilege; services may have to be protected from automation and be given social status; leisuretime activities may have to be invented in order to give new meaning to a mode of life that may have become "economically useless" for a majority of the populace.

45.14.4 Eugenics

Finally, to mention a problem which, though not upon us as yet, will require more forethought and wisdom, there is the possibility—now just below the horizon but expected to be realized within a generation or two—of selectively extending an individual's life span through biochemical methods and of selective eugenic control through molecular genetic engineering. The potential dangers of mismanaging these capabilities are too obvious to require formulation.

45.15 Convergence of Opinions

We now turn briefly to an examination of some of the methodological features of our experiment.

Many of the questions put before Panels 1, 3, 4, and 6 were asked more than once. This gave us an opportunity to determine the amount of opinion convergence that was taking place in the process of interrogation.

A convenient measure of the spread of opinions is the quartile range, QR, of the responses. Figure 18 shows a scatter diagram of the final quartile range, QR_2, versus the original quartile range, QR_1, for each repeated question. (The numerals used to spot these points refer to the panel number.)

It can be seen at a glance that the quartile range decreased, since the majority of the points lie well below the 45° line. The median ratio of QR_2/QR_1 is almost exactly 5/8.

A number of questions were not pursued because of their relative unimportance in the face of an initial highly divergent response. We cannot guess whether a satisfactory process of convergence would have been observed, had we taken the trouble to continue the inquiry on these topics. Also, in a number of cases in which a question was pursued through several rounds, a considerable divergence of opinions persisted. To cite just two examples, the Science and Automation panels each disagreed on predictions regarding the feasibility of direct electromechanical human-machine symbiosis (medians: 2020, 2010; quartile ranges: 1990-never, 1985-2600, respectively); and in the Space panel there was a dissensus as to when (but not whether) propel-

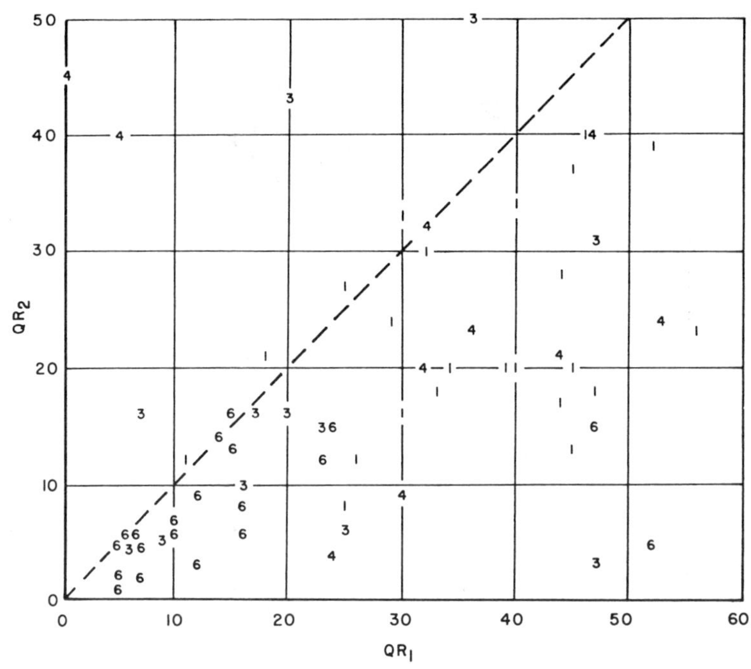

FIGURE 18

lant materials might be mined and manufactured on the Moon (median: 1990, quartile range: 1980-2020).

Whether or not the convergence observed in the Delphi procedure compares favorably in amount and rationality with that obtained by more traditional modes of consensus formation, such as a round-table discussion, is a moot question. We submit, however, that even if the effectiveness of the Delphi technique in producing a consensus is not superior to other methods, it can conceivably offer considerable advantages in cost and reliability—the former by avoiding the need for assembling the experts in one place, the latter by not subjecting them to the persuasiveness of oratory or to the bandwagon effect of prominent authority and of face-to-face confrontation with majority opinion, but merely to the milder form of anonymous social pressure exerted by the feedback of some information on the range of opinions held by the group.

45.16 Prediction Precision as a Function of Time

The precision with which a panel as a group predicts the date of a future event, as measured by the narrowness of the quartile range, must be expected

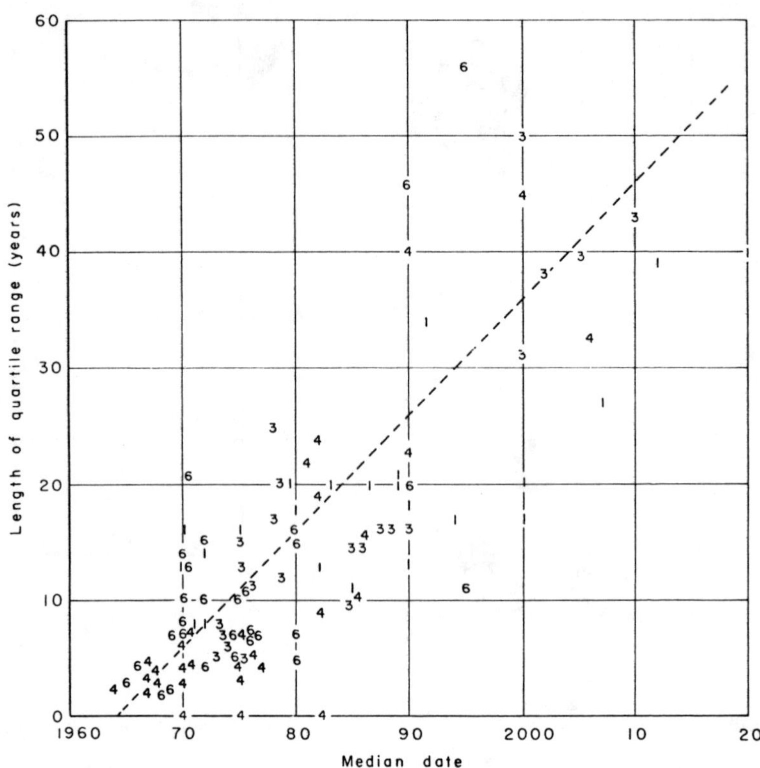

FIGURE 19

to diminish with increasing distance in the future. The scatter diagram in Figure 19, which covers all items with a median date no later than 2020, not only confirms this but reveals the additional fact that the size of the quartile range on the average is about equal to the expected distance in the future. (The numerals again refer to the panel numbers.)

We mention in passing that the position of the median within the quartile range, on the average, is about one-third of its length from the lower end (see Figure 20). Hence, if an event has a median predicted date x years in the future then, on the average, the corresponding quartile range will span the interval from 2/3 x years in the future to 5/3 x years in the future (e.g., for an event with a median year of 2000, the ends of the quartile range would average approximately 1988 and 2024 [note that this statement was written in 1964]).

45.17 Confidence as a Function of Predicted Date

The members of Panels 1, 3, and 4 were asked, in several questionnaires, to state not only the year by which they thought an event had a 50 percent probability of occurrence, but also by what year they felt 90 percent confident that the event would occur. In Figure 21, we have plotted the medians of these 90 percent confidence years against the medians of the corresponding 50 percent confidence years for all events for which the latter was no later than 2000.

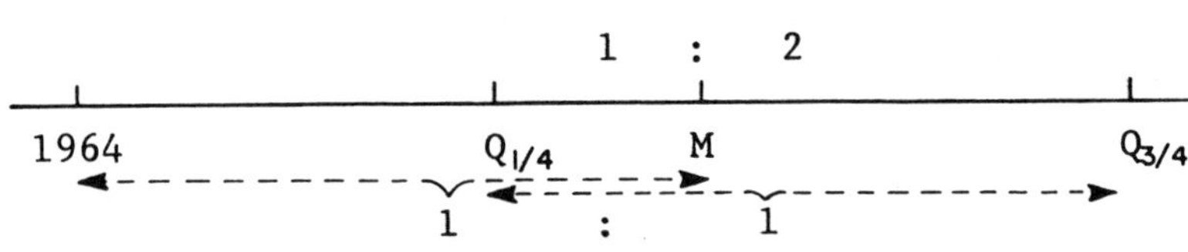

FIGURE 20

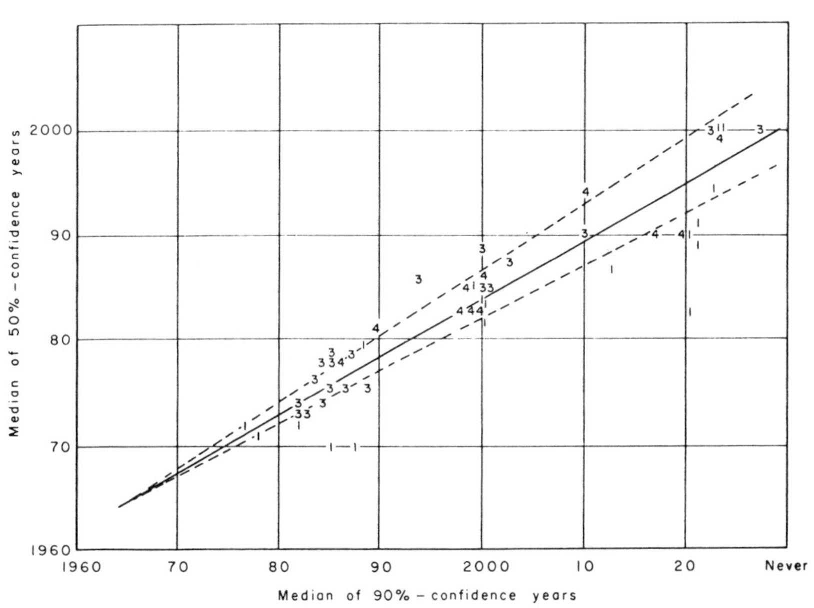

FIGURE 21

The graph, not unexpectedly, shows a close correlation. Denoting the distances in the future of the medians of the 50 percent and 90 percent years by $M_{.5}$ and $M_{.9}$ respectively, we note as a matter of curiosity that

$$\text{median}\ (M_{.9}/M_{.5}) = 9/5 = 1.8$$

with a corresponding quartile range from 1.6 to 2.0, as indicated by dotted lines in Figure 21.

45.18 *Critique of Experimental Procedure*

The procedure we have followed in this experiment is open to many criticisms. Some shortcomings we were aware of from the beginning, some became clear as we went along, others were brought to our attention through comments by our respondents, still others will undoubtedly occur to the readers of this report.

It is precisely because of our conviction of the basic soundness of our approach that we wish to devote some space to a critical discussion of our procedure. In particular, we would like to establish, for possible future reference, which deficiencies could have been corrected and thus are in principle avoidable, and which others are weaknesses inherent in the method.

45.18.1 Instability of Panel Membership

The makeup of each of our six panels of respondents fluctuated considerably; some early participants dropped out, and others were added after the initial round. While in principle we see no objection to some changes in panel membership—in fact, scientific progress in general relies on the constantly changing collaboration of many contributors—we have no doubt that the convergence of opinions is impeded by too many substitutions. To eliminate the latter entirely would be virtually impossible in view of unforeseeable circumstances and of the many competing demands on their time to which a group of experts is bound to be subjected. One means of keeping changes in personnel within reasonable bounds for the duration of an experiment might be to have some form of contractual arrangement with the participants. [In contradistinction to many later Delphi studies, no payment had been offered to the respondents.]

45.18.2 Time Lapse

Too much time elapsed between successive rounds, the average lapse having been about two months. Better advance organization plus possibly the omission of overseas respondents might have reduced this to one month per round. The excessive length of time presumably was partly responsible for some of the dropouts mentioned in Section 45.18.1; it also may have caused some genuine shifts of opinion due to the mere passage of time, with its concomitant change in the state of our knowledge generally.

45.18.3 Ambiguous Questions

Many of the questions put to the respondents, perhaps even a majority, were worded ambiguously. To some extent we regard this as unavoidable, because precision of meaning can often be bought only at the expense of legalistic phraseology, whose cumbersomeness would be repellent to many respondents. But an even greater effort should be made, by being reasonably specific, to avoid the possibility that two respondents may form widely disparate interpretations of the same question. We are conscious of having violated this prescription in several instances—for example, when we asked for a specific date for the occurrence of an event that was inherently a matter of gradual development.

45.18.4 Respondents' Competence

The questions put to each panel ranged over a large field. With all due regard for our eminent respondents, it is not reasonable to expect that each could be equally competent with regard to all of the areas touched on by our questions. Thus the answers by highly competent experts were somewhat diluted by less highly informed estimates on the part of others. This effect was even slightly enhanced by including among the responses those of volunteers from other panels who submitted answers to questionnaires not addressed to their own panel. There are several remedies for this defect. On the one hand, the members of a panel might be selected for their known expertise within a narrowly defined area, and questions can be confined rigidly to the latter. On the other, the respondents might be encouraged to leave blanks in the questionnaires whenever they feel unsure of their judgment, thus leaving the matter of their qualification to their own discretion. Our own preference would be in the direction of this second alternative, with the possible further modification that the respondents answer every question but add in each case a self-appraisal of their degree of competence in answering it. Precisely how this should be done is an open question that might be made the subject of a separate study. We merely mention that there are problems concerning scale comparability of different respondents' self-appraisals and concerning the optimal use of such self-appraisals in devising a consensus formula.

45.18.5 Self-Fulfilling and Self-Defeating Prophecies

If a person of great authority and trustworthiness were to announce that the condition of the U.S. economy for the foreseeable future is excellent, the strengthening effect on business morale might be such as to improve the state of the economy, thereby making the statement to some extent a self-fulfilling prediction. Conversely if, say, it were announced that we are about to lose our race with the Russians to the Moon, the effect might be a redoubling of our effort, thereby turning the statement into a self-negating prediction. It has been objected by one of our panelists that some of the predictions we solicited might be of one of these types. Leaving aside the implication—

to which we emphatically do not subscribe—that the publication of the answers to some of our questions might in fact affect the future course of history with regard to the subject of the questions (e.g., by hastening or retarding a predicted event), there still remains the possibility that a respondent's answer might be biased by his expectation (whether conscious or not) that the announcement may affect the truth of the prediction's content. If this were so, then the respondent would cease to be acting as a pure predictor but would in part become a would-be manipulator of the future; in addition, so it has been said, the very act of his stating a probability for some future event would involve a logical circularity, because by stating it he would affect it. While the first possibility, of attempting to play politics as it were, must be admitted to be a real one, which may place a respondent in the position of having to choose between what he thinks is right and what he thinks is true, there seems to us to be no real evidence of a logical circularity. In other words, if a respondent wishes to make an objective forecast, he can do so without getting involved in a logical fallacy. To see that this is so, let us consider the case in which the probability of the event E at some future date is to be estimated. Let e be the probability, according to the respondent's opinion, that E will occur provided no public announcement of the outcome of the questioning process is made, and let f(x) be his estimate of that probability, if an announcement is made stating that the probability has been estimated to be x. Then, if the announcement in itself were ineffectual, we would have $f(x) = e$ for all x. If it were self-fulfilling or self-defeating, f(x) would be monotonically increasing or decreasing, respectively, as shown in Figure 25. In either case, there will be at least one point (in the second case, exactly one point) x_o for which

$$f(x_o) = x_o$$

so that a forecast of x_o as the probability of E induces a probability x_o, thus making x_o a logically consistent estimate.

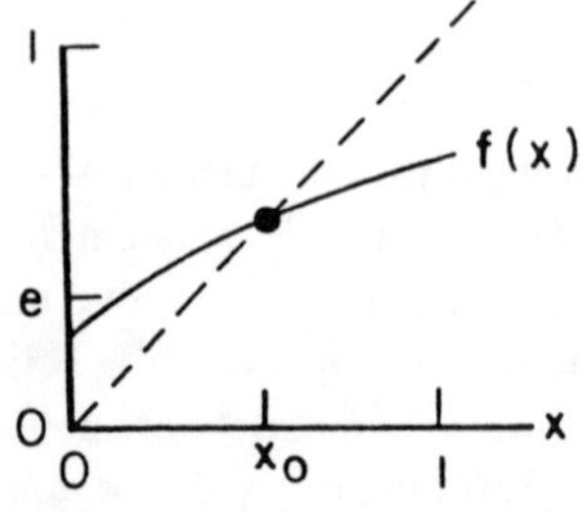

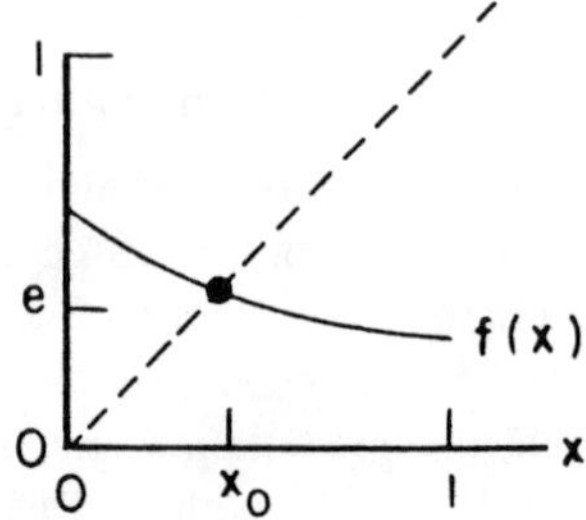

FIGURE 22

45.18.6 Consensus by Undue Averaging

The objection has been raised that the emphasis we place on the median as a descriptor of the group opinion and on the quartile range as a measure of the degree of consensus biases the outcome unduly against the far-out predictor, whose judgment may after all prove to be right while the majority opinion may be wrong. We regard this objection as not entirely unjustified with respect to the present experiment, but as invalid as a criticism of the technique in general. It should be remembered that it is an essential feature of our method that a respondent who disagrees with the majority is invited to state his reasons for such disagreement, and that all the members of the panel are given an opportunity to accept or reject such reasons and to reevaluate their opinions on the basis of whatever merits they believe these reasons deserve. Thus a far-out opinion is in principle rejected only if its proponent fails to justify it before the rest of the panel. The valid part of the objection against the overly averaging influence of our procedure appears to us to be directed at our not having sufficiently observed this principle in practice. In retrospect, it seems that we should indeed have been more insistent on eliciting explicit reasons for minority opinions, and should have provided an opportunity for explicit critique of such reasons, even at the expense of an additional round if necessary. We might thus have retained items that were rejected early and explored them more thoroughly through further questioning.

45.18.7 Substantive Breadth

The foregoing points are all concerned with method. Substantively, although we had aimed for coverage of most of the major aspects of the world of the future, we would have done better in this respect had we also included in our survey a panel explicitly devoted to exploring the future of international relations. The War Prevention panel, of course, was concerned with perhaps the most important issue in this area, and other panels incidentally touched on various aspects of the international scene, but it would have been greatly desirable to attempt a more systematic examination of this subject.

45.19 Conclusions

In trying retrospectively to assess the merits of our experiment in forecasting, we may summarize the outcome as follows:

45.19.1 Substantive Forecasts

For many items whose occurrence is generally expected within the next few decades, the predicted time of this occurrence has been narrowed down somewhat. For others in the same category, we have found that even among experts there is little agreement as to the date, indicating perhaps that relatively greater uncertainties are involved, which preclude more precise predictions at this time. As for the more remote future, we have observed that some events are definitely expected to happen (though at an uncertain date), some are considered of dubious realizability, and still others have been ruled out altogether by our respondents. None of these predictions should be endowed with excessive reliability, because of the smallness of the sample of respondents, the variability of their expertise, and the possible intervention of unforeseeable breakthroughs. Still, the number of surprises in store for us may have been reduced a little.

45.19.2 *Warnings of Potential Dangers*

Among the contingency forecasts implicit in the responses were indications of potential danger areas that call for preventive action. Among these are the possibilities of war, of a continuing maldistribution of food and other commodities in the face of plenty, of social upheaval due to progressive automation, and of unbridled biological applications of molecular engineering.

45.19.3 *Effect on the Participants*

Although the filling in of our questionnaires must have had its nuisance aspects, there is evidence—or at least we like to think so—that the questions were thought provoking to many of our respondents, who may have found some reward for their labor through the mental stimulation to which the experiment exposed them.

45.19.4 *Expediency of the Method*

Nothing that occurred in the experiment seemed to us to discredit the method in principle, and at least moderate consensus was usually obtained without excessive effort. The dependence of the outcome on certain subjective features, such as ambiguity in the wording of questions, uncertainties regarding the degree of expertise among the respondents, and the possibility of deliberate or subconscious bias in the answers, while not totally avoidable, is equally present—if not more so—in traditional modes of reliance on expert judgment in decision-making.

45.19.5 *Feasible Improvements in Method*

The experiment has pointed up the need for various kinds of methodological and procedural improvement. Some of these could be introduced without much difficulty. In particular, one would want to see to it that the panel membership remain reasonably stable, that the time between questionnaires be held within more acceptable limits, that questions be phrased with greater care to avoid unnecessary ambiguity, and that enough cycles be provided to allow for adequate feedback, not only of the primary reasons for opinions, but also for a critique of such reasons.

45.19.6 Potential Improvements through Further Research

A more effective use of experts in a Delphi context might be achieved through further methodological research in several areas: (i) improvements in the systematic selection of experts; (ii) experimentation with various schemes for the respondents to give a self-appraisal of competence, either absolute or relative to that of their fellow respondents; (iii) methods of improving reliability of forecasts through suitable consensus formulas, possibly based on appropriate self-ratings; (iv) experimentation with various methods of feeding back information, in order to learn more about the sensitivity of opinion changes to both the form and the contents of such feedback; (v) comparative analysis of social pressure and persuasive reasoning as determinants of opinion convergence; (vi) formulation of a statistical model of the question-and-answer operation of an expert panel, in which the latter would be viewed as a measuring instrument for the substantive quantities that form the subject of the questions; each respondent would here have to be represented by an error distribution, and some hypotheses would have to be stated as to the relative independence of the measurement thus obtained; and (vii) development of techniques for the formulation of sequential questions that would probe more systematically into the underlying reasons for the respondents' opinions, in a deliberate effort to construct a theoretical foundation for the phenomena under inquiry. ■

46 THE FUTURE OF SCIENCE

What follows is an excerpt from an article I wrote for the October 1967 issue of the British *Science Journal.*[2] The forecasts contained in it were not derived from any systematic inquiry, Delphi or otherwise, but reflect my own opinion at the time, based on information gleaned from the literature:

Of all scientists who ever lived, it has been said, 90 percent are living today. The same statement can probably be made about astronauts, pop singers, and Californians. It means simply that the scientific profession, except for a few pioneers, is a modern one. Its growth has been rapid, its methods multiplying, its purview expanding explosively.

We are still in the midst of this fascinating development, and it is certain that the future state of science will be utterly different from what it is today. Much of what might be said about its future has to be speculative; yet there are recognizable trends that give some substance to speculation. In this article I intend to discuss a few of these trends and their implications for the last third of this century.

2. This material, first appearing in *Science Journal,* London, the weekly review of science and technology (now called *New Scientist*), is reprinted with permission of New Science Publications.

A rough estimate of the number of scientists and engineers in 1967 is 2 million in the United States and 5 million worldwide. Population growth alone would raise these figures to almost 4 and 10 million respectively by the year 2000. In addition, a doubling of the number of scientists and engineers per head of population has been observed to take place every twenty years thus far in this century. Even if this rate of increase slows down somewhat, we may expect by the year 2000 to have about 10 million scientists and engineers in the United States and 25 million worldwide.

Another factor that contributes considerably to the output of the scientific community is the increase in what may be called the labor productivity of the individual researcher. This, of course, is a quantity that is only vaguely defined, yet there can be no doubt that its value, however imprecisely determined, has been rising rapidly due to the advent of high-speed computers and of scientific instruments of steadily increasing sophistication. I am firmly convinced that we have not nearly reached the point in time where the rate of increase in this factor will begin to slow down. Taking, however, a very conservative view of the effect of this factor, and assuming a mere doubling of per-capita researcher productivity between the present and the end of the century, we arrive at the estimate that the total scientific and engineering productivity will rise by a factor of ten by the year 2000.

Only in the past few years has a wholly new attitude toward the future become apparent among policy planners and others concerned with the future of our society, resulting in a new intellectual climate in many parts of the world. Customary planning horizons are being extended into a more distant future, and intuitive gambles—as a basis for planning—are being replaced by systematic analysis of the opportunities the future has to offer.

In view of the accelerating momentum of its capabilities, the research community, in particular, is realizing the enormous power and responsibility it has in selecting among the multitude of possible futures of our society those whose probability of occurrence it ought to influence through appropriate policy recommendations. This rising social consciousness among scientists, based on a sense of urgency as well as a sense of their own strength, is propelling them in new directions that promise to relate their activities more closely to policymaking. The search for truth per se will thus be replaced or at least augmented, for better or worse, by a search for what is both morally right and attainable. The purists' motto, "science for science's sake", will carry less weight than the pragmatists' "science for society's sake".

To translate such new aspirations into fact will not come easily, however inevitable the commitment to this trend. The process will involve rather fundamental changes in method and quite noticeable changes in the routine behavior patterns of scientists.

During the next ten years or so the relative decay of fatalism will complete itself; the growing ability to do something about the future, from which the scientific community's new sense of social responsibility derives, will come to full fruition. The reason for this trend can be seen in two revolutionary developments that are currently unfolding.

One is what may be called the second computer revolution. It took just twenty years for the first computer revolution to be completed, from the mid-1940s to the mid-1960s. During this time the computer was transformed from a mere bookkeeping device to a highly versatile data processor and research tool. Furthermore, the size and the cost of electronic computer components decreased by factors of 100 and 100,000 respectively, and their speed increased by a factor of 100,000. The second computer revolution . . . will consist of . . . the relative automation of the computer, in the sense of doing away with many of the cumbersome aspects of computer programming, and the invention of numerous highly versatile display devices, tied directly to the computer. These two trends will constitute the beginning of a true symbiosis between human and machine, where in a very real sense human intelligence will be enhanced through collaboration with a computer.

The other revolution in the making is . . . the reorientation that is beginning to take place within the so-called soft sciences. [See Chapter III, Section 9.]

We can expect substantial changes in the future in the way in which science is actually transacted. These will profoundly affect some of the traditional behavior patterns of the scientist.

46.1 Conferences

The utility of conferences began to deteriorate decades ago; now, when attendance by the thousands has become the rule, we are faced with a situation that is absurd and ludicrous. Scientific congregations have to be reduced to reasonable proportions, and new ways have to be found to make more constructive use of the talents and knowledge of those who do congregate. Novel conference styles are beginning to be experimented with, and it may safely be predicted that, particularly with the aid of electronic computing and display devices, new forms of conference workshops will evolve in which the participants' role will have been changed from that of spectators to contributors.

46.2 Researcher/Computer Symbiosis

As a result of the second computer revolution referred to earlier, the use of a console tied to a time-shared computer and to banks of data and of mathematical models will become part of the scientist's daily routine. The computer's role will thus rise to that of a quasi-colleague, and this person/machine team's productivity may be expected far to exceed that of today's scientist. (I earlier gave a factor of two as a highly conservative estimate.)

46.3 Interdisciplinary Teams

There are signs today that the complex problems involved in shaping the future of our society are multidisciplinary in character and that their solution will therefore require the collaboration of scientists and technologists from many different fields. Thus far, however, little more than lip service is being paid to this need for interdisciplinary cooperation, partly because effective methods for encouraging and facilitating such joint attacks on problems are still in the explorative stage. However, such quasi-experimental techniques as operational gaming and other simulation workshop approaches offer great promise in this direction. It has been demonstrated that a simulation laboratory environment facilitates cross-disciplinary communication; further, a participant's interaction with persons representing viewpoints different from his own presents him with new insights into the problem that might otherwise have eluded him. Based on today's promising beginnings, organized interdisciplinary team approaches to major problems will become common modes of operation, especially when such interaction among specialists—even in geographically distinct locations—can take place through a computer acting as an intermediary and simultaneously providing access to a central data bank.

46.4 University Reform

The universities are unable to spearhead this movement toward true interdisciplinary cooperation, largely because scholars are discouraged from devoting too much time to enterprises that do not find their rewards within the departmentalized promotion system. While this situation, by default, has left it primarily to industry and to government-sponsored nonprofit corporations to carry out interdisciplinary pioneering work, there are strong indications that the universities will undergo the necessary administrative and curriculum reforms to enable them to resume the lead in this type of research.

46.5 Publications

Scientific and technical publications, like conferences, have gotten completely out of hand; through sheer volume they have become self-defeating. There are two principal motivating forces for publishing articles in the technical journals: the incentive structure (where again the universities are the main, but not the only, villains) and the genuine need for communication with the rest of the scientific community. Fortunately, we can expect radical changes in the methods of scientific communication, although it may well take another decade to see real progress. Eventually, the traditional form of communication through the printed word will be replaced by placing a record of the material to be communicated in a central data bank and making this material available to other researchers through highly sophisticated data retrieval devices.

46.6 Popularization of Science

Despite the expected continuation of the explosive growth in scientific knowledge, which might on first thought seem to widen the gap of understanding between scientist and nonscientist, I venture to predict that during the 1980s, at the latest, we shall enter a new era of popularization of science. For one thing, the scientists themselves, in order to be able to communicate effectively across disciplinary boundaries, will require a certain amount of popularization of what their colleagues in other fields are doing. This process will be greatly aided by computer-controlled instruction and advanced data retrieval systems that will make it increasingly possible to extract information about an area without already having to be an expert in that area. Once such facilities are generally available and many households are equipped with consoles tied to central computers and data banks, the general public—with its expected increase in leisure time—will be ready to accept the acquisition of popularized scientific knowledge as a new hobby. This trend toward public enlightenment will be reinforced by the scientific community's desire, discussed earlier, to be more policy-oriented in its activities: A more thorough analysis of the options for improving society on their part will remain ineffective unless there is a better-informed public that can exercise these options intelligently through the democratic process. ■

47 LIKELY FUTURE SOCIETAL DEVELOPMENTS

Before taking a very general look, in the next chapter, at the future of the United States, I would like to include in the present chapter a few remarks on the problems associated with societal, as opposed to technological, forecasts and to provide just a few illustrations of such societal forecasts in the form of brief excerpts from a report by Raul de Brigard and myself, *Potential Societal Developments—1970–2000*.[3]

The study reported in this paper applied the Delphi technique, using a multi-disciplinary panel of 34 respondents,

- to identify major current societal trends,
- to ascertain the panelists' expectations regarding possible future societal developments; and
- to assess the likely societal implications of a number of expected breakthroughs in physical and biomedical technology.

It has to be understood from the outset that an inquiry into as complex a subject as the future of our society, when compared to a technological fore-

3. Report R-7, Institute for the Future (1970).

casting study, inevitably has certain drawbacks, which should be taken into account in the interpretation of results. Many of these shortcomings, quite aside from the relative inexperience in attempting societal, as compared to technological, forecasts, can undoubtedly be traced to the difficulty in matching, in the social sciences, the crispness associated with statements in the physical sciences. For instance, while the question of when electric power plants driven by thermonuclear fusion will come into existence is reasonably unambiguous, the same could not be said of the question of when the alienation and impersonality of urban life will reach its maximum. There are two differences here. Societal terminology is not as precise as physical terminology, so that in general the circumstances under which a statement could be considered true are not as clearly determined. In addition, there is a certain inevitability about many physical developments, the only question being one of the precise time at which they will come to fruition, whereas for most societal developments their occurrence or nonoccurrence depends greatly on the presence and form of human intervention. Thus the future of society, factually as well as semantically, is less determinate than the future of technological progress.

With this in mind, then, I reproduce below a few short excerpts from the 1970 study.

47.1 Current Trends

Here are a few examples of current [i.e., 1970] societal trends identified by the Delphi respondents:

> *Urban problems:* The benefits of technology to cities, which used to be high and then declined, are beginning to rise again. . . . There is an unresolved conflict in urban policy between programs requiring centralization (transportation and land-use planning) and decentralization (health and welfare). . . .
>
> *Family structure:* There is a greater acceptance of change and flexibility . . . and a greater demand for sexual expression. . . . Abortion is becoming more acceptable. . . .
>
> *The economy:* There is a manpower revolution, in the sense that high economic returns on the uses of labor are required, with manpower for marginal economic activities becoming unavailable. . . . The thesis that economic development will take care of poverty via filtering down of benefits is being disproved. . . . The income aspirations of the below-average economic class are growing ever faster and more demandingly. . . . There is an increasing understanding of the role of innovation. . . .
>
> *Education:* There is a rising need of professionals for retraining. There is a growing disillusion with the idea of the school as agent of total socialization. . . . Student challenges to authority, although sometimes excessive, may be a vehicle through which major changes into the education process are introduced. . . .
>
> *Food and population:* We are on the verge of a great breakthrough in applied agriculture technology as well as in pure-food and protein research. Some new

adaptive agricultural research efforts have begun to pay off, particularly in fertilizers and new seed hybrids.

International relations: Atomic armament by such states as Israel and Egypt is in the offing. The expectation gap in underdeveloped countries is further threatening any prospect for international stability. The rise of China and France as nuclear powers is upsetting "reciprocal nuclear deterrence". . . .

Government and political structure: There is a growing interest in institutionalizing "social accounting". . . . The noneconomic aspects of societal decision-making are becoming more important than the economic ones.

Division in American society: There is a rapid acceptance of "black pride" by liberal whites. There are substantial advances in civil and political rights of the "disadvantaged" and an increase in integrated employment. . . .

Values and mores: There is a greater acceptance of a multicultural society, with search for new forms of values and expressions, especially in the younger generation.

Science and technology: Control of technology (rate, variety, and permitted use) is increasingly being taken from the private sector and subjected to public control. Significant advances are being made in decision sciences and behavioral knowledge, toward a possible "policy science".

47.2 Future Developments

The following are a few among the panel's expectations regarding possible future societal developments:

Urbanization: The panel expected a gradual abandonment of the concept of the city as a discrete and definable entity as metropolitan areas merge into a growing megalopolis. . . . Though the panel was rather hopeful about our increased ability to carry out effective, responsive, and visionary central planning and large-scale urban development, there was strong disagreement as to the likelihood of a major redirection of resources from military and space programs to urban programs. . . . The majority of respondents foresaw continuing disorder and disequilibrium as well as an increase in the alienation and impersonality of urban life. . . . Efforts at integration were generally expected to be increasingly successful toward the latter part of the century. . . . The institution of the communiversity was envisioned as one possibility for improving community life and providing cultural enrichment for the aged and unemployed.

The family: The panel expected the family eventually to take on many aspects of a "leisure-activity unit". . . . The availability of methods to preselect the sex of children was considered increasingly likely toward the end of the century. Nonmarital methods for rearing children were expected to gain acceptability. . . . New careers for women were expected gradually to appear in the areas of education and social services. . . . With respect to the elderly, it was thought that, especially in the near term, their relationship to their families may suffer due to the financial problems of runaway inflation. However, they expected that throughout the re-

> mainder of this century community service, second careers, and travel would progressively help in reducing the alienation of the elderly.
>
> *Leisure and the economy:* The respondents differed on whether technological change would substantially contribute to future alienation in society by significantly increasing unemployment. . . . Similar disagreement appeared over the extent to which a full-employment economy would remain a publicly avowed goal. . . . Most respondents agreed that the standard age of retirement would probably decrease to 60 or less, although some felt that the opposite trend would appear after 1980.
>
> *Education:* There were some respondents who foresaw a significant trend toward educational systems that combine work with education for adolescents. . . . The elimination of grades and credit, at least as known today, was considered likely, with evaluation of students possibly done with the aid of independent testing services. . . .
>
> *Food and population:* There was agreement that large-scale production of synthetic food substitutes will increase steadily throughout the remainder of the century. Agricultural improvements, together with new sources of food (such as the oceans or artificial protein), would contribute to a moderate reduction in the famine problem. There was little doubt that birth control would be widely adopted and that world population growth would begin to diminish slowly in the next twenty years.
>
> *International relations:* There was considerable agreement that substantial proliferation of nuclear armaments would take place before 1990, causing perhaps some moderate but very important changes in the balance of power. . . . The panel also thought that the 1980s might see a high rate of Chinese economic and territorial expansion. . . . World trade and investment were expected to increase steadily through the rest of the century. It was anticipated that space programs and the peaceful organization of the world may bring about a moderate increase in technological cooperation in the 1980s and 1990s, but probably not in the more immediate future.

47.3 Implications of Technology

A list of possible physical and biomedical breakthroughs was presented to the panel in the first round, and each respondent was asked to state potential societal consequences of such breakthroughs. Subsequent rounds then inquired into the conditional probability of these consequences—conditional on the assumption that the triggering breakthrough had indeed occurred. Here are a few examples of likely implications, as foreseen by the panelists:

> *Triggering breakthrough:* Demonstration of large-scale desalination plants capable of producing useful water economically for agricultural purposes (possible date: 1980).
>
> *Probable consequences:* The food supply would be raised throughout the world. Productivity of Near Eastern countries would increase, making them less dependent on foreign aid. To establish such plants would become a major form of aid from rich to poor countries.

Triggering breakthrough: Establishment of a central data storage facility (possible date: 1980).

Probable consequences: Important improvements in law and medicine would result. Grave privacy problems would be created.

Triggering breakthrough: Availability of cheap electric power from fusion power plants (possible date for laboratory demonstration: 1985).

Probable consequences: Living standards would increase generally, due to a rise in the use of consumer durables powered by electricity. There would be greater dispersal of urban areas. The birth rate would decline as TV and the electric light become widespread.

Triggering breakthrough: Individual portable telephones, carried by most Americans (possible date: 1990).

Probable consequences: Traffic control would be aided. Persons would be subjected to intrusion at all times. Many more mobile forms of work would come into existence with many individuals "in the field" rather than in offices.

Triggering breakthrough: Feasibility of limited weather control, in the sense of predictably affecting regional weather at acceptable cost (possible date: 1990).

Probable consequences: Dissention within a community would be created (as, for instance, between ski resort owners and farmers). Weather would become a political issue between countries. This development would be conducive to more outdoor living and recreation, thus improving health.

Triggering breakthrough: Availability of a computer that comprehends standard IQ tests and scores above 150 (possible date: 1990).

Probable consequences: The automation of a substantial portion of today's tasks would be likely in certain industries. Computers would be used to perform what today are considered routine medical and psychiatric diagnoses. The concentration of knowledge in the hands of the technical elite would be further increased.

Triggering breakthrough: Demonstration of nonsurgical techniques by which the sex of babies may be chosen with 90 percent reliability (possible date: 1980).

Probable consequences: The initial effect in the U.S. would be an increase in the number of males. This development, in combination with birth control, would diminish the tendency of couples to have more children in hopes of changing an all-girl or all-boy family.

Triggering breakthrough: Demonstration of chemical control of the aging process, permitting extension of life span by fifty years, with commensurate increase in number of years of vigor (possible date: 2010).

Probable consequences: A more complex society would result, organized around different maturity and interest levels of its member groups. A new aristocracy would be established, if access to control of aging is not available to all. The normal work career would become multistaged, the stages being separated by several extended retraining/resocialization periods. There would be a demand for major innovations in social welfare. There would be profound implications for inheritance laws and individual landownership.

Chapter IX

On the Future of the United States

Most of the remainder of this book will deal with explorations of the future of three major areas of concern: the United States, international relations, and economics. The first of these is the subject of the present chapter, which consists of three parts: portions of my essay, "On the Future State of the Union",[1] followed by two shorter sections, one a 1976 address to a congress of educators, the other a resume of the report on a study of the future of transportation in California.

48 ON THE FUTURE STATE OF THE UNION

48.1 Introduction

This report is addressed to the many persons in this country who are concerned over the direction in which our society should be moving and especially to those experiencing a growing sense of frustration and alienation because of the rapid changes in the world around them, the seeming remoteness of governmental decision-making, and the difficulty of relating the vast knowledge that is being offered by our educational institutions to an understanding of our society and its future.

In a country as immense, as complex, and as populous as the United States, it is not reasonable to expect that each of its citizens should be active, outside the polling booth, in the affairs of government and, thus, in one of the main forces that shape the future of this nation. Nonetheless there is a need for the thoughtful individual to have better means than he is likely to have at present for understanding more clearly what options there are for the future course of our society, of his community, and, within that ambient culture, of his personal life. Without such improved understanding, he will not only fail to act wisely when voting on national or community matters or when making decisions affecting his own or his family's future, but his sense of dignity, of being more than a cog in an unintelligible machine, of having some measure of control over his personal destiny, will suffer intolerably.

Thus, as the pace of change accelerates and the complexity of societal problems grows, the need is becoming increasingly urgent for giving our-

1. Report R-27, Institute for the Future (1972).

selves, individually and as a nation, an accounting of what major options are available to our society. A thorough awareness of such options and of the courses of action that might be pursued to attain them would give a larger fraction of the public a new chance to participate in the formation of its own future and provide decision makers with a more rational planning basis.

This essay has the sole purpose of making a contribution to this greater awareness of future options and thereby improving our chances, even if only slightly, for greater rationality in planning for the future.

The subject matter of this report is the future state of the Union. In speaking of "the future" in this context, emphasis will be placed not on the months and years that lie immediately ahead or on the far distant future many decades or centuries hence, but on the middle range of from five to thirty years from now. Enough has been said by others about the more immediate future; moreover, its main features are already rather firmly fixed and not so susceptible to deliberate interventive planning as are those of the period beyond, say, the next five years. Beyond a few decades, on the other hand, our ability to forecast even our major options diminishes rapidly and, in any case, present actions aimed at affecting that far future are likely to be superseded and obliterated in their effects by later ones, so that preoccupation with the period, say, beyond thirty years from now becomes largely an academic exercise.

Of course, it goes without saying that the appropriate time horizon for planning depends on the precise matter of concern. But if we look at some of the typical ones among the major issues confronting our society today—pollution, the drug culture, urban deterioration, race relations, education, poverty, crime, international antagonisms, the population explosion—none offers much hope of radical improvement in just a few years, yet all seem to be characterized by an increasing and even accelerating degeneration that makes interventive action within the next decade or two mandatory without question. It is the trends in areas like these, their effect on the state of the Union and on the state of the individual within it, and the policies and programs that might be enacted to deal with these trends that forms this essay's subject matter.

To explore these matters fully in their true and vast complexity would be an enormous undertaking, one far beyond our intent and capability. And we must seek ways of bringing this task down to manageable proportions—if, indeed, that is possible without depriving the effort of meaning.

Forecasts concerning the future state of the Union, in order to be at least plausible if not credible, must take their departure from the present and, through the dynamics of development scenarios, reveal how various possible future conditions of our society might evolve from the present one. This implies, among many other things, that we must have a vocabulary for describing the state of the Union at a given time and for comparing states of it at different times. Such a vocabulary, moreover, must permit us to discuss the mechanisms of change through which one given condition is transformed into another. The implications of this requirement in terms of conceptual analysis and data collection are formidable.

It might be said without exaggeration that the full execution of what we have set out to do would require:

- attempting to present a somewhat detailed description of the present state of the Union;
- elucidating this description with a presentation of the levels of selected economic indicators, comparing them with those of the past, and analyzing the implications of their movement;
- including in our report, along with this economic accounting, a similar "social accounting", framed correspondingly in terms of certain social indicators;
- augmenting these statements with similar ones covering the political state of affairs, both domestic and (particularly) international, in terms of selected political indicators;
- forecasting changes in technology, the physical environment, social trends, and foreign relations;
- anticipating the potential effects of such changes on the future state of the Union;
- describing the options for the future of our society that it may exercise either through the formal channels of government or through a diffuse multitude of informal and decentralized influences, pressures, and actions;
- assessing the interactions between these diverse trends and the reactions to them and thereby identifying major potential societal developments; and
- thus tracing the probable future courses of the economic, social, and political indicators, in terms of which the present state of the Union was described.

Since the full realization of this program is clearly beyond our aspirations, a choice must be made between concentrating on some of the subtasks and attempting to give at least some attention to all aspects. The spirit in which this whole present exercise is being conducted is one of a systems approach, that is, of ascertaining the complex interactions among events in areas that are not necessarily seen to be closely related and of presenting an integrated overview of future societal potentialities. Consequently, our decision must inevitably be in favor of the latter alternative. That is, even at the risk of initial superficiality, we will have to confront every one of the component tasks just outlined and seek to establish at least the structural framework into which perhaps at first only sketches of the required elements can be inserted, to be replaced eventually, it is hoped, by more detailed descriptions.

Thus the present effort should be looked upon as a first stepping stone in a sequence of successive approximations toward a more comprehensive statement of possible futures; that is, it should be read with the presumption that it will be succeeded at a later time by other, like-minded efforts that, perhaps by building on the present one, may be able to cover the subject more aptly and fully.

48.2 *The Problem of Describing the State of the Union*

A full description of the state of the Union at a given time—whether past, present, or future—is not possible. We cannot describe—nor are we remotely interested in describing—the location and condition of every thing or person in the country. It is preferable to be highly selective with regard to the items to which we want to pay particular attention.

What principle should guide our selection?

The purpose of giving an account of the future state of the Union, or of several possible future states of the Union, is more than to satisfy our curiosity; it is primarily to aid the planning and decision-making process through which the course of events will be influenced. This means that our aim ought to be to describe possible future states of affairs in a way that will allow us to compare these with regard to their desirability and, thereby, to help identify those decisions that will enhance the probability of realization of desirable states and reduce the probability of occurrence of undesirable ones.

The description we are seeking must, therefore, clearly be in terms of what is important from the point of view of creating a more satisfactory state of the Union. This suggests two guidelines for our procedure.

One is that the discussion of the present and potential states of the Union should be in terms of descriptions that do not place the emphasis on an inventory of what is or might be there but on the satisfaction felt by people (or groups of people) with a given state of affairs or on the desirability expressed by them for a potential state of affairs. A set of satisfaction indices selected for this purpose is presented and discussed in Section 48.5.

The other procedural guideline requires that, throughout any dimension of our considerations, the items in question be rank-ordered with respect to their societal importance so as to permit ourselves to limit our attention to those items that lie above a chosen threshold of importance. This applies equally to, say, scientific advances, technological developments, environmental changes, domestic political trends, international developments, changes in people's values and preferences, or any other events that might affect the future of the nation. Thus we might begin by selecting for consideration only those few potential developments in each of the areas just enumerated that might be regarded as most important in view of their probable societal implications. [For our present purposes, in making this selection, we may be guided by some of the work presented and discussed earlier in this volume; see Sections 45 and 47 in Chapter VIII, and Gordon and Ament, 1969.]

Developments, it should be noted, very often represent opportunities for action, for an action may generally be interpreted as an effort to enhance or slow down a specific development. Since it is through interventive actions that we attempt to influence the future, the effectiveness of such control depends on the wisdom with which developments have been singled out for consideration. Thus the very selection of developments involves a learning process of linking alternative states of the future with effective vehicles of choice.

Developments, of course, cannot be considered singly, that is, in isolation from one another, if we wish to construct an integrated image of a possible future state of this nation. For one thing, the occurrence of one development may have a profound effect on the occurrence of another; for example, a breakthrough in cancer therapy, obviously, may increase life expectancy. For another, the significance of one development often cannot be fully appraised except in the context of others; for instance, a proliferation of the drug culture may appear in a very different light depending on whether the economy is thriving or ailing.

Consequently, later, particular attention is paid to the relationship between potential developments, especially the effect that the occurrence of one development has on the direction or probability of occurrence of another.

48.3 Today's Dominant Issues

It may be well to begin by recounting the all too familiar: the major issues confronting our society today. In so doing, the stage is being set for an appraisal of how good or bad things are at present and of what aspirations we may reasonably have for improving things in the future. An attempt to quantify such appraisals in terms of satisfaction indices is made in the next section.

The word "issue", in this context, implies the imminence of confrontation with a choice, the choice being between alternative policies or courses of action for dealing with a given problem situation. Occasionally there are issues that are highly controversial, in the sense that clearly defined, but incompatible, alternatives are being advocated by opposing groups; a current example [this was the year 1972] is the issue over how to bring the war in Vietnam to an acceptable conclusion. More often, issues are problematical rather than controversial, since circumstances may prevail that clearly require amelioration, without there being a single, not to mention more than one, clear-cut course of action for dealing with them; an example is the crime issue, that is, the problem of how to achieve a deceleration in the rate of crimes, particularly crimes of violence. In the case of a problematical issue, the choice is apt to be between doing nothing (often made by default) or taking *ad hoc,* piecemeal actions designed to temporize until a more satisfactory, decisive plan has been devised. While controversial issues present options of choice, problematical issues above all indicate the need for inventions.

Given below is a list of major current issues. The large majority of them are problematical rather than controversial. The invention of ways to deal with them and the choices that must be made among available alternatives will dominate the nation's political life in the next few decades and will, more than anything else, determine the kind of society that will emerge during that period.

The issues are roughly arranged in descending order of societal importance [as determined at the time by the judgment of staff associates of mine at the Institute for the Future]:

Major Current Issues

(1) the unsatisfactory condition of the economy
(2) foreign entanglements
(3) urban deterioration
(4) pollution
(5) the crime rate
(6) inadequate housing
(7) the drug problem
(8) poverty
(9) deficiencies in the educational system
(10) infringement of civil liberties
(11) inadequate health care delivery
(12) international antagonisms
(13) the problem of the aged
(14) transportation and communication breakdown
(15) uncontrolled science and technology
(16) the need for preservation of the environment
(17) the difficulty of adjusting to changing value systems
(18) governmental disorganization
(19) race relations
(20) alienation from governmental processes
(21) deficiencies in the Social Security system
(22) institutional decay
(23) the desire on the part of the young for radical change
(24) widespread anomie
(25) the demand that corporations change their role in society
(26) the population explosion
(27) the impoverished cultural environment
(28) the difficulties in overcoming sexual discrimination
(29) inadequate opportunities for self-fulfillment
(30) the deterioration of friendships and family ties

48.4 The Concept of Satisfaction Indices

The presence and relative severity of issues such as those enumerated above are clues to the degree of dissatisfaction felt by Americans with the present condition of their country. These dissatisfactions, in turn, are the driving force behind aspirations for improvement; they give rise to the formulation of goals for the future and of policies for the attainment of such goals.

Theoretical debates in the area of subjective preferences, goals, and policies tend to suffer at least as much from semantic disagreements as from substantive ones. A clear terminology, therefore, can do much to clarify discussion.

In particular, it will be expedient from here on to draw a reasonably clear distinction between goals and objectives, on the one hand, and, correspondingly, between satisfaction indices and social indicators, on the other.

Let us understand by "goals", very roughly, those conditions that a person (or group or nation) might strive to attain in order to maximize or at least enhance his (or a group's members') state of satisfaction with the world. Goals are thus closely related to what is referred to as the "quality of life", taking that term in its widest sense. The quality of life is a multidimensional entity, consisting of such components as the quality of the environment, the quality of health care, the quality of education, the quality of interpersonal relations, and so on. Deficiencies in these, particularly when it is sensed that they could be overcome, precipitate the articulation of goals. The quality of life, or the degree of goal attainment, is measured (or perhaps we should say, might be attempted to be measured) by ascertaining the levels of subjective satisfaction that people feel with the components of the quality of life (of which a few have just been enumerated). These measures of what people "really" want, or at least are convinced that they want, are referred to as "satisfaction indices".

We will not go into a lengthy discussion at this point of the difference, if any, between what people want and what they think they want (not to mention the differences between ascertaining what people want and ascertaining what they think they want). It would seem rather obvious that what people think they want is affected in some measure by the process of education, both by changing their predilections and aspirations and by increasing their awareness of what may or may not be reasonably attainable. Thus, while there may at first be a sizable gap between what people impulsively think they want and what, on further consideration, they really want, we might say with all due caveats that the process of education (be it formal or not) may tend to close that gap. The principal caveat consists in the need to point out that, for this to be entirely true, the educational process itself would have to be assumed to be free from bias and propaganda—an assumption that will rarely be justified.

In order to attain a goal (say, better health care), certain "objectives" may be formulated (e.g., so many hospital beds per capita, or a certain reduction in the death rate from lung cancer). Such objectives are stated in terms of objectively defined and objectively measurable quantities, known as "social indicators". Thus a social indicator is a quantity of such a kind that, all else being equal, an increase (or decrease) in its numerical value is expected to constitute a contribution to some aspect of the quality of life. Hence, while a social indicator is an objective parameter, its selection is warranted solely on the basis of its expected subjective effect. The primary problem with which workers in the social-indicator field are confronted may perhaps be described as that of identifying in each satisfaction category a set of social indicators that has the property of being both necessary and sufficient to determine the level of the corresponding satisfaction index.

It may be well to extend our terminological stipulations into the decision-making area. In the present context, a "policy" is a statement of goals and of the relative weight to be attached to each goal; it therefore is an articulation of subjective (individual or group) preferences to be realized. A policy is translated into a "plan" by specifying the objectives to be attained, the degree of their attainment being measured in terms of social indicators. A proposed set of specific actions intended to implement a plan is called a "program".

For example, the mayor of a city may have among his goals an increase in the physical safety of its inhabitants and improvements in housing conditions. A policy declaration might announce that these goals are to have priority over all other goals. A plan seeking to implement this policy might specify the objectives of (a) reducing the rate of crimes of violence in the city as well as the death rate from traffic accidents by 25 percent and (b) providing an additional 10,000 housing units. A program would spell out in detail the actions to be taken to achieve these objectives, which might include, say, increasing the police force by 1000 officers and providing city-backed long-term loans to construction firms.

Thus, to repeat, a policy specifies goals; a plan specifies objectives; a program specifies actions. The attainment of a policy is measured in terms of satisfaction indices; the attainment of a plan is measured in terms of social indicators. As for programs, which are means of implementing plans, the word "attainment" does not apply; they can be discussed in terms of feasibility, cost, and effectiveness.

Suppose now that we had ascertained the goal preferences and priorities of each population segment within the nation. How should decision makers proceed to formulate policies, plans, and programs responsive to these desires? The selection of a policy requires a dual process of aggregation, namely, the reconciliation of possibly incompatible preferences of different population segments into one set of national goals and the combination of goals into one policy by setting the weights (i.e., relative effort levels) to be allocated to these goals. There is no unique magic formula by which, in a democracy, these aggregations can be carried out. They are, in fact, at the heart of the political process, and differences in the emphasis given to the desires of various groups and in the political judgment involved in translating these desires into policies lead to different political platforms.

We note in passing the attractiveness, yet inadequacy, of one seemingly "democratic" procedure for arriving at a set of weighted goals and thus at a policy: Suppose it were possible (and within reasonable limitations it is) to ascertain the average weight that the citizens wish to attach to each of a set of possible goals. The policy consisting of the goals thus weighted, which might be called a "proportionate policy", has considerable merit, particularly in that it establishes benchmarks against which the goal attainments promised by other policies can be measured. What makes a proportionate policy as such unacceptable in a democracy is that it pays insufficient attention to the needs of minorities (e.g., the urban poor, various racial or ethnic groups, the elderly). It is one of the characteristics of a modern democracy that, in addition to the resolution of issues by majority vote, it offers certain basic elements of protection for the rights of minorities (all the way down to the rights of the individual) against what has been called "the tyranny of the majority". This means that a national policy, aside from seeking "proportionate satisfaction" in some measure, must also include provisions for what might be called "equitable satisfaction".

The degree of equitability of satisfaction that our intuitive ethical standards require depends on the particular goal that is to be satisfied. While many people will feel that we are doing well if all but 10 percent of our population are reasonably satisfied with the condition of housing or of education, these same people may feel that in the matter of poverty we are not doing well until all but 1 percent are reasonably well satisfied; and when it comes to questions of justice under the law, the percentage required to give an equivalent feeling of doing well may drop to well below one-thousandth of 1 percent.

These reflections suggest that, in addition to the "standard" indices of satisfaction (satisfaction with education, housing, the environment, and so on), we might seriously consider introducing an index of "satisfaction with the general equitability of satisfaction". (Alternatively one might go one step further by establishing, for each standard index of satisfaction, a companion index measuring the satisfaction with the equitability of satisfaction in that particular area.)

The use of one or several indices of satisfaction with the equitability of satisfaction may mitigate Bertram Gross's (1969) concern over "aggregatics", which he voiced with regard to social indicators and no doubt would apply also to nationally aggregated indices of satisfaction; for a low value of an equitability index, even in the presence of a high average satisfaction level, would represent a warning to policy makers that all is not well and would draw attention to the need for less aggregated examination.

The question may be raised whether there is not another, similar type of "metasatisfaction", namely, that associated with rising levels of satisfaction. But here we must be careful lest we fall into a logical trap. It is true that generally an individual, in order to be happy in the long run, requires occasional increments in the levels of compliance with his aspirations (rising living standard, perhaps improved interpersonal relations, increased access to cultural amenities, and so on). But we must not attempt to express this requirement by stating that he will be unhappy unless his happiness steadily increases. This paradox arises only if we fail to distinguish between objective and subjective assessments. A logically acceptable way to express the intent of the phenomenon under discussion is to say that the social indicators selected to measure a certain aspect of society may stay at a constant level and yet the individuals affected by this aspect may experience a drop in the associated level of satisfaction; or, conversely, that in order to maintain a given level of satisfaction over a long period, some of the associated social indicators may be required to rise rather than stay constant.

48.5 A Specific Set of Satisfaction Indices

We now return to the tasks of selecting appropriate satisfaction indices in terms of which to describe the quality of the state of the Union and of assigning to each such index a value reflecting the degree of satisfaction felt with today's conditions and the issues implied by them.

A suggested set of satisfaction indices, listed in descending order of importance, is given below. They were obtained from a Delphi survey conducted among the research staff of the Institute for the Future. In judging priorities among these indices, the participants were asked to ignore their personal preferences and to think, instead, of what seemed to be more important from the point of view of the nation as a whole, considering today's state of affairs and today's value system:

(1) *Personal physical security* from violence, disease, accidents
(2) *Economic prosperity:* economic well-being in terms of quality and variety of available consumer goods (including food, in particular) and reasonable expectation of future increments in prosperity
(3) *Justice under the law:* effectiveness, equality, conformity with accepted moral standards, protection against injustice
(4) *National security* from external as well as internal enemies
(5) *Social security* with respect to old age and sickness
(6) *Spiritual well-being as an individual:* self-fulfillment, variety of experiences, harmonious relations with family and friends, prospects of a long and satisfying life
(7) *Involvement of the individual in society:* social mobility, status, pride in belonging to a particular societal group, dignity, influence, participation in government, reasonable control over one's personal future within a range of available socioeconomic lifestyles
(8) *Equality of opportunity* with respect to education, employment, housing, recreation
(9) *Quality of the cultural environment:* education, the arts, entertainment, recreation, leisure, the mass media
(10) *Civil liberties:* voting franchise, free speech, free assembly
(11) *Quality of the technological environment:* transportation, communication, housing, household equipment, utilities, office machines, factory equipment, farm equipment, hospital equipment, teaching machines
(12) *Quality of the physical environment:* esthetics, freedom from pollution

In addition, as mentioned before, we may add a thirteenth index measuring the satisfaction with

(13) The general *Equitability of satisfaction.*

(The placement of this special index at the end of the list does not imply a judgment that it is inferior in importance. Since it is a "meta-index", it cannot logically be treated on the same level with the other twelve.)

Juxtaposed to the foregoing static notion of importance is a dynamic one, that is, one based on the operational consideration of which indices should be given the most attention in terms of the national effort that ought to be expended on them in order to hold the line or to achieve improvements over their current levels. These allocations of effort should reflect both the urgency of attaining a level of satisfaction in excess of what it would be without such an effort and the degree of expectation that the effort would, indeed, bring about the desired benefits.

In the internal survey at the Institute for the Future, the staff participants were also asked to give their opinions on this dynamic notion of importance. The medians of their effort allocations, normalized to add up to 100 %, are recorded in the following table:

(1) Personal physical security	15
(2) Economic prosperity	8
(3) Justice under the law	11
(4) National security	7
(5) Social security	6
(6) Spiritual well-being as an individual	3
(7) Involvement of the individual in society	9
(8) Equality of opportunity	10
(9) Quality of the cultural environment	9
(10) Civil liberties	8
(11) Quality of the technological environment	6
(12) Quality of the physical environment	8
	100

Thus, for example, the relative effort that the promotion of equality of opportunity deserves was judged to be higher than the static-importance rank of this item would indicate. Conversely, the opposite is true of spiritual well-being as an individual. This presumably reflects the feeling that governmental action could readily produce a beneficial effect on the first but not nearly as easily on the second.

The next step that is required is to assign to these indices some values representing the current state of the Union. To accomplish this, one might conduct an opinion survey among a representative sample of the American population, asking each respondent how satisfied he felt with respect to the twelve areas corresponding to the satisfaction indices. However, the average valuation thus obtained would be analogous to the "proportionate policy" discussed in Section 48.4 and subject to similar objections. A preferable method would be to conduct a Delphi study among a set of carefully selected experts (sociologists, psychologists, lawyers, educators, artists, philosophers), seeking their opinions, not as to their personal feelings of satisfaction with the condition of our society, but of where the nation as a whole stands with regard to it. Despite the vagueness of such an inquiry, preliminary findings derived from queries addressed to Institute staff members and consultants suggest that a reasonable consensus would not be too difficult to obtain.

For the purposes of the present report, such a Delphi survey was merely "simulated", in that staff members of the Institute acted as "experts" and, through an abbreviated, in-house Delphi procedure, arrived at valuations for the twelve indices. In fact, such an assessment was carried out in 1970, with corrections made for 1971 to account for interim changes in conditions. Values were chosen on a scale from 0 to 100, where 0 denoted an utterly catastrophic state of affairs and 100 denoted a state of utopian bliss. The results, rounded to the nearest multiple of 5, are shown below:

	1970	*1971*
(1) Personal physical security	60	55
(2) Economic prosperity	70	60
(3) Justice under the law	50	50
(4) National security	65	70
(5) Social security	60	60
(6) Spiritual well-being as an individual	60	55
(7) Involvement of the individual in society	50	55
(8) Equality of opportunity	35	40
(9) Quality of the cultural environment	50	50
(10) Civil liberties	75	75
(11) Quality of the technological environment	75	75
(12) Quality of the physical environment	40	40

While no exaggerated significance should be attached to the absolute magnitudes of these values, the relative difference between values ascribed to different indices clearly reveals that the panelists were aware of considerable variations in their own feelings of satisfaction with different aspects of the quality of life. In other words, regardless of their absolute valuation, the panelists very clearly conveyed through their relative valuations what aspects of the quality of life in our society they found most urgently in need of amelioration. Similarly, the increases or decreases since 1970 (though expectedly small) in the values of some of the indices clearly indicate that the participants had differential perceptions of changes in various aspects of the quality of life. For instance, while the economy in 1971 was in worse shape than it had been (Index 2), more people were taking an active and effective interest in community affairs (Index 7). In the case of Index 12, the positive effects of environmentalist efforts were probably thought to be offset by the further deterioration of the state of water pollution, resulting in no net change of that index.

It is well to note that a low current value of an index does not necessarily entail a high importance rank (under either the static or the dynamic notion of importance). For instance, the quality of the physical environment was rated at only 40, yet it ranked lowest in static importance (indicating presumably that, while judged to be quite low compared with what it might be, it is not yet considered intolerably oppressive); similarly, its dynamic importance rank, while not nearly so low, was low enough to indicate that potential efforts to improve satisfaction with the quality of the physical environment were not viewed by the panelists as offering a high degree of cost-effectiveness.

The pilot panelists (in 1970) were next asked to consider each index once more, not from the viewpoint of the nation as a whole, but from the viewpoints of minority groups that might feel either singularly worse or singularly better about that particular index. To be specific, the respondents were asked to assign to each index a "1 percent value" and a "99 percent value", meaning those values which the index is estimated to have in the eyes, respectively, of that 1 percent of the population which would be least satisfied, and that 1 percent which would be most satisfied, with respect to the quality measured by that index. On the basis of the resulting valuations, and taking into account the shifts in the basic state-of-the-Union values between 1970 and 1971 (as displayed above), the following estimates were obtained (the 1971 state-of-the-Union values being repeated for comparison):

	1% value	*1971 state-of-the-Union value*	*99% value*
(1) Personal physical security	30	55	65
(2) Economic prosperity	10	60	70
(3) Justice under the law	20	50	70
(4) National security	50	70	70
(5) Social security	20	60	80
(6) Spiritual well-being as an individual	5	55	75
(7) Involvement of the individual in society	10	55	80
(8) Equality of opportunity	15	40	65
(9) Quality of the cultural environment	25	50	75
(10) Civil liberties	25	75	90
(11) Quality of the technological environment	40	75	80
(12) Quality of the physical environment	5	40	60

The difference, particularly, between the 1 percent values and the values for the nation as a whole provides some clues as to what the value of Index 13 (satisfaction with the equitability of satisfaction) should be. It might, in fact, simply be defined as a weighted average of the 1 percent values divided by the total-population values. However, it is debatable whether such a simple linear expression will represent more than a first approximation of what is intended.

A simple calculation shows that, under the suggested definition, if all the weights are assumed equal, we obtain $I_{13} = 36$. If weights are chosen that decline slightly as we go from I_1 to I_{12}, the resultant value of I_{13} will be slightly larger; but its precise value is relatively insensitive, within wide limits, to the choice of weights.

48.6 Predictions, Forecasts, and Actions

The listing given earlier of major current issues together with the estimated 1971 values of the satisfaction indices convey a very grossly aggregated picture of the present state of the Union and of the needs for changes and improvements as currently felt.

Turning now to the future, an attempt will be made to present a reasonably comprehensive, though again grossly aggregated, description of the major facets in the spectrum of potential developments.

The purpose here, of course, is not to make "predictions", that is, firm assertions of precisely what will happen at what time in the future. Such statements are best left to soothsayers and clairvoyants. Instead, we shall be concerned with what has in contradistinction come to be referred to as "forecasts", that is, statements about the future that are couched in probability terms, often are of the conditional ("if-then") form, and consequently suggest the concept of alternatives.

While forecasts may be less informative than predictions, their operational utility to a decision maker may actually be greater. A prediction would, at best, provide a portion of the background against which plans have to be laid. A forecast, on the other hand, points up alternatives and therefore often carries with it a suggestion of possible action: If the forecast is a simple probability estimate ("Event E will occur by time t with probability p"), it may suggest actions as being desirable because they would raise or lower the probability estimate (or, equivalently, advance or retard the anticipated time) of occurrence; if, moreover, the forecast is of the conditional form (e.g., "The occurrence of Event E′ will cause a substantial rise in the estimated probability of occurrence of Event E"), it makes explicit the means by which the event's probability estimate can be affected (namely, by bringing about or preventing the occurrence of the triggering event).

As pointed out earlier (see Section 47), technological forecasts come close to predictions, inasmuch as they tend to be about technological breakthroughs that are firmly expected to happen sooner or later, the only question being the precise time of occurrence. Societal forecasts, by contrast, are less certain, mainly because they are much more subject to human intervention. Admittedly, the occurrence of technological developments or "breakthroughs" can only be influenced (rather than determined) by human decisions (i.e., they can be promoted but not assured by increased investment), and some societal developments clearly fall in this class, too; but others do not. Whether a societal development can be influenced only or fully determined by interventive action depends on who the actor is and whether in fact there is a single actor or a multiplicity of actors. For example, if the development is the passage of a tax reform bill and the actor in question is the U.S. Congress, the development is fully determinable, since the Congress can carry out the development by enactment. By contrast, widespread sabotage of airplanes can be influenced negatively by the government (through enactment of laws and support of countermeasure development) as well as positively by would-be saboteurs, but neither actor can fully determine this development. Thus the notion of "action" cannot be separated from the identification of the "actor". Any actor has some things under his control, whereas others are only subject to his influence. This distinction is not being disregarded in the Future State of the Union game discussed in a later section of this chapter: There, the set of actions at a player's disposal, as opposed to the events he can forecast and, at best, influence, depends very definitely on what particular role he is playing.

[The original text at this point went on to list a large number of potential scientific, technological, and societal developments, with estimated dates of occurrence (in the case of events) or estimated values over the next thirty years (in the case of trends). Most of these consisted of updated items gleaned from the earlier studies reported in Chapter VIII, Sections 45 and 47, or from Gordon and Ament (1969), and they will not be included in this present excerpt. Instead we proceed immediately to a discussion of the application of such forecasts to long-range planning purposes.]

48.7 Possible Futures and Planning

The utility of such forecasts should be seen in their serving as background material for planning, but the need for caution in using them for this purpose must be reemphasized here. To the long-range planner interested in composing images of possible future states of the world and constructing potential scenarios of developments leading to such future states, the forecasts may perhaps provide some initial guidance. However, before proceeding to the design of detailed plans and interventive action programs, the planner would be well advised to bear in mind the following considerations:

- The forecasts are based on opinions, and even expert opinions can be wrong.
- Even if the probability estimates assigned to potential future events were quite reliable, they would still be merely probabilities; that is, of all events stated to have, say, a 60 percent probability of occurrence by a certain date, only 60 percent should be expected actually to take place by that time.
- The occurrence of any one event will affect the probability of the subsequent occurrence of others; these cross-impacts should be taken into account in constructing scenarios and, by implication, in making plans for the future.
- The actions the planner is contemplating would, if implemented, alter the probabilities of some of the forecasted developments; the cross-impact feedback from these hypothetical self-generated events should be taken into consideration when deciding between alternative plans.
- The list of events under consideration is confined to ones having assigned to

them a moderate to high probability of occurrence during the next three decades. A planner must, in addition, pay some attention to low-probability events of such high importance that their expected impact, were they to occur, would be comparable to that of the original events. These are the potential catastrophes and "anticatastrophes" (i.e., low-probability events that are highly beneficial). A good plan, clearly, seeks to minimize the consequences of potential catastrophes and to take advantage of the opportunities offered by potential anticatastrophes.

- It is well to beware of myths, which, in this context, mean foregone conclusions about supposedly high-probability developments that in fact appear to be either decidedly low-probability or whose probability, though not necessarily negligible, depends heavily on the form of as yet uncertain human intervention. Such myths abound in considerations of society's future, and a few will be listed presently.
- The quality of planning depends not only on a clear understanding of the probabilities attached to future developments and of the probabilistic cross-impacts among them but equally on imagination and inventiveness. Our options often are obscure and frequently must be invented rather than discovered. The encouragement and systematization of social inventions is crucial to our progress (and this essay will have served an important purpose if it succeeds in making a small contribution to this effect).

In the next three sections we shall deal briefly with some of the topics just mentioned: catastrophes, anticatastrophes, and myths. Then, in subsequent sections, we shall turn to interventive opportunities and the options they provide.

48.8 Potential Catastrophes

Listed below are some potential developments which, if they were to occur, would have catastrophic consequences for the future of our society. The dimensions of the catastrophes vary from a substantial decrease in the quality of life to total annihilation. To most of the items listed one would assign a probability that is quite low but still too high for comfort. They have been arranged approximately in descending order of "expected impact" (that is, impact if occurring times the probability of occurrence during the next thirty years).

- World War III
- a war involving the United States at the level of the Korean and Vietnamese wars
- a serious revolutionary attempt to overthrow the U.S. government
- significant loss of individual civil rights for the sake of maintaining social order
- more than 12 percent unemployment
- destruction of a large American city by an accidental nuclear explosion or by the accidental release of radioactive or chemical or biological warfare material
- large-scale famine in the world (resulting in more than 100 million deaths in one year)
- extinction of at least half the marine life in the world's oceans
- covert illegal use of biogenetic or of personality engineering, for the purpose of altering the attitudes or actions of some societal groups

- a further widening of the poverty gap (as measured by the amount of money needed annually that would raise the income of all families above the poverty level)
- a civil war involving at least one million people in armed conflict
- a major breakdown, lasting a month or longer, in the functioning of at least one large American city or of a region involving at least one million people
- ecological instability of the biosphere
- a doubling of the current rate of psychotic dysfunction because of sensory overload
- extinction of most fish in America's lakes and rivers
- a change in the average temperature of the earth's atmosphere by at least 2°C
- a runaway price inflation
- unforeseen biochemical consequences of commonly used medications, causing death, serious illness, or genetic damage to a substantial portion of the population
- inadvertent firing of a nuclear missile by us against others or by others against us
- a further doubling of the per-capita rate of crimes of violence
- a substantial plant blight, reducing food production in the United States by at least 20 percent
- air pollution becoming one of the major causes of death in the United States

No probabilities have been stated for the occurrence of these catastrophes, because any such estimates would be considered highly controversial. The reader may wish to form his own opinion about these and then make some assessment of the changes that the occurrence of each catastrophe would induce in the values of the satisfaction indices enumerated earlier.

48.9 Anticatastrophes

Anticatastrophes are low-probability developments that derive their expected importance from their highly beneficial rather than their highly detrimental implications. It appears that anticatastrophes fall into three classes: (a) those that are essentially the direct opposites of catastrophes; (b) those that represent unexpectedly accelerated technological breakthroughs; and (c) those that are the result of changes in human attitudes.

Some anticatastrophes of each of these classes are listed below. Within each category, an effort has been made again to arrange them in descending order of expected societal impact.

Class a

- prompt termination of the war in which the United States is currently engaged [remember that this was written in 1972]
- reduction in unemployment to less than 2 percent
- essential eradication of poverty in the United States
- resuscitation of America's inland waters
- reduction in the per-capita rate of crimes of violence to less than half its current value
- reduction of air pollution to harmless levels

Class b

- early availability of a new source of cheap energy
- a cure for cancer
- availability of immunization against bacterial and viral diseases
- availability of pesticides having no harmful side effects
- economic feasibility of commercial manufacture of synthetic protein for food
- a breakthrough in genetics, leading to prenatal correction of hereditary defects in humans
- possibility of growing replacement limbs and organs through biochemical stimulation
- a breakthrough in physics, making it economically feasible to manufacture many chemical elements from subatomic building blocks

Class c

- continuance of the change in attitude among young American couples concerning the desirable number of children to have, leading to a further reduction in the present 1 percent annual population growth rate
- a reduction in chauvinistic nationalism throughout the world, resulting in reduced belligerency among nations
- greater acceptance among Americans of the need for appropriate training to increase one's sensitivity to, and understanding of, other persons
- advent of increased acceptance of population segments different from one's own, resulting in open housing and decreased job discrimination
- a substantial rise in the level of debate on public issues, due to improved education and better access to information
- institution of major educational reforms at all levels

As in the case of catastrophes, the estimation of both the probabilities of occurrence of these anticatastrophes and their effect on satisfaction levels if they were to occur is left to the reader.

48.10 Myths

To recognize claims about the future as unlikely may be as important to rational planning as to be aware of likely developments. It is for this reason that we present, below, a certain number of myths about the future, which are asserted from time to time. Far from being foregone conclusions, they portend occurrences of questionable, if not negligible, probability.

The following list, therefore, is a compilation of what in the author's opinion are "nonforecasts", arranged under seven headings. In each case, a comment is added to suggest why the statement does not deserve to have a high probability of occurrence attributed to it.

Myths about the economy

- The standard of living in the United States and in the world is falling. (Comment: Technological advances are continuing to provide labor-saving, health-improving, and pleasure-enhancing devices that are apt to be taken for granted.)

- The income gap between the rich and the poor in this country is increasing. (Comment: The ratio between the median income of the top decile and that of the bottom decile has in fact been declining; moreover, the future size of the gap will be considerably influenced, and might be further decreased, by future legislation.)
- Efforts to lower the rate of price inflation will raise unemployment, and vice versa. (Comment: The classical, unidisciplinary models of a national economy, which support this view, have been greatly discredited by their failure to predict correctly the consequences of monetary and fiscal policies enacted by the last two administrations.)
- The effort invested in the space program is nonproductive; hence the economy will benefit from having it reduced. (Comment: The same argument would condemn the entertainment industry, which is not economically productive in the sense of directly contributing to our basic needs or material wealth; moreover, the space program has produced innumerable side benefits of direct economic value.)
- The length of the workweek will be steadily reduced, resulting in greatly increased leisure time. (Comment: The choice between a "leisure economy", such as predicated here, and a full-employment economy is one of the major decisions about the future facing our society. Which way it will be made will depend on the emerging social climate and its effect on work motivation and on the role of women in the labor force. A major involvement, say, in raising the level of the underdeveloped part of the world, combined with a reinforced space program, would provide enough work for full employment.)

Myths about the quality of life

- We are suffering from too much technology; hence the quality of life will rise if technological progress is slowed. (Comment: Technology may have to be redirected, particularly toward pollution abatement, but the case for wholesale condemnation of technology has not been established; see earlier comment on the "falling" standard of living.)

Myths about population

- The world population explosion cannot be halted by the year 2000. (Comment: Contraceptive devices are improving, and propaganda for family planning is beginning to show results, though as yet insufficient. However, it does not take an enormous change in attitudes to produce a preference for, say, one child less per family than had been the case, and such a shift would do much to attenuate the population explosion.)
- The U.S. population growth rate cannot be brought down close to zero by the year 2000. (Comment: The previous comment applies even more in this case, because the present growth rate is already only about 1 percent per annum and declining.)
- The median age in the United States will be decreasing to less than 25. (Comment: On the contrary, in view of declining birth rates and rising life expectancy, the median age is rising.)

Myths about resources

- Mass world famine before the end of the century is inevitable. (Comment: While this is a distinct possibility, ongoing all-out efforts to avoid such a catastrophe should not be discounted. The Green Revolution, plus family planning, plus possibly new sources of food, such as large-scale ocean farming and artificial protein, may succeed in averting the disaster.)

- Mineral resources are being depleted so fast that the world's economy will revert to medieval levels by the year 2000. (Comment: The situation is indeed growing serious, but the effect will be to force us into more recycling and the exploitation of much-lower-grade ores than are being utilized now. Also, there is the off-chance that large-scale transmutation of elements may become economically feasible by 2000.)
- The exponentially increasing demand for energy will lead to catastrophic shortages before the end of the century. (Comment: It is true that energy demand is rising much faster even than the population, but new sources of energy, such as solar, nuclear, tidal, and geothermal may be utilized in time to meet the demand.)

Myths about the environment

- Man has already modified the atmosphere to the extent that the temperature of the earth may be expected to fall dangerously by virtue of reduced sunlight. (Comment: See next item.)
- Man has already modified the atmosphere to the extent that the temperature of the earth may be expected to rise dangerously by virtue of the carbon dioxide greenhouse effect. (Comment: It is not clear to what extent this effect and the one referred to in the preceding item may balance each other.)
- Heavy air pollution is a necessary concomitant of modern technology, and it will take a major breakthrough before the trend toward heavier pollution can be reversed. (Comment: Stricter laws and law enforcement have cleared up London's atmosphere.)

Myths about international relations

- The controversy between capitalism and communism can be resolved only by the victory of one system over the other. (Comment: There are numerous indications that the two economic systems are converging in many respects and, to the extent they are not, are quite capable of coexisting; the real problem has shifted from considerations of preference for one or another economic system to one of military standoff between superpowers trying to maintain what Albert Wohlstetter has called "a delicate balance of terror".)
- The gap in affluence between the developed and the underdeveloped countries will continue to grow. (Comment: Whether this trend will continue will depend greatly on the future foreign-aid strategies adopted by the industrialized nations.)

Myths about war and peace

- There will always be wars. (Comment: We may be approaching the historical point where war will become obsolete. Most nations have already discarded it as a deliberate tool for advancement, and the problem of war prevention has largely become one of avoiding accidental and preemptive outbreaks and of keeping preventive maneuvers from escalating.)
- If the majority of people in the United States want peace and make their wishes known strongly enough, the United States will be at peace. (Comment: Few

members of the "establishment" need any longer be convinced that deliberate resort to war offers no advantage; the problem of how to avoid an unwanted war cannot be solved by wishful thinking; see previous comment.)

By classifying these statements as "myths" we do not wish to indicate that they should be dismissed from consideration in thinking about the future. For myths can materialize for a variety of reasons. In some cases we may be extrapolating into the future our growing awareness of a problem area that may well have existed for a long time. In other cases these myths reflect a change in aspirations. Since changes in awareness or in aspirations are fundamental to our evaluation of the quality of life, changes in this list of non-forecasts may serve as an additional indication of elements contributing to our assessment of satisfaction. As an example, it may be that the poverty gap in the United States seems to be getting wider, simply because our aspirations are heading toward greater economic equality. Many of the myths listed here can be considered from this point of view.

48.11 Impediments to Social Progress

Having presented in the preceding sections a compendium of potential future developments, both likely and long-shot, and a warning against the rash acceptance of certain myths, we should now proceed to a consideration of the options for the future that, in view of those forecasts, are available to us and among which we, as a society, will choose—whether deliberately or by default.

Before going on to an examination of specific alternatives, however, it may be well to reflect briefly on the overall societal planning situation and to interject a few remarks of a general philosophical nature.

A good way to gain an overview of what our real options are is to ask ourselves what is wrong with the way in which this nation, or any nation for that matter, goes about the business of achieving societal reforms. What are, in fact, the impediments to social progress, here and throughout the world?

Considering the rapid advances in the physical sciences and physical technology during the last hundred years, the social sciences—not to mention social technology—have by comparison been advancing at a snail's pace, and many attribute the ills of the world to this achievement gap between the soft and the hard sciences. There are, of course, good reasons for this differential attainment. But instead of dwelling on them, it may be more constructive to consider positive steps that might be taken in order to ameliorate the present situation and to attempt to narrow the gap between our abilities to cope with things and to cope with people. There are several points to be made here.

One has to do with the intellectual attitude among social scientists, a matter that has been discussed in greater detail elsewhere (see the section on social technology in Chapter 2). The way to catch up with the physical sciences is not to emulate their methods directly: the construction of neat theories, their subsequent application to predicting the consequences of alternative courses of action, and the achievement, thereby, of a measure of control over the future are not readily transferable, and such attempts have led to unnecessary frustration. By going in the opposite direction and relying largely on historical and interpretative analyses, on the other hand, as so many social scientists are doing, they are doing themselves an injustice and are being less effective than they might be in affecting the future course of events. A slight redirection of emphasis would seem to hold great promise of opening up the enormous reservoir of intuitive insight into human interactions accumulated in the social-science domain and making it available to those responsible for societal decision-making. The aspects that perhaps need to be stressed in this reorientation include a greater use of modeling and other operations-analytical techniques, such as simulation, Delphi, and the cross-impact method; and a more deliberate encouragement of inventiveness, so as to match some of the innovations introduced by physical technology with sorely needed social inventions. With regard to physical technology, the conviction is now prevalent that virtually nothing is impossible. One cannot help but feel that in social technology, too, where there is a will there is a way to solve most of the pressing problems of our time.

A second, related point—however obvious—is that it is insufficient to concentrate on reforms without paying equal attention to the implementation of reforms. For instance, modifications in welfare legislation, or educational reforms, or improvements in the health care delivery system, no matter how obviously desirable they are, require the cooperation of groups and individuals who are the potential agents of change but whose vested interests may cause them to resist such change vigorously. Thus, along with proposed social remedies in any of these areas, we need innovative approaches designed to overcome such opposition. Simulation, incidentally, may be helpful as a tool in exploring implementation alternatives.

Third, because of the complex nature of integrated societal planning, which requires a multidisciplinary as well as a multi- (government-) departmental approach, certain institutional innovations would be highly desirable. These include the creation of a national goals institute and of a technology assessment center. [The latter, of course, has since been realized in the form of the Congressional Office of Technology Assessment.] The former would be charged with the identification of alternative sets of national priorities that are both feasible in view of existing resource limitations and responsive to reasonable demands; the latter would have the task of anticipating important future technological developments, forecasting their societal implications, and recommending appropriate research strategies, legislation, or regulative measures. Along with the institution of these agencies, there ought to be a change in university graduate school curricula, placing greater emphasis on interdisciplinary cooperation and on an appreciation of the mutual cross-disciplinary effects of societal developments.

A further point, which is again closely related to the first one, concerns the essential difference in subject matter between the physical and the social sciences, namely, the fact that the latter deal with the relations between people and groups of people. [This point, having to do with a fuller implementation of the "social contract", was discussed in Section 42.1.]

Finally, in the discussion of impediments to social progress and of approaches to their removal, a few remarks may be indicated on a point which is rather different from the others, in that it has to do not with the methods that societal planners might use, but with the structure of the governmental decision-making process. It is disturbing, in this era of ever-increasing complexity of the processes of government, to hear a clamor for governmental decentralization. Behind this is an understandable and well-meaning, but sadly mistaken, desire to return to a state of affairs in which average citizens understand what needs to be done to run their country and participate directly in the decision-making process. What many do not seem to realize is that governing has more than ever become a matter for experts, who must be able to trace the implications of alternative courses of action across disciplinary and departmental boundaries before making their decisions. Moreover, decentralization, far from bringing the processes of government within easier reach of understanding by the average person, adds to the complexity (as evidenced by the overlapping of jurisdictions of many local authorities, which has made it virtually impossible to manage our cities) and leads to suboptimization and consequent inefficiency. Thus, if there is to be any hope for national reforms of our social institutions, we need greater, rather than less, centralization. This does not by any means imply that the people have to resign themselves to being governed by what they must view as an unintelligible machine. In a democracy, every effort must be made to disseminate relevant information widely and to promote an understanding of important issues, so that the public will be enabled and encouraged to discuss these issues intelligently and to assert their considered choices among the available options through the formal and informal modes of the democratic process.

48.12 National Opportunities for the Future

It may be debatable whether the quality of our future depends more heavily on our own decisions or on events and developments over which we have no control or whose causes and effects elude our comprehension. However, while the uncertainty and impenetrability of these exogenous influences may be considerable, they are not so dominant as to warrant an attitude of fatalism. Much of the future of our society will depend on the wisdom and imagination with which we, through our government, select the policies and programs that will affect the shape of things to come.

A somewhat better grasp of the extent to which we, in fact, control our destiny can perhaps be gained by factoring this question into its components: the opportunities open to this nation during the coming decades, the options available to us in view of these opportunities and of existing resources, and the responsiveness of our government to the people's preferences among these options.

To take up the last point first very briefly, there appears to be an increasing feeling of alienation of the general public from the affairs of government, in the sense of being unable either to understand the complexity of public affairs or to cause the government to comply with the wishes of the people. This seeming disenfranchisement of the general public in regulating its own affairs has moved some, particularly among the young, to proclaim that the United States is rapidly heading toward an autocratic form of government. This view ignores that the present predicament, real though it is, seems to result primarily from the inability of a governing bureaucracy, however well-meaning, to extricate itself from the inertia of the existing system rather than from a juxtaposition of the people at large and a small group that wishes to rule dictatorially. While much of the inflexibility of the system, admittedly, can be traced to the vested interests of certain individuals, there is no evidence to point to the existence of a concerted effort, a plot, to seize dictatorial power.

Some of the foci of vested interest are only too obvious: the congressional seniority system and the concomitant traditional privilege of congressional committee chairpersons to prevent pending legislative bills from reaching the floor; the "tenure" system for governmental agencies, under which new agencies can easily be created but existing ones are hard to abolish or even to reduce in size—with the result that annual budgetary allocations generally have to be made within the limitations of narrowly constrained marginal adjustments; and the so-called states' rights and analogous local rights (not excluding local school boards' rights), which often, under the guise of returning decision-making power to the people, strive to retain parochial privileges at the expense of efficiency and effectiveness.

How to correct these largely inadvertent abuses of the democratic system is one of the issues with which our society is confronted today. There are a variety of ways in which such correction might be achieved. For the present, no detailed alternatives will be suggested, and we shall merely list the possibility of appropriate governmental reform as a specific one among the opportunities for the future. Having thus noted the problem, without resolving it, we shall discuss national opportunities in general as well as the options arising from them, without specifying whether these opportunities and options are open to the people or to its government.

First, to clarify the terms "opportunity" and "option": It is possible to have the opportunity for a manned exploration of the planetary system; it is possible also to have the opportunity to prevent large-scale famine in the world. But the resources may not be available to pursue both opportunities, hence, an option has to be exercised as to which, if either, of these opportunities to select. The existence of an opportunity can be determined in isolation while the availability of an option requires examination of opportunities in the presence of one another and in the light of existing physical and human resources.

The opportunities before us are vast in number. The forecasts presented earlier in this report surely convey a feeling of technological optimism—a conviction that virtually anything within reason can eventually be attained and that it is merely a question of what resources we are willing to devote to the effort that will determine how soon it can be done. This, at least, applies to matters of physical technology. The lag in achievements requiring social technology has been pointed out here earlier, but there are now signs that the shift in social-science effort toward pragmatism is gaining momentum rapidly, and cautious optimism even here is not unwarranted.

The material presented in earlier sections suggests ample specific opportunities for the future. A brief summary at this point may suffice as a reminder:

First, there are many potential scientific and technological breakthroughs whose occurrence could be hastened by increased governmental support. For example, while the median year for which the production of commercial energy through controlled thermonuclear fusion has been predicted is 1990, a well-funded crash program might possibly advance this event to the mid-1980s. Similarly, additional governmental investment might accelerate the development of the means for prenatal correction of hereditary defects, the conquest of the major diseases, the perfecting of personality control and intelligence drugs, the achievement of economical water desalination, the depollution of air and water, the reliable forecasting and even controlling of the weather, the adaptation of the communication/computer symbiosis to the many needs of society, the exploration of the planetary system, and so on.

Second, beneficial societal events and trends might be promoted either by governmental support or private initiative. Among the many possibilities in this area, the following might be among the more important ones to be given consideration: a guaranteed annual income and lifelong medical care; measures reducing the rate of crimes of violence; a reorganization of the system of criminal justice; reform of the system of higher education; revival of genuinely participatory democracy; the provision of new cities and housing for 50 million more people; improvement in ethical standards in business and the professions; a drive for real equality of opportunity; reorientation of the socioeconomic system away from the profit motive as a dominant incentive; subsidies or other incentives for waste elimination at the source or conversion of waste products into salable commodities; and a serious effort toward worldwide alleviation of hunger, poverty, and disease.

Third, active steps might be taken wherever possible to forestall potential societal catastrophes (see Section 48.8), such as war, a disastrous unemployment level, or an ecological cataclysm; or to enhance the likelihood of anti-catastrophes (Section 48.9), such as the resuscitation of America's lakes and rivers or the abolition of war.

Fourth, there are opportunities at a metalevel that may be worthy of consideration. They are those which would create conditions that, in turn, might be conducive to generating new and worthwhile opportunities. What is being referred to are measures that would address themselves to the generic problem of raising levels of satisfaction within the general population. Examples are the creation of a permanent institution for the systematic and continual reordering of national priorities, a reorganization of government at all levels so as to be more responsive to the people's preferences in regard to national priorities, and the institutionalization of technology assessment as an aid to the formulation of national priorities.

Many of the opportunities referred to above have been suggested by the forecasts recorded earlier. A point that needs to be made most emphatically in this connection is that the suggestive role of forecasts is but one of the sources of ideas for national opportunities. The other, equally important, one is the inventiveness of individuals, both in devising the means of implementing suggested opportunities and, even more so, in originating ideas for social inventions that will constitute novel societal opportunities. Inventions in physical technology, through the patent system, usually carry their own reward. This is not often the case with regard to social inventions. Hence the creation of an institution that would encourage, evaluate, disseminate, and reward social inventions is another metaopportunity to be added to those listed under the fourth heading.

48.13 Specific Options

In principle, a catalogue of specific options is obtained from a list of opportunities (such as those referred to in the preceding section) by the process of estimating the cost of each opportunity and then composing sets of these opportunities, such that for each set the combined cost of implementing the opportunities in the set does not exceed a given, available budget. Each such set would then represent a set of compatible options.

The actual process of identifying options is, of course, not quite so simple. There are a number of reasons for this. For one thing, opportunities are often stated in very general terms ("depolluting the water"), and costs cannot be estimated until a specific plan of action has been proposed. Moreover, the manner of implementation, and hence the cost, may depend on the state of technology. Another consideration is that a particular opportunity may be exploited to different degrees, depending on the amount of the investment that one is prepared to make in it. In addition, various contemplated measures may be interdependent by being complementary or at least mutually supportive, or by being substitutable for one another, with the result that the costs of implementing the components of a set of opportunities are not additive.

Aside from these practical difficulties in dealing with individual sets of specific options, the planner is faced with an overwhelming number of alternative sets from which to choose. For example, if there were 100 opportunities, each implementable, say, at three levels of intensity, and if each set of options consisted on the average of 10 such opportunities, the total number of alternatives would be approximately 10^{18}—a completely unmanageable quantity, even by a high-speed computer.

This suggests that a realistic approach to a survey of options must not attempt to scan all feasible sets of options but use some other systematizing device, which can act as an aid to the ingenuity of intuitive judgment. Just such a device is presented later in this report in the form of a simulation game.

For the moment, instead of attempting to deal with specific options at the action level, we will confine ourselves to listing some of the major options at the overall policy level that seem to recur most often in discussions of national objectives. They can perhaps best be stated in terms of choices between alternatives at our disposal.

48.13.1 Full-Employment Economy vs. Leisure Economy

Productivity in this country may be about to reach such a point that considerably less than a forty-hour work week will suffice, at least in theory, to support a reasonably high living standard for all Americans, especially if we manage to stay out of any further wars. Thus increasing amounts of time could be freed for so-called leisure activities. On the other hand, there are many alternative pursuits that could keep us well occupied at present levels of working hours per week if we choose to engage in them. Foremost among them are the eradication of poverty in America, to the point where all families are brought up at least to the present-day level of middle-class comfort; the exploration of the solar system; and the development of the Third World to the point where hunger, poverty, and large-scale disease are eventually eliminated. The choice between these alternatives—leisure versus full employment—is ours; they may be the most important options affecting the future state of our society.

Even in a relatively full-employment economy (at present standards), not to mention a more leisure-oriented economy, our options may not include the simultaneous full-scale pursuit of the three major areas just enumerated (domestic-poverty eradication, space exploration, development of the underdeveloped nations), so that choices between these alternatives may still have to be made:

48.13.2 Space Exploration vs. Social Needs

Despite the rising moral pressure to shift public funding from space exploration to tending to our urgent social needs, the adoption of a policy to this effect has been slow. There are several reasons for this, notably the existence of vested aerospace interests (reinforced by their close ties to military interests), the difficulty of avoiding the economic disruption that a major reallocation of government funding may cause, and the lack of an adequate understanding of just how the social ills of this nation can be effectively cured. These impediments might eventually be overcome, possibly by letting the aerospace industry with its reservoir of systems-engineering talent transfer some of its effort to societal problems, and by converting some of the academically oriented social-science manpower to the applied field of social technology. Our choice here is whether, as a nation, we wish to make this move away from space exploration ventures and toward a constructive approach to social reform, and if so, how fast; or whether these two efforts should be forcefully pursued in parallel.

48.13.3 International Cooperation vs. Isolationism

As in the previous case, resource constraints as well as a desire for more leisure time may force a stipulation of priorities between domestic and foreign pursuits. Some strengthening of international institutions may be mandatory for reasons of self-protection; in particular, cooperative measures to halt further pollution of the oceans and of the atmosphere will be indispensable for survival. As for a decision, if any, in favor of more extensive foreign aid directed toward the development of the Third World, it might be implemented in many ways, ranging from a unilateral increase in financial and technological support for developing nations to a joint approach to these problems, either in collaboration with other advanced nations or through the equivalent of an international income tax levied and distributed by the United Nations.

Another choice in the domain of international relations that may for the first time in history be within our reach is the following.

48.13.4 War as an Instrument of Foreign Policy vs. the Obsolescence of War

We live in an era of transition, in which fewer and fewer nations still consider going to war as a deliberate instrument of foreign policy, while others—including the United States—have not yet learned to avoid being inadvertently drawn into military conflict, either through unintended escalation of military support designed to be preventive of war, or by the occurrence of an accidental or preemptive outbreak of war. For some pairs of nations, such as Canada and the United States, it is currently unthinkable that disputes between them might be settled by war; others, even including former archenemies such as France and Germany, are well on their way toward the same state of mutual abelligerence. The choice for the United States is either to continue on its traditional course of spending a sizable fraction of its resources each year on war preparedness (on the assumption that inadvertent outbreaks of war must still be contemplated in our national planning) or to make an all-out effort, possibly even through partial or total unilateral disarmament, to create an atmosphere of trust generally that is comparable to our relations with Canada, so as to relegate the idea of war to the aberrations of the past.

Within the area of domestic improvements, there are many options open to us. Some of the more important ones are these:

48.13.5 Bigger Cities vs. New Cities vs. More Uniform Population Density

Estimates of population increase in the United States during the last three decades if this century, which had been in the neighborhood of 100 million, tend of late to be closer to 50 million. Even to accommodate this smaller increment, either our present cities have to be allowed, as they have in the last few decades, to sprawl in laissez-faire fashion, or provisions have to be made for large numbers of sizable new cities, or some positive inducements have to be offered that will cause people to settle more uniformly over the inhabitable portions of this country. While, presumably, some mixture of these possibilities will occur, the quality of life in our future society will depend a good deal on which alternative will receive the greatest emphasis. If there is no definite policy, the urban-sprawl alternative will win by default. If there are to be new cities in quantity, a public-private partnership may be required in order to create the institutional mechanism for encouraging the enormous investments that will be necessary. If, finally, the goal is a more evenly distributed population, this will require better access by high-speed ground transportation to what are still largely rural areas—and thus, again, large investments possibly necessitating cooperation between the public and private sectors.

48.13.6 The Old vs. the New Vision of the "Good Life"

Increasing numbers of people, particularly among the younger generation, are replacing in their vision of what constitutes a good life the traditional goal of good income, material wealth, and social status by that of an inner sense of "spiritual" self-fulfillment and a measure of social and cultural participation. This trend can be strengthened or discouraged, with results that will affect preferences among other options, notably those discussed under Sections 48.13.1, 48.13.5, and 48.13.9.

48.13.7 Centralized vs. Decentralized Government

There are conflicting sentiments regarding the issue of centralized versus decentralized government, which have already been alluded to briefly in Section 48.12. On the one hand, the growing complexity of public affairs and the narrowing decision deadlines entailed by the general acceleration in the pace of change make for greater centralization of governmental decision-making functions and, in particular, for the abolition of overlapping governmental jurisdictions that have proliferated at the local and regional levels. On the other hand, even today's degree of concentration of power in federal agencies has generated a feeling of alienation and frustration among the general public—alienation because of the remoteness and incomprehensibility of governmental processes, frustration because of the apparent unresponsiveness of governmental decision-making agencies to the preferences of the people. A compromise between these tendencies toward centralization and decentralization will have to be found, possibly through the invention of new political institutions, that will satisfy the needs both for greater governmental efficiency and for greater participation of the public in its government.

48.13.8 Integrated vs. Polarized Society

There are currently trends toward a racially more integrated society as well as certain trends toward polarization, both racially (black separatist and white supremacist movements) and by age groups (youth culture, retirement communities). Forecasts differ as to whether integration or polarization will dominate in the long run, and the societal structure that will emerge by the end of the century will depend greatly on which of these trends we elect to promote or suppress.

48.13.9 Continuing Technological and Economic Expansion vs. Leveling Off

Closely related to, but not identical with, the options described under Section 48.13.1 is the choice between planning to continue on the path of technoeconomical expansion and planning to level off gradually before the depletion of natural resources and the pollution of the environment reach catastrophic dimensions. The choice is a difficult one, because the feeling prevails that the next two decades might bring many technological hopes to fruition. We seem to be on the verge of being able to exploit the progress in transportation, housing, and communications/computer technologies to improve the quality of life for large masses of the American people by an order of magnitude. The amount of freedom in this choice may depend largely on how soon a new, economical source of power (such as might be derived from thermonuclear fusion) will become available, for the scarcity of raw materials can be expected to be overcome by recycling and by extracting metals and food from low-grade ores and soils as well as from the oceans—all of which require large amounts of energy.

48.13.10 Competitive-Market Ethics vs. Public-Interest Ethics

The moral climate in the world of business, labor, and the professions is felt by many to have deteriorated to the point where the public interest is in serious jeopardy. This decline in deference to the common good seems to derive more from the normal operation of competition in a free economy than from the nefariousness of individuals. The choice here is one of permitting the gradual deterioration to continue until the public clamor for reform can no longer be ignored, or of anticipating the inevitable before a crisis is reached and cooperatively recreating a climate in which business, labor, and the professions can thrive while not disregarding the public interest. To pursue the option represented by the second alternative would require submission to social audits and adherence to standards of conduct and performance laid down by either government or self-regulation.

This list, of course, is not complete and could be extended indefinitely. Among many other examples of areas in which additional choices among alternative options could be formulated, the following may deserve special mention: the ongoing revolution in sexual mores; the nascent pharmacological revolution; the problem of adolescent socialization; the redirection of formal education toward greater relevance; the overdue reform of internment facilities (prisons, hospitals, institutions for the mentally or physically handicapped and the aged); and political reforms involving possible abandonment of the present congressional seniority system, controls over lobbying activities, and the conduct of political campaigns.

In looking back over the alternative options presented on the preceding pages, a few conclusions seem to emerge very clearly.

First, the choices are real. That is to say, the outcome in each case will depend less on chance or on unforeseeable and uninfluencible turns of events than on deliberate decisions made by individuals acting singly or through their government. In some cases, these choices need by no means to be uniform for everyone. Thus, some people may prefer to live in the present cities, others in new cities, still others in the countryside (Section 48.13.5); similarly, there is no compulsion for an individual to declare for one or another vision of the "good life" (Section 48.13.6); nor is there a reason why we should not eventually see the development, in parallel, of both racially integrated and uniracial communities and, correspondingly, communities that are integrated or segregated in terms of age or other differences (Section 48.13.8).

Second, the choices to be made with regard to this country's future socioeconomic posture, as discussed in Section 48.13.9 for the shorter term and in Section 48.13.1 for the long term, are paramount; for they affect the feasibility or infeasibility of much that Americans may wish to accomplish in the decades to come. Regardless of whether they will wish to settle down and rest on the laurels of past technological achievements or whether their pioneering spirit will continue to prevail, the crucial question, as has been pointed out, is whether new sources of cheap energy will be unlocked before the old ones give out; and this is itself again only partly a matter of chance and at least equally so a matter of deliberate pursuit.

Third, precisely because so much of this nation's future lies in its own hands, because—in other words—the future is so much more a matter of invention than of discovery, it has become a social responsibility of highest order to create the intellectual and institutional tools with which to explore the potentialities of the future, to generate a greater public awareness of feasible options, and to encourage the invention of sociotechnological devices with which to implement societal aspirations. This essay, as stated in the introduction, has been written with the intention of making a contribution, however small, toward assuming that responsibility. Thus far, it has presented no more than a checklist of important events and trends that may affect our society and of some of the major policy options that must be given serious consideration by anyone who wishes to participate in the planning for America's future.

It is not the purpose of this treatise to advocate any particular policy. Its sole intent is methodological: to present aids to the would-be societal planner (or even just to the conscientious voter) in the complex process of thinking ahead, of recognizing the needs, of ranking them by their relative importance, of identifying and, when necessary, inventing possible remedies, of judging their feasibility, of arraying the overall options, and, finally, of selecting a plan of action.

Perhaps the most difficult aspect of this planning process is the ever-present need to take account of interrelations, sometimes obvious but often obscure, between different planning factors. The occurrence of an event, or the taking of an action, may affect the occurrence of other events, the feasibility and cost of other actions, the rise and decline of related trends. The planner cannot afford to overlook any of these effects, whether direct or secondary. But the number of potential repercussions is so large that many will go unnoticed unless a systematic effort is made to scan the entire field. A device for accomplishing just that is cross-impact analysis [see the presentation on this subject in Chapter VI].

48.14 Considerations of Cost, Satisfaction, and Cross-Impacts in Planning

In planning the future of a highly complex organization, such as a nation or a city (or even a corporation, school, or hospital), it is necessary, in addition to considering individual measures and assessing them in terms of their cost and effectiveness, to take a comprehensive systems approach which takes account of the interrelations between measures and of their joint cost and joint effectiveness. The cross-impact concept outlined earlier is helpful in this context, but the overall planning process still is an exceedingly complicated and imperfect one, and we can here only attempt to give an outline of the steps involved in it and point out a few of the conceptual difficulties that still await resolution.

An orderly planning process will involve, among others, the following steps (though not necessarily precisely in this order):

48.14.1 *Determination of Satisfaction Indices*

In order to give proper direction to the planning effort, it is clearly necessary to have an understanding of the goals of the organization. The degree of goal attainment finds its expression in terms of the degree of satisfaction that is felt with certain aspects of the organization. In the case of planning the future of the United States, a suggested set of twelve satisfaction indices has been presented in Section 48.5. If the organization in question were a corporation, appropriate satisfaction indices might be current profit, expected future profit, return on investment, and some measure of the "image" of the firm. At any rate, a set of appropriate satisfaction indices must be identified, their current values must be assessed, and *ceteris paribus* estimates of their future values must be made so as to have benchmarks against which to measure the success of any contemplated plan of action.

48.14.2 *Compilation of Relevant Potential Developments*

The time period for which plans are to be made must be determined, and potential developments during that period must be listed whose occurrence or nonoccurrence might have an important influence on plans. These developments may be in the nature of events (either one-time-only occurrences, such as a scientific breakthrough, or repeatable occurrences, such as a riot) or in the nature of trends (time series, such as GNP, or more vaguely defined currents, such as attitudinal changes). The list of these developments should include external events, over which the planner (or the decision maker on whose behalf plans are being prepared) has no direct control (for instance, a natural disaster or actions taken by an antagonist), as well as developments that can be affected (such as a technological advance, which can be accelerated by investment in research and development) or even fully controlled (such as an executive action).

48.14.3 *Forecasts*

For those developments which are not, or are only partly, under the planner's control, probabilistic forecasts should be made for the extent of the planning period. For events, these would be in the form of probability distributions for the event's occurrence; for trends, these would be in the form of trend projections, with indications of the probabilistic uncertainty attached to future values.

48.14.4 *Cost Estimates*

For measures contemplated for inclusion in a plan of action, cost estimates have to be made. For several reasons, such costs should at first merely be roughly estimated. Many measures will generally be eliminated as too costly on that basis; moreover, precise cost estimates will depend on other developments (including other measures eventually incorporated in the

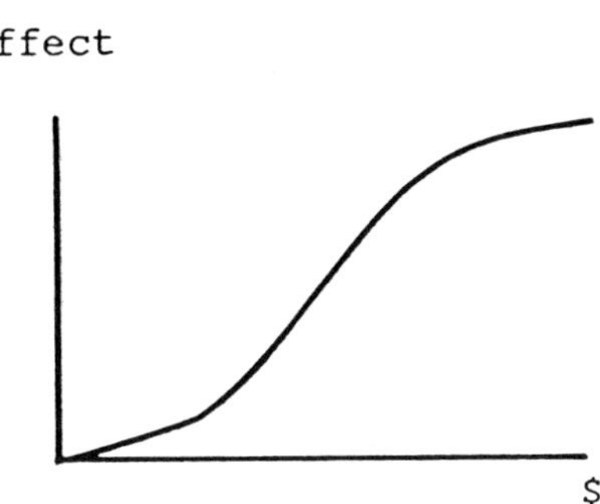

FIGURE 23

plan), so that a prematurely "precise" estimate would be misleading. For a clearly defined measure (say, raising all enlisted men's pay by 10 percent), the cost would be a single number. More often, a proposed measure is stated more flexibly, allowing for an unspecified degree of enactment (such as raising all enlisted men's pay, or investing in additional research aimed at producing controlled thermonuclear energy). In these cases, estimated cost curves have to be obtained that relate expected effects to expenditures. Such curves are generally S-shaped, as illustrated in Figure 23. If the expenditure is intended to promote a particular event, the effect is best expressed in terms of the resultant increase in the probability of occurrence; if it is intended to alter a given trend, the effect would be gauged in terms of the expected deviation of the trend from the values otherwise anticipated.

48.14.5 Cross-Impacts

Next, the potential interactions among anticipated developments have to be examined; this is best done by setting up a cross-impact matrix of the type described in Chapter VI. In addition to the factual cross-impacts manifested in changes in event probabilities or trend levels, it may be well, for those developments that are under consideration as measures to be taken or to be promoted, to record estimates of cross-impacts affecting their costs or their effectiveness in contributing to a rise in the levels of satisfaction indices. The latter type of cross-impact would be indicative of some degree of complementarity or substitutability among contemplated measures.

48.14.6 Sensitivity Determination

Having obtained factual cross-impacts, it is important to determine how sensitively the future will depend on particular developments, hence, how a desirable future can be most effectively attained through the promotion of selected developments. If estimates of cross-impacts have, in fact, been recorded in the form of a cross-impact matrix, a comprehensive sensitivity study can be carried out as suggested in Section 33. If not, reliance has to be placed on the planner's acuity in identifying such sensitivities intuitively.

48.14.7 Preliminary Selection of Allocation Alternatives

Given an overall policy (i.e., a set of goals expressed in reference to certain satisfaction indices) and budgetary constraints that must be observed, the planner will now be in a position to formulate some tentative plans, that is, some preliminary alternative allocations of the given budget over a selected set of measures. These selections will have to be based on the sensitivity considerations in Section 48.14.6 and the costs discussed in Section 48.14.4 as well as the planner's perception of the selected measures' potential effects on satisfaction indices.

48.14.8 Expected Alternative Outcomes

Using the cross-impact approach, each plan of action can be interpreted as a set of measures consisting either in the enactment of certain events or in the promotion of event probabilities or trend changes. With this interpretation, each alternative plan can be analyzed as to its expected outcome, that is, the change in the future state of the world that may be expected if that plan is selected for implementation. As the result of these computations, some of the plans under consideration are likely to stand out as deserving more detailed examination, in view of the superior quality of their expected outcomes.

48.14.9 Revised Selection of Alternatives

For this subset among the original set of alternative plans, a more careful analysis must now be made utilizing whatever information has been collected, not only on factual cross-impacts, but also on cost and effectiveness cross-impacts, that is, on the effects of (partial or total) complementarities and substitutabilities on effectiveness increases and cost reductions. Using refined cost estimates as well as refined assessments of the impact on satisfaction levels, new (factual) cross-impact runs should now be carried out for this revised set of alternatives.

48.14.10 Final Selection of a Plan

The expected outcomes which, on the basis of these computations, are associated with the revised set of alternative plans can be used as a basis for the final decision. If one outcome emerges clearly as superior to all others, the choice is obvious. When there is no such clear dominance, either because the results are close or because one outcome favors one dimension of satisfaction over another while another outcome does the opposite, then the decision maker may have to give consideration to such factors as the relative variance in cost or effectiveness that must be expected of each plan, or to the relative weight that should be given to each satisfaction index (which is a matter of political preference), in order to arrive at his final choice.

This barest outline of the considerations that must enter into the planning process for a complex organization makes it apparent that this process is highly intricate and that there are a number of points requiring further conceptual clarification or methodological analysis before it may be considered a wholly rational activity. Among the difficulties yet to be entirely overcome are the following.

• *The need to develop methods of handling cost cross-impacts:* There are potential cost cross-impacts (a) among the elements of a plan of action and (b) between external developments and action measures. Case a arises when the cost of two or more measures is less than the sum of their costs, their joint pursuit offering certain savings. This is a possible source of double accounting, and systematic methods for avoiding it must be found. Case b, in which the cost of an action is affected by external developments, is equally common. Here, in particular, a technological breakthrough may reduce costs. On the other hand, the mere passage of time tends to alter the original intent of a proposed measure, often increasing its cost by the need of adaptation to new, unforeseen circumstances. These cost uncertainties, too, should not be neglected by a conscientious planner.

• *Complementarity and substitutability:* There is, similarly, the possibility that effectiveness assessments of contemplated measures may be distorted by neglecting the effect of complementarities and substitutabilities. In the case of two measures being complementary, their joint enactment contributes more than the sum of their separate contributions to the rise in satisfaction levels, while in the case of (complete or even partial) substitutability the joint contribution would be less than the sum. While obvious instances of this kind will generally be accounted for by an astute planner, there often are subtle complementarity and substitutability relationships that escape the planner's notice for lack of a systematic method of searching for them.

• *The open-endedness of the planning process:* It is difficult enough to compose action plans by selecting measures from a given list of candidate measures and to identify a preferred one on the basis of an assessment of their relative costs and merits. But even if this process were executed faultlessly, the result might still represent a far-from-optimal solution, because the quality of the candidate measures may be inadequate. It is a common pitfall for a decision maker to be convinced that a particular plan is optimal, simply because it compares favorably with all other rival plans that have come to his notice. But whether the plans under consideration include any that are close to an optimal solution will depend largely on the inventiveness and ingenuity of the plan proposers. Often far too little attention is paid to the systematic elicitation of novel ideas for the resolution of a particular issue.

• *The multidimensionality of cross-impacts:* As pointed out before, the approach presented here takes only pairwise cross-impacts into account. In practice, the effect, say, of A on B may be different in the presence and in the absence of C; in other words, there are potential cross-impacts, not only among two but also among three or more developments. An extension of the present two-dimensional treatment to a multidimensional one meets with some conceptual, but mostly with formidable practical, difficulties related to the sheer size of the task.

• *The multidimensionality of satisfaction:* The utility of a proposed plan is measured in terms of its expected effect on a set of satisfaction indices. Hence, of two plans one is clearly preferable only if it "dominates" the other, in the sense of enhancing some satisfaction levels while degrading none. In order to establish preferences among plans for which this dominance criterion is not met, it is necessary to resolve the usual problem of multidimensional utility vectors. This can be done by assigning weights to the components of the vector (here, to the individual satisfaction indices) and using their weighted sum as a master index. More sophisticated alternatives to this linear method might also be considered. It is important to recognize that there is, in principle, no objective way of performing this aggregation of several indices into one master index but that this procedure is at the heart of the political process. Satisfactions are, after all, multifactional: The importance attached to particular satisfaction indices will differ from political faction to political faction, and the choice of a specific mode of aggregation amounts to the affirmation of a political platform. Having recognized this fact, though, there still remain the problems of (a) devising, for a given political orientation, an appropriate aggregation algorithm that reflects this orientation accurately and (b) finding a reasonable way of compromising between several factions.

This list of unresolved difficulties, long as it is, is far from complete and should serve merely as an indication of numerous areas for further research.

48.15 Scenarios of the Future

This report is intended to be exploratory rather than definitive, and no reader should therefore expect a systematic and exhaustive presentation of possible scenarios for the future history of the United States. The emphasis here is on the exploration and discussion of methods by which a gamut of representative scenarios might be constructed, using as building blocks some of the forecasts of potential developments presented earlier as well as the listings of dangers, opportunities, and consequent options at our disposal.

This section will be devoted to the presentation of a sample of three scenarios. They are illustrative only and are by no means intended to be representative of the spectrum of possibilities. Each has a low probability of resembling the actual future course of history—as does any scenario; yet none is implausible in the sense that it postulates events that are altogether unlikely to occur. A means of generating additional scenarios is provided in the form of the future-state-of-the-Union game to be described in Section 48.16.

The main determinants of a scenario of the future are three: chance, the choice among major policy options, and the selection of specific actions.

We speak of chance in referring to developments that are not under our control. Natural catastrophes fall into this category; so do wars, at least to a large extent. Another chance factor must be seen in the luck (or lack of it) that scientists and engineers may have in achieving scientific or technological breakthroughs.

Major policy options, though eventually formalized through legislative or executive or judicial actions, are generally exercised by the public at large through the electoral system or other, less direct, political processes.

Specific actions, finally, are measures taken by agencies of the government (the Congress, the president, a city council, and so on) or by representatives of specific interests (a corporation, a labor union, a civic organization, a minority group, and the like).

Each of the following scenarios contains ingredients of all three kinds.

Scenario A

1972-1982: Many current trends continue through this decade: The average work week declines slowly in length, per-capita GNP moves up slowly, the general moral climate deteriorates further, the urban sprawl continues unchecked, crimes of violence increase, the defense budget continues high. Major breakdowns of metropolitan areas (due to strikes, power shortages, riots) increase in frequency toward the end of the decade. Air and water pollution reach unacceptable levels and begin to be among the primary contributing causes of ill health and death. Consumerism, though on the rise, has as yet little far-reaching effect. A large diversification of lifestyles is practiced and tolerated, but the total fraction of the population devoted to unconventional family or community structures is still quite small. Marijuana is legalized and in widespread use; the open sale of hard drugs continues to be prohibited, and their use has continued to increase slightly. Noticeable technological advances are made in biomedicine, most notably in the laboratory demonstration with vertebrate test animals of the possibility of cloning and of genetic correction of hereditary defects through molecular engineering. In the field of education, mandatory school busing has been abandoned, many educational experiments are being carried out at all levels, encouraged at the primary and secondary levels by a nationwide system of educational vouchers, permitting parents to send their children to schools of their choice.

1982-1992: Many intolerable trends are reaching explosive levels by 1984; among these are pollution, urban congestion and failure of urban services, race riots, unemployment, and the crime rate. A new administration takes over and institutes many reform measures, which, after numerous false starts and against the resistance of many vested interests, result in noticeable improvements by the late 1980s. A guaranteed minimum income and other social reform measures are introduced, including a thorough overhaul of the system of criminal justice. The development of new sources of energy is being promoted. Famine conditions prevail in parts of southern Asia and South America, and the United States and the Soviet Union divert part of their defense allocations to massive relief and joint foreign-aid programs. The sex of babies can be preselected, and the production of numerous identical offspring through cloning has become possible; legislation is passed to prevent abuse of these possibilities.

1992-2002: The economy improves rapidly. Large-scale centralized data banks are set up to aid in the administration of the Social Security and criminal-justice systems and to assist business firms in their long-range planning. International relations have improved to the point of permitting the defense budget to be lowered, freeing substantial funds for the building of new cities and of a network of high-speed ground transportation and automated highways. Virtually every home is equipped with two-way communication terminals, usable for education, entertainment, shopping, financial transactions, and many business and professional activities. The first power plant based on thermonuclear fusion begins operation in the year 2000. The length of the workweek declines to an average of thirty-two hours. The population growth rate is zero, with the total U.S. population leveling out at approximately 280 million.

Scenario B

1972-1982: Defense expenditures are reduced sharply, releasing funds for a guaranteed minimum income and other Social Security reforms, as well as for urban renewal and the building of new cities, improving the transportation system, and initiating a crash program for the construction of breeder-reactor power plants and the development of fusion power plants. Strict antipollution measures are passed, and a federal technology-assessment institute is set up, primarily to forestall future abuses of new technologies that might have polluting or other detrimental side effects. The average workweek continues at about thirty-eight hours. Government-sponsored research leads to many breakthroughs in biomedicine (especially genetics and new drugs). By the end of the decade most households are equipped with two-way communication terminals. Central data banks are set up, and cash transactions are becoming quite rare. Child-care centers are available in all urban communities, permitting many more women to enter the work force. Per-capita income rises slowly at first, rapidly toward the end of the decade. The population growth rate is close to zero.

1982-1992: The fast rise in GNP in the early 1980s permits the reinstitution of a vigorous space program and a large-scale effort directed at the prevention of famine and disease in the Third World and at the modernization of agriculture and industry in those countries. Reliable weather forecasts and the construction of economical plants for desalination of sea water have become possible. Fusion power plants, producing virtually unlimited electric energy at low cost and without hazard of radioactive or thermal pollution, are beginning to operate in the late 1980s. An effective cure for cancer and means of immunization against most bacterial and viral diseases have been found, resulting in an increase of life expectancy at birth by five years. The birth rate has dropped sharply.

1992-2002: Rapid progress in technology, especially in the information processing and computer fields, while having virtually eliminated poverty in America, has created an affluence gap. Dissatisfaction among the less affluent increasingly leads to riots, having strong evidence of racial overtones. Civil rights are temporarily suspended in efforts to quell civil uprisings. Some tax reforms are carried out, including a substantial rise in the guaranteed minimum income level. Biomedical progress continues, leading to the possibility of successful implantation of artificial organs. Numerous experimental scientific laboratories in earth orbit are succeeded by orbital sanitariums and power stations. Most Americans carry portable telephones, and several types of sophisticated household robots have come into use. The population in the year 2000 reaches 250 million. The international situation is tense, for reasons similar to those causing domestic disorder, namely, growing dissatisfaction with apparent inequities in affluence and, in particular, insufficient access to education and to immunization against, and cure of, diseases. Around the turn of the millennium, these tensions lead to the outbreak of several wars in regions of the Third World, which, because of the intervention by several of the major powers (including the United States), threatens to bring about World War III in the year 2002.

Scenario C

1972-1982: The movement, initiated in the late 1960s by radical students and groups of environmentalists and aimed at reemphasizing the other-than-profit aspects of a good life, has grown into a major force that is reshaping American society fundamentally. There is, on the one hand, a new emphasis on ethical standards in politics, business, and the professions, and regular social audits of corporations and of public agencies are designed to compel such organizations to act in socially responsible and politically responsive ways. As far as people's private lives are concerned, on the other hand, there is much experimentation with new lifestyles. While many are earnestly seeking patterns for a new morality, others are turning to hedonistic self-indulgence and the use of hallucinogenic drugs. Interracial marriage is widely practiced. There is a guaranteed minimum income, but barely above the poverty level. The defense budget is reduced substantially, and the per-capita income remains nearly constant throughout the decade. As a consequence of a falling birth rate and a migration back to the countryside of many of the new "pioneers", some of the larger metropolitan areas have ceased to expand.

1982-1992: The early 1980s see a gradual breakdown of the cities and of government at all levels. There is a sharp reduction in scientific and technological progress. The romanticism of the early back-to-nature movement is fading. Drug use and crime are on the increase. Dissatisfaction with urban conditions and with the low living standard in nonurban communes is the cause of many riots and other civil disturbances. The general deterioration, in 1992, causes a new president to be elected on a platform of restoring law and order and revitalizing the economy. While in the United States the population growth rate is now negative, the Third World nations have still been expanding rapidly, and severe famine conditions in the late 1980s are found in southern Asia, South America, and parts of Africa.

1992-2002: The average workweek, which had been around thirty hours, begins to rise. Per-capita GNP, by the mid-1990s, recovers and begins to increase noticeably. A comprehensive technology-assessment effort and a national goals institute are sponsored by the government. Renewed support of scientific research and of technological development gradually pays off, leading to overdue breakthroughs in medicine, information technology, and power generation. A vast, modernized transportation network is constructed to encourage a continuing pattern of a more uniformly distributed population than had been the case in the middle of the century. The population growth rate rises above zero, and, by the year 2000, the population reaches 260 million and is rising.

If the set of these three scenarios gives the impression that their composition was not based on any systematic principle of selecting events, trends, and options from the material presented earlier, this impression is correct. The purpose in presenting them was merely to convey what is perhaps obvious, namely, that possible—and, in fact, quite plausible—future courses of history may show vast differences from one another. To what extent each of the three main determinants—chance, policy choice, and specific action—accounts for this variability can only be conjectured at this point. To obtain a firmer appreciation of their relative roles requires a more systematic treatment of possible scenarios.

Systematic treatment of the future of our society calls for the construction of a model that captures the essential facets of the subject. This essay has merely provided some of the ingredients for such a model, in the form of both substantive inputs and suggestions for methodological structure. A first approach to putting some of these elements together is offered in the form of the game to be discussed in the next section.

48.16 The "Future State of the Union" Game

As a supplement to the present report, a Future State of the Union game has been designed, which can be used for teaching, research, and planning purposes. The game can serve, among other things, to generate scenarios for the future of the United States, similar to those presented in the preceding section.

[Instead of a complete description of the game, as given in the original report, only a brief summary will be included here, based on excerpts from that report. The reader will realize that the game, except for subject matter and size, resembles in structure and purpose the Global Resources game presented in Section 32.]

The primary application of the game is as a teaching tool, since it can be readily used as a focusing device in seminar treatments of future societal developments. It provides not only an appreciation of the multiplicity of possibilities that the future holds but also an insight into how potential events are interconnected, how the future might be affected by legislative intervention, and to what extent it is influenced by sheer chance.

The game constitutes a socio-politico-economic model of the United States and as such can be employed by the researcher as a tool for analyzing the relationships among trends and among events and for studying the mutual effects between trends and events. And while the present model still has simplistic features, it has the advantage of being thoroughly interdisciplinary and of lending itself to continual amendations and refinements suggested by new research findings.

The game, finally, can be used as a simulation device by planners, because it affords a means of considering alternative policies and plans and of comparing their likely societal implications, and thus represents an aid in the selection of a preferred set of such policies and plans.

The game deals with the interactions among 50 potential future developments, of which 30 are events and 20 are (societal) trends. These developments, all of which have been mentioned previously in this report, are the following:

E_1: controlled thermonuclear fusion
E_2: mass-administrable contraceptives
E_3: genetic manipulation
E_4: conquest of major diseases
E_5: state of war
E_6: societal computer simulation
E_7: intelligence drugs
E_8: breakdown of a city
E_9: harmless pesticides
E_{10}: computer-aided instruction
E_{11}: food from artificial protein
E_{12}: suspension of civil liberties
E_{13}: home computer terminals
E_{14}: computerized diagnosis
E_{15}: life expectancy up five years
E_{16}: mass-produced housing
E_{17}: reliable weather forecasts
E_{18}: personality-control drugs
E_{19}: human cloning
E_{20}: personnel data banks
E_{21}: high-speed interurban transport
E_{22}: high-IQ computers
E_{23}: automated highways
E_{24}: nonpolluting automobiles
E_{25}: minimum income for all
E_{26}: medical service for all
E_{27}: elimination of nonvictim crimes
E_{28}: reorganization of criminal courts
E_{29}: technology assessment
E_{30}: educational vouchers

T_1: new vision of a good life
T_2: state of revolutionary tension
T_3: population growth rate
T_4: international tension
T_5: insistence on social responsibility
T_6: citizen lobbies
T_7: per-capita GNP
T_8: federal expenditure on new cities
T_9: protection of the environment
T_{10}: defense budget
T_{11}: racial tension
T_{12}: crimes of violence
T_{13}: percentage female of labor force
T_{14}: unconventionality of lifestyles
T_{15}: price inflation
T_{16}: child-care centers
T_{17}: unemployment rate
T_{18}: private/public amalgamation
T_{19}: strikes
T_{20}: education of culturally deprived

The game covers a thirty-year period and proceeds in ten triannual move cycles. At the beginning, as well as at the end of each three-year cycle, the state of the Union is assessed by the players in terms of twelve satisfaction indices (which are identical with those presented in Section 48.5 of this chapter).

Each event has a stated anticipated probability of occurrence in any particular three-year time period; similarly, each trend has an anticipated value at the beginning of each such move cycle. These probabilities and values, however, are subject to change in the course of the game, depending on (i) chance, (ii) the players' intervention, and (iii) the cross-impact effects of the occurrence or nonoccurrence of other events or of changes in the anticipated values of other trends.

The game can be played as a one-person (more properly, in fact, a one-team) game "against nature", that is, a planning exercise simulating the actions of the federal government; in other words, moves by the playing teams would simulate either congressional acts, or executive presidential decisions, or possibly judicial actions by the Supreme Court. In an extended version, additional playing teams can be introduced, representing, say, the separate branches of the federal government, industry (possibly further subdivided into several industrial sectors), labor, consumers, and possibly various population segments with partly or wholly opposed interests.

[As much can be learned from constructing a game such as this as from playing it. Since all the details of the Future State of the Union game have been omitted above, a good classroom exercise in future studies would be to fill in those details. Some of the more important steps in such a construction would be:

- the choice of events and trends to be portrayed;
- forecasts of their anticipated probabilities and values, respectively;
- stipulation of their mutual cross-impacts; and
- determination of the actions at the players' disposal and of their impacts.

Aside from these substantive decisions, procedural rules for playing the game will have to be formulated; these will depend in part on whether the game is to be played entirely by hand as a board game or the group is ambitious enough and allots enough programming talent to construct a computerized version. In the latter case, allowance has to be made for human-machine interactions, since the players must (i) feed in their moves in reaction to the changing situation and (ii) periodically assess the status in terms of satisfaction indices, best done by mini-Delphi among all players.]

48.17 Summary

This essay represents at best a first attempt to bring together some of the raw materials for an examination of the future state of the Union. Some of these raw materials are substantive, some methodological.

The substantive material includes a large number of probabilistic forecasts, of both scientific and technological developments and of societal trends and innovations, and a collection of nonforecasts (myths). Also presented are a list of the major issues demanding solutions and, in view of these, a statement of some of the options among which we have to choose and of opportunities that we may wish to seize. It is hoped that these opportunities, in their totality, convey a reasonably accurate picture of the multitude of potential strands out of which the future history of the United States will be formed.

On the methodological side, a number of rudimentary devices have been suggested with which to refine the quality of the substantive items, analyze their interrelations, and improve their utility for understanding and planning the future. The concept of a set of satisfaction indices has been suggested as a useful tool—however subjective and intuitive—for describing and comparing different states of the Union. For obtaining panel estimates of present and projected satisfaction levels as well as of forecasts of future trends and events, the Delphi method has been found a useful device. In order to overcome, at least to some small extent, the absence of a theoretical corpus explaining the interdependencies among societal developments, the notion of a cross-impact matrix has been introduced, by means of which intuitive estimates of such relationships can, if nothing else, be systematically elicited and processed. As a direct application of the cross-impact concept, a simulation game has been outlined, which can serve as a teaching, planning, and research tool with which to explore potential scenarios of the future. ■

49 EDUCATION FOR THE FUTURE

Education, because of its profound role in any civilized society and in view of the long lead times involved in its planning, is a natural and challenging subject for futurists to consider. There have, indeed, been a number of studies, often employing Delphi as a procedural vehicle, that have attempted to explore the future of education (to name just two, Shane, 1973; Adelson, Alkin, Carey, and Helmer, 1967). Here I will confine myself to reproducing a talk I gave in Seattle in 1976 to the Northwest Association of Schools and Colleges:

If it were not for the decimal system, nobody would pay any special attention to the year 1976 as the two hundredth birthday of this nation. In this age of the computer, the binary system may soon become the order of the day, and the next really big celebration may be in what we now call the year 2032. At that time, this nation, decimally speaking, will be 256 years old; 256 being 2^8, that will, in the binary system, be the occasion of its one hundred millionth birthday.

But one numerical fetishism provides as good an occasion as any other to devote some thought to reflection—reflection, that is, on the state of the Union and on the state of education in particular, as well as on the direction in which we will be moving between this two hundredth decimal anniversary and the one hundred millionth binary anniversary fifty-six years hence. How good, or bad, are things now? Are they getting better or worse? Opinions on the present state of the Union and on its future prospects range all the way from euphoria to despair. There are, no doubt, some grounds for both.

The system of government in this country, with all its faults, has endured remarkably well, and the number of people throughout the world who look with envy on American standards of affluence and personal freedom is enormous. Culturally, too, we are in the forefront in many respects. Among many other areas, this country has been in the lead in the last fifty years in such diverse fields as space technology, music, and biomedicine. This year, the fact that America has garnered every single Nobel prize (except for one, which remained unawarded) is further evidence of singular achievements.

However, there is the other side of the coin: Government does, after all, have its faults. Many feel that it has become too big and intrudes altogether too much into our lives; and there are laws on the books, especially in the areas of taxation and social welfare, that promote and perpetuate highly undesirable inequities. Our affluence is being steadily eroded by inflation, unemployment, and, most of all, an insufficiently growing rate of productivity. And the cultural highlights represented by a few outstanding individuals are offset by an increasing functional illiteracy among our youngsters and the inability of even many graduate students to spell correctly or to carry out simple arithmetical calculations. Above all, there is, in every layer of our society, a moral decay at work that gives substance to the claims of those most pessimistic who foresee the imminence of the decline and fall of the American system. Who is right? The euphoric enthusiasts or the doomsday prophets? And what are the role and fate and responsibilities of the educational establishment in this context?

I confess that I am poorly qualified to answer these questions. I am not a sociologist and, although I have taught a few students in my time, I do not consider myself an educator. My credentials are those of a concerned citizen and of a methodologist in that part of the field of operations research that has become known as futures research. As such let me address these questions by giving voice to some of my citizen's concerns and by trying to indicate in what way a new approach to educational planning might make a small contribution toward solving some of the problems with which we are faced.

First of all, let us distinguish between comparing social conditions in the United States with conditions elsewhere and comparing conditions in the United States with what they might be.

Compared to most other countries, we are still doing extremely well, both in terms of per-capita income and in terms of the general quality of life. There are, admittedly, two or three small countries where the per-capita income is even higher, and in about two dozen countries the infant mortality rate is lower than in the United States. But, in terms of most of the standard indicators of a good life, we are comparatively well off.

However, if we consider the economic, the intellectual, and the cultural potentialities in this country and ask ourselves to what extent today's realities measure up to them, the verdict must be—I think—that conditions are utterly disgraceful. What excuse is there, in a supposed democracy as affluent as ours, for 26 million people, by the government's own standards, living in poverty; for many people, even among the middle-income families, having to think twice before consulting a doctor when they are sick; for crime so rampant and protection so inadequate that many sections of our cities have to be shunned for fear of violent death; for many of our schools having become custodial rather than pedagogical institutions? Why do we have to put up with so many forms of pollution in our lives? The fish are dying in our rivers, the lives of city dwellers are appreciably shortened by air pollution, and if that does not kill us, the pollution of the airwaves is threatening our sanity with its inane, ungrammatical, deceitful, and endlessly repetitious commercials. Why, most seriously of all, have ethical standards in this country deteriorated so abysmally in all walks of life, from the lowliest welfare cheats to the highest officials in the land?

I suspect that at the root of these troubles there is a basic dishonesty that has spread through our culture, a dishonesty that goes far beyond misdeeds that are legally actionable, a dishonesty that is basically an intellectual one. Serious issues tend to be decided not by cogent arguments but by empty slogans; scapegoats are seen everywhere; a free-for-all scramble has taken the place of the social contract, which means that the tragedy of the commons, where the public land is overused by all, has become a characteristic disorder of our time; and drugs, both legal and illegal, are the great escape from the resultant, unfortunate reality.

Among the manifestations of this intellectual dishonesty are certain peculiarly illogical attitudes, reminiscent of some of Lewis Carroll's tongue-in-cheek logic in *Alice in Wonderland*, with which important public issues are tackled. Let me cite half a dozen examples.

When inflation first began to get out of hand, the word was passed around that "our economy must be slowed down" (although, to be sure, it was prices rather than overproduction that needed attention). To achieve this slowing down of the economy, interest rates were raised, with the result that this added cost of capital was passed on to the consumer in the form of even higher prices. The end effect, of course, was that the economy indeed slowed down, simply because consumers could no longer afford to buy as much and caused a large part of our productive machinery to lie idle. Thus the policy, with its slowing-down intent, was "successful", and one would have expected the perpetrators of that policy to be pleased with themselves. Far from it though. Instead of pointing with pride at their achievement, the very same people soon began to raise a hue and cry over the decrease in GNP,—as though that had not been the ostensible aim of their effort.

In much the same vein, it has become the custom, if some goods or services do not sell, not to lower their price in order to make them more attractive to buyers but to raise it instead, presumably on the theory that that was the way to maintain the same profit level at a reduced volume of sales. This attitude has been prevalent in many areas, perhaps most notably in residential housing, which has been highly overpriced; the automobile industry, where sales have been far from satisfactory in recent years; and the construction trade, whose workers have priced themselves so far out of the market as to cause the greatest unemployment rate in their recent history.

Another absurdity, close to my own heart because of my approaching official senility, is the matter of the retirement age. There has been a public clamor to reduce the retirement age, based on the mistaken notion, I suppose, that our rising productivity rate permits us to confer the benefits of leisure on a larger segment of the population. Not only is this premise false (productivity is not keeping pace with rising living-standard expectations), but people live longer and retain their faculties longer, so that what is called for is a raising rather than a lowering of the retirement age. For one thing, such a measure would largely solve the rising problems of Social Security financing, because people would continue to pay premiums into the system over a period of additional years during which they now receive annuity payments.

As a fourth example, let me mention that of nuclear parity, where we can perhaps least afford to indulge in self-deceptive slogans. Parity here does not mean, as some orators would have it, an equal number of warheads deliverable on the enemy. Rather it means that if the enemy were insanely to initiate a nuclear war, it should be inconceivable that, after the first such assault, we should not have enough missiles left over to destroy the enemy's major cities. This is what deterrence amounts to. Since a single H bomb dropped on a large city would destroy it virtually completely and eradicate almost all of the life in it, a few dozen missiles securely hidden in silos and submarines would provide that parity, even in the face of heavy enemy defenses. Nuclear stockpiles of thousands of weapons are, in fact, counterproductive since they merely perpetuate and escalate the arms race and thereby increase the probability of eventually triggering an accidental outbreak of nuclear war. Thus our national security could actually be enhanced if only we discarded the parity slogan for true parity and diverted some of our military expenditures to our social needs.

Another example of lopsided thinking concerns the matter of educational opportunities for the so-called culturally disadvantaged minorities. While the insistence on equal chances is something of which all right-minded persons heartily approve, the way in which this is being implemented amounts to a de facto quota system, which is working to the disadvantage of all parties concerned and, if continued, will lead to a national disaster. What the minorities want, and need, and have every right to get, is the opportunity to attain levels of training and competence completely on a par with that of the majority. But preferential certification and the creation of job opportunities based on group membership rather than individual competence is, from the minorities' own point of view, utterly counterproductive in the long run because it removes the incentive for acquiring competence. Furthermore, it creates an expectation of incompetence where none exists; that is, those who have in fact attained high competence against heavy odds are unjustly deprived of due credit for their effort since they often are assumed to have obtained accreditation merely because of membership in their minority group.

As a final excursion into the illogical wonderland, let me briefly mention the subject of public services or, rather, the pervasive reluctance to pay for the public services. Better transportation, cleaner air, protection against crime, improved health care, and—yes—a more meaningful system of education are high on everyone's list of desirable amenities. As we move into what has been called the postindustrial age, the quality of our lives will be determined more and more by those intangible services rather than by tangible merchandise. However, people show a profound unwillingness to put their money where their avowed priorities are, the usual rationale being that this would mean higher taxes and thus bigger government. The government may, indeed, not be the most efficient purveyor of such services. But the question of whether they should be subcontracted to private entrepreneurs is really secondary. The point is that the required services, whether performed publicly or privately, are in fact, public in nature because they serve the needs of society as a whole rather than the needs of individual citizens. In the meantime, the mix of goods and services we irrationally acquire because we pay too much attention to antigovernment slogans represents a very poor reflection of our actual needs and preferences.

These six examples of cases in which we are intellectually less than honest with ourselves could easily be augmented in number. My purpose in dwelling on them was to focus on several related observations. First, these examples serve as illustrations of the many things that are wrong with our society today, faults that most of us feel ought to be eliminated. Second, they show that we often go about the task of applying corrective measures in a peculiarly illogical way and that, as a society, we somehow will have to make a more concerted and, above all, a more honest effort to put things right. And third, these examples lend emphasis to the fact that the educational establishment has both a stake and an obligation in seeking to bring about the intellectual and moral climate in which solutions to our great social problems can be found.

Let me now briefly address the question of what educators in fact might be able to do in order to achieve some improvements in this state of affairs. What redirection in educational planning is indicated at the local and federal levels that might help put our society back on the right track?

I hasten to say that I do not have the answers to these questions—and I doubt if any one person can be expected to have all the answers. To solve these problems will take an enormous cooperative effort, goodwill, and much patience. Now that a new administration is about to take over in Washington, it may be as good a time as any for all of us to think positively and to attempt to come up with constructive suggestions for educational reforms. All I can do here along this line is to put a few suggestions of my own into the hopper for general consideration.

My first suggestion has to do with the problem of relevance, and it is directly related to the kind of less-than-straight thinking I tried to illustrate. It seems to me that we ought to pay more than lip service to the need for developing an ability to solve real-life problems rather than overemphasize the storing up of masses of data in the brains of our youngsters. We are, after all, on the verge of an electronic revolution where comprehensive data banks, two-way television, and highly sophisticated data retrieval systems will be available. Since machines are better than humans at storing information, we ought to leave that chore largely to them, and what is needed instead is extensive training in data retrieval, so that we will be able to make the most of this new capability both for enriching our lives and for solving the complex problems with which we are faced. But problem-solving obviously calls for more than just efficient data retrieval; it requires straight thinking of the kind that, I believe, can best be learned by "training on the job", that is, by getting into the habit, from an early age, to look at real-world problems squarely, identify the issues, learn to recognize and discard phoney arguments, and seek a fair solution. It has been stated frequently in recent years that the GNP is a poor measure of the national well-being and that other measures ought to be substituted for it that come closer to a real assessment of that multidimensional entity we loosely call "the quality of life". If the ecologists have taught us anything, it is that the world is more complex than many of us realized—that everything depends on, and affects, virtually everything else. Therefore, in order to resolve societal problems fairly, we have to pay attention to these cross-connections and their repercussions, or else we are in danger of improving just one facet of the quality of life at the expense of others. This is a lesson that even the ecologists themselves have not wholly absorbed.

It seems to me it would be well worthwhile, even at the secondary school level, to institute regular courses in problem-solving, ranging all the way from family and school issues to mock sessions of the state legislature, the Congress, or the United Nations. At the college level, these should take the form of well-organized, possibly computer-aided, planning simulation exercises, with particular emphasis on interdisciplinary approaches.

I do not mean by this suggestion that everyone ought to become a generalist, and that specialized training ought to be abandoned. By no means. The intricacies of modern science and technology require the existence of a great many narrowly specialized experts. But we need to recognize that most of the problems with which our society is faced are highly complex and require for their solution the cross-disciplinary collaboration of different kinds of specialists. Not only do our schools and universities fail to provide sufficient opportunities for such interdisciplinary team approaches, but the present disciplinary compartmentalization sets up nothing but disincentives for such cooperative efforts.

My second suggestion concerns the relationship between federal and local educational planning. We are here faced with two countervailing trends. On the one hand, there is the current revulsion against overly big government and the consequent desire to place responsibility for planning in the school boards and college or university administrations. On the other hand, because of the growing complexity of our society, the data requirements for adequate planning are so vast and the interconnections between different societal facets are so intricate that a local planning organization cannot be expected to do justice to the demands of a proper planning activity. These trends toward centralization and decentralization, however, only appear to be irreconcilable—again, I think, because of some basically fuzzy thinking. There is a need to distinguish more clearly between the planning function as such, which can be (and usually is) merely advisory, and the decision-making function that uses the results of the planning effort as an input. If we look on the situation in this light, there is no reason why the planning activity could not be highly centralized while still leaving the actual decision-making to the local authorities.

To implement this idea, I suggest that the federal government be urged to set up a national simulation laboratory for educational planning. Its function would be manifold: It would collect relevant statistical data; it would provide trend projections based both on extrapolation from past time series and on the forecasts of selected experts; it would collate the experience gained at individual schools and colleges with various experimental programs; and it would disseminate all this information to educational planners throughout the nation and use it to facilitate the building of educational planning models. The way I visualize its operation, it would involve the employment of a national computer network, linking the local educational planning organizations to the national laboratory. The network would be used by local planners to explicate their planning problems to the national center, and the latter would collect through it specific local information, in the form of both factual data and indications of aspirations and preferences. These would be adjoined to the national bank of data and forecasts and used to construct a custom-made planning simulation model to fit the local facts, prospects, and needs. The results of running such a model, possibly with remote participation via computer terminals of the local decision makers, would be fed back to the requesting organization, which could then base its detailed decisions on the suggestions implicit in the outcome of these computer runs.

A third suggestion, finally, has to do with my own field, futures research. I would like to urge the educational establishment to adopt a more explicit orientation toward the future, to engage more systematically than at present in long-range planning, and to avail itself of some of the methods of futures research in order to move in that direction.

There is no major field of human endeavor in greater need of an orientation toward the future than education. This has not always been so. It used to be the case until not so long ago that societal and technological changes from one generation to the next were not very noticeable, and it would have made sense for a would-be educational reformer, even as late as in the nineteenth century, merely to ask himself what was wrong with the then-present educational system, or even with the past system to which he had been exposed as a youngster, and thereupon propose reform measures that might improve those conditions. Today such an attitude would be inappropriate. We are living in a world of fast and still accelerating change, a world of "future shock", as it has been called; and for any reform proposals to make sense they must take into consideration expected changes in the future environment. In fact, the educational planner finds himself in the unique position of having to work with two planning horizons: the time, perhaps ten years in the future, by which he might hope to see any major reform proposals adopted and implemented; and the time, perhaps extending fifty or more years into the future, during which the students exposed to the proposed new system would live out their lives and put what they have learned to good use.

These dual planning horizons mean that we need, first of all, forecasts concerning the next decade or so, particularly regarding technological breakthroughs in the still explosively progressing computer and communications revolution, but also regarding societal developments—including, in particular, demographic redistributions and changes in lifestyle—that may affect school attendance and educational aspirations. Second, because the students of that time will live out a large part of their lives in the first half of the twenty-first century, we need to foresee some of the social and technological developments of the next fifty to seventy-five years in order to make the education that will be offered relevant and meaningful for them.

To suggest that all these forecasts be made by local planning agencies would be quite unreasonable. The size of such an undertaking would exceed the time and resources at their disposal, especially if we consider the numerous, complex interactions between forecasts and educational plans. That is to say, not only will contingency plans depend on the forecasts regarding the future operating environment, but the type of education we are planning to offer will, in turn, have a feedback influence on those external conditions. To give proper consideration to these mutual effects (i.e., cross-impacts) would require an elaborate analysis best conducted through a computer-assisted simulated-planning effort. Thus, my third suggestion ties in very directly with my second one, of setting up a national laboratory that could perform simulation studies as a service for individual, local planning agencies.

To sum up: Education in America at present, just like societal conditions generally in this country, is not in good shape. There is reason for cautious optimism regarding the future, however. Improvements, though, will not come easily and certainly not without great, concerted effort. The beginning of a new federal administration may be a good time at which to voice constructive criticism. ■

50 A STUDY RELATED TO THE FUTURE OF TRANSPORTATION

As an example of a futures study concerned with a much more narrowly defined subject matter than the preceding one, I include the following brief account of some research done at the University of Southern California in 1975.[2]

50.1 Introduction

The future is always uncertain. But, transportation policy and planning depend critically on sound assessment of future developments. These assessments involve not only the anticipated events and trends in transportation technology, but also the societal environment that transportation will serve. A variety of techniques have been developed in recent years that permit planners and policymakers to do more than simply project current trends indefinitely into the future. In this paper, the use of two of these techniques—Delphi inquiry and cross-impact analysis—is illustrated.

This paper is based on the results of a specific study undertaken at the Center for Futures Research at the University of Southern California, sponsored by the California Department of Transportation (CALTRANS). CALTRANS began work in 1973 on a statewide multimodal transportation plan to be presented to the Legislature by January 1, 1976. Early in its work, CALTRANS recognized that, since this plan can affect the course of transportation in California beyond the year 2000, the planning effort would have to be undertaken in the context of the future of the state. It was to provide this needed context that CALTRANS turned to USC.

50.2 Delphi Inquiry

A total of forty-six experts from a broad range of backgrounds participated in the Delphi inquiry. These experts were polled on the following seventeen societal areas:

- value changes
- science and technology
- institutional changes
- the economy
- resource allocation
- communications
- international affairs
- regulatory measures
- natural resources
- employment
- domestic politics
- demography
- communities
- transportation of people and goods
- leisure and recreation
- education
- health and welfare

Initially the panel was asked to concentrate on developments that, in their opinion, have a high degree of "expected relevance". Developments were to

2. Paul Gray and Olaf Helmer, "The Use of Futures Analysis for Transportation Research Planning", *Transportation Journal,* vol. 16 (1976).

include (i) events that have a reasonable chance of occurring within the next thirty years that would have a major impact on transportation planning if they occurred, and (ii) trends that have a reasonable chance of deviating from commonly accepted values where such deviations would have a major impact on transportation planning. The initial inquiry of the panel resulted in identification of 263 developments (93 events and 170 trends). The second round of the Delphi inquiry provided a reasonable consensus on 146 of the developments; the remaining 117 were resolved in a conference of twenty-one of the panelists.

In addition to completing the Delphi inquiry, the panelists selected 36 developments out of the 263 that they believed most relevant for transportation planning and estimated the magnitude of the cross-impacts among developments in areas of their expertise. A few of these 36 developments and the forecasts made for them are illustrated below:

	Forecast Year of Occurrence		
Events	*Earliest*	*Most Likely*	*Latest*
Introduction of free rapid-transit facilities in California's major cities	1990	2000	never
Development of a practical high-energy density battery or fuel cell, making electric automobiles economically competitive for urban use	1983	1983	2000
Introduction of automated highways on a more than experimental scale	2000	2000	2020

	Trend Value in			
Trends	*1974*	*1985*	*1995*	*2000*
The demand for rapid transit	100	150	200	275
The percentage of persons in California who are opposed to further freeway construction	15	25	40	43
The degree of air pollution in California	25	20	15	10

Examination of the panelists' contributions to the Delphi inquiry indicated that their concerns were focused particularly on the future state of the economy and on legislative and regulatory developments as they affect transportation. Their outlook on the economy was, on the whole, pessimistic. A severe depression was considered likely by the 1980s, and labor and agricultural productivities were expected to increase only slightly over the next thirty years. The GNP, on the other hand, was expected eventually to rise above three trillion in constant 1974 dollars. The panelists also foresaw considerable proliferation of governmental regulation and increased governmental planning, particularly in the areas of environment and transportation.

With regard to transportation modes, the panelists gave the greatest attention to mass transportation, with little consideration given to highways and virtually none to sea and air transportation. They appeared to view mass transportation as a near-term solution to both the energy and environmental problems. They were also quite hopeful that energy availability will increase and pollution will decrease over the next thirty years.

50.3 Cross-Impact Analysis

Cross-impact analysis is a method for evaluating the effects of interactions among trends and events over time. The occurrence of an event (e.g., development of a steam car) may change the likelihood of occurrence of other events (e.g., development of an electrically powered car) or the values of trends (e.g., rapid-transit use). Similarly, major deviations from anticipated trend values such as population estimates can affect other trends and events.

The number of cross-impacts may be quite large. Even with the aid of a large computer, it is not practical at present to perform a cross-impact analysis on all the developments considered in the Delphi inquiry. The present study was therefore limited to the interactions among the thirty-six most relevant events and trends. Estimates of the magnitude of the cross-impacts were obtained from a subset of the panelists.

The cross-impact model can be used for three purposes: sensitivity studies, scenario development, and comparative policy analysis. In sensitivity studies, the effects of changes in one development (resulting from unforeseen events or from deliberate policy action) affect other developments in the long term. Understanding the effects that such changes have makes it possible to identify the major contingencies with which plans have to cope and to compare the effectiveness of alternative policies and action programs.

A scenario is a particular time sequence of event occurrences and changes in trend values. An immense number of scenarios can be generated with the cross-impact model. All of these contingencies could not possibly be taken into consideration in planning. To reduce the task to manageable proportions, it is necessary to select a few typical representative scenarios, chosen in such a way that a decision-making agency, by considering just these representative contingencies, can feel reasonably confident that the results of its planning effort will fare well no matter which scenario turns out to be correct. The decision-making agency will be particularly concerned about contingencies over which it has little or no control.

A rough measure of the overall effect of each development is obtained by taking the total of all cross-impacts exerted by the development. This is displayed in the first column of the following tabulation for some representative developments:

Development	*Impact*	*Estimated CALTRANS Infl.*	*Contingency index= Impact × (1 − Infl.)*	*Infl. Index= Impact × Infl.*
Free rapid transit	5.5	.5	2.75	2.75
Fuel cells	2.3	.1	2.07	.23
Automated highways	1.7	.6	.68	1.02
Economic depression	8.2	0	8.20	0
Oil and gas rationing	5.8	.1	5.22	.58
Demand for rapid trans.	2.5	.3	1.75	.75
Freeway opposition	1.3	.2	1.04	.26
Air pollution	6.5	.1	5.85	.65

Developments having high impact may be considered "driving forces" of the system and therefore the most important for sensitivity analysis. The table also shows estimates, made by the USC team, of the degree of influence CALTRANS has on each development. (Here 0 denotes no influence and 1 denotes complete control.) These estimates are tentative and any conclusions derived from them are illustrative only. By multiplying the impact by (1 − influence), an estimate (labeled "contingency index") is obtained of the relative importance of contingencies over which CALTRANS has little control. (For example, if CALTRANS has a degree of influence of 0.3 over a development, then (1 − 0.3) = 0.7 is a measure of the degree of lack of control over the development.) The three most important contingencies were an economic depression, the level of air pollution, and the imposition of oil and gas rationing.

For purposes of developing a state-wide transportation plan, these three developments serve to define the beginning of a relevance tree. Each branch of the relevance tree represents a major contingency scenario worth examining:

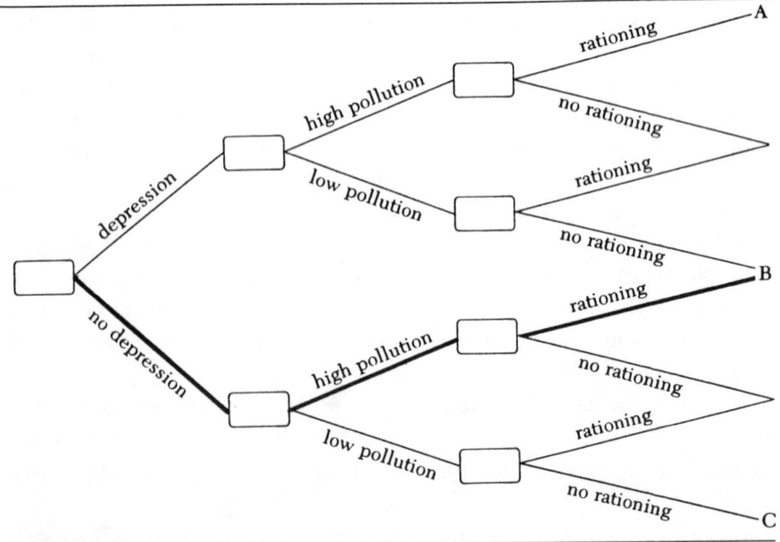

FIGURE 24

The following table shows illustrative results of making sensitivity and scenario runs using the cross-impact model. In each case, the table shows the effects of changes between 1975 and 1980 on the values of six trends in the year 2000. A + indicates a significant increase, a − a significant decrease, and a blank indicates little effect. The symbols ++ and −− indicate the largest changes observed for the trend:

Development	Transit demand	Pollution	Energy supply	Population	Transit availability	Leisure
Free mass transit by 1980	++	-		+	+	
Depression by 1980		+		-		-
No depression by 1980	+			+	+	+
Gas rationing before 1980	+		--			--
No gas rationing by 1980	-	+	+		-	
More air pollution 1975	+				+	
Less air pollution 1975	-				-	
Population increase 1975	+			++	+	
Population decrease 1975	-			--	-	
More mass transit 1975	+	--		+	++	
Less mass transit 1975	-	++		-	--	
Branch A of relevance tree	+	+	-		+	
Branch B of relevance tree	+	+		+	+	++
Branch C of relevance tree	--		++		-	

The table shows that, among the trends considered, long-term transit demand and transit availability are most affected, whereas energy supply and leisure are least affected by the developments included in the model.

The cross-impact model can also be used to examine the effectiveness of alternative policies. Here it is natural to concentrate on those developments that have a strong impact and can be subjected to some measure of influence by CALTRANS. These developments can be identified by taking the product of impact and influence (labeled "influence index"). The most important are public transportation availability, institution of free rapid transit, and establishment of a set of statewide transportation priorities. Since any planning effort has to take into account not only the potential merits of various options but also their associated costs, policy analysis using the cross-impact model requires testing various combinations of measures and levels of intensity of implementation within given budgetary constraints. Such analyses were, in fact, recommended as the next step CALTRANS should undertake. The use of the cross-impact model in this manner, while certainly not constituting the last word, can be looked to for providing insights into determining the most promising transportation policies to be examined more closely.

50.4 Limitations

This study extended to a future horizon of thirty years and dealt with a broad range of societal issues. As with any such study, the numerical results have to be viewed as being indicative of what can be anticipated rather than as absolute predictions.

In an exploratory Delphi inquiry such as this, the developments included depend on the responses of the panelists. The responses, in turn, depend on the choice of panelists. A different panel might have added other developments and left out some that were included here. The panel, an outstanding group of individuals, consisted largely of middle-class professionals. The emphasis could have been the result of predispositions on their part; however, in our judgment, such bias, if any, was slight.

Cross-impact analysis is still in an early stage of development. The present study is one of the largest applications of this method to date. Several improvements in the methodology (particularly the measurement of cross-impacts in terms of standard deviations to reflect the degree of uncertainty regarding future values) were made during this study. It can be anticipated that additional improvements in cross-impact analysis will be made in the future. The cross-impact results should therefore be regarded as indicative of changes in the trend directions rather than the precise trend values to be anticipated.

50.5 Conclusion

Recognizing the limitations inherent in the data obtained from the panelists and in the methods employed, the results do establish a general societal background that is being used in transportation planning in California. A number of scenarios have been selected for inclusion in the statewide transportation plan. These scenarios, based on the results of the study, were reviewed to detect early warning signals of changes to be anticipated and to assess the policy implications of the developments identified. The planning effort is still under way. As the plan develops, these scenarios will serve as a yardstick against which to measure the effectiveness of the final statewide transportation plan. Since this process is still ongoing, it is much too early to be able to judge the success of the technique in this application.

It is quite clear, however, that California has attempted a major step forward in the planning process. Whereas historically transportation plans have considered future developments in transportation technology and operational concepts, most efforts of this magnitude have either ignored issues outside of transportation or have attempted arbitrarily to define a single scenario that represents the future environment. Scant attention has usually been paid to societal changes and value changes. Charged with developing a long-range plan, the planning group has tried to put the plan into a much larger framework, namely, the future societal environment which it is to serve. They have recognized that not only does transportation affect large areas of society, but large areas of society affect transportation.

The present study has shown that modern techniques of futures analysis can be used to aid in long-range planning and policy formulation. The success of the study indicates that other policy planning groups could benefit from using these techniques.

Chapter X

On the Future of International Relations

A potentially rich field of applications of methods of futures research is that of foreign policy. The first section, below, is a reprint of a paper that discusses this subject in rather general terms, followed, in the next section, by a further elaboration of approaches to forecasting and planning in this area. The third section represents an early (1948) attempt to clarify some of the notions involved in the concept of national security, to be followed, in the last section, by some thoughts, formulated 25 years ago, on deterrence, which may still have some relevance to today's military planning.

51 POLITICAL ANALYSIS OF THE FUTURE[1]

The title of this paper is ambiguous—and deliberately so. It could and, indeed, is intended to refer to the analysis of potential future political developments as well as to the future of political analysis as an intellectual endeavor. The remarks I intend to present will have some bearing on both of these subjects, for I shall concern myself, first, with new approaches to forecasting future developments and the role of such forecasts in political analysis and, second, with the effect that a more deliberate orientation toward the future might have on the future of political science as a professional activity.

I hasten to say at once that my statements are those of an outsider to the profession. I am not a political scientist and consider myself a devout methodologist with a bent toward operations analysis. This makes for a certain detachment, which has obvious advantages and disadvantages. While promising the possibility of a refreshingly novel point of view, it is apt to be afflicted with a good deal of naïveté. I hope, and fear, respectively, that what I have to say will have some of both of these qualities.

51.1 Futures-Research Opportunities in Political Analysis

Political science, to this outside observer, presents a picture that, in highly simplified terms, exhibits two major tendencies. One is that it appears to be

1. Publication P-1, Institute for the Future (1969). This paper was prepared for delivery at the 1969 annual meeting of the American Political Science Association.

oriented primarily toward the past and present and not toward the future, explicit prediction usually being limited to the immediate consequences of present events that historical evidence may suggest. Consideration of the more distant future, five, ten, or fifty years ahead, seems rare, except in rather abstract utopian terms, in which case the time horizon is apt to be quite indefinite. The other notable tendency is that of theory-building, the results of which often provide a profound intuitive understanding of the political scene. But precisely since these are intuitive, the observer is left with the impression that the authors of such theories must have a sense of frustration because their theories lack the intersubjectively testable character of their counterparts in the physical sciences and consequently do not have the directly predictive quality of physical laws. This perhaps explains the regrettable reluctance to make fuller use of the often enormous intuitive insights derived from subjective theories based on historical consideration and to apply them to a political analysis of the future.

The standard objection to attempting any analysis of the future, especially in the political sphere, is the claim that prediction is impossible since the state of the future is dominated by the occurrence of unforeseeable events, such as the death of a statesman, the rise in power of a dictator, the irrational behavior of a political negotiator. While it is true that such singular events are largely unpredictable, it is a misconception of the nature of scientific prognostication to conclude that therefore an effective analysis of the future is not feasible.

I cannot but regard such a position—of rejecting the explorability of the future—as untenable. When placed in its proper perspective, an analysis of the future is both possible and necessary. It is necessary, because—whether we like it or not—whenever long-range plans have to be made, we inevitably do rely, in our choice among alternative actions, on forecasts of their probable consequences. For instance, in the case of such long-term commitments as are involved in the acceptance or rejection of an antiballistic missile system or in the selection of a strategy for foreign aid, we clearly anticipate that our actions will affect the future more than randomly, or we would not bother taking them. Since our anticipation of the future, even the long-range future, does indeed enter our decision-making processes, it clearly makes sense to go about the analysis of future potentialities in an orderly and deliberate fashion rather than to rely on the haphazard and often hurried inclinations of a political decision-making body.

Of course, recognizing the desirability of an orderly analysis of the future does not guarantee its feasibility, which I will consider next. In order to discuss this, we need to have a clearer understanding of what may reasonably be expected of an analysis of the future and what may not. The first thing to acknowledge is the uncertainty of the future and hence its unpredictability in principle. There are two main reasons for this uncertainty: One is that our knowledge is insufficient to predict singular yet influential events of the type mentioned earlier. The other, which is the rationale underlying all planning, is the partial dependence of the future on our choice of action.

It is therefore inappropriate to speak of the future (in the singular) as something to be discovered, be it through crystal balls or through analysis. Rather, there are many possible futures, which can be considered in terms of probabilities, and it is through planning decisions and through invention that we may hope to affect these probabilities in the desired direction, raising the probabilities of those potential future states of the world that are preferable and lowering those that are not. An analysis of the future, then, should include the following objectives:

- It should provide a survey of possible futures in terms of a spectrum of major potential alternatives.
- It should ascribe to the occurrence of these alternatives some estimates of relative a priori probabilities.
- It should, for given basic policies, identify preferred alternatives.
- It should identify those decisions that are subject to control, as well as those developments that are not, whose occurrence would be likely to have a major effect on the probabilities of these alternatives.

Once these objectives have been achieved, the groundwork will have been laid for the operational application of political analysis, that is, for its use in the selection of appropriate courses of action toward the implementation of given policies.

The question, now, is whether these objectives are in fact attainable.

My contention is that they are, or at least that considerable strides can be taken in the direction of their attainment. However, in order to move in this direction, a reorientation of some of the traditional political science effort will be required. Thus far these seems to be evidence of a growing recognition of the need for such a reorientation but of only a few relevant pioneering efforts; that by Ivo and Rosalind Feierabend on the correlation between literacy and belligerence is a good example.

What is necessary, I think, and long overdue in political analysis is a deliberate move toward greater acceptance of the attitudes and methods of what has become known as operations analysis. Such a step, however much it may be approved of in principle, is more difficult than it sounds, for the basic attitudes of the operations analyst are in considerable conflict with the work habits of the majority of social scientists. Specifically, operations analysis, as its name implies, is operationally oriented. That is, its practitioners place emphasis on the pragmatic aspects of implementing policies; they are planning-oriented and, therefore, future-oriented. They also tend, of necessity, to take a highly interdisciplinary systems view of things and, primarily because of methodological requirements, to favor quantitative approaches.

Among the methods prevalent in operations analysis I would like to mention three categories. There is, first of all, the use of so-called mathematical models, including in particular the extrapolation into the future of past time series through correlation analysis. I note in passing that this involves the whole new area of social indicators, in terms of which we can estimate various aspects of the past and present states of affairs and make contingency forecasts of future developments. Other mathematical models include the formulation of so-called behavioral equations (well-known in economics), which attempt to reflect the expected reactions of people to changes in their environment. A special case of a behavioral model that particularly deserves mention in a political-science context is one that might be considered an extension of non-zero-sum games. Such an extension would adjoin to the concepts normally included in such games that of the behavioral changes among "players" having to cope with a succession of individual conflict situations, where the behavior in any particular situation is influenced by the behavioral pattern exhibited by other players in previous situations. I shall turn later to a brief discussion of the rather obvious application of such a model to the international scene.

The second category of operations-analytical tools is concerned with expert opinions. Since many of the inputs into operations analyses derive from the intuitive insights of subject area specialists, methods are needed to extract such expert judgments as effectively as possible. Among these methods are scenario construction, the Delphi technique, and simulation. "Scenarios", as I use the term, are descriptions of plausible sequences of events leading from the present to the future; they are in the nature of thought experiments that serve to explore intuitively the realism of an imagined future state of affairs. The Delphi technique, now widely used in government and industry, is a means of extracting group judgments from a panel of experts, using a procedure that involves successive questionnaires and a controlled opinion feedback process. As a third method for the utilization of informed judgment, I mentioned simulation. I meant here specifically manual (or personal as opposed to computer) simulation, also sometimes referred to as gaming. It requires that a group of experts engage in playing the roles of decision makers and thus simulate, under assumed conditions, the planning decisions that their real-life counterparts would be expected to make under comparable circumstances.

In the third category of operations-analytical methods I would like to mention the cross-impact technique, which is still under development and which offers a promising systematic means of examining the mutual effects of a set of potential future developments. . . . A cross-impact matrix, when applied to potential political developments, may be looked upon as the nearest thing to a model (or theory) of interactions among political events.

An operations-analytical approach then, in summary, implies an interdisciplinary and future-oriented systems view of the subject matter, and it brings to bear such methods as mathematical models of many kinds, simulated planning techniques, the systematic use of expert judgment, and the cross-impact technique for examining the mutual influences of potential future developments.

Having thus sketched the attitudes and methods of operations analysis, it is necessary to describe briefly how the adoption of this approach might in concrete terms affect the pursuits and products of political-science research. Can this help bridge the gap in comparative progress between the physical and the social sciences?

With respect to the physical sciences and technology, it has been estimated that between now [i.e., 1969] and the end of the century we may expect a tenfold increase in R & D productivity, due to the continuing rise in the number of scientists and engineers and in the number and versatility of computers. The resulting changes in science and technology are bound to be enormous. Nevertheless, precisely because we have already reached such a high level on the scale of scientific and technological development, we may find that further progress in this area will be harder and harder to come by. In the social sciences and in their applications to societal problems—that is, in social technology—we have not nearly reached that point where diminishing marginal returns for our efforts have to be expected. I am firmly convinced that, with the adoption of a more pragmatic and future-oriented viewpoint and, with it, some of the methods mentioned earlier, there is an excellent chance that in the next few decades social-science research, and political-science research especially, will be able to make fundamental contributions to the betterment of the human condition and thus to begin to match the progress that has characterized physical technology in this century.

Specifically, let me list some of the areas where a renewed and redirected effort promises substantial rewards.

51.2 International Political Indicators

With indicators generally there has been a tendency to prefer those that lend themselves to easy objective measurement. This can lead to absurd results, as when we measure the status of the cold war against the Soviet bloc in terms of the number of people under Communist domination, an indicator which is a carryover from an earlier period when population pressure was a political asset rather than a liability. Similarly we tend to measure our performance in Vietnam in terms of enemy soliders killed vs. U.S. soldiers killed; this accounting not only conveys an inadequate description at best, but it fosters the misconception that the killing per se of as many enemy soldiers as possible is one of our primary goals. What we badly need is an appropriate set of indicators, that are in accord with our long-range goals as a nation, in terms of which we can assess how well we are doing on the international scene. Here, the Delphi technique for obtaining a consensus among experts may be very helpful, for it permits us to include indicators which require intuitive appraisal rather than measurement in terms of observable quantities.

51.3 National Goals

National goals, just mentioned in connection with political indicators, form a hierarchy. The goals at any given level are merely indicative of the policies chosen to implement the goals at the next higher level. The only absolute goals, at the very top, are probably simply the old cherished ones of life, liberty, and the pursuit of happiness. The President has recently established a National Goals Research Staff that will presumably concern itself with these problems. The work of this group could make notable contributions to the decision-making processes at the presidential level if it would state this nation's goals and subgoals in relation to appropriate political indicators, so that the degree of attainment of such goals expected from proposed policies could be estimated and stated in terms of these indictors. Aside from again making systematic use of expert opinion for this purpose, the cross-impact technique might be applicable, as it would afford a means of examining the joint effects of a set of measures on a set of indicators.

51.4 Capitalism vs. Communism

As a particular case, a reappraisal of our national goals should include a more future-oriented assessment of our relations with the Communist world. One sometimes wonders whether we have not forgotten what the entire quarrel was about. What started out as a difference in ideology on certain economic principles has inadvertently turned into a power struggle for world domination. Our economies, meanwhile, are converging, each adopting some of the methods of the other; what is more, as affluence steadily increases on both sides of the iron curtain, we will all, before we know it, be entering the age of post-industrial society, where there will be a common search for new principles by which to order our economic processes, and the old quarrel will have become totally meaningless. This suggests that the proper way to a rapprochement with the Soviet Union may well be via futurism, since our long-range goals are much more compatible than our short-range (and often short-sighted) subgoals. There are, in fact, indications that the cultural exchange is already proving relatively most successful in areas concerned with the long-range future.

51.5 Cost-Effectiveness Analysis of Foreign Policy

A well-chosen set of international political indicators and a clear statement of national goals in terms of such indicators would eventually put us in a position where we could begin to think of making foreign-policy choices on the basis of cost-effectiveness considerations. For our foreign policy to make cost-effectiveness sense, it is essential to attempt the impossible, namely, to take a systems view of our operations in the foreign-policy field. This means that we have to create the conceptual as well as the administrative apparatus for across-the-board comparisons of marginal benefits to be derived from investing a million dollars, say, in aid to Indonesia, in our military effort in Vietnam, in military intelligence about China, or in improved cultural relations with Poland. What is more, these estimates of benefits must include comparisons of immediate vs. long-term benefits. To tackle this immense, but I hope not really impossible, task we shall need many of the methods that operations research has to offer,—in particular, simulation, the systematic use of expertise in many areas, and the cross-impact technique for studying, in Michael Spicer's words, "the complex ricochet effects of particular policies".

51.6 Negotiation

Two comments seem appropriate on the subject of international negotiation. First, while so-called "crisis gaming" (dealing with anticipated cold-war crises or with the threat of hot war) has been in vogue for some time and been of some utility to our foreign-policy planners, there is little evidence that such simulation is being applied specifically to important forthcoming international conferences. Our negotiators on such occasions might conceivably derive considerable benefit from pre-conference gaming, in which their prospective adversaries are simulated with verisimilitude. The development of appropriate simulation models for this purpose might be a worthwhile undertaking. Second, and perhaps more importantly, in playing the international non-zero-sum game, we do not always seem to be fully aware of the difference between short-term and long-term gains. In game-theoretic terms, this difference is one between immediate expected payoff in the game that happens to be going on at the moment and restructuring the game into one which promises increased payoffs to both sides; such restructuring can often be achieved by changing the flow of information or by augmenting (or diminishing) the opportunities for negotiation. As I have suggested earlier, the accommodation of such applications may require an extension of traditional non-zero-sum game theory, as we are here no longer dealing with a single game but with the behavior pattern of adversaries engaged in a dynamic sequence of successive conflict situations.

These five very brief examples from the foreign-policy field suffice to make my point—that there is some promise in the transfer of operations-analytical techniques to political analysis; and it would be easy to give similar examples relating to domestic-policy problems.

A reorientation of political analysis toward the future, through the adoption of some such techniques, is likely to make it a more effective tool for policy formation, especially in the area of foreign relations. In analogy to the application of physical science to physical technology, this development may lead to the establishment of "political technology" as an activity explicitly devoted to the pragmatics of the political scene. ■

52 INTERNATIONAL RELATIONS FORECASTING[2]

Future developments in the arena of foreign politics depend so much on individual unforeseeable events (an assassination, the outcome of a close election, the result of a negotiation, even the weather) that political scientists show an understandable disinclination to engage in prophesies.

To mitigate this reluctance in deference to the demands of foreign-policy planning, it is helpful, I think, to remind the would-be prognosticator of the following points:

- No predictions but merely (probabilistic) forecasts are expected.
- The stakes are so high that a substantial payoff can be expected from only a slight improvement in statistical reliability over the average person's expectations.
- Longer-range (say, ten- to thirty-year) forecasts are less dependent than short-range (say, one- to five-year) ones on unexpected and unforeseeable occurrences.
- No single prognosticator should be required to undertake the task of political forecasting alone, but the responsibility should be shared among experts.

A convenient tool for implementing this latter prescription is the Delphi method. While it could be applied to any specific topic, let me choose as an illustration the case of the future of Soviet-American relations during the next twenty-five years.

Imagine a well-selected panel of about ten specialists in Soviet-American relations, including some who are not just political experts in the narrow sense but well versed in closely related fields such as economics, cultural relations, and military developments. Using the intellectual resource represented by such a panel, a Delphi inquiry might best be initiated by conducting an open-ended first round, using something like a "twenty questions" approach:

Step 1: Ask each participant to list those twenty political developments (events or trend changes) that, in his opinion, have a reasonable chance of occurring during the next twenty-five years and that, were they to occur, would either have a profound impact on Soviet-American relations or be significant indicators of the status of those relations.

Step 2: Collate the responses, weed out essential duplicates, eliminate others that are comparatively less relevant, and thus obtain a reduced list of trends and political events that form the input into the forecasting inquiry proper. (If time and

2. The following is an excerpt from "The Use of Expert Opinion in International-Relations Forecasting", a chapter I contributed to *Forecasting in International Relations*, edited by Nazli Choucri and Thomas Robinson (San Francisco: Freeman, 1978).

resources permit, this selection process could be carried out with the aid of the panelists, by interjecting another round, requesting a ranking of items by expected importance. Here "expected importance" is defined as the product of the probability of occurrence and the importance if occurring, where importance is measured on some convenient, intuitive scale, say, from 0 to 10.)

Step 3: For the events on the list, ask for probability distributions of their occurrence over time (most conveniently in terms of the years by which each attains a probability of .1, .5, and .9, of having occurred). For the trends, ask for projections over the next twenty-five years, with some indication of the uncertainty of the estimate (possibly again in terms of not just the .5 curve but also the .1 and .9 curves).

Step 4 and Succeeding Steps: Continue through several rounds of inquiry, following the standard pattern of a Delphi procedure.

The result will be a set of forecasts, with indications of the uncertainties attached to them. Some of the forecasts will represent a narrow consensus, others merely the median of relatively widely dispersed responses, accompanied, however, by indications of the reasons for such divergencies of opinion. Analysis of these reasons will reveal whether a lack of consensus is due to semantic causes (i.e., different interpretations of the questions that had been posed), to factual disagreements, or to the exercise of wishful thinking in the face of genuine uncertainty. To the political decision maker, who will have to base his plans on expert advice, the forecasts representing a narrow consensus will of course be most helpful. But he will profit, too, knowing about real uncertainties and, especially, about the reasons why different experts, in some cases, hold widely divergent views on some aspect of the future; for this will give him clues as to where he has to tread with particular caution and what areas are in need of further research.

The utility to the planner of a set of forecasts, such as might be obtained through a straightforward Delphi inquiry, may be far from negligible; yet it will be limited because such isolated forecasts, by themselves, shed no light, except incidentally (via the respondents' explanatory arguments), on the reasons for prospective happenings. If the planner wishes to proceed on a basis of more than just a blind trust in the forecasting reliability of a panel of experts and desires a better understanding of the causal relationships among potential developments, he needs, ideally, to be provided with a theory consisting of generalized propositions. That would put him in a position where statements regarding particular situations could be derived by him from the general case by specifying the appropriate parameters.

While such generalized propositions, as stated before, are as a rule unavailable, a modicum of an integrated overview, and therewith of quasi-theoretical insights into underlying causalities, can be attained by an application of the cross-impact technique.

In order to see how a cross-impact model might be considered the next best thing to a theory, let us return to the illustrative case of Soviet-American relations. Suppose, for simplicity, that, among the developments about which forecasts were earlier assumed to have been obtained, the twenty most important events and, similarly, the twenty most important trends had been selected. These could be made the subject of a cross-impact inquiry (possibly using the same expert respondents who had provided the original individual forecasts); that is, a 40 × 40 cross-impact matrix could be constructed in which the expected impact of the occurrence of any of the events or of the deviation of any of the trends from its anticipated values on any of the other developments would be recorded. This task, of course, is a difficult one, but it may be made somewhat easier by subdividing the estimation requirements for the 1560 matrix items (40 × 40, minus 40 for the diagonal) and distributing these among subpanels selected for their particular expertise with regard to the pairs of items whose cross-impacts are to be estimated.

Also, it should be noted that many of the cells will remain blank, because for many pairs of developments the impact of the first on the second may be nil or negligibly small. With regard to many of the entries, even experts will be relatively uncertain as to what assessment of the impact to make; but at least each pair of developments will be given some reflection, and even an uncertain estimate by experts will be better than no estimate at all, which would be tantamount to totally neglecting the effect by default. For example, suppose that one of the trends is "the GNP of the U.S." and one of the events is "a free-trade agreement between the U.S. and the Soviet Union". It may be hard to assess the effect, all else being equal, of an unexpected rise of the former on the probability of the subsequent occurrence of the latter or equally of the occurrence of the latter on the subsequent rise of the former; yet a planner will have some implicit conception of what these impacts may be, and it will be better if this matter is given explicit consideration not only by himself but by his panel of expert advisers.

It may be further argued that an examination of forecasts and cross-impacts in their mutual context, rather than separately, will provide a check on systemic consistency. That is, if any counterintuitive implications seem to arise as a result of running the cross-impact model, either some of the forecasts or some of the cross-impacts will be seen to require adjustment, and the input estimates may thus be improved.

Generally speaking, however, the cross-impact approach, as a theory-building device, may leave much to be desired. For one thing, in its present form it permits examination of the influences among pairs of developments only, when in reality it is often the case that it is the joint effect of two or more developments that affects some other event. Moreover, at best, the approach is a casuistic one that attempts to build a theoretical system out of a mosaic of individual sparks of insight without necessarily producing an overall understanding of the causalities that characterize the subject domain in question.

Actual trial applications will have to determine whether, on balance, the systems orientation of this method outweighs its simplistic features in importance.

It may be noted, in this context, that the system-dynamics approach, as it was applied by Dennis Meadows et al. (1972) to the world resources problem posed by the Club of Rome, can well be viewed as a cross-impact model of certain trends (population, food production, pollution, and the like). That model, suggestive though it is, suffers from the shortcoming of not including events in addition to trends. If the model were extended so as to incorporate events such as technological breakthroughs or governmental interventions, it would gain in realism, and its value as a forecasting and policy-testing tool might increase immensely.

There is one general point that should be made here that applies to any theory-building attempt in the social sciences but is particularly pertinent in the case of a cross-impact analysis. I am referring to the fact that there are circumstances under which subjective social indices or, in the case at hand, subjective political indices can have considerable utility. The social-indicator movement is replete with instances in which an attempt is made to capture an intuitive concept in terms of a set of carefully defined objective indicators (e.g., "the quality of education" in terms of "teacher-to-pupil ratio", "number of college graduates", and so on), but we are often aware of the artificiality and inadequacy of such attempts. When using a cross-impact approach, since we are dealing with intuitive expertise in any case, we may as well forego the cumbersome process of translating subjective indices into corresponding sets of objective indicators and deal directly with the original, intuitive concepts. Examples of such concepts in the foreign relations field are "degree of belligerency" (of a nation), "level of technology", "degree of democracy", and so on, none of which lends itself to direct, objective measurement, but all of which are capable of intuitive estimation once some reasonable scale of measurement has been introduced. The use of such indices, it will be noted, is entirely in keeping with the epistemological style of the cross-impact approach, which after all seeks to accomplish a systematization of intuitive judgmental information.

Turning now to applications to foreign-policy planning, this, like planning in any other area, requires the following ingredients:

- An inventory of the current situation, in terms of appropriate objective indicators and subjective indices, including past time series to indicate trend directions.
- The identification of possible futures, in terms of scenarios of event sequences and trend changes, that may come about if no deliberate interventive action is taken. Since the number of such scenarios can literally be infinite, it may be convenient to select a relatively small set of "representative scenarios", in the sense that any actual scenario is sufficiently close, for planning purposes, to one

of the representative ones so that policies and plans designed to cope with these representative contingencies can reasonably be expected to be adequate for any contingency that may arise.

- A statement of policy, in terms of priorities among general goals to be achieved.
- A statement of objectives in pursuit of these goals, formulated in terms of specific events to be brought about or of specific trend levels to be achieved.
- The identification, including the invention, of actions that may be taken in pursuit of such objectives.
- An assessment of the costs (monetary and other) of such contemplated actions, at various levels of intensity of enactment, including an estimate of "cost cross-impacts" (i.e., of savings, if any, accruing from the joint implementation of several actions).
- The selection, within given resource constraints, of alternative action programs.
- The determination of an optimal program among those selected.

The planning process, as laid out here, can clearly benefit from the techniques described earlier. Since judgment is involved at all stages, the Delphi technique can be invoked whenever it is felt that the judgment of more than one person should be utilized. This may apply particularly to the statement of objectives, the identification of actions for pursuing the objectives, and the estimation of the costs of such actions. Even when it comes to inventing actions, and perhaps especially then, the Delphi approach can be helpful; for strategic moves suggested by individual planners can thus be conveniently submitted to their peers for evaluation in terms of feasibility, desirability, and cost.

A potential role for the cross-impact technique in the planning process may be seen in the development of noninterventive scenarios, leading to the identification of a set of representative scenarios that provide a planning benchmark, and in the testing of alternative action programs for the purpose of singling out an optimal one among them.

The techniques described here thus have considerable potential utility. It is still an open question whether their present quality, or the quality they may eventually acquire through continuing improvement, is high enough to justify their employment in the context of international relations forecasting and, by implication, in foreign-policy technology. ■

53 OBJECTIVES OF A THEORY OF NATIONAL-SECURITY PLANNING[3]

The following brief essay, written in 1948 and thus long before any of the specific techniques of futures research had been thought of, contains some concepts which later turned out to be of some utility in the search for effective methods of long-range planning in the public sector. Some of the ideas

3. From a Rand Corporation memorandum, G4-MW-260 (dated July 1948), under that title.

contained in this paper were no doubt influenced by conversations I had at the time with John D. Williams, under whose guidance I was working at the then nascent Rand Corporation.

53.1 Principal Factors Involved in Planning

The purpose of a theory of national security planning is not to tell the national policymaker what to plan but rather to aid him in how to plan. National planning consists in the formulation of alternative courses of action, in an appraisal of the merits of the alternatives in the light of the national objectives, and in making a decision in favor of one of the alternatives. Consequently, the principal factors involved in planning are these:

- the underlying values that constitute our national security, or with the furtherance of which our national security is to be concerned;
- the possible alternative courses of action in a given situation;
- the judgment involved in making a choice among these alternatives; and
- the use of authority to take whatever action is called for by this choice.

Some comments on these four factors will be given in the four following sections.

53.2 Underlying Values

A decision is based on a preference for one among several alternative courses of action. This preference, in turn, must flow from value considerations—national values in the case of decisions concerning national security and military values in the narrower case of strictly military decisions. Increments in these values, or at any rate a preservation of these values, may be looked upon as the objectives behind our decisions.

The national values are determined, in a manner requiring further study, by the preferences of the individuals constituting the nation. These personal values may, for instance, be described in terms of the four freedoms proclaimed in the Atlantic Charter or, more simply, in terms of an adequate standard of living and an adequate standard of civil liberties.

The level of attainment of personal values may be called "individual satisfaction". An action or event may be said to have a certain "individual worth" to a certain person, measured by the (actual or expected) increment of his individual satisfaction. The level of attainment of national values may be called "national security", and an increment in national security due to a given action or event represents the latter's "national worth". Similarly we may speak of the "military worth" of an action or event, as representing the resulting increment in (relative) "military strength".

The six terms just introduced call for strict definition. It would be desirable to define them in such a manner that the three notions of worth are numerical measures of utilities in the sense of the theory of games; a minimum requirement, on the other hand, would be that they impart to the possible events in a given situation a total order, so that of any two events A and B it is clear which has greater worth or whether they are of equal worth.

A considerable amount of conceptual analysis as well as empirical study of preferences will have to be carried out before satisfactory definitions of these terms are obtained. In particular, the problem of defining national security in terms of individual satisfaction is one of extreme difficulty, since neither a method of averaging nor one of accepting a majority vote appears to yield a satisfactory concept of national utility. Possibly, if attempts to define national security directly in terms of individual satisfaction should fail, an indirect method may have to be used, whereby a group of experts would define national security in a manner best suited, in *their* judgment, to take proper account of individual satisfactions. Another problem is the relation of military superiority to national security. The former presumably can best be defined in terms of our ability to ward off damage inflicted on us by an enemy and to reduce his capacity of damaging us in the future (rather than in terms of the damage we can do to him). If this suggestion for defining military superiority is accepted, then it becomes necessary to establish the precise relationship between "damage" (to us) and national security.

53.3 Alternatives Calling for Decisions

A decision may concern anything from an overall strategy (of warfare or peacefare) to an individual action. In many instances the alternatives confronting the decision maker are obvious. It is important to realize, however, that just as often this is not the case, so that it may take a great deal of ingenuity to recognize the potentialities of a situation; and in assessing the qualifications, say, of a general, his imaginativeness in this respect may well outweigh in importance his ability to decide in favor of the correct alternative—not because the final decision is of minor importance but because the choice of an alternative may become obvious once that alternative has been recognized as such.

An important distinction between two types of decision may be pointed out here, namely, between what may be called "absolute decisions" and "conditional decisions". The former are to the effect that such and such an action be taken; the latter merely direct that a certain action be taken *if* such and such a situation is encountered. The authority to make decisions of these two types is usually vested in different persons, and more will have to be said about this below, particularly with reference to the question concerning which decisions are capable of automatization.

In the case of absolute decisions, the alternatives are often obvious, while conditional decisions are apt to make higher demands on the intuitive power of the decision maker to foresee the possible alternatives that may arise.

53.4 *Judgment Involved in Decisions*

A choice between given alternative actions would require no judgment if there were a clear-cut definition of the national and military worth of an action. However, the best one can hope for regarding a definition of worth is likely to be a criterion stated in terms of expected consequences of the proposed action. This at once introduces probability considerations in the form of observational estimates of the actual situation, anticipation of the opponent's counteraction, prediction of consequences, and so forth.

Thus there is good cause for the decision maker to avail himself of a staff of experts, who can advise him in a variety of ways: They can supply intelligence regarding the present state of affairs (including possibly the present intentions of an opponent); they can forecast future events that are likely to happen independently of the decision at hand; and they can predict the respective consequences of various contemplated courses of action.

Military and national worth, as construed here, do not attach to a state of affairs as such but rather to a change in a given state of affairs. If the salient features of a situation of conflict (armed or peaceful) can be described in terms of several parameters, some of these parameters may be under the control of one opponent, the rest under the other's. A change in the situation is then determined by a pair of decisions, one by each opponent, regarding the values of the parameters, and to speak of the military worth of one opponent's decision by itself may be without meaning. In this case we have a typical game situation, the payoff being the military worth of a pair of strategies. (The game need not be zero-sum or even constant-sum, since the military worths for the two opponents may not be linearly related.) Many tactical situations are undoubtedly of this type; questions of military or economic strategy, on the other hand, lend themselves less readily to an interpretation of this kind, and the precise extent of the applicability of the theory of games is an open problem.

Whenever the planner is confronted with a situation in which the theory of games is applicable, he will need among his "expert advisers" a mathematician (possibly in the form of a computing machine) and a chance mechanism—the former to compute on the basis of game theory the strategy yielding maximal expected worth, the latter to make random decisions within the prescriptions of the chosen (mixed) strategy.

53.5 *The Structure of Authority*

Ideally the decision process could be completely automatic. For this to be the case it would be necessary that:

- the national values be set down once and for all in a national constitution;
- in a situation calling for a decision, the relevant intelligence be made available instantly;

- all feasible alternatives be determined automatically (with the understanding that such an alternative may be a mixed strategy in the game-theory sense);
- the expected consequences of each alternative be computed by machines;
- the worth of each alternative, in view of its consequences, be evaluated automatically on the basis of the given national values; and
- the alternative having greatest worth be chosen and put into effect.

In none of these six respects has the ideal situation even approximately been attained. In practice, therefore, the place of what should be automatic decisions is taken by a chain of decisions carried out by decision makers appointed and authorized to make such decisions.

These decisions include stipulations of national values, by interpretation or decree, by representatives of the judiciary and legislative branches of government. Next we have decisions in the form of broad statements of policy by the president and his cabinet. These are again subject to interpretation on the part of commanding generals and officials in charge, who translate them into directives usually taking the form of conditional decisions. On the working level (which may not be reached directly but possibly through a long chain of command), a final interpretation takes place regarding whether the conditions required by the conditional decision handed down are in fact present, resulting at last in an absolute decision and corresponding action.

This well-known and rather complicated structure of decision-making authority is a far cry from any automatic decision process, and it would be an illusion to expect any fundamental deviations from this system in the near future. But just because this is so, it becomes of prime importance to inspect the present set-up very closely with a view to improvements in the direction, if not of automation, then at least of speeding up the decision process.

Speediness of decision has in many fields become a crucial matter. In order to accelerate the decision process it might not be out of place to conduct what is known in the industry as a time-study analysis. In particular, when a decision maker is called upon to act, it happens only too often that he finds himself in need of expert advice, which itself may have to be based on lengthy empirical studies. It is obvious that these studies should be initiated in anticipation of their demand; yet this is frequently not the case, even when the need might have been foreseen.

Apart from a gradual increase in efficiency due to an improved timing pattern for the components entering the decision process, it may not be too early to make a survey of the points in the decision structure at which eventually—namely, with the arrival of push-button warfare—a radical reform will become a matter of absolute necessity. These changes will have to be of two types: automatization and decentralization. The need for the former will arise because the approach of high-speed missiles with atomic warheads will barely leave time for identification and counteraction initiated automatically by electronic devices; the latter because the central links in the authority pattern may have been eliminated by previous enemy action. ■

I conclude this chapter with a set of somewhat aphoristic statements on the subject of deterrence. Though written a quarter of a century ago, they still are relevant to the debate on this topic that continues to be controversial.

54 DETERRENCE[4]

(1) Deterrence, as applied to warfare, relies on the potential enemy's belief that, should he start a war, retaliation would be so heavy that the probable outcome would compare unfavorably with what he might have achieved without war.

(2) To accomplish increased deterrence, therefore, it is necessary either to strengthen the enemy's belief that continued peace will be more rewarding or to strengthen his belief that aggression will be severely punished.

(3) The former alternative, which emphasizes peaceful prospects, must be well distinguished from appeasement, which affords little if any deterrence in the long run. Appeasement involves a sacrifice without positive recompense on the appeaser's part; it is thus in the nature of a ransom payment, having at best a delaying effect. A deterrent policy based on the expected payoffs of continued peace, on the other hand, must call for cooperative efforts entered into by both sides for mutual benefit.

(4) The advent of nuclear weapons has had two effects, and it is debatable to what extent they offset one another as far as the probable long-run implications are concerned: It has raised the catastrophic aspects of all-out war, but it has by mutual deterrence enormously lowered the probability of the occurrence of such a war.

(5) Mutual military deterrence from nuclear war among the central powers encourages peripheral wars for, to the extent to which it is effective, it reduces the fear that a small war might grow beyond control into an all-out central war.

(6) Deterrence for peripheral war, therefore, is a separate problem and should be given separate attention. It is in fact becoming the more important problem, since central deterrence is already moderately well established, whereas the risk remains that a peripheral war, after all, may inadvertently turn gradually into a central war.

(7) As for peripheral deterrence, our policy has tended to go to one of two extremes, namely, either to underplay our willingness to intervene in the peripheral theater or to threaten central retaliation. Neither of these attitudes is compatible with a policy of deterrence. This is obvious for the first (Hitler's attack on Western Europe and the invasion of South Korea being clear examples); and the second is only too readily put down to bluffing, since a peripheral situation will rarely involve a sufficiently vital interest to warrant initial reply by all-out central war with all its catastrophic implications.

4. From a Rand Corporation research memorandum, RM-1882 (dated March 1957), under that title.

(8) For peripheral deterrence we must rely on an expressed willingness and a demonstrated capability of instant peripheral intervention in the case of aggression, being careful to avoid a tie-in with central deterrence but otherwise keeping the enemy guessing as to precisely what form of military response to aggression he should expect.

(9) The belief, on the part of the enemy, on which military deterrence rests can be broken down into two parts: his belief that the deterrer has the capability of heavy retaliation, and his belief that the deterrer may have the intention of carrying it out.

(10) Since deterrence is a matter of belief as well as of fact, it follows that it is not logically necessary that deterrence be based solely on an actual capability and an actual intent.

(11) Actual capability is more accessible to enemy intelligence than is actual intent. Moreover, the former is highly stable, while the latter can change overnight.

(12) The enemy intelligence apparatus cannot be expected to be greatly deluded regarding actual U.S. capabilities. Feints can have only marginal effects, slightly increasing or decreasing enemy estimates of U.S. capabilities.

(13) Feints regarding U.S. intentions (say, by diplomatic maneuvers or planted leaks) are more promising, on the other hand, and careful consideration must be given to the strategic implications of this possibility.

(14) An enemy, faced with the possibility of war, will weigh his chances of winning if he attacks against those if he should be attacked. Deterrence, in this case, will be ineffective if the enemy is led to conclude that retaliation, though massive, would still give him a chance while he would have none were he to be attacked first. Hence the very opposite of deterrence is achieved by demonstrating a high aggressive capability that, at the same time, appears to be vulnerable if the enemy gets in the first strike.

(15) Conversely, deterrence would be highest if the enemy could be convinced that he who strikes last strikes best. While it is unlikely that the first strike can ever be made to appear disadvantageous, one of the most important aspects of a deterrence policy must be to minimize (actually and by feint) the reduction that one's retaliatory capability would experience as a result of a first strike by the enemy.

(16) Public pronouncements emphasizing the dependence of instant retaliation on democratic processes of government (congressional and presidential approval) are at variance with a policy of deterrence; so is any public discussion stressing the response delay caused by the intricacies of the military decision-making apparatus.

(17) The seemingly autonomous position of the Strategic Air Command, to the extent to which it may succeed in convincing an enemy of its relative independence of democratic decision-making processes, constitutes a powerful support for a policy of deterrence.

(18) It is a matter of controversy whether the bombing of a nation's civil-

ian population causes a rise or a decline in that nation's will and ability to resist. A policy of deterrence should foster the belief that the effect would in fact be a rise (the "wounded buffalo" hypothesis).

(19) In order to demonstrate a high retaliatory capability (even to ourselves), it is necessary to prepare detailed war plans emphasizing the reprisal effect. There is no reason why such deterrent war plans should actually be carried out once their motivation, namely deterrence, has failed.

(20) Deterrent war plans either emphasize the destruction of cities or rely on the inevitability of high urban damage and thus increasingly promote a spirit of indifference about the choice of precise targets. There is a danger that the deterrence motivation makes us lose sight of the prime goal of a war plan, namely, that of winning the war in the sense of best defending our national values and institutions.

(21) If we had nothing but a war plan based on the assumption of an inviolate retaliatory force and designed to produce deterrence by the horror of urban annihilation (and one sometimes wonders if this is not all we have), we should be committing a double mistake: Since our retaliatory force is in fact not invulnerable, such a plan would invite rather than deter a first strike by the enemy, who would thereby force us to adopt a makeshift strategy derived from the hypothetical war plan by adaptation to the real situation; moreover, by carrying the original deterrent intent to the absurdity of locking the barn after the steed has been stolen we might fail to salvage anything by insistence on revenge rather than self-protection.

The main points in the foregoing considerations may be summarized in the following maxims: Demonstrate a flexible and highly invulnerable retaliatory capability. Neither state precisely nor understate the retaliatory intentions. Base actual war plans on the assumption not of an inviolate base of operations and a deterrent target system but of a partly damaged base and a target system chosen to minimize destruction at home. Promote peripheral deterrence separately. Emphasize attractive alternatives to war and thus tie in a deterrence strategy with a positive policy toward peaceful international pursuits of mutual benefit. ■

The foregoing little "editorial" clearly does not in itself represent an illustration of the application of futures-research techniques to planning. What prompted me nevertheless to include it is my conviction that there is little point in engaging in any kind of long-term public-sector planning unless we include in it some effort to reduce the likelihood of nuclear war. The above section merely attempts to sort out some of the terminology involved in discussions of deterrence and, I hope, may help in providing some of the conceptual basis for conducting a thoroughgoing futures analysis of the subject matter, using Delphi for both factual and normative forecasting and using simulation gaming for testing alternative deterrence strategies.

I may add that, in one factual respect, the basic assumptions of today's deterrence debate have changed from what they were when the foregoing statements were written, namely, regarding the matter of so-called parity. Once the nuclear arsenals on both sides have reached the enormous sizes extant today, we need to realize the fact—rarely acknowledged by the advocates of further military build-up—that, for deterrence purposes, the realm of sharply diminished marginal returns has long been reached, and it may even be argued that our build-up of the nuclear stockpile to its present size has been counter-productive. All that is needed for effective nuclear deterrence is an awareness on the part of a potential aggressor that, even after he has carried out a massive first strike, there is a high probability that we will still have a few missiles left that are deliverable on his cities. If, as in fact is the case, we have a nuclear arsenal vastly in excess of that basic deterrent posture, the enemy can merely conclude that our intentions are, more than to deter aggression, to prevail in an extended nuclear conflict, with the result of exacerbating the arms race. Parity, for purely deterrent purposes, is achieved when a few dozen warheads can be expected, with high probability, to survive a first enemy strike, and that capability is assured even when, numerically, our stockpile of missiles is smaller by an order of magnitude than the enemy's.

Chapter XI

On the Future of the Economy

Closely related, through cause and effect, with the previous topic, international relations, is economics. Much of diplomacy these days, especially between nations fortunate enough to have leaders endowed with a modicum of sanity, is concerned with the elimination of economic friction and the establishment of modes of economic interaction that are of mutual benefit.

A nation's domestic economic problems, too, are largely inseparable from global ones, as evidenced once again by the current depression afflicting all countries of the world with virtually no exception.

The basic reasons for the economic turmoil throughout the world are not difficult to see and have been stated often. The economies of the developed nations are suffering, and will continue to suffer for some time, from the effects of two simultaneous, related transitions, namely, from an industrial to a postindustrial, or service-oriented society, and from human-machine cooperation to increasingly robot-oriented methods of production and, eventually, also of service operations. This transition is aggravated by the increasing scarcity of mineral raw materials and, at least during the 1980s, of new sources of energy, as well as by the unwillingness of the working population, long spoiled by decades of satisfied rising expectations, temporarily to forego further increases in their living standard in the interest of possibly order-of-magnitude improvements at a later time. The economic problems in the developing countries, though different, are equally severe, if not more so. There, neither the modernization of agriculture nor the acceptance of birth control is proceeding fast enough to avert large-scale malnutrition and even famine conditions, and the situation is much aggravated by two factors: the enormous rise in the price of petroleum, which they simply cannot afford but need more than ever, and the phenomenon of instant worldwide communication, which causes people in the poor countries to have unsatisfiable aspirations to living standards comparable to those in the rich countries rather than to relish the (often considerable) improvement over conditions in their own country a generation or two ago.

There are a number of reasons why the subject of economics is ripe for the kind of analysis that futures research has to offer. It clearly is an area in need of a systems approach, and that it requires an interdisciplinary futures orientation goes without saying. It is involved in, and even controls, so many aspects of our society that economic planning will inevitably have to concern itself with an operating environment that may undergo sizable changes over time, a fact that makes economics a prime candidate for futures research. Among the social sciences, economics unquestionably is the most quantitatively oriented and thus lends itself particularly well to some of the quantitative techniques offered by Delphi and cross-impact analyses. Also, because of the presence of economic actors with partly opposed interests, it is a subject that practically invites examination through operational gaming. Perhaps most important, the numerous attempts on the part of economists in recent decades to develop theories by which to explain, predict, and control economic phenomena (such as inflation, unemployment, and international trade and competition, to name a few) have not been singularly successful. Consequently, even those who may look on the promise of futures-research methods with some skepticism may decide "to try everything once" and, in this spirit, give futures researchers a chance to show what they might be able to contribute to the resolution of some of the pressing economic issues of our time.

In this chapter, I include, first, a joint paper with my former Rand colleague, Ed Quade, on the possible application of gaming techniques to the problems of developing countries. This is followed by the description of a game dealing with the world economy, which I constructed while at the International Institute for Applied Systems Analysis (IIASA). The final section is devoted to a detailed proposal, written for the University of Southern California's Center for Futures Research, to study the American economy through gaming.

55 STUDYING A DEVELOPING ECONOMY THROUGH OPERATIONAL GAMING[1]

55.1 Introduction

This paper considers the possible use of operational gaming, or simulation involving human players, to examine an economy as a whole. It is our belief that this operations-research technique could become an extremely useful tool for the study of a developing economy. In the present state of the art, however, it is not going to provide, with confidence, direct recommendations on what to do about matters of national policy. Rather it is an educational device, providing both ideas and insights, useful for the generation and preliminary comparison of alternative economic policies.

Operational gaming, like other operations-research techniques, undoubtedly is most fruitful when applied with a clear objective in mind to well-structured problems based on abundant data. Such a situation is more likely to be found within an industry or a single firm. Nevertheless, our present

1. A Rand paper, P-2718 (1963), by O. Helmer and E. S. Quade.

discussion of gaming techniques will be entirely in terms of their applications to national economic planning. We believe this approach to hold a greater promise in this difficult area than any other available technique.

55.2 The Role of Operations Research

In principle, the problems to which operations research may be applied in the economies of the so-called developing countries are similar to and no more challenging than their counterparts in the highly developed countries. On the other hand, while, in the highly developed countries, custom, the belief in laissez-faire, and the vast intricacies of the national economy ordinarily restrict the applications of operations research to the "tactical" scale of economic planning within an industry or firm, the less sophisticated structure of a newly emerging economy and a greater faith in planning greatly enhance the chances of employing operations research on a "strategic" level. One may even hope that, if operations research could be successfully applied to the analysis of developing economies, the insights gained might provide useful leads concerning the application of similar methods to more highly developed nations. Thus analysts primarily interested in the exploration of highly sophisticated national economies may be well advised to divert some of their attention to the study of more primitive economies and to use the experience gained in modeling the latter to achieve eventual progress in predicting economic effects in more intricate contexts.

Before planning can be applied effectively on a national scale—say, to do long-range resource allocation for the general advancement of an emerging economy or to determine foreign-aid policy for such an economy—it would seem to be a clear prerequisite that the planner have a thorough understanding of how the economy works as a whole, not merely how it works on an institutional or on an industrial scale. One would want to be able to predict, for example, how economic measures, applied nationwide, such as tax cuts, or subsidies, or price controls, or tariffs, or interest rates, would influence the workings of the economy as a whole and how they would differentially affect the various sectors of the economy. Unfortunately, such predictions cannot be made with great assurance. Most economists attribute the difficulties to the many factors and complex relationships involved. Some, however, feel this is due to the lack of a consistent theory.

If an adequate theory of national economic phenomena were indeed lacking, it could be precisely for that reason that operations research is being called into action. Industrial and military operations research also has had to function without the benefit of a comprehensive accepted theoretical foundation. It has done this with great success, relying on the systematic utilization of a large body of only partly articulated and largely intuitive judgment by experts in the field. The standard operations-research technique for such utilization is that of constructing an appropriate model of the situation; such a model—by introducing a precise structure and terminology—serves primarily as an effective means of communication and thereby, through a feedback process, helps the expert to arrive at a clearer understanding of his subject matter. The hope is that the same approach will meet with similar success in the area of national economic phenomena.

55.3 Simulation

The economist does not have, and cannot be expected to have, the precise and flexible means available to the physical scientist for testing his models experimentally. He can seldom, for example, experiment with an actual economy. He can, of course, make good use of experiments that are conducted by the economic system itself. That is, he can search out and observe situations in which the variables behave somewhat in the way he would expect them to behave in an actual experiment. In addition, he has other techniques available; one of these, "simulation", may provide a substitute means for exploring the implications of his theories and for comparing alternative hypotheses.

Simulation, although relatively new in wide-scale applications, is an established operations-research technique, which uses quasi-experimentation in an artificial environment as a substitute for actual experimentation in the real world. The more the artificial environment is representative of the real world—that is, the better it simulates the relevant factors—the more reliably will a theory about the real world be tested in the simulative experiment and the easier will it be to apply insights gained to an understanding of the real situation under study.

The defects of simulation are that it is not ordinarily an efficient technique and that it yields only a quasi-empirical form of knowledge, inferior to the functional relationships built up through the more traditional approach of using an analytical model. Its outstanding virtue is that it can be used to tackle seemingly unmanageable or previously untouched problems where a traditional analytic formulation appears infeasible. Simulation is a device appropriate to use before one has an adequate theory, for it provides a means of using the intuition and advice of experts in a systematic fashion.

If a reasonably adequate simulation of the national economy of one of the "developing" countries were achieved, one might, for example, use it to examine a given development plan for consistency and technical feasibility. This would be accomplished by observing within the model the effects of changes in the plan or of alternatives to it on such things as personal income or gross national product. Thereby a clearer insight into the nature of the underlying problems might be achieved and some ideas might begin to suggest themselves as to the sort of measures likely to be helpful in the real world.

55.4 Computer Simulation

A number of attempts have been made to simulate economic systems using high-speed digital computing equipment (for an example, see Holland,

1962). The ideal is to devise and program a model of the national economy under study that is complete in every important detail and responds to stimuli provided by the operators exactly like the real one but on a much condensed time scale. Practical considerations, of course, impose many simplifications in the representation of the economy, requiring the use of aggregate variables and the omission of many details. One possible approach is first to program separately the operation of each of the several sectors of the economy (consumer, industrial, financial, government, agricultural, labor, and so on), then to attempt to express their interrelationships, and, finally, to try to tie the various sectors together in a combined program. Carefully done, this can lead to a computer program that represents the workings of an economy in much more realistic detail than any model that can be examined by conventional analytic techniques.

Computer simulation is open to a number of objections:

(i) Certain human factors, of great importance in the real world and hence not negligible, are extremely difficult to quantify: pride, loyalty, resistance to change, religious prejudice, and so on. Elaborate models adapted for high-speed computers are not likely to take these factors into consideration with proper emphasis and subtlety.

(ii) Assuming that our knowledge of economics is sufficiently firm so that in principle we know how to effect the simulation, it requires several years and the work of many people to program the model in realistic detail. It would thus not only be expensive but, more important, rigid. This inflexibility may be too high a price to pay for the precision with which a computer-programmed model represents an economy. The theory on which the model is based, after all, could not be expected to be in completely final form but would inevitably call for successive corrections indicated by more up-to-date information or suggested by the learning process that parallels the application of the model. Such corrections would be likely to require elaborate and time-consuming changes in the computer program.

(iii) The learning process just referred to is hindered rather than enhanced by the use of a computer model. It is in the nature of a high-speed computing process that only highly selected stages of the computations are visible to an observer while most of the intermediate steps remain hidden in the "black box" of the machine. Hence the direct influence of variables on one another, the knowledge of which is crucial in any intuitive reappraisal of a given theory, is generally not observable but must be inferred indirectly.

In view of these limitations, it is questionable whether, with our present knowledge of economic theory, any computer simulation, no matter how elaborate, can answer questions such as:

(a) In initiating development, should emphasis be on investment and capital or on the attitudes and motivations of the people? Are there forces that can catalyze economic growth in an underdeveloped country?

(b) How does an underdeveloped country begin economic growth? Are limited

capital, low productivity, inadequate rates of saving and investment the dominating constraints, or are they the attitudes and motivations of the people?
(c) What effects do government regulations in the form of taxes, subsidies, and restrictions on foreign investment and trade have on the economy?
(d) If the country is receiving foreign military assistance, how can the latter be modified, without significantly reducing military effectiveness, to generate substantially improved economic (and political) side effects?

What is needed is some scheme that can give proper weight to the difficult-to-quantify social and political factors. One possibility is to introduce human players into the simulation.

55.5 *Gaming*

In analyses of major questions of public policy, it may well be worth the sacrifice of precision to gain other benefits. Among these would be a representation which at least potentially—though perhaps with inadequate emphasis—included the political, economic, social, and military factors relevant to the analysis that might at first be overlooked or thought to be of insufficient importance. Another aspect it would be desirable to take into account is the possibility of "feedback" of the type mentioned earlier which might lead one to want to modify the model in accordance with changes in the theory on which it is based. For the "developing" countries, where the situation is poorly structured and where we have little firm knowledge of the existing facts and relationships, a possible approach would be through an unsophisticated simulation, or "game", in which the various sectors of the economy would be represented by human simulators in the form of specialized experts. These experts would be expected, in acting out their roles, not so much to play a competitive game against one another but to use their intuition as experts to simulate as best they could the attitudes and consequent decisions of their real-life counterparts. It may well be necessary, in order to do justice to the intangible intricacies of the situation, to rely on the varied expertise of several specialists (e.g., an anthropologist in addition to an economist) for obtaining an acceptable degree of realism.

One objective of such an "unsophisticated" simulation would be to learn how to model an economy in the first place as well as to draw conclusions about the economy from an existing model. Thus, the underlying game structure would, at least at first, be left flexible. Only when there is reasonably general agreement about the basic economic forces and trends would they be built firmly into the model; when there is not, we would attempt, in playing the game, to examine various economic hypotheses and rely on the considered expert judgment of the players to arrive at tentative conclusions. Thus the construction of the final model would become part of a mutual learning process, utilizing synthetic experience in lieu of actual experience when the latter is unavailable or insufficient.

Comparative rather than absolute results are the aim. Emphasis on this more modest aim provides an important hedge against mistaken assumptions about unknown parameters (especially those relating to human factors mentioned before) which are highly important in the real world.

The formal structure of a simulation exercise in the form of an operational game would automatically subject any model or theory of the operation of the countries' economies to detailed critical review. Since the environment of a game forces the players to take active roles, they are compelled to take specific and concrete actions in situations in which a person sitting in his office or participating in a discussion around a conference table might fail to consider the full range of possibilities or to carry through the argument beyond the opening steps. It is easy to be vague in talking about theory or doctrine, but a game shares with the analytically formulated computer model the quality of concreteness—there can be no vague moves in a well-formulated and well-run game. Moreover, controversial parts of the model that are likely to be buried and forgotten in a computer program remain visible.

Simulative gaming of the kind referred to above has been successfully employed in the past, though applied to different subject matters. We may mention the following three studies to illustrate the degree of sophistication of subject that can be captured by such relatively unsophisticated methods:

- An examination by Charles Wolf and a staff of military and scientific experts of the effectiveness of military-assistance programs, based on limited-war gaming. (See Wolf, 1962.)
- Cold-war gaming, in which the players simulate the decisions of heads of government and thus jointly engage in modeling certain international relations. Such gaming was first used at Rand and has subsequently been carried out at the Massachusetts Institute of Technology, at Northwestern University, and most recently at the Western Behavioral Institute at La Jolla. (See de Sola Pool, 1961; Goldhamer and Speier, 1959.)
- Military R & D and procurement gaming, exemplified by the SAFE (Strategy and Force Evaluation) game developed at Rand, in which the players simulate the peacetime planning activities of the defense establishments of two major powers, their prime concern being the development, procurement, and operation of military weapon systems. (See Helmer and Brown, 1962.)

All of these efforts have certain features in common: The use of computers is minimal or even absent; reliance is on intuitive expertise of specialists; emphasis is on clearer problem formulation and on merely a first survey of possible solutions rather than on obtaining definitive answers.

55.6 Gaming a National Economy

We would now like to indicate some suggestions for how one might go about designing a simulative game model for the purpose of investigating economic problems on a national scale. It should be understood that these suggestions are tentative and should be interpreted as merely indicative of the spirit in which we would like to see this problem approached and are approaching it ourselves.

The first question that arises in attempting to game a national economy is what roles are to be assigned to players. The decisions of the players are to simulate economic decisions in the real world and thus are of two types: One is the deliberate decision by single individuals or groups acting as individuals, such as corporations, labor unions, the national government, or parliament. The other type of player decision simulates the aggregate effect of the multitude of decisions made by the members of an entire economic sector, such as agriculture, industrial labor, or consumer goods manufacture. In the first role, a player's decisions would be relatively unconstrained; in the second role, his "decisions" would not so much represent free acts of choice but estimates of how a certain economic sector might respond to a new situation.

For gaming purposes it would seem convenient to aggregate the economy into a relatively small number of sectors, say eight to ten, and to let a player (or a weighted combination of players) correspond to each such sector; in addition, certain selected institutions may each be represented by a player. A possible breakdown of an economy into sectors might look as follows:

(1) agriculture
(2) mining
(3) labor
(4) power industry
(5) basic industry
(6) investment goods industry
(7) consumer goods industry
(8) services
(9) foreign commerce

In addition to the players representing these sectors of the economy, depending on the particular problem under study, there will have to be players representing the national government, foreign investors, the voting public, or even the revolutionary underground. In particular, a government player might be needed to study the effect of governmental regulation of the economy, a player representing foreign investment to determine the effect on the economy of specific allocations of such investment. An alternative to handling these influences via the decisions made by the players assigned to these tasks is to leave these manipulations of the economy entirely to the control team running the game and to observe the effect of predetermined operations by the domestic government or the foreign investor through the reactions of the sector players.

Actually, of course, the precise lineup of players and what they are to represent depends critically on the particular economy being investigated and the question under study. A pregaming phase in which the sectors and initial conditions are assigned somewhat arbitrarily and a few preliminary moves are planned is likely to be very helpful for the later, more permanent, formulation. During this phase, the important questions about aims and objectives that determine the whole character of the exercise can be discussed.

For example: Is the aim in the development to become economically independent or to become prosperous—and what does that mean?

A next step in the construction of a game model would be to obtain an input-output matrix reflecting the initial annual flows of goods among the sectors of the economy. If no appropriate reliable statistics are available, estimates by qualified experts would have to take their place (perhaps best obtained through a mini-Delphi procedure).

Next, and perhaps most difficult, would be the derivation of a production function for each sector, describing the annual production as a function of inputs (including labor) and investment. Here, in particular, heavy reliance on expert judgment would be almost inevitable. In cases where a general acceptable production function could not be obtained, it might be necessary—as the game proceeds—to defer to expert judgment in estimating the production resulting from a particular combination of inputs and investments. One would hope, in that case, that such casuistic assessment of production would eventually lead to the construction of general production functions.

Real-life factors affecting the economy in the form of taxation and of legislative supports and constraints would have to be reflected in the rules of the game. Similarly, natural effects (especially climatic) might be simulated by appropriate randomization schemes incorporated in the rules. These rules, incidentally, need not be static but can be modified from play to play or even during play.

Using either ready-made production functions or *ad hoc* production estimates, the players could go through the motions of operating the economy over a series of annual cycles, each making periodic decisions on such things as prices to be charged for their products, purchases of inputs, and reinvestment of profits. In this way one might hope to gain insight into the probable "normal" development of the unmanipulated economy or to arrive at broad-brush productions of the effect of deliberate manipulation by legislative means or foreign investment.

Incidentally, players with definite beliefs regarding the workings of the economy would be able to examine their hypotheses quasi-experimentally, with the possibility of receiving salutory feedback from observing the consequences of their simulative actions. Conversely, a feedback in the opposite direction might be made observable in the case of economic policies that have a self-fulfilling component; for instance, a highly pessimistic policymaker might transmit his pessimism to the economy, and thus his beliefs might in fact influence the future course of the economy in a direction that would (unjustifiably) confirm his belief.

It should be noted that the resort to expertise in the construction, the playing, and the administration of such a game is not necessarily a liability but may be an asset. It does, admittedly, make the predictive quality of such an exercise very much a function of the quality of intuitive insight provided by the experts involved. On the other hand, by allowing for the introduction of judgment at every step, this approach provides an opportunity to take into account those human factors usually considered completely intangible. This is true both of the player, who can let his economic decisions be influenced by his appraisal of the human effects of the simulated environment, and of the expert on the control team, who may be called upon to assess the effect of changed economic conditions on the productivity of labor in a given situation. For example, the success or failure of a plan may depend on the assumptions about the mobility of the population and the flexibility in the allocation of materials. For a computer simulation, decisions about these things must be made in advance; in a game they can be made as the need arises.

A great disadvantage of a gaming exercise using human players is the time required to carry it out. In contrast, a computerized simulation can run through thousands of cases in far less time, once it has been programmed. The gaming process can be speeded up by introducing a computer for routine phases; whether this is economical or not depends on the scale of the exercise.

We will readily admit that anyone using the approach we have described can set up some kind of a model in terms of which players can make moves analogous to the operations that take place in an economy. The results, however, may be meaningless or completely misleading if the model does not adequately simulate what it is supposed to. Yet even in the absence of the right numerical input values or of reliable functional relationships, as long as the right qualitative features are present (e.g., dependencies, time lags, nonlinearities, and not readily quantifiable aspects such as human factors), experience in other fields indicates that a great deal of insight can be gained concerning what modes of behavior are likely and what parameters are critical. It is a useful way to uncover alternatives and to organize arguments supporting a particular theory.

55.7 Concluding Remarks

By way of conclusion, we make the following observations.

In considering the possible application of operations research to problems of national planning, one should view any scheme proposed today which promises an immediately usable output with a great deal of skepticism. As expressed by Charles Hitch (1957), "Problems of national economic planning in underdeveloped countries are at least as intricate, as ridden with subtle political and sociological traps, as complicated by plural, interdependent, and conflicting objectives, and therefore as little amenable to current operations-research techniques, narrowly defined, as high-level problems of national security."

As an aid to counseling on high-level problems of national security, it is becoming increasingly clear that "current operations-research techniques, narrowly defined" are not adequate. Piecemeal component optimizations and cost-effectiveness comparisons of competing postures and strategies are extremely useful, but they must be supplemented by an overall treatment in which emphasis is placed on an integrated simultaneous consideration of all the major relevant factors.

It seems reasonable, nevertheless, to look for an approach to national planning that has a capability of development to a point at which it can provide policy guidance in real situations. Our feeling is that the most promising approach is through some form of gaming. The more conventional analytic techniques or simulation by computer program, even though potentially they may have greater validity, are not sufficiently flexible. Moreover, even in cases where they provide correct guidance, they may still be lacking in conviction, for we have the uneasy feeling that any solution to a problem in this area exclusively formulated and solved by outsiders, using what is essentially a "black box", may not be readily accepted as a solution. By contrast, an important aspect of an unsophisticated simulation by the type of gaming we are advocating and trying to formulate, which has not been much exploited, is that the decision maker or his representatives can actually participate.

In the area of national planning, the problems are likely to be ill-formulated and not of the type to which established optimization techniques can be applied without considerable preliminary work, if ever. The operations-research analyst usually tries, using mathematics or logical analysis, to help a client improve his efficiency in a situation in which everyone has a fairly good idea of what "more efficient" means. In contrast, here he is likely to be faced by problems whose difficulties lie in deciding what ought to be done or even in what the problems are rather than in simply how to proceed. In such a situation, far more attention must be devoted to establishing objectives, values, and criteria. The total analysis is thus a complex and untidy procedure, with little emphasis on mathematical models, no possibility of quantitative optimization over the whole problem, and great dependence on considered judgment.

To summarize further, the three main points of our argument are as follows:

(1) Putting people in an appropriate environment provides a means of effective communication and thereby creates an opportunity for the systematic employment of the knowledge and insight of experts with diverse specialities.
(2) A gaming approach establishes a possible means of providing "feedback" from the economy, resulting from the effects of the beliefs about it held by those who are trying to direct its course.
(3) It provides a means of systematically taking into account relatively intangible factors that are compounded of economic, social, political, military, and psychological considerations. ■

Following the publication of the paper reproduced above, its authors carried out a few simple gaming experiments at Rand, using a highly simplified four-sector model of a national economy, each presided over by one player. While the results of these trial runs looked promising (at least to us), we were not able at the time to lay our hands on the resources necessary for a full-size effort.

The game reported on below was not concerned with the exploration of one developing country but sought to simulate, however inadequately, the workings of the global economy. Some of the ideas represented in it clearly have their roots in the earlier work by Quade and myself. I may mention that this game was played quite successfully by an international group of graduate students at IIASA. Even in its still very primitive form it was found to be a highly instructive educational tool.

56 GEM: AN INTERACTIVE SIMULATION MODEL OF THE GLOBAL ECONOMY[2]

56.1 Subject Matter and Purpose of the Game

The GEM game was developed to acquaint the research staff of IIASA with the potentialities of simulation gaming as a preanalytical research tool.

GEM, whose acronymic name stands for Global Economic Model, is a six-person interactive simulation model (or game) intended to generate intuitive insights into the economic interactions among six world regions over the next fifty years.

Each player is responsible for manipulating the economy of one of these regions. To do so, he has to make resource allocation decisions (between sector inputs, capital investment, investment in R&D, and supplies to consumers and to government); in addition, he may trade commodities with the other five participants and conclude long-term agreements with them concerning trades, loans, investments, and technology transfer.

The six regions, designated by the letters S, E, C, O, N, and D, which are intended to resemble very roughly six real-world regions obtained by aggregation from the ten regions of the Mesarovic-Pestel (1974) model, may be characterized as follows:

- S: a highly developed, centrally planned economy with substantial energy resources (the Soviet bloc)
- E: a highly developed market economy with greatly limited energy resources (Western Europe, Australia, and Japan)
- C: a developing, centrally planned economy with substantial energy resources (China)
- O: a small developing market economy with very substantial energy resources (the member countries of OPEC, the Organization of Petroleum Exporting Countries)

2. A paper under this title, by O. Helmer and L. Blencke, was put out as a research report, RR-79-4, by the International Institute for Applied Systems Analysis in 1979. Blencke's role was that of writing the computer program for this game. Some assistance was supplied by Igor Zimin, a Russian economist assigned to IIASA at the time. The above description is based closely on the IIASA report but omits many of the numerical specifics.

N: a highly developed market economy with substantial but inadequate energy resources (North America)

D: a developing economy with underdeveloped energy resources and a rapidly growing population (the developing countries of Latin America, most of Africa, and South and Southeast Asia)

The economic structure of each of these regions is highly aggregated and is represented in terms of eight economic sectors.

The GEM game is played over a simulated fifty-year period, starting with the present. The fifty years are broken up into ten five-year scenes; each scene represents one move cycle in the game.

The purpose of such simulation gaming generally is not so much to solve problems directly as it is to lead to a better intuitive understanding of the problem structure and thereby to help the analyst in the development of models that gradually become more and more appropriate for dealing with the real-world problem situation. Thus a simulation game is preanalytic in nature; it is not intended in itself to be either predictive or decisional. An essential part of the routine of playing a simulation game is a constructive debriefing or review session in which the participants are asked to engage in a self-critique ("What would I do differently if I were to play the game again?") and in a critique of the game ("What numerical inputs or what structural components of the game should be altered in order to achieve greater realism?").

As a result of such inquiries, the game is almost invariably changed in some respects between plays. The gaming activity, therefore, should not be viewed as a series of trial runs of a particular simulation model but as a dynamic process in which a more and more realistic conception of the world gradually evolves. A simulation game must have the built-in capacity for such self-correction.

In order to accommodate such self-corrective amendments, it is important that the game be designed flexibly. While it is usually easy to change numerical inputs within wide limits, it should also be feasible to alter structural features of the model without extensive reprogramming. This is true of many aspects of the GEM game, making it possible, in particular, to adjust the degree of detail (e.g., the number of players, the number of economic sectors, and the length of the basic time unit) as well as the move sequence within each game cycle (i.e., the order in which economic activity-level decisions, international trade, and output allocations are handled).

GEM's primary function is that of a demonstration game (in line with its intended mission at IIASA). It is for this reason that emphasis has been placed not on obtaining the most precise and up-to-date statistics to serve as input data for the six regions considered in GEM but rather on including in the game model as many important factors descriptive of global economic interactions as are compatible with the requirement of keeping the game simple enough to be played easily. GEM in its present form, therefore, should definitely be thought of as a "Mark 1" version. The absence of precision in the initial choice of numerical inputs—if this is considered a defect—can be easily remedied later by substituting more precise data when these become available. With regard to selecting factors for inclusion in the model, special attention was paid to IIASA's particular areas of interest, such as the world food and energy situations.

56.2 Move Sequence

The GEM game is played in ten move cycles, called "scenes", each simulating five years of real time. The record of a particular play of GEM is a scenario, consisting of scene-by-scene descriptions of decisions made by the players as well as of event occurrences (such as technological breakthroughs or discoveries of new basic-resource reserves) and of notable changes in trend values (such as capital investment or labor unrest).

The move structure of each scene is as follows (where P indicates player moves; I, information given to the players; and R, random effects):

I: information on start-of-scene status
P: tentative allocation of resources
I: information on expected output resulting from these allocations
P: definite decisions on activity levels
R: random effects: weather, labor unrest
I: information on actual output
P: world trade and negotiation session
I: updated status information
P: final-supply allocation (to consumers and government)
R: random effects: technological breakthroughs, population increase

It should be particularly noted that, as shown above, the game features certain stochastic elements. Some of these reflect influences entirely exogenous to the model, such as those controlling the weather and the growth of population. Others, such as technological breakthroughs or the amount of labor unrest, are endogenous in the sense that, while they are the result of random (i.e., Monte Carlo) decisions, their probabilities of occurrence can be affected by player actions. The effect of the presence of these stochastic features is that the players have to plan in the face of some uncertainty as to the results of their decisions. In this respect the model differs markedly from standard econometric models, in which economic output is determined solely by input allocations—and it is hoped that it differs in the direction of realism.

56.3 The Economic Sectors

The eight economic sectors, in terms of which the economy of each of GEM's six regions is described, are as follows:

(1) mining (other than fuel)
(2) intermediate products
(3) durable goods
(4) consumption goods (other than food)
(5) food
(6) fuels
(7) electric energy
(8) services

The singling out of food as a separate sector and the decision to have energy represented by two sectors (6 and 7) reflect the special importance attached to long-range planning in these areas at IIASA and elsewhere.

To express input/output transactions among the sectors of the economy, it is convenient—and, in view of the high degree of aggregation, virtually mandatory—to use monetary units in order to be able to add together otherwise incommensurable quantities. Of course, the production process requires certain physical quantities as inputs to obtain a specific physical output, and the monetary value of these inputs and outputs may change as prices fluctuate. A simple way to deal with this situation is to choose a monetary unit and then to define one physical unit of the output of Sector i as that quantity of the ith commodity whose price, at the outset of the game, is one monetary unit. As the monetary unit we choose $1B (one billion dollars).

The operation of the economy is described in terms of an input/output matrix that, for the purposes of GEM plays, can be presented in the format shown in Figure 25. The standard format for an input/output matrix is shown in the left-hand side of the figure. This side of the figure can be filled in either with technical coefficients or with actual flow coefficients. The technical coefficients indicate the physical quantity produced by the sector on the left that has to flow into the sector listed above in order to produce one physical unit of output in that sector. The actual flow coefficients are expressed in monetary units (which, it should be remembered, are initially equal to physical units). When actual flow coefficients are used, the matrix provides an accounting of actual inputs and outputs and of the resultant surplus available for final supplies; that is, each amount entered in the "available for final supply" column is the sum of the three quantities listed in the columns to the left as well as equal to the sum of the five final-supply items listed in the columns to the right.

In order to change from technical coefficients to monetary flow coefficients, it is necessary to multiply the column vector of technical coefficients corresponding to the ith sector with the activity level of that sector and then to form the inner product with the vector of current prices.

In applications to the real world, an input/output matrix can be interpreted as representing either the rates of flow at a given time or the average rate of flow over a given period (such as a year). In the context of GEM, for game-playing purposes the fiction is maintained that the economy of a region operates in two successive stages. In Stage I, the activity levels of the industrial sectors are chosen by the player directing that region, the required inputs for these activity levels are calculated, and the net product (i.e., the

		Into sector								Total req'd. inputs	Net product (= output – req'd. inputs)	Old inventory	Net imports	Available for final supply	Consumption	Government	Hard capital	Soft capital	New inventory
		1	2	3	4	5	6	7	8										
Input from sector	1																		
	2																		
	3																		
	4																		
	5																		
	6																		
	7																		
	8																		
Cost of inputs																			
Value added																			
Value of output																			

FIGURE 25

total output minus the required intermediate inputs) is determined. This, together with existing inventories and net additions derived from imports, constitutes the resources available to satisfy final demand. Given this information, the player, in Stage II, decides how to allocate these supplies between consumers, government, inventories, and capital investment (both "hard" and "soft"). Hard-capital investment consists in the expansion of production facilities, using existing technologies. Soft-capital investment represents R&D effort; it consists in promoting certain technological breakthroughs by attempting to enhance their probability of occurrence.

It should be noted that the options available to a player in both Stages I and II are subject to certain obvious absolute constraints. The activity levels chosen in Stage I are constrained by the capacities of the sectors, the total amount of effective labor available, and the requirement that net production plus inventories must be nonnegative. In addition, in the special cases of Sectors 1 and 6, there are limits on known resource deposits, and production may not exceed the extraction of such known deposits. The allocation made in Stage II is subject to the constraints that final supplies must be nonnegative and that the final supplies must add up to the total available for this purpose.

In playing GEM, the options available to a player, as well as any constraints on his allocations, are clearly displayed to him. The constraints include the absolute ones just mentioned as well as "advisory constraints". The advisory constraints inform the player about the amount of hard-capital investment required to offset capital depreciation, the level of supplies (food and other commodities) to consumer households necessary to prevent death from starvation and civil unrest, and the level of supplies to government necessary to prevent deterioration of government services.

In standard econometric models the output of the economic sectors is completely determined once their activity levels have been set (provided, of course, that proper feasibility constraints have been met); this is not so in GEM, since there are two built-in random elements affecting the output. One is the uncertainty of the amount of labor unrest, which affects the size of the effective labor force and thereby indirectly affects the output of each sector. The other is the regional harvest conditions (weather, crop and cattle diseases, pests, and so on), which are simulated as follows: For each region and each scene, a random deviate d is drawn from a normal distribution with quartiles at $\pm.05$, and the nominal food output for that region and scene is then multiplied by $1 + d$.

56.4 Population and Labor

For each region, an essentially fixed population growth rate per scene (of five years) is assumed, which differs from region to region:

Region	S	E	C	O	N	D
Growth rate (in %)	4	2.5	7.5	10	4	10

Superimposed on these basic growth rates are random fluctuations plus certain cutbacks in case of inadequate food supply.

Each region's total labor force is somewhat arbitrarily set at 45 percent of its population (which happens to be a not-too-unrealistic figure). From this theoretical total labor force, an "effective labor force" is calculated by taking into account the amount of labor unrest, which in turn is affected by the per-capita supply to households as well as by random fluctuations.

A fraction of the effective labor force is skilled. The higher this fraction, the greater is the labor productivity assumed to be. The skill fraction is determined, in part, by the government's level of efficiency (see below).

56.5 Government

The government requires final supplies from Sectors 3, 4, 6, 7, and 8 in fixed proportion. The activity level of this supply vector determines government efficiency. The government efficiency, in turn, affects the skill level of the labor force, the capital coefficients (both hard- and soft-capital), the rates of inventory depreciation, and the quality of information on commodity quantities available to the player for planning purposes.

56.6 Capital Investment

As previously stated, there are two kinds of capital investment, "hard" (using existing technology), and "soft" (R & D). Both require inputs in fixed (but different) proportion from Sector 3 (durable goods) and Sector 8 (services).

56.7 Technological Breakthroughs

It is assumed that each sector's production process is capable, in principle, of technical improvement resulting in a more economical method of production. Such an improvement is the consequence of a technological breakthrough, which is treated as an event having, for each scene, a certain probability of occurrence that can be estimated and also can be influenced by investment in appropriate R & D ("soft capital investment").

When a technological breakthrough in a sector occurs, it causes the technical-coefficient vector for that sector, which specifies the input and labor quantities required to produce one unit of output, to be changed to a different vector, specifying a more economical mixture of inputs and labor.

Specifically, the potential technological breakthroughs included in GEM are these: First of all, for each sector there are what may be considered normal technical-improvement breakthroughs, which for simplicity we standardize by assuming that the effect is a reduction in inputs from Sectors 6, 7, and 8 as well as in labor by 10 percent. Each of these technological breakthroughs may occur repeatedly (but only once in each scene). Aside from these eight, there are six other potential breakthroughs, three of which are also production-process breakthroughs (but going beyond normal technical improvements). The remaining three are other developments improving the state of the economy:

- *Re Sector 1:* the detection of hitherto unknown mineral reserves within the region, increasing the amount of known reserves by 100(r+1) units, where r is a random integer drawn from a uniform distribution over the set from 0 to 9.
- *Re Sector 5:* the feasibility of large-scale nonagricultural food production.
- *Re Sector 5:* the feasibility of controlling the weather, resulting in an improvement in average harvest conditions that cause the harvest to be increased by 1 percent in the following scene, by 2 percent in the scene thereafter, and so on, over what it would have been otherwise.
- *Re Sector 6:* the detection of hitherto unknown fuel reserves within the region, increasing the amount of known reserves by 100(r+1) units, where r is a random integer (as before).
- *Re Sector 7:* the feasibility of producing electric energy from solar power plants.
- *Re Sector 7:* the feasibility of producing electric energy from fusion power plants.

Of these, the second and the last two are production innovations; none of these is repeatable. Of the other three events, the first and fourth are repeatable, while the third is not.

All of the potential breakthroughs have stated probabilities, per scene, of occurring; these probabilities have certain values for the highly developed regions S, E, and N, lower ones for C and O, and still lower ones for D. Soft-capital investment in a sector raises the probabilities of the breakthroughs pertaining to that sector.

Technological breakthroughs are region-specific. However, once a breakthrough has taken place somewhere, all scene probabilities related to that breakthrough in other regions are automatically enhanced. Moreover, a new technology can be transferred to another region if the donor contributes the service portion of the required capital investment during the first scene when such investment is undertaken.

56.8 World Trade

During each scene, after the players have received information on their economy's actual output and before final-supply allocations are made, there is a formal trading session. To facilitate cash flow during this session, each player is provided with a small amount of international currency. It is expected that the players will balance their imports and exports sufficiently to stay within their cash-flow limitations. If they cannot do so, they will have to rely on negotiated loans or gifts from other players.

All trades involve an expenditure in services (reflecting the cost of transportation, finance, and so on). In GEM both buyer and seller are assessed .025 units of services for each commodity unit traded.

Since it is generally not easy to simulate a market-clearing mechanism realistically, the following description of the formal trading session is included for the benefit of a reader who may be particularly interested in this phase of the game: For each commodity (1 through 6), the latest world price p_1 is announced (at the start of the game it is 1.00 for each commodity), and the players are invited to state their bids, that is, the quantities of each of Commodities 1 to 6 they wish to sell (supply) or buy (demand). If, for a given commodity, the total supply and demand are s_1 and d_1, respectively, a second price

$$p_2 = \frac{\max(d_1, s_1/2)}{\max(s_1, d_1/2)} \cdot p_1$$

is announced. (Note that this formula implies that $\frac{1}{2}p_1 \leqslant p_2 \leqslant 2p_1$.) New bids are then solicited. If $p_2 > p_1$, it is usually, but not necessarily, the case that, for the new total supplies and demands, we have $s_2 > s_1$ and $d_2 < d_1$, and it may indeed happen that a "crossover" occurs as shown in Figure 26. The same is true for $p_2 < p_1$, with the s- and d-inequalities reversed.

If, indeed, a crossover occurs, the next price, p_3 (corresponding to the crossover point), is computed by the formula

$$p_3 = p_1 + (p_2 - p_1)\frac{d_1 - s_1}{d_1 - s_1 + s_2 - d_2}$$

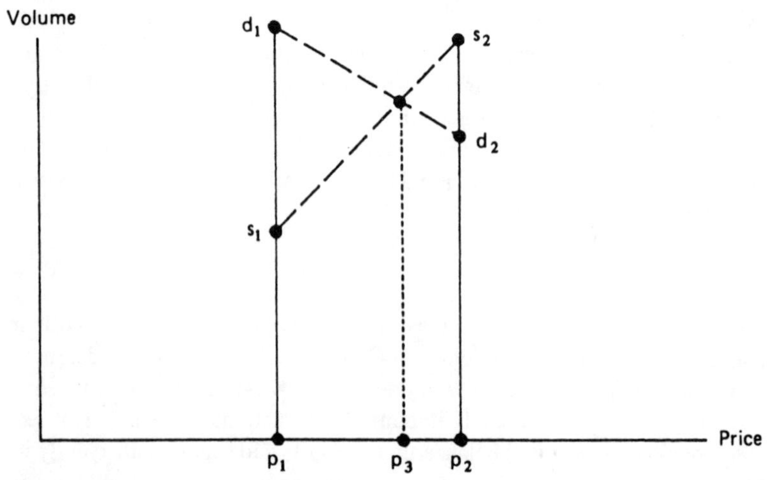

FIGURE 26

(The case $p_2 = p_1$, incidentally, is counted as a crossover, and in this case it is seen that $p_3 = p_1$.)

If no crossover occurs, the next price is computed as in the first step, except that the price is constrained by the original price interval: $\frac{1}{2}p_1 \leq p_3 \leq 2p_1$.

This procedure of computing new prices and obtaining new bids is iterated several times, subject, however, to these additional constraints: (i) If the successive prices for a commodity are $p_1, p_2, p_3, \ldots$, and the final price is p^*, then $p^* = p_j$ where $j \leq 5$ (in other words, there are at most four iterations); (ii) The process continues at most until, for each commodity, a crossover has occurred at some time; (iii) The bounds of the price interval, which at first are $\frac{1}{2}p_1$ and $2p_1$, shrink with each iteration. These shrink as follows: a price p_i, in the next iteration, becomes a new lower (or upper) bound if the price movement is in an upward (or downward) direction.

Once the final prices p_j have been reached, they are announced to the players, who then place their final bids at these prices. For each commodity, the total volume traded is the smaller of the quantities s_j and d_j, and allocations between several buyers or several sellers are in proportion to their bids.

It should be noted that the above procedure for arriving at updated world prices lends itself to exploitation by a wily player, who may open the bidding with a first bid designed merely to drive the price in a direction more favorable to himself. Such behavior should be discouraged by properly instructing the players. In fact, throughout the play of GEM, a player should not attempt to "beat the rules" (as he might if this were a parlor game) but to use whatever expertise and insight he can bring to bear on the play of the game to simulate reality as closely as his ability permits. The purpose, after all, of playing a game such as GEM should not be to "win" but to use the process of human-machine collaboration as a means of gradually producing an increasingly realistic model of real-world interactions.

56.9 Dummy Players

Provision has been made to carry out plays of GEM when there are fewer than six players by automating the actions pertaining to one or more of the regions. This is done by prescribing specific policies to be followed by such "dummy players".

The advantage of this provision is not only to accommodate groups of fewer than six participants, but also to offer the important possibility of systematically exploring the relative value of preset policies by repeatedly exposing them to the vicissitudes of random events and interventions by opposing players.

For this purpose, the choice of a "policy" is defined as the assignment of importance ratings, from 1 to 4, to each of the eight industrial sectors and to each of the three final-demand categories (households, government, capital investment); here, a rating of 1, 2, 3, or 4, respectively, indicates no, slight, moderate, or great importance.

A strategy is then designed for the dummy player that, in making allocations and trade decisions, gives highest priority to a "maintenance operation" (see below) and otherwise follows the instructions implied by the importance ratings.

A maintenance operation consists in running the economy in such a way-that

- the per-capita food supply remains at its present level;
- the government efficiency remains at its present level;
- the capacities of the eight industrial sectors remain at their present levels;
- depreciated inventory is replaced; and
- the level of supplies to households rises at the rate of 5 percent per scene (which prevents labor unrest from increasing).

It should be mentioned that the provisions for automating the operation of a GEM region can also be invoked if a player wishes to have the information about the course of action that would be prescribed by the automated pursuit of a set policy, or if, after participation in several rounds, he wishes to relinquish further active participation in favor of merely setting a policy and turning over the further management of his region to automatic control.

57 INTERACTIVE JUDGMENTAL SIMULATION OF THE AMERICAN ECONOMY

I conclude this chapter with the following essay, written under the auspices of the Center for Futures Research at the University of Southern California and previously published by the World Future Society.[3] This is, in fact, a project proposal that differs from the usual kind in that it is not addressed to a prospective sponsor but to the scientific community at large.

Let me begin by explaining my motivation for writing this. As a methodologist, I have tried to invent methods and procedures that might be used to address complex planning problems in the real world. Such problems, regardless of whether they occur in the private or public sector, invariably are multidisciplinary and future-directed—multidisciplinary because they typically involve considerations of technology, economics, politics, psychology, and often numerous other areas; future-directed not only in the obvious sense that all planning refers to the future, but rather because complex plans tend also to be long-range, meaning that the operating environment at the time such plans might come to fruition will differ markedly from the operating environment at the time the plans are being made. The implication of

3. *WFS Bulletin*, vol. 14 (1980).

these two combined characteristics often fails to be fully recognized: There are no general laws, or even well-established, law-like regularities, to provide reliable guidance to interdisciplinary long-range planning, and the planner has to rely to some extent, or even largely, on the intuitive insight by experienced practitioners, rather than on theory-based findings. It is for this reason that the often prescientific methods of operations research offer more promise of success than purely scientific approaches, which would of course be preferable if they were available.

All the methods to which I am alluding involve, in some measure, the systematic application of expert judgment. Specifically, these include interactive simulation (also called "operational gaming"), Delphi surveys, and cross-impact analysis. To these might be added what is not in itself a research method but a newly available communication technique conducive to interdisciplinary cooperation—namely, computer conferencing.

The case I suggest be examined in this light—and that is what this "proposal" is all about—is that of the future of the American economy. The present state of our economy provides ample testimony to the failure on the part of the economists to make accurate forecasts and to devise measures for, say, the reduction of unemployment and inflation. The primary reason for this unsatisfactory performance, I venture to say with only slight fear of exaggeration, lies not in the failure of the laws of economics, but in the manner in which they have been applied: unidisciplinary, and without adequate future-directedness (i.e., without taking into proper account impending changes in the economically exogenous operating environment). The fault is not the economists' as such; it lies, rather, in the continuing intellectual compartmentalization along disciplinary lines generally and in the virtual nonexistence of "laws" that provide connections between phenomena belonging to traditionally separate academic disciplines. It is essential to recognize that the complexity of the world has increased to such an extent that a cross-disciplinary dialogue and a joint, interdisciplinary treatment have become necessary prerequisites for success in this area.

The suggestion of a new approach is certainly not intended to imply that economic expertise should be discarded and replaced by some new body of supposedly superior but untried knowledge. On the contrary, an operations-analytical attack, as proposed, on what are basically economic problems would merely attempt to provide an interdisciplinary framework and a set of facilitating procedures that would allow an economist to practice the "art of conjecture" more effectively and to examine how his own conjectures harmonize with those of other specialists in related disciplines.

To turn now from generalities to specifics, let me outline a possible mode of procedure. Some of its details are intended to be suggestive only and may well be modified if desirable.

The procedure involves principally three of the techniques referred to earlier: operational gaming, Delphi, and computer conferencing. In a subsequent postgame analytical phase, it may also utilize cross-impact analysis, to which I shall return later in this section.

The format of the study would be an "open" game, that is, a game in which the consequences of player moves are not generally computable from prestated formulas (as they would be presumed to be in a "closed" game), but are determined judgmentally by an umpire team. This format is well known to the military, who have used it successfully on many occasions to simulate conflict situations. The choice of an open-game format to study the national economy reflects the conviction that neither the behavioral reactions of some of the economic "players" to governmental intervention nor the resultant effects on economic indicators are sufficiently understood to be predictable. To be sure, this does not preclude an expert, *qua* player, from using information derived from what he considers valid and applicable economic theory to form the opinions to be fed into the simulation process by him. Regardless of whether intuitive or theory-based estimation is employed in the open-game format in examining the implications of interventive actions on a case-by-case basis, the improved understanding thus gained will justify the hope that, eventually, general relationships in the form of mathematical functions can be derived from these individual cases.

For example, in a period such as the present, where consumer prices are subject to heavy inflationary pressures, with little more than "jaw-boning" governmental intervention, it is well-nigh impossible, using traditional economic approaches, to predict the future supply-and-demand situation in this country. In a gaming simulation it might be possible to proceed in small steps in order to gain some insight into the successive interactions among the relevant economic entities. Thus, faced with rising prices and in consideration of other facets of the overall situation, the playing team representing the consumers will arrive at some estimate of changes in buying habits, in the proclivity to save, and in the willingness to fight for higher wages. (Note that these decisions involve psychology as much as economics.) The team representing industry will, in turn, have to consider the resultant changes in demand, in the cost of labor, and in the availability of capital—not to mention the general operating environment—when deciding what prices to set, what capital expansion to engage in, whether to deplete or refurbish their inventories, how much to spend on R & D, and what effort to put into lobbying and advertising. (Note the relevancy, again, of psychology, as well as of politics and engineering technology.) At this stage the government team may decide to intervene in any one of many ways (e.g., by setting wage and/or price ceilings, adjusting the interest rate, changing the tax structure, providing subsidies, introducing regulatory measures, or changing the rules for foreign commerce). The overall result of the interacting decisions by these three types of economic players (consumers, producers, and government) will make itself felt in changes of all sorts of economic indicators (consumer price index, average wage, unemployment, productivity, rate of capital investment, balance of trade, and so on), some of which may be computable, while most will have to be estimated. Together, these new values will provide a picture of the state of the economy and thus set the stage for the next move cycle of this game.

While it cannot be pretended that the forecasts for the future state of the economy that result from this procedure are reliable (even when the participating players are singularly well informed and imaginative), there is nevertheless reason to hope—particularly if the game is played not once but repeatedly—that the simulated environment of the game and the continual observation of other players' reactions to one's own moves will provide the participants with an improved understanding of how the economy works and what indirect repercussions may be associated with specific economic decisions. It is these insights, derived from the pattern evolving after many plays of such a game, that might eventually enable the analytically minded of the participants to begin to formulate general laws describing the complex, longer-range impacts among the economic variables under consideration.

In detail, the construction and play of the proposed game would proceed as follows:

Item 1: Participants. A group of knowledgeable individuals, willing to participate in the proposed exercise over an extended period (say, six months or a year), have to be recruited. These will be divided into four teams (umpire, consumer, producer, government), with each team, aside from at least two appropriate economists, comprising representatives of the required skills other than economics. Each team, as a minimum, should have four members, although a somewhat larger number would be preferable. One of the members of each team will be designated its chairperson. A subteam of the umpire team, consisting of three persons, will be the steering committee. The chairperson of the steering committee, also referred to as the game director, must be essentially full-time; his two colleagues on the steering committee might be thought of as half-time contributors. For all other participants, probably no more than 10 percent of their time will be required during most of the exercise.

Item 2: Move Sequence. Playing the game will involve an initial phase, a series of move cycles, and a postmortem phase.

The initial phase serves a number of preliminary purposes:

(a) A basic set of economic and other numerical indicators must be selected that need to and can be estimated and in terms of which the state of the economy can be roughly characterized. These indicators should not be quantities that are under the full control of one of the actors in the game, because they could then be observed, rather than merely be estimated. Their number should be between ten and twenty. They may well include, in addition to such indicators as the GNP and the cost-of-living index, certain intuitive measures, such as the quality of life, the degree of labor unrest, and so on.

(b) Once the identity of the basic indicators has been established, their initial values need to be estimated.

(c) If the game is not being played for the first time, the initial phase may also be used to agree on some changes in the game structure, such as the number of playing teams, the precise move sequence, and the voting procedure.

(d) The time horizon has to be established, that is, the maximum length of the period that is to be simulated. (The umpire team may later use its discretion in terminating a particular play prematurely.)

(e) Potential technological breakthroughs as well as important foreign developments (e.g., wars not involving the United States, trade agreements, famine conditions in developing countries) that ought to be monitored have to be identified. For each selected event, probabilities of occurrence have to be estimated for the period under consideration, so that appropriate random procedures can later be invoked in order to determine the occurrence or nonoccurrence of each event in each succeeding year. Similarly, for each selected trend, its expected course and its probable dispersion around the expected values need to be estimated.

Each move cycle consists of eight steps, all of which will be further explicated below:

- determination of random fluctuations,
- government moves,
- umpire reactions,
- producer moves,
- umpire reactions,
- consumer moves,
- umpire reactions, including choice of initial time for the next cycle, and
- estimation of new values of basic indicators.

The postmortem phase will provide an opportunity for all participants to voice

- their criticism of specific moves ("What should we, or some other player team, have done differently?"),
- their criticism of umpire decisions,
- their criticism of the game structure (including constructive suggestions for improvement), and
- their ideas on correlations, implications, or repercussions among various economic factors that the play of the game may have suggested and that may possibly carry over to scenarios other than that represented by the play just terminated.

Item 3: Decisions and Estimations. As the game proceeds, the participants will be called upon to make certain judgments. These will concern either playing-team decisions on what moves to make or umpire-team decisions on reactions to, or assessments of, the consequences of such moves, or estimation of the new values of the basic economic and other indicators. All such group judgments will be arrived at through the device of a mini-Delphi. The group, in each case, will consist of the members of one of the four teams, except in the case of the values of the basic indicators, which will be estimated by the combined membership of all four teams.

It would, of course, be too much to expect that the Delphi process, especially in the case of umpire adjudications, will yield unanimous judgments. However, by breaking the causal sequence down into small steps, as necessitated by the requirements of the gaming format, the experts' opinions are less likely to diverge as much as they would if the overall outcome of a lengthy cause-and-effects chain had to be estimated. Moreover, in cases in which there are substantial substantive disagreements, the simulation process offers the interesting option of following up the implications of two, possibly diametrically opposed, views as to the consequences of a particular move.

Item 4: Voting Procedure. Votes on all decisions, assessments, and estimations, as stated above, are to be taken by mini-Delphi. For the purposes of this game, there are two versions of mini-Delphi: simple and modified. The simple version applies when the result is expressed in numerical form (which includes the case of yes/no decisions, since these can be represented as choices between 1 and 0). The procedure, in the case of the simple version, consists of the three steps described in Section 26.2. In the case of qualitative moves (e.g., deciding on the identity of the basic indicators to be used and on the random developments to be monitored, or taking certain measures to deal with an issue that has arisen) or qualitative assessments by the umpire team of the consequences of player moves, the modified version of mini-Delphi is employed. In this case, the three steps of the simple version are preceded by an additional preliminary step:

Step 0: The group members are invited to suggest appropriate measures (in the case of player team actions) or consequences of player actions (in the case of umpire assessments).

A list of such items is then submitted to the entire group, whose members, using Steps 1 to 3, accept or reject the suggestions (choice of 1 or 0) or decide, if appropriate, on the intensity i (where $0 \leq i \leq 1$) with which the measure is to be enacted or the consequence is judged to occur. (For example, the decision to plow a larger share of industry profits into R&D is subject to quantitative specification, the intensity being 0 if none and 1 if all of the profits are thus allocated; similarly, the decision to raise the prices of consumption goods by, say, 20 percent may be judged to increase the U.S. trade deficit by x billion dollars, where the quantity x needs to be estimated.) At the option of the group's chairperson, a further intermediate step between Steps 0 and 1 may be inserted: If a large number of measures (or consequences) have been suggested, it may be expedient, before adjudicating each separately, to subject the entire set to a rank-ordering by importance so as to introduce a cutoff point that will help reduce the set of items to be considered to manageable proportions.

Item 5: Game Play. The regular move cycles that constitute the play of the game will normally begin in the present, so that the players may be expected to be reasonably familiar with the initial game situation, since it corresponds to the current state of the economy. They may derive further aid from the values of the basic indicators, which will have been determined during the initial phase.

At the beginning of each move cycle, certain random developments are decided. These include the year's harvest conditions, as well as some random events selected in the initial phase for inclusion in the game. Harvest conditions, in particular, are determined by drawing a random number h from a uniform distribution over the interval from $-.1$ to $+.1$ and multiplying the expected harvest output by $1+h$.

While the three playing teams may, of course, have simultaneous sessions in which to consider their moves, the results of their deliberations will be taken up by the umpire team in sequence: government first; then the producers; last, the consumers. The players on each of these teams could think of themselves as multiple decision makers and thus, in deciding on their moves, wear different hats in succession as necessary. Thus the government team represents both the President and Congress (and possibly state and local authorities in addition); the producers' team represents the industry and agriculture and banking (each possibly broken down further into subsectors of the economy); and the consumers' team represents the consumers as such, as well as the labor sector (possibly broken down by employment and income categories). (An obvious alternative would be to have these various subsectors represented by different teams, an option that may in fact be elected in the initial phase of a later play of the game; but for the time being, in order not to proliferate the number of participants, it was thought better to limit the number of playing teams to three.)

A team may always decide to pass. This will be interpreted as meaning that no significant changes in previous policies are contemplated. Examples, easily augmented, of moves that a team may announce are as follows:

Government: specific changes in tax legislation, subsidies, import duties; changes in the interest rate set by the Federal Reserve Bank; regulations; legislation affecting unions or industry; allocation of resources to R & D; and so on.
Producers: decisions affecting prices, inventories, capital investment; cartel formation; foreign operations; concessions to labor demands; investment in R & D

and in the search for new sources of raw material; and so on.

Consumers: allocation of income between saving, housing, food, and the like; changes in procreation rate; product boycotts; wage demands and strikes; insistence on environmental standards; and so on.

Any proposed move requires ratification by the umpire team. The latter may reject a proposed move, either if it is considered not to be within the particular team's jurisdiction or if it is judged to be too unrealistic to match any possible such occurrence in the real world. A rejection should take place quite rarely and must be accompanied by an explanation of the reasons. The playing team then has the right to submit an amended move. Once a move has been accepted, the umpire team assesses its implications (largely in qualitative terms) and communicates them to all participants.

After the consumers' move has been made, accepted, and assessed, the move cycle is concluded with an estimation, by all participants, of the new values of the basic indicators, after which the scene is set for the beginning of the next move cycle.

Item 6: Cycle Length and Play Termination. A move cycle normally covers one (fiscal) year; however, the umpire team has the option of announcing changes in this schedule, either slowing it down because realism may demand that reactions to a particular move ought to be observed sooner than after the lapse of a year, or stipulating that two or more years be allowed to pass before the next move cycle in order to observe the longer-term effects of a particular move.

The umpire team may also, at the end of a move cycle, terminate the play of the game although the preset time horizon has not been reached, either because it is felt that enough has been learned from that play of the game or, of course, simply because available time has run out.

Item 7: Postmortem. Conducting a postmortem, as outlined under item 2, after termination of a play is an essential part of the game. It should generally be anticipated that the game will undergo slight changes—to be sure, improvements, it is hoped—between one play and the next. The postmortem should be looked to for providing guidelines for such amendments, which may concern numerical inputs, structural aspects, and procedural rules.

The umpire team has the responsibility for preserving adequate records for each play of the game, including the results of the postmortem session.

The purpose of repeated plays of the game is to provide, as a minimum, new insights into the workings of the economy that may be of help to economic planners. Beyond that, it is hoped that analysis of the results of many plays will help in the establishment of new theoretical constructs that may advance the general state of the science of economics.

In physics and biology, the standard mode of scientific progress is through repetitive, controlled experiments. This is possible because the individual phenomena in these fields often are relatively easy to isolate and thus lend themselves to study one at a time.

In the social sciences, by contrast, we have learned that such compartmentalization is not possible. Everything depends, virtually, on everything else. Hence the phenomena in which we are interested in the social sciences have to be studied in the context of each other. The system in its entirety needs to be observed, rather than individual, disconnected aspects. But the entire system—in our case, the economy of the United States—is the real world in which we live; it "happens" only once, and repetitive observation under controlled conditions is not one of our options.

Seen in this light, the device of gaming simulation is of great potential importance, because it offers the possibility of what may be called "pseudo-experimentation" (experimentation, that is, not in the real world, but in the simulated world of the game model). The game players, in systematically carrying out a joint Gedankenexperiment, gain a good deal of surrogate experience and thereby acquire a body of synthetic knowledge that may well be the next best thing to the kind of knowledge derived from real experience if such could be attained.

To carry out such an exercise in pseudo-experimentation would not be forbiddingly expensive, especially when its potential payoff is considered. The details given above of a possible format for a gaming exercise should make it clear that the manpower demands for such an effort would be modest, particularly if computer-conferencing facilities were used, which would make it possible for relatively high-level personnel, located in geographically separate places, to participate very effectively as players without a substantial commitment of time.

An interactive simulation effort of this kind might well focus on specific economic policy issues by having the government team introduce appropriate interventive moves and observing the simulated reactions of various economic entities in the ensuing play of the game. A few important examples of questions relating to such policy issues, some of which have been under public debate for many years, are the following:

- Do efforts to lower the rate of inflation necessarily raise the rate of unemployment?
- What are the relative merits of the so-called trickle-up versus the trickle-down approaches to improving the state of the economy?
- What would be the effects on the standard of living of instituting wage and price ceilings?
- What are the implications of the relationship between tax rate and tax revenue, as expressed by the Laffer curve?
- What are the direct and indirect effects of raising interest rates?
- What would be the effect of no longer subjecting earned interest to income tax?
- What would be the long-term effects of legislation requiring that the federal budget be balanced?

To study such issues through operational gaming means, in effects, to subject them to technological assessment. Each issue, after all, concerns the wisdom of the potential introduction of a social technology through legislation, regulation, or governmental directive; and the gaming procedure consists precisely in the step-by-step exploration of the primary, secondary, tertiary (and so on) implications of instituting such a new policy.

After several plays devoted to a particular issue have been carried out, an analysis of what transpired during these plays might be undertaken, and an attempt could even be made to construct a rudimentary theory of the effects caused by various governmental interventions.

To try to achieve this, it is suggested that a cross-impact model be constructed, which would interrelate the occurrences of events and the fluctuations of trends over the time period of interest (say, the next five or ten years). The trends would include those basic indicators that recurred in many of the individual plays, the harvest conditions, and those among the exogenous trends (whose random fluctuations were monitored during individual plays) that are judged to be especially relevant. The events would consist, similarly, of relevant exogenous events monitored during individual plays, as well as of important decisions made by the producers' or consumers' playing teams. The mutual impacts among these events and trends would have to be estimated, such estimates being based on observations of occurrences during game plays.

The expectations one should have with respect to a "rudimentary theory", as I called it, that might be constructed in this way should, of course, be no higher than that regarding any operations-analytical model. Such models generally are intended to be tentative manifestations of the experts' best understanding to date and subject to amendment as additional insights accrue. But even at worst, if the model obtained in this case is very temporary, the joint simulation effort leading to its construction will have contributed greatly to the mutual, cross-disciplinary education of the participants and, in all probability, will have enhanced the quality of their judgment. Thus, the proposed activity, of applying interactive simulation to the study of the American economy, is likely to produce increased understanding, at the very least, and may even generate some new profound ideas sorely needed by our economic planners. ■

Chapter XII

Looking Forward from the Mid-1980s

58 REVIEW AND PREVIEW

The emphasis in this book has been on providing an orderly conceptual framework for looking forward into the future. Thus, much of this volume has been concerned with forecasting and planning techniques, the identification of feasible and desirable futures among the possible ones, the importance of interdisciplinary and systems thinking in the exploration of the future, and the indispensable role of intuitive expertise in this process.

Many of the conceptual and methodological essays included in this book, especially in its first half (Chapters I through VII) are of the generic type; that is, they presented concepts and methods applicable regardless of the particular subject matter. Chapters VIII and IX dealt more specifically with technological, sociopolitical, and economic forecasting and planning, and in the course of these discussions some explicit statements about probable future developments were included. Whatever probability estimates for these were indicated may, of course, be obsolete by now, since they came from studies conducted ten to twenty years ago (although in many cases current estimates would not turn out to be too different).

I would like to conclude this volume by briefly making some personal forecasts, both factual and normative. As for the factual forecasts, I do not claim any particular wisdom in this respect, and I merely state the result of my attempt at integrating the current thinking of the forecasting community, probably tinged with a superimposition of my own short-term pessimism and long-term optimism. Mostly, in presenting these thoughts, I hope to stimulate the readers and challenge them to generate their own, reasoned, and possibly dissimilar forecasts.

The normative forecasts, by contrast, express my own wishful thinking, not as to some utopian world of the future, but as to measures that ought to be taken in the near future (say, during the remaining 1980s) in order to achieve a better future beyond. Here, even more than in the case of factual forecasts, the readers' diverse sets of preferences and priorities are apt to produce somewhat different desiderata for the future.

59 SOME PERSONAL FACTUAL FORECASTS

I am not about to give a listing of forecasts, comparable to those presented in Chapter 8, with my personal probability estimates attached. Let me merely comment on two of the earlier forecasts of technological developments: (i) With regard to obtaining commercially useful energy from controlled thermonuclear fusion, the median date of 1985 turns out to have been much too optimistic, in that the technical impediments to a breakthrough had been greatly underestimated. Although experimentation continues and shows encouraging results, the experts are still uncertain as to when to expect ultimate success, and the present consensus, if any, appears to be that we may well have to wait until after the turn of the century. (ii) Forecasts concerning progress in space exploration, by and large, have also been on the optimistic side. Except for the highly successful unmanned planetary flybys (that sent back, among other things, remarkable pictures and information on the rings and moons of Saturn), a fuller exploration of the solar system and the anticipated colonization of the Moon have been delayed not by technical obstacles, but by the unavailability of appropriate funding. As for other forecasts, previously presented, those pertaining to the period up to the present, by and large, have not been too far off the mark; and those referring to the future that still lies ahead would, on the whole—as I said before—receive slightly, but not very, different probability estimates.

Instead of indulging in personal forecasts of individual technological breakthroughs or of specific changes in societal trends, I will limit myself to some general remarks on the overall picture of what lies ahead for our society over the next two or three decades and on the interconnections among discernible developments.

For the remainder of the 1980s and possibly the early 1990s there are, in my opinion, some serious grounds for pessimism. All of these are fundamentally economic in nature. The industrialized world is faced with a very difficult period of transition toward a postindustrial society, which is expected to be highly commmunication-, service-, and leisure-oriented, with more and more of the jobs requiring physical labor and routine chores being taken over by robots. But to get to that state, anticipated by some (possibly mistakenly) as blissful, some very sizable obstacles have to be overcome:

- Our industrial plant, including its infrastructure, is in disrepair and, in many cases, obsolete. Even without robotization, updating the system would require a formidable amount of capital investment. But precisely because so much of our industry has become inefficient, this would be the right time to take the step toward large-scale robotization—which means even more capital investment. Another form of capital investment, overdue improvements in the educational system, needs to be added.
- Decades of comparative affluence during the prime of the industrial age have

raised personal expectations of ever-increasing affluence to the point where it has become exceedingly hard to convince the working population that a major switch from immediate gratification, in terms of consumer goods and services, to delayed gratification, based on long-term capital investment, is needed. Without such renewal, productivity will decline further; and without rising productivity levels, the basis for rising real wages will vanish.

- Not only have many factories become obsolete, but so too have many manufacturing skills. Many of the millions currently unemployed in the industrial countries across the world will never be employed again unless they first undergo extensive retraining, a process to which many of them are reluctant or even unable to submit, especially if their governments provide inadequate budgetary allocations for this purpose.
- The situation is further aggravated greatly by the paranoia that has seized the leadership of, especially, the superpowers, causing them to engage in an escalating arms race that draws enormous amounts of resources away from desperately needed socioeconomic investment. (The military priorities here are grossly misplaced in any case. Neither side, if only for reasons of effective deterrence, can rationally have the slightest intention of attacking the other. But each seems to fear attack by the other and feels compelled to add to the already vastly excessive deterrence posture. The real danger, it seems to me, comes not from the opposing superpower but from small nations that may be acquiring insane leaders along with nuclear capabilities. The superpowers, instead of vying with each other for supposed superiority, could enhance their national security far more effectively by engaging in a joint effort at stopping nuclear proliferation.)
- Meanwhile, the so-called Third World of developing countries, with their still-exploding populations, is faced with the real possibility of large-scale famine, not to mention the inability to provide enough consumer goods to satisfy the rising aspirations of its people. The demands for transfer of some of the wealth of the developed to the underdeveloped world will constitute a further severe drain on the industrial nations. Some of these demands will be met for purely humanitarian reasons; others, because previous loans to Third World nations have to be protected by additional loans; still others, in response to explicit terrorist blackmail or in order to appease nascent terrorism. The inevitable, at least partial, fulfillment of these demands will further slow down the economic recuperation of the industrial nations and their efforts to cope with the birth pains of the postindustrial age.

These obstacles to reaching "postindustrial bliss" amount to a bad ten years or so ahead, with severe deprivations for some segments of the populations of both developed and underdeveloped countries. Technologically, I expect to see a consolidation of past breakthroughs (in energy, computers, and biomedicine) rather than a continuation of the last few decades' explosive accrual of new breakthroughs.

My intuitive long-term optimism, based on no more than an unfounded belief in humankind's ultimate predisposition to rationality, tells me that, after muddling through for perhaps another decade, ways and means will be found to cope with the two major tasks before us: to defuse the arms race and to reorganize the structure of our economy so as to provide work for all who want it and goods and services for all who need them.

Once these dominant causes of concern are essentially under control, the way will be open to seeking a new and higher plateau for the quality of life throughout the world, by pursuing new breakthroughs in numerous areas of technology, including social technology above all. But this, at best, is not around the corner; it amounts to a new millennium's resolution.

60 SOME PERSONAL NORMATIVE FORECASTS

Normative forecasts ideally consist in proposals for action measures, to be taken by a specified decision-making agency, which have been checked out for technical and financial feasibility. I am not planning to be that specific in what I have to propose, but, on the other hand, I will not fall into the opposite extreme of blue-sky utopian fantasy. What I am advocating are types of measures (rather than detailed specific measures) that I personally regard as entirely feasible (though others may not) and that could, and should, be carried out within, say, the next five years. Their nature is largely determined by the factual assessments I tried to make in the preceding section. They all are addressed to the U.S. federal government (the Congress and the president) as the decision-making agency.

Heading my list of proposals is a realistic reassessment of our national priorities. For example, the average American, these days, is much more likely to be killed by a street mugger than by a Russian; yet our outlays on crime prevention are minuscule in comparison to our defense expenditures.

Based on such a reassessment, we need to undertake a thorough reallocation of our resources, both those under direct government control in the form of revenues and those whose allocation can be influenced by appropriate legislation. Among the primary beneficiaries of such a reallocation I would expect to see the educational establishment, basic research, crime prevention and law enforcement, the robotization of many of our industries, and the social-services establishment, whose standards have lagged lamentably far behind those of Western Europe.

Along with this redistribution of resources, we need a fundamental restructuring of our economy and of the government's fiscal apparatus, with a view to easing the transition to a postindustrial society. Fiscally, we need to distinguish clearly between out-of-pocket, nonrecoverable expenses (such as on armaments and on old-age pensions) and investments expected to pay for themselves and possibly even increase net revenues (such as education and retraining, basic research, plant modernization, health care, and possibly even space exploration). Only then can the government be run like a business and a reasonable assessment of supportable budget deficits be made. As for the tax structure, rather than reducing taxes across the board in an effort to stimulate the economy (which has inflationary side effects), selective tax incentives might be offered that promote investment in desired sectors of the economy, possibly including tax reductions on earned interest.

To ease the unemployment situation (which looks grim for many years to come), a three-part plan such as the following might be offered in hard-hit industries that the government considers worthy and capable of being saved: (i) If a plant is on the verge of having to close down, offer its worker an option of staying on at half their wages, in exchange for equivalent shares in the company; (ii) let workers accepting this arrangement be entitled to half the unemployment payments they would receive if indeed they were unemployed; (iii) have the government underwrite low-interest loan guarantees for plants that have accepted such an arrangement with their workers, to enable them to invest in modernization of their equipment. Under this three-way cooperation between management, labor, and government, the plant's viability is likely to be reestablished; increased productivity would undoubtedly result from the combination of government-supported modernization, reduction in payrole expenses, and employees' added incentives derived from part ownership.

Generally, and in the same spirit, management-labor contract negotiations should be encouraged to place emphasis on indexing wages with respect to plant productivity (rather than with respect to the cost of living).

Internationally, high priority should go to arms-limitation negotiations, aimed at order-of-magnitude reductions; these might well be tied in with proposals for joint proliferation control measures. Other, more positive joint ventures might include space exploration and the organization of effective aid to the Third World.

61 THE FUTURE OF FUTURES RESEARCH

There are difficult times ahead for our society. Its problems are numerous and complex beyond precedent, and their solution is urgent. Traditional piecemeal approaches have proven to be sterile, and what is needed is a new type of massive, imaginative, and interdisciplinary effort. Our resources are limited, and any such effort, to be successful, must be highly cost-effective. Moreover, the world situation is in a state of constant flux, so that conditions are ever changing. Consequently, any reform plans must be based not on currently observable conditions, but on anticipated future conditions.

These, as the reader is well aware by now, are precisely the defining characteristics of futures research. There is, therefore, no shortage of important tasks for futurists.

First of all, the methods of futures research need to be further refined. Delphi, cross-impact analysis, and operational gaming, together with the traditional methods of systems analysis, are in need of and unquestionably susceptible to conceptual as well as procedural improvement. In addition, the search for new methods, possibly more effective and efficient ones, should be vigorously pursued. Among these, a more sophisticated use than hitherto of extrapolation from historical findings, facilitated by modern data-processing capabilities and combined with the judicious use of intuitive expertise, may well deserve attention. Futures research, to date, has been remiss in foreseeing many developments that have later proven to be major influences in shaping our society. The oil crisis, the socioeconomic implications of the transition to postindustrialism, the increasing functional illiteracy of a large segment of the American population, the enormous public-sector deficits, the antinuclear movement, the extent of the pollution from toxic wastes, the deterioration of the industrial infrastructure—all these are obvious examples of trends that might have been foreseen by a few individuals but to the perils of which the general public has not been alerted in good time and forcefully enough to take concerted countermeasures. While there is unquestionably a class of future events that cannot reasonably be expected to be predicted—notably those dependent on the irrational actions of an individual or on the windfall of a miraculous technological breakthrough—the community of futures researchers ought to develop a reliable capability of examining potential future trends (of the kind illustrated above) systematically and regularly and of assessing both their probabilities and their likely impacts.

In these pursuits, because of the unavoidable reliance, in part, on expert judgment, greater accessibility to the "advice community" across the land through the institution of a national D-net would represent a distinct advance.

With this expected increase in effectiveness, futures research should be in a position to make decisive contributions to the solution of many of the world's most pressing problems during the next few decades.

Bibliography

American Management Association. *Top Management Decision Simulation.* New York: American Management Association.

Adelson, M., Alkin, M., Carey, C., and Helmer, O. "Planning Education for the Future," *American Behavioral Scientist*, vol. 10, 1967.

Alter, S. "The Evaluation of Generic Cross-Impact Models," *Futures*, vol. 2, 1979.

Ament, R. "Comparison of Delphi Forecasting Studies in 1964 and 1969," *Futures*, vol. 2, 1970.

Arrow, K. *Social Choice and Individual Values*. New York: Wiley, 1951.

Ayres, R. *Technology Forecasting and Long-Range Planning*. New York: McGraw-Hill, 1969.

Bellman, R. "On the Construction of a Multi-Stage Business Game," *Journal of the Operations Research Society*, vol. 5, 1957.

Brown, B., and Helmer, O. "Improving the Reliability of Estimates Obtained from a Consensus of Experts," Rand Publication P-2986, 1964.

Caldwell, Coombs, C. H., Schoeffler, S., and Thrall, R. M. "Linear Model for Evaluating the Output of Intelligence Systems," *Naval Research Logistics Quarterly*, vol. 8, 1961.

Choucri, N., and Robinson, T. (eds.). *Forecasting in International Relations*. San Francisco: Freeman, 1978.

Cushen, W. E. "Operational Gaming in Industry," in Closkey and Coppinger (eds.), *Operations Research for Management*, vol. 11. Baltimore: 1956.

Dalkey, N. "An Elementary Cross-Impact Model," *Technological Forecasting*, vol. 3, 1972.

Duperrin, J. C., and Godet, M. "SMIC 74," *Futures*, vol. 7, 1975.

Enzer, S. "Cross-Impact Techniques in Technology Assessment," *Futures*, vol. 4, 1974.

Enzer, S. "An Interactive Cross-Impact Scenario Generator for Long-Range Forecasting," doctoral dissertation, University of Southern California, 1979.

Finetti, B. de. "Does It Make Sense to Speak of 'Good Probability Estimates'?" in I. J. Good (ed.), *The Scientist Speculates*. New York: Basic Books, 1962.

Frankel, C. "Explanation and Interpretation in History," *Philosophy of Science*, vol. 24, 1957.

Gabor, D. *Inventing the Future*. New York: Knopf, 1964.

Gabor, D. *The Mature Society*. London: Secker & Warburg, 1972.

Goldhamer, H., and Speier, H. "Some Observations on Political Gaming," *World Politics*, October 1959.

Gordon, T., and Ament, R. "Forecasts of Some Technological and Scientific Developments and Their Social Consequences," Institute for the Future, Report R6, 1969.

Gordon, T., and Hayward, H. "Initial Experiments with the Cross-Impact Matrix Method of Forecasting," *Futures*, vol. 1, 1968.

Gross, B. "Urban Mapping for 1976 and 2000," *Urban Affairs Quarterly*, December 1969.

Helmer, O. "Cross-Impact Gaming," *Futures*, vol. 4, 1972.

Helmer, O. "An Agenda for Futures Research," Chapter 17 in W. Boucher (ed.), *The Study of the Future*. Washington, DC: Government Printing Office, 1977a.

Helmer, O. "Problems in Futures Research," *Futures*, vol. 9, 1977b.

Helmer, O., and Brown, T. A. "SAFE," Rand Research Memorandum RM-3827, 1962.

Hempel, C. G., and Oppenheim, P. "Studies in the Logic of Explanation," *Philosophy of Science*, vol. 15, 1948.

Hitch, C. "Operations Research and National Planning—A Dissent," *Journal of the Operations Research Society*, vol. 5, 1957.

Holland, E. "Simulation of an Economy with Development and Trade Problems," *American Economic Review*, vol. 52, 1962.

Huxley, A. *Brave New World*. London: Chatto & Windus, 1932.

Jantsch, E. *Technological Forecasting in Perspective*. Paris: Organization for Economic Cooperation and Development, 1967.

Jouvenel, B. de. *The Art of Conjecture*. New York: Basic Books, 1967.

Kahn, H., and Wiener, A. *The Year 2000*. New York: Macmillan, 1967.

Kaplan, A., Girshick, A., and Skogstad, A. "The Prediction of Social and Technological Events," *Public Opinion Quarterly*, 1950.

Kennedy, J. L. "A Display Technique for Planning," *Proceedings of a Symposium on Personnel Training*. Washington, DC: 1956.

Linstone, H., and Turoff, M. (eds.). *The Delphi Method*. Reading, MA: Addison-Wesley, 1975.

Loye, D. *The Knowable Future*. New York: Wiley, 1978.

Martino, J. *Technological Forecasting for Decisionmaking*. New York: Elsevier, 1972.

Meadows, D., et al. *Limits to Growth*. New York: New American Library, 1972.

Mehl, P. E. *Clinical vs. Statistical Prediction*. Minneapolis: University of Minnesota Press, 1954.

Mesarovic, L., and Pestel, E. *Mankind at the Turning Point*. New York: Dutton, 1974.

Mitchell, R. B., Tydeman, J., and Georgiades, J. "Structuring the Future," *Technological Forecasting*, vol. 4, 1979.

Mood, A. M., and Specht, R. D. "Gaming as a Technique of Analysis," Rand Publication P-579, 1954.

Orwell, G. *1984*. London: 1949.

Rescher, N. "On Prediction and Explanation," *British Journal for the Philosophy of Science*, vol. 8, 1958.

Scheffler, I. "Explanation, Prediction, and Abstraction," *British Journal for the Philosophy of Science*, vol. 7, 1957.

Shane, H. *The Educational Significance of the Future*. Bloomington, IN: Phi Delta Kappa, 1973.

Shapley, L. "Simple Games: An Outline of the Descriptive Theory," *Behavioral Science*, vol. 7, 1962.

Sola Pool, I. de. "Cold War Modeling," *Proceedings of the Military Operations Research Symposia*, vol. 1, 1961.

Thomas, C. J., and Deemer, W. L. "The Role of Operational Gaming in Operations Research," *Journal of the Operations Research Society*, vol. 5, 1957.

Thrall, Coombs, and Caldwell. "Linear Model for Evaluating Complex Systems," *Naval Research Logistics Quarterly*, vol. 5, 1958.

Toffler, A. *Future Shock*. New York: Random House, 1970.

Toffler, A. (ed.). *The Futurists*. New York: Random House, 1972.

Toffler, A. *The Third Wave*. New York: Morrow.

Winthrop, H. "Social Systems and Social Complexity in Relation to Interdisciplinary Policy-making and Planning," *Policy Science*, vol. 3, 1972.

Wolf, C. "Defense and Development in Less Developed Countries," *Journal of the Operations Research Society*, vol. 10, 1962.

About the Author

Best known for his development of the famous Delphi forecasting procedure, Olaf Helmer is the originator of cross-impact analysis and other predictive techniques now used by government, business, and research organizations worldwide. His contributions to systems analysis, simulation gaming, and operations research are recognized as being of first-order importance.

One reason *Looking Forward* will appeal to students of futures research is that Dr. Helmer tells them about the historical context in which many of his classic studies originated—at the Rand Corporation, UCLA, the Institute for the Future (which Helmer co-founded), the International Institute for Applied Systems Analysis in Austria, and the Center for Futures Research at the University of Southern California.

Dr. Helmer now resides in Carmel, California, and travels extensively for purposes of lecturing, consulting, and pleasure.